Wittgenstein's Metaphysics offers a radical new interpretation of the fundamental ideas of Ludwig Wittgenstein. It takes issue with the conventional view that after 1930 Wittgenstein rejected the philosophy of the *Tractatus* and developed a wholly new conception of philosophy. By tracing the evolution of Wittgenstein's ideas Cook shows that they are neither as original nor as difficult as is often supposed. Wittgenstein was essentially an empiricist, and the difference between his early views (as set forth in the *Tractatus*) and the later views (as expounded in the *Philosophical Investigations*) lies chiefly in the fact that after 1930 he replaced his early version of reductionism with a subtler version. So he ended where he began, as an empiricist armed with a theory of meaning.

  This iconoclastic interpretation is sure to influence all future study of Wittgenstein and will provoke a reassessment of the nature of his contribution to philosophy.

WITTGENSTEIN'S
METAPHYSICS

WITTGENSTEIN'S METAPHYSICS

JOHN W. COOK

CAMBRIDGE
UNIVERSITY PRESS

Published by the Press Syndicate of the University of Cambridge
The Pitt Building, Trumpington Street, Cambridge CB2 1RP
40 West 20th Street, New York, NY 10011-4211, USA
10 Stanford Road, Oakleigh, Melbourne 3166, Australia

First published 1994

Printed in the United States of America

Library of Congress Cataloging-in-Publication Data

Cook, John W. (John Webber), 1930–
    Wittgenstein's metaphysics / John W. Cook.
        p.   cm.
    Includes bibliographical references and indexes.
    ISBN 0-521-46019-0
    1. Wittgenstein, Ludwig, 1889–1951.   2. Metaphysics.   I. Title.
B3376.W564C66   1994
110'.92—dc20   93-28603
                                                                    CIP

A catalog record for this book is available from the British Library

ISBN 0-521-46019-0 hardback

For
Frank B. Ebersole

A man will be *imprisoned* in a room with a door that's unlocked and opens inward; so long as it does not occur to him to *pull* rather than push it.

Ludwig Wittgenstein
Culture and Value

Contents

Part V: The Past, Memory, and
The Private Language Argument

Preface

This book is an exposition and critique of Ludwig Wittgenstein's basic philosophical ideas. The interpretation it offers differs greatly from that current in the philosophical community today. At one time I was myself a party to the received view of Wittgenstein's philosophy and was among those who helped to foster it. My views began to change during the 1970s, but it was not until 1984 that I came fully to the realizations that form the basis of this book. In that year an early draft of the book was completed. Since then several people have read and commented on the original and succeeding drafts. Some expressed doubts about my interpretation, and their skepticism forced me to dig deeper and provide additional documentation. I offer them my thanks, and I hope that what I have now produced will meet with their approval. Others applauded my efforts, and I am most grateful for the encouragement they provided. I am especially indebted in this regard to William Davie. Special thanks are due to Frank Ebersole, to whom this book is dedicated. Without the benefit of his philosophical contributions over the last three decades this book could not have been written.

My wife, Annie, has provided constant encouragement and editorial assistance, without which this project might never have reached fruition. For this and much more she has my deepest gratitude.

In articles published over the past dozen years I have discussed some of the topics dealt with in this book. Articles dealing especially with the topics of Chapters 14 and 15 include:

"Notes on Wittgenstein's *On Certainty*," *Philosophical Investigations*, Fall, 1980, pp. 15–27.

"Malcolm's Misunderstandings," *Philosophical Investigations*, Spring, 1981, pp. 72–90.

"The Metaphysics of Wittgenstein's *On Certainty*," *Philosophical Investigations*, April, 1985, pp. 81–119.

In "Wittgenstein and Religious Belief" (*Philosophy*, October, 1988, pp. 427–452, esp. Sec. III) I have tried, in a way quite different from anything found in this book, to bring out the behavioristic character of Wittgenstein's view of language.

Chapter 11 is a revised version of a paper read at the Oregon Annual Colloquium in Philosophy in 1982. Parts of Chapters 8 and 12 are derived from a series of lectures delivered at the University of Swansea in 1985.

Captiva, Florida
October, 1992

List of Abbreviations

Abbreviations used to refer to Wittgenstein's writings, notes and lectures in roughly chronological order

NB   *Notebooks, 1914–16*, eds. G. H. von Wright and G. E. M. Anscombe, trans. G. E. M. Anscombe (Oxford: Blackwell, 1961).

TLP   *Tractatus Logico-Philosophicus*, trans. D. F. Pears and B. F. McGuinness (London: Routledge and Kegan Paul, 1961).

RLF   "Some Remarks on Logical Form," *Proceedings of the Aristotelian Society*, Supplementary Volume 9 (1929), pp. 162–171, reprinted in *Essays on Wittgenstein's Tractatus*, eds. Irving M. Copi and Robert W. Beard (London: Routledge and Kegan Paul, 1966), pp. 31–37.

WVC   *Wittgenstein and the Vienna Circle*, shorthand notes recorded by Friedrich Waismann, ed. Brian McGuinness, trans. Joachim Schulte and Brian McGuinness (Oxford: Blackwell, 1979).

EL   "A Lecture on Ethics," *Philosophical Review*, LXXIV (1965), pp. 3–12.

RGB   "Remarks on Frazer's 'Golden Bough'," trans. A. C. Miles and Rush Rhees, *The Human World*, No. 3, May 1971.

PB   *Philosophische Bemerkungen* (Oxford: Basil Blackwell, 1964).

PR   *Philosophical Remarks*, ed. Rush Rhees, trans. Raymond Hargreaves and Roger White (Chicago: University of Chicago Press, 1975).

PG   *Philosophical Grammar*, ed. Rush Rhees, trans. Anthony Kenny (Berkeley: University of California Press, 1974).

WL32   *Wittgenstein's Lectures: Cambridge, 1930–1932*, ed. Desmond Lee (Chicago: University of Chicago Press, 1982).

WL35   *Wittgenstein's Lectures: Cambridge, 1932–1935*, ed. Alice Ambrose (Chicago: University of Chicago Press, 1982).

BB   *The Blue and Brown Books* (Oxford: Blackwell, 1958).

NFL   "Wittgenstein's Notes for Lectures on 'Private Experience' and 'Sense Data'," ed. Rush Rhees, *Philosophical Review*, LXXVII (1968), pp. 271–320.

LSD   "The Language of Sense Data and Private Experience – I" and "The Language of Sense Data and Private Experience – II," notes taken by Rush Rhees in Wittgenstein's 1936 lectures,

Philosophical Investigations, Vol. 7, No. 1 (January, 1984), pp. 1–45, and Vol. 7, No. 2 (April, 1984), pp. 101–140.

LC   *Lectures and Conversations on Aesthetics, Psychology and Religious Belief*, ed. Cyril Barrett (Oxford: Blackwell, 1966).

CE   "Cause and Effect: Intuitive Awareness," *Philosophia*, Vol. 6, Nos. 3–4, pp. 391–408, Sept., Dec., 1976. Selected and edited by Rush Rhees. English translation by Peter Winch.

LFM   *Wittgenstein's Lectures on the Foundations of Mathematics, Cambridge, 1939*, ed. Cora Diamond (Hassocks: Harvester Press, 1976).

RFM   *Remarks on the Foundations of Mathematics*, revised edition, eds. G. H. von Wright, R. Rhees and G. E. M. Anscombe, trans. G. E. M. Anscombe, (Cambridge: MIT Press, 1983).

PI   *Philosophical Investigations*, eds. G. E. M. Anscombe and R. Rhees, trans. G. E. M. Anscombe (Oxford: Blackwell, 1953).

Z   *Zettel*, eds. G. E. M. Anscombe and G. H. von Wright, trans. G. E. M. Anscombe (Oxford: Blackwell, 1967).

RPP, I   *Remarks on the Philosophy of Psychology, Vol. I*, eds. G. E. M. Anscombe and G. H. von Wright, trans. G. E. M. Anscombe (Chicago: University of Chicago Press, 1980).

RPP, II   *Remarks on the Philosophy of Psychology, Vol. II*, eds. G. H. von Wright and Neikki Nyman, trans. C. G. Luckhardt and M. A. E. Aue (Chicago: University of Chicago Press, 1981).

LW, I   *Last Writings on the Philosophy of Psychology, Vol. I*, eds. G. H. von Wright and Heikki Nyman, trans. C. G. Luckhardt and Maximilian A. E. Aue (Chicago: University of Chicago Press, 1982).

LW, II   *Last Writings on the Philosophy of Psychology, Vol. II*, eds. G. H. von Wright and Heikki Nyman, trans. C. G. Luckhardt and Maximilian A. E. Aue (Oxford: Blackwell, 1992).

WL47   *Wittgenstein's Lectures on Philosophical Psychology: 1946–1947*, ed. P. T. Geach (Chicago: University of Chicago Press, 1989).

ROC   *Remarks on Colour*, ed. G. E. M. Anscombe, trans. Linda McAlister and Margarete Schattle (Berkeley: University of California Press, 1977).

OC   *On Certainty*, eds. G. E. M. Anscombe and G. H. von Wright, trans. D. Paul and G. E. M. Anscombe (Oxford: Blackwell, 1969).

CV   *Culture and Value*, ed. G. H. von Wright, trans. Peter Winch (Chicago: University of Chicago Press, 1984).

Introduction

It has been common to regard Wittgenstein as being, in his later years, an ordinary language philosopher in some fairly obvious sense of that phrase. The reason for this is that in his later writings he frequently admonished us to consider how words are actually used. And he declared that the philosopher's task "is to bring words back from their metaphysical to their everyday use" (PI, §116). All of us, I suppose, have noticed that Wittgenstein persisted in the metaphysical use of various words. But these failures have commonly been regarded as nothing more than isolated errors he would have been happy to correct. No one, I think, saw in these a pattern indicative of a pervasive metaphysical theory. And yet this, I will argue, is precisely what these seeming lapses actually were. Wittgenstein, if I am right, never rejected the empiricist metaphysics that forms the basis of the *Tractatus*. By 1916 he had embraced that version of empiricism that William James called "radical empiricism" and Bertrand Russell later called "neutral monism." From that date until his death his fundamental views changed very little. In his later writings he did revise the *Tractatus* account of language, but beyond that he merely tinkered with empiricism, adjusting both it and ordinary language until he could bring them to a conformity that suited him.

Many philosophers would dismiss this interpretation of Wittgenstein's later work. There are two principal reasons for this. One is that most philosophers have remained happily ignorant of Wittgenstein's early views, especially his adoption of neutral monism as the means of avoiding skepticism. The other reason is that numerous myths have dominated the way in which Wittgenstein is viewed. I will here list some of these myths so as to provide an orientation for the chapters that follow.

1) The basic myth, the one largely responsible for the others, is that in the *Tractatus* Wittgenstein showed little, if any, interest in epistemology. As will be shown in the chapters that follow, better sense can be made of the *Tractatus* if we recognize that its author was very much concerned with epistemology, especially skepticism, and that his linguistic doctrines were intended to subserve his epistemological convictions.

2) A second myth, related to the first, is that when writing the *Tractatus*

Wittgenstein had no definite ideas about the "simple objects" that he posits there, aside from the necessity of their being simple. The truth of the matter is that Wittgenstein had very definite ideas about the epistemological role of his "objects": nothing may count as a Tractarian object unless it is given in immediate experience.

3) A third myth is that Wittgenstein cannot have thought of Tractarian objects as being sense-data. As with many myths, this one contains a grain of truth, for Wittgenstein, as we will see, did not share the usual, i.e., Moore's and Russell's, conception of sense-data. Once we understand his own conception, there can be no doubt that the 'objects' of the *Tractatus* are sense-data (or what he elsewhere calls "the material of experience"). This is important for understanding not only Wittgenstein's early writings but also such later works as *Philosophical Investigations* and *On Certainty*. For with only minor changes Wittgenstein retained the same ontology throughout his life: 'reality' and 'immediate experience' are one.

4) It is a pervasive myth that at some point after returning to philosophy in 1929 Wittgenstein wiped the slate clean and developed a philosophy that is independent of and indeed opposed to the fundamental ideas of the *Tractatus*.[1] This fourth myth is a direct product of the first, of the view that in the *Tractatus* Wittgenstein had no interest in epistemology and was chiefly concerned with the philosophy of language. Anyone holding this view will think that, because the *Investigations* criticized at length the Tractarian account of language, a fundamental change had taken place. The truth of the matter, however, is that the empiricist views that dominate the *Tractatus* and significantly determine its account of language play the same role in the *Investigations*. In both books an important question for Wittgenstein is this: By what account of meaning (or grammar) can one reconcile empiricism and ordinary language? This question is answered differently in the two books, but that is a comparatively minor matter. Wittgenstein's fundamental views changed very little after 1916, i.e., he remained a neutral monist.[2]

The myth that Wittgenstein's thinking underwent a fundamental change in the 1930s has led to the misconception that one can understand his later writings – in particular, *Philosophical Investigations* and *On Certainty* – without having mastered the basic ideas of the *Tractatus*, such as his conception of objects, his treatment of solipsism, and his Humean view of causation. The general acceptance of this myth has rendered worthless most of what has been written about Wittgenstein's so-called "later philosophy." One cannot, for example, properly understand the way in which Wittgenstein, in the *Investigations*, deals with the problem of other minds or criticizes the idea of a "private language" without seeing that he remained committed to the ontology of the *Tractatus*. Nor can one understand the epistemological problems addressed in *On Certainty* without recognizing that they are problems generated by that ontology, i.e., phenomenalism.[3]

5) A myth that has dominated much of the thinking about Wittgenstein's later work is one that links his thought after 1929 closely with that of G. E. Moore.[4] Nothing could be further from the truth. As will become apparent in the chapters that follow, Wittgenstein held a metaphysical view of the world that was fundamentally opposed to Moore's. If we are to find similarities between Wittgenstein and his contemporaries, we will do better to look to Russell and the neutral monists, especially Ernst Mach and Karl Pearson. The neutral monists, Wittgenstein believed, provided an ontology that showed how to escape solipsism and solve the problem of other minds. And it was Russell's distinction between grammatical and logical form that provided him with the view of language that, in a fundamental way, guided him for the rest of his life.[5] Although he later modified this distinction, along lines anticipated by Berkeley, it remained fundamental to his conceptions of language and philosophy. He also accepted uncritically certain other of Russell's views. But as for Moore, Wittgenstein said this: "Moore? – he shows you how far a man can go who has absolutely no intelligence whatever."[6] And he remarked to Malcolm that "he did not believe that Moore would *recognize* a *correct* solution [to a philosophical problem] if he were presented with one."[7]

6) Perhaps the gravest misunderstanding of Wittgenstein is the myth that he became an ordinary language philosopher. An ordinary language philosopher, as I understand this, is one who tests his philosophical ideas against examples drawn from the discourse of everyday life, including the discourse of scientists. Wittgenstein was never an ordinary language philosopher in this sense. Rather, he brought his philosophical preconceptions to his encounter with language and then adopted a theory of meaning to show how his empiricism could be reconciled with what plain men say. When he found that we say things that conflict with his preconceptions, he declared that here ordinary language (including that of scientists) is misleading. Far from letting himself be guided by ordinary language, he found himself at odds with it. "Philosophy," he declared, "is a battle against the bewitchment of our intelligence by means of language" (PI, §109).

The myth that Wittgenstein's later writings belong to the tradition of ordinary language philosophy has fostered a particular way of explicating those writings, one that ignores a great many passages and focuses exclusively on those in which he claims (often inaccurately) to be pointing out how certain words are actually used. This selective reading displaces his later writings from the tradition in which they can best be understood, namely, the philosophical developments of the early years of this century. It overlooks the fact that Wittgenstein was a philosopher of his times whose early work inspired Logical Positivism and whose philosophical intimates in the early 1930s were members of the Vienna Circle. The standard reading disregards the many similarities between Wittgenstein's later work and the neutral monism of Ernst Mach, William James, and Karl Pearson.[8] We ignore these cues at our peril, for much that Wittgenstein wrote in his later years was written for the benefit of philosophers who, like Rudolph Carnap, shared his empiricist assumptions but whose ideas about language he sought to correct.[9] If we would understand Wittgenstein, we must read his later writings, not in the light of recent ordinary language philosophy, but in the historical context in which they were written.[10] This, I realize, is none too easy a thing to do, for in the sixty years that separate us from *Philosophical Investigations* many views that were widely accepted then have lost their air of plausibility. But those who insist that Wittgenstein *could not* have held such views because they are so ridiculous merely reveal a lack of historical perspective. The views of the neutral monists were commonplace from 1900 to 1940.

7) The final myth is that Wittgenstein was an original thinker, a philosopher without precedent.[11] One cannot deny, of course, that there is originality in the way Wittgenstein developed or used his predecessors' ideas, such as neutral monism and Wolfgang Köhler's Gestalt theory of perception. At bottom, however, he was merely an empiricist, and, as will be shown in Chapter 8, his later views about language and the nature of philosophy amount to little more than a generalizing of the position already taken by Berkeley, the position that says: while the grammar of ordinary language is on many points philosophically misleading, this is no defect because the plain man does not *mean* what the grammar suggests, for grammar is arbitrary and the plain man's meaning is determined by the use he makes of words in the practical affairs of life. Following his return to philosophy in 1929 Wittgenstein systematically invoked this 'use' theory of meaning as a means of reconciling empiricism and ordinary language. In short, he was carrying on in the tradition of Berkeley, whom he regarded as a "very deep thinker."[12] It was not modesty that led him to say: "I think there is some truth in my idea that I really only think reproductively. I don't believe I have ever *invented* a line of thinking. I have always taken one over from someone else. I have simply straightaway seized on it with enthusiasm for my work of clarification" (CV, pp. 18–19). And again: "I believe that my originality (if that is the right word) is an originality belonging to the soil rather than to the seed. (Perhaps I have no seed of my own.) Sow a seed in my soil and it will grow differently than it would in any other soil" (CV, p. 36). These remarks seem to me to be accurate self-assessments. Wittgenstein spent his life tinkering with empiricism, but while some of

his tinkering was indeed novel, it was bound to leave him essentially where he had begun: as an empiricist armed with a theory of meaning.

That these seven myths, and other misunderstandings, should have grown up around his philosophy is largely the fault of Wittgenstein himself. For while his fundamental views were, for the most part, borrowed from earlier empiricists, he rendered them obscure by the aphoristic style in which he wrote. Moreover, as his ideas developed, he constantly took it for granted that his thinking had followed a perfectly natural and inevitable course, so that he needn't spell out for his readers what his starting points had been. What struck him as obvious should also, he thought, be obvious to others. Wittgenstein said in 1948: "Nearly all of my writings are private conversations with myself. Things that I say to myself tete-à-tete" (CV, p. 77). The result is that his later writings fail to mention the assumptions he was making throughout, and with those assumptions hidden from view his remarks often lend themselves to interpretations inconsistent with his actual views. This is why it is necessary to follow his thinking chronologically, beginning with the pre-*Tractatus* notebooks. Only in this way can one see how much metaphysical baggage he carried with him throughout his life.

One other impediment to reading Wittgenstein critically should be mentioned here and that is the fact that we live in an age still dominated by empiricism or by certain of its conceptions. A few philosophers – preeminently Frank Ebersole – have worked themselves free from that tradition, but to the extent that we remain its captives (e.g., as believers in 'logical possibilities'), we will fail to recognize the extent to which Wittgenstein systematically misunderstood ordinary language because he looked at it through empiricist spectacles. This has posed a problem for the writing of this book. Should I rely on the maxim that to expound is to expose, or must I accompany my chronicle of Wittgenstein's views with a critique of empiricism? I am not confident that I have solved this problem satisfactorily. In some cases, and especially on the topics of causation (Chapters 11, 12, and 13) and "logical possibility" (Chapter 14), I have provided the philosophical critique; in other cases I have not. In particular, I have taken it for granted that all those theories of perception (and the 'proper objects of perception') that philosophers have found attractive must be scrapped. (While I feel some discomfort at having left this matter unargued, Ebersole's work in this area has been so impressive that I could add nothing to it.) Accordingly, I hold no brief for such terms as "sense-datum," "sense impression," "visual picture," and the like that are so essential to empiricism. The fact, then, that these terms occur throughout my exposition of Wittgenstein's views should not be construed as an endorsement of them. The same holds for the other philosophical terms – "proposition," "grammar," "criterion" and others – that are required for exposition. While empiricists may find these terms unproblematic, I do not, and I have tried to indicate this even where I have omitted criticism of them. This book is written, then, from a point of view outside empiricism, and I can only hope that this will not strike the reader as question begging.

A word about sources and chronology is in order here. Throughout the book I have identified the sources of quotations from Wittgenstein by means of the abbreviations listed on pages xiii–xiv, which are given there in roughly chronological order. Wittgenstein's early ideas are set out in his pre-*Tractatus* notebooks (NB) and in the *Tractatus* itself (TLP), which was published in 1921. For the next seven years he stayed away from philosophy. When he returned to it in 1929, he held a series of conversations with several members of the Vienna Circle, which continued into 1932. Friedrich Waismann recorded those conversations, and they were eventually published as *Ludwig Wittgenstein and the Vienna Circle* (WVC), together with Waismann's "Theses," which the latter composed as a compendium of Wittgenstein's views in the early 1930s. This is a valuable source for identifying the changes that were taking place in Wittgenstein's thinking in the years 1929–1932, as is *Philosophische Bemerkungen* (PB) – in English, *Philosophical Remarks* (PR), which Wittgenstein wrote during this period. By 1930, when he began lecturing at Cambridge, his new ideas had begun to gel, and we are fortunate in having a rather complete record, in the form of students' notes, of the lectures Wittgenstein gave during the years 1930–39 (WL32, WL35, LSD, and LFM). (Some of his own lecture notes (NFL and CE) have also been published.) We also have from this period *The Blue and Brown Books* (BB), which he dictated during the years 1933–34 and 1934–35. (The Blue Book is a sustained exposition and refinement of neutral monism.) *Philosophical Grammar* (PG) was composed, and underwent several revisions, during the years 1932–34. It contains many passages that were later incorporated into Part I of *Philosophical Investigations* (PI). Wittgenstein's last lectures were delivered in 1946–1947, and the copious notes of three of his students, published as *Wittgenstein's Lectures on Philosophical Psychology* (WL47), show that he had not abandoned the radical empiricism (neutral monism) he was so plainly espousing in the early 1930s.

The date of composition of the *Investigations* requires some explaining. In the "Editors' Note" (PI, p. vi) we are told only that Part I was completed by 1945 and that Part II was written between 1947 and 1949. This has left some readers with the impression that the *Investigations* was composed during the mid- and late-1940s – an impression that helps to sustain the belief that Wittgenstein's development included three periods: the *Tractatus* phase, the phenomenalistic phase of the 1930s, and his later philosophy of the 1940s. This, however, was certainly not how Wittgenstein himself regarded his work. Discussing the history of the

Investigations with Oets Bouwsma in 1949, he said that he had begun it "eighteen years ago," i.e., in 1931.[13] From this we can infer that in 1949 Wittgenstein saw his book as being of a piece with the neutral monism he was so clearly espousing in the early 1930s. As I remarked above, the *Investigations* contains many passages taken directly from *Philosophical Grammar*, which was completed by 1934. (These are found mainly in the middle portion of Part I, where Wittgenstein again expounds and refines his neutral monism.) Moreover, the first 189 sections of the *Investigations* were composed in the mid 1930s,[14] and accordingly these sections, too, must be interpreted in the light of the views Wittgenstein was expounding in his notes and lectures of that period. Part II of the *Investigations*, written between 1947 and 1949, is largely derived from the notes later published as *Remarks on the Philosophy of Psychology* (RPP I and RPP II) and *Last Writings on Philosophy of Psychology* (LW, I). (The notes comprising these volumes are, to a large extent, concerned with developing a theory of perception that Wittgenstein first adopted in 1930.) *Zettel* (Z), which Wittgenstein regarded as the repository of important remarks, is also mainly a selection of material from these last-mentioned notes and can therefore be mainly credited to the final years of his life, but it also contains passages he had preserved from as early as 1929.[15] *On Certainty* (OC), written during the last eighteen months of Wittgenstein's life, shows him struggling with a problem he had mentioned in his conversations with Waismann in 1929 (WVC, p. 47) but had left largely uninvestigated, namely, whether one can "*know* truths, not only about sense-data but also about things" (OC, §426).

Notes

1. Thus Norman Malcolm describes the *Investigations* as "an assault upon the fundamental conceptions of Wittgenstein's first book" and goes on to say that "Wittgenstein purged himself of the thinking of the *Tractatus* and created a revolutionary new philosophy" [*Nothing is Hidden* (Oxford: Blackwell, 1986, 1986), pp. vii and ix]. In a well-known essay D. A. T. Gasking and A. C. Jackson declare: ". . . in the last twenty or so years of his life Wittgenstein turned his back on the *Tractatus* and went on to produce and to teach at Cambridge a whole new way of philosophizing" ["Wittgenstein as Teacher," reprinted in *Ludwig Wittgenstein: The Man and His Philosophy*, ed. K. T. Fann (New York: Dell, 1967), p. 49].

2. In 1948, just three years before his death, Wittgenstein remarked to Drury: "My fundamental ideas came to me very early in life" [quoted by M. O'C. Drury, "Conversations With Wittgenstein," in *Recollections of Wittgenstein*, ed. Rush Rhees (Oxford: Oxford University Press, 1984), p. 158]. He could hardly have spoken in this way in 1948 if what were then his fundamental ideas had come to him only after 1929, when he was forty years of age. It is noteworthy that Wittgenstein chose as his motto for the *Investigations* a passage from Nestroy that can be translated: "It is in the nature of progress that it appears much greater than it actually is." The significance

of this lies in the fact that Wittgenstein intended (see PI, p. x) that the *Tractatus* and the *Investigations* should be published in a single volume, so that this motto, sandwiched between them, would serve as a warning that the difference between the two books is not as great as it may appear.

3. I am going to use the term "phenomenalism" to mean any theory that maintains that there can be nothing 'beyond' immediate experience and, in one way or another, reduces material things to sense-data.

4. G. A. Paul, for instance, began an essay on Wittgenstein by saying that "He follows Moore in the defence of Common Sense and in a regard for our ordinary language" ["Wittgenstein" in *The Revolution in Philosophy*, A. J. Ayer et al., (London: Macmillan, 1956), p. 88]. John Wisdom also discounted differences between Moore and Wittgenstein [*Paradox and Discovery* (New York: Philosophical Library, 1965), p. 156]. And Gilbert Ryle said of Wittgenstein: "Like Moore, he explores the logic of all the things all of us say. . . . What had, since the early days of this century been the practice of G. E. Moore has received a rationale from Wittgenstein; and I expect that when the curtain is lifted we shall also find that Wittgenstein's concrete methods have increased the power, scope and delicacy of the methods by which Moore has for so long explored in detail the internal logic of what we say" [Ludwig Wittgenstein," reprinted in *Ludwig Wittgenstein: The Man and His Philosophy*, op. cit. pp. 122 and 124].

5. Norman Malcolm reports that "Wittgenstein believed that the Theory of Descriptions was Russell's most important production . . ." [*Ludwig Wittgenstein: A Memoir* (Oxford, 1958), p. 68]. What he valued in the Theory of Descriptions was its distinction between logical and grammatical form.

6. F. R. Leavis, "Memories of Wittgenstein" in *Recollections of Wittgenstein*, ed. Rush Rhees, (Oxford: Oxford University Press, 1984), p. 51. Leavis indicates that he is uncertain whether Wittgenstein said these exact words or only said something that could be expressed in these words.

7. *Ludwig Wittgenstein: A Memoir*, op. cit., p. 66.

8. The views closest to Wittgenstein's, both early and late, are those found in Ernst Mach's *The Analysis of Sensations* (fifth ed., 1906; English trans., 1914), Karl Pearson's *The Grammar of Science* (third ed., 1911), and Moritz Schlick's *Gesammelte Aufsätze* (1938).

9. Thus, we find Wittgenstein writing in 1947: "There just are many more language-games than are dreamt of in the philosophy of Carnap and others" (RPP, I, §920). That Wittgenstein meant to address only those who shared his philosophical perspective was made explicit in his notebooks:

> If I say that my book is meant for only a small circle of people (if it can be called a circle), I do not mean that I believe this circle to be the elite of mankind; but it does comprise those to whom I turn . . . because they form my cultural milieu, my fellow citizens as it were, in contrast to the rest who are *foreign* to me (CV, p. 10).

10. An example of the misunderstandings that arise from an ignorance of Wittgenstein's fundamental ideas is Norman Malcolm's *Nothing is Hidden*, op. cit. Malcolm advances an account of Wittgenstein's later work that bears scant resemblence to the truth. More egregious examples are noted below.

11. This was certainly the received view among those close to Wittgenstein. G. H. Von Wright, for example, says: "The later Wittgenstein, I should say, has no ancestors in the history of thought. His work signalizes a radical departure from previously existing paths of philosophy" ["Biograph-

ical Sketch" in Norman Malcolm, *Ludwig Wittgenstein: A Memoir* (op. cit.), p. 15].

12. Quoted by M. O'C. Drury, "Conversations with Wittgenstein," op. cit., p. 157.

13. O. K. Bouwsma, *Wittgenstein: Conversations 1949–1951* (Indianapolis: Hackett Publishing Co., 1986), p. 9.

14. G. H. von Wright tells us: "In August 1936 Wittgenstein began a revision, in German, of the Brown Book which had been dictated in English one year earlier. He called the revision *Philosophische Untersuchungen*. He soon abandoned work on it as unsatisfactory, and made a fresh start in the autumn of the same year. What he then wrote is substantially identical with the first 189 sections of the *Investigations* in its printed form" ("Biographical Sketch," op. cit., pp. 14–15).

15. See the editors' preface (Z, p. iv). RPP II contains an appendix (pp. 123–130) showing correspondences to both *Zettel* and the *Investigations*.

I

From Idealism to Pure Realism

1

Wittgenstein's Philosophical Beginnings

Wittgenstein arrived in Cambridge in 1911 to study with Russell, having a background in engineering and no formal training in philosophy.[1] Since 1908 he had been enrolled in the Engineering Department of Manchester University, where he had begun work on the design of an aircraft engine. His interest in this work was eventually supplanted by an interest in mathematics and the foundations of mathematics when a fellow student directed him to Russell's *The Principles of Mathematics*. This began a chain of events that led him to Cambridge in October 1911, where he spent the next five terms at Trinity College as Russell's student and protégé.

At Cambridge his interest in the foundations of mathematics was augmented by Russell's concern with epistemology. This was not completely new territory for Wittgenstein, for, as Anscombe reports: "As a boy of sixteen Wittgenstein had read Schopenhauer and had been greatly impressed by Schopenhauer's theory of the 'world as idea' (though not of the 'world as will'); Schopenhauer then struck him as fundamentally right, if only a few adjustments and clarifications were made."[2] Similarly, Von Wright reports: "If I remember correctly, Wittgenstein told me that he had read Schopenhauer's *Die Welt als Wille und Vorstellung* as a youth and that his first philosophy was a Schopenhauerian epistemological idealism."[3] This is confirmed by a passage in Wittgenstein's pre-*Tractatus* notebooks, in which he describes his philosophical development as having begun with idealism (NB, p. 85). With such a philosophical orientation he must have received a rude shock at Cambridge, for idealism had recently come under attack by both Moore and Russell.

What Wittgenstein encountered there can be partly inferred from Russell's account of his own development.

During 1898, various things caused me to abandon both Kant and Hegel. . . . But these motives would have operated more slowly than they did, but for the influence of G. E. Moore. He also had a Hegelian period, but it was briefer than mine. He took the lead in rebellion, and I followed with a sense of emancipation. Bradley argued that everything that common sense believes in is mere appearance; we reverted to the opposite extreme, and thought that *everything* is real that common sense, uninfluenced by philosophy or theology, supposes real.[4]

What Russell fails to mention here is that he and Moore did nothing to challenge the idea that what we perceive (or 'directly perceive') are sense-impressions, not tables, chairs and people. The result was that they both embraced mind–body dualism, and, moreover, they took this to be the "common sense view of the world."[5] In doing so, they departed from the tradition, beginning with Berkeley, that seeks to overcome philosophical skepticism regarding 'the external world' by embracing phenomenalism. As a result, they were obliged to address the various forms of skepticism that dualism introduces.[6] Yet Russell and Moore dealt with these problems in distinctly different ways.

In crediting Moore with leading the rebellion, Russell was no doubt referring to Moore's essay "The Refutation of Idealism," published in 1903,[7] and over the years Moore continued to sharpen his attack on idealism. In his 1910–1911 lectures, published much later as *Some Main Problems of Philosophy*, he undertook to criticize phenomenalism as well, maintaining that both theories are not only untrue but are sharply at odds with the way the plain man, the nonphilosopher, thinks of himself and the world – at odds, as he put it, with "the Common Sense view of the world." In 1914, in "The Status of Sense-Data," Moore presented a somewhat improved version of what he had said in 1910, arguing this time that phenomenalism fails to accommodate "the natural sense" of certain of our everyday words.[8] (In particular, he argued that, contrary to Berkeley, a counterfactual analysis of such a sentence as "The pot boiled over while no one was watching" misrepresents what the plain man would mean by that.) In the same essay Moore maintained that the only plausible account of the relation of sense-data and material things is the Lockean view that material things are distinct from, and the cause of, sense-data. And yet he acknowledged that such a view presents a major problem, for it makes it difficult to see *how* we could ever know that there are material things causing our sense-data and how we could know what qualities material things have.[9] This is a difficulty Moore never satisfactorily overcame.[10]

Russell, although he may have been goaded by Moore to abandon idealism, followed a very different route. By 1914, in *Our Knowledge of the External World*,[11] he had adopted a position quite the opposite of Moore's, for he rejected the causal theory of perception and devised a reductionist account of material things. On one point, however, he agreed with Moore: he allowed that the plain man *believes* in the existence of a world of material things beyond sense-data. Russell's reductionist account, then, was not intended to rescue common sense from skepticism. On this point he was prepared to say only that "*in so far* as physics or common sense is verifiable, it must be capable of interpretation in terms of actual sense-data alone,"[12] thus leaving himself the option of declaring that the plain man regularly believes things and says things that cannot be known to be true. The maxim, as he called it, for his style of philosophy was this: "Whenever possible, logical constructions are to be substituted for inferred entities."[13] Here we see Russell's indifference to ordinary language: his logical constructions were not intended to analyze things the plain man says but to provide (verifiable) substitutes for them wherever "inferred entities" are mentioned or presupposed. As for skepticism, Russell could only say that, while no one tries to live by this philosophy, it is "logically irrefutable."[14] This, one could say, was the principal difference between Russell and Moore: while Moore labored to defend (his dualistic version of) common sense against skepticism, Russell was sure that no such defense can succeed and so concerned himself with devising logical constructions that bore only a distant resemblance (or none at all) to what the plain man thinks and says.

This, then, was part of the philosophical atmosphere in which Wittgenstein found himself at Cambridge, and it will be instructive to consider how he reacted to it. Although deeply influenced by idealism, he must have been impressed by the fact that Moore and Russell were arguing that idealism is a very peculiar view, one that is certainly at odds with the way we all normally think of ourselves and the world. And yet Moore and Russell were not in agreement on the proper alternative to idealism. There was, therefore, much that remained unsettled, and Wittgenstein was obliged to make some fateful choices at this early point in his career, choices that shaped not only the *Tractatus* but his later writings as well. To understand the choices he made, we need to consider the alternatives available to him.

First of all, it never occurred to Wittgenstein to challenge the very idea of sense-impressions (or sensible qualities), and that fact limited his options in a most important way. It forced him into a choice between joining Moore in embracing Locke's causal theory of the relation of sense-data and material things or following other empiricists in adopting a reductionist (phenomenalist) account of the 'external world.' This choice could not have been difficult to make, for like other philosophers of the period Wittgenstein must have been dissatisfied with the causal theory of perception. Russell, in his 1914 essay "The Relation of Sense-data to Physics," stated the objection as follows:

But how is the correlation itself [between physical objects and sense-data] ascertained? A correlation can only be ascertained empirically by the correlated objects being constantly *found* together. But in our case, only one term of the correlation, namely, the sensible term, is ever *found*: the other term [i.e., the supposed physical cause] seems essentially incapable of being found. Therefore, it would seem, the correlation with objects . . . is itself utterly and for ever unverifiable.[15]

This argument, which Wittgenstein was later to state as his own (see

WL32, p. 81), had far-reaching consequences in Wittgenstein's think-ing. For the argument can be generalized as an objection to *any* view that holds that we have inductive evidence for something *essentially* unverifiable. (To state the matter using terminology Wittgenstein later adopted, Russell's argument is that one could not have a reason to treat Xs as *symptoms* of Ys unless Xs and Ys had been regularly observed to go together, which would be possible only if Xs and Ys are *both* observable phenomena.[16]) There cannot, then, be *evidence* for the existence of anything that transcends experience, and so (assuming that beliefs arise from evidence) it can't be the case that anyone *believes* in anything that transcends experience. Accordingly, when Wittgenstein explained the *Tractatus* to Frank Ramsey in 1923, he said that it is "nonsense to believe in anything not given in experience."[17] Or, as he said later, "It isn't possible to believe something for which you cannot imagine some kind of verification" (PR, p. 89).[18]

This point has an obvious bearing on what Moore and Russell held in regard to 'common sense': both maintained that the plain man holds a dualistic view of the world. Because this saddles the plain man with be-liefs in a variety of transcendent entities, Wittgenstein was obliged to dis-miss this account as nonsensical. (For the same reason he could not have agreed with Russell that the philosopher's job is to substitute logical con-structions for what the plain man says, for this view of philosophy also derives from the assumption that the plain man constantly assumes the existence of various transcendent – or "inferred" – entities.) Later, in *The Blue Book*, Wittgenstein made this point explicit by saying that "the com-mon-sense philosopher [i.e., Moore] . . . n.b. is not the common-sense man, who is as far from realism as from idealism" (BB, p. 48). This comes to: the common-sense man is not a realist in that he does not speak of things that transcend experience but is also not an idealist in that he does not doubt (or deny) the existence of tables, chairs and other people.[19]

In reviewing Wittgenstein's options, then, there are various things we can rule out: the Lockean view of perception, the dualistic view of 'common sense,' and the idea that philosophers must content them-selves with inventing logical constructions. What can we rule in?

In Wittgenstein's pre-*Tractatus* notebooks there is a group of remarks, dated 1 May, 1915, in which Wittgenstein contrasts his own views with Russell's. The most significant of these are the following:

Scepticism is *not* irrefutable, but *obvious nonsense* if it tries to doubt where no question can be asked.

For doubt can only exist where a question exists; a question can only exist where an answer exists, and this can only exist where something *can* be said. . . .[20]

My method is not to sift the hard from the soft [as Russell claims to do], but to see the hardness of the soft (NB, p. 44).

In the first of these remarks Wittgenstein is clearly dismissing Russell's view (see above) that skepticism is "logically irrefutable." Taken together, however, these remarks are a commentary on Russell's distinction between "hard and soft data." In *Our Knowledge of the External World* Russell explained this as follows:

> I mean by "hard" data those [beliefs] which resist the solvent influence of critical reflection, and by "soft" data those which, under the operation of this process, become to our minds more or less doubtful. The hardest of hard data are of two sorts: the particular facts of sense, and the general truths of logic. . . .
> Certain common beliefs are undoubtedly excluded from hard data. Such is the belief . . . that sensible objects persist when we are not perceiving them. Such also is the belief in other people's minds . . .[21]

What Russell here calls "critical reflection" he identifies on a later page as philosophical skepticism, saying that it is essential to philosophy "to practise methodological doubt, like Descartes" in order to subject our naive beliefs to "the ordeal of sceptical criticism."[22] By this process, says Russell, we discover which of our beliefs are "capable of a true interpretation," i.e., which are "hard data." For Russell, then, a central question of philosophy was this: Which of the propositions of ordinary language are (as he put it) capable of interpretation in terms of actual sense-data alone? And, owing to his dualistic view of 'common sense,' he was obliged to hold that *some* of these propositions – *some* of the things we commonly say – fail this test. It was in opposition to this that Wittgenstein said that his own method, by contrast, "is to see the hardness of the soft." By this he meant that his method is to show that all the propositions of our everyday language belong to a phenomenological language.[23] At the time of the *Tractatus* he took this to mean that what the plain man says in speaking of tables and chairs can be analyzed into propositions about phenomenal entities. Later on, as I will show, he came to think that the *Tractatus* version of reductionism was mistaken and, under the influence of Wolfgang Kohler, replaced it with a subtler form of phenomenalism.

To make good this position, what Wittgenstein found himself in need of was not a new solution to skepticism regarding 'the external world,' for other empiricists – beginning with Berkeley – had already blazed that trail. What he needed was a way of embracing phenomenalism without falling into solipsism, i.e., without remaining a skeptic in regard to other minds.[24] Because Russell at this time remained a dualist, he was prepared to leave other minds in limbo: he rejected the argument from analogy and concluded that one cannot know whether any other person exists.[25] Finding this unacceptable, Wittgenstein turned for a solution to a radical form of empiricism which was much in vogue at the time: neutral monism.[26] This theory, which originated with William James and Ernst Mach, holds that the world consists, not of mind and matter, but of "pure experience." Or as Mach put it, "the world consists only of our sensations."[27] The radical feature of neutral monism is that, unlike idealism, it does not hold that everything is mental or *in* a mind. On the contrary, it claims to eliminate altogether the (Cartesian) mind or ego, thus doing away with the subjectivity of experience. In this view, then, there is nothing that is subjective (or private) and therefore there is nothing that is unknowable: not only are such things as tables and chairs given in immediate experience, but so, too, are the thoughts, feelings, desires, etc. of other people.[28] This, then, was the view Wittgenstein adopted in the *Tractatus*.

In the next chapter I will provide a fuller account of neutral monism and evidence of Wittgenstein's adoption of this view. Before turning to that, however, there is a misconception regarding the *Tractatus* that I must address here.

Anscombe, in her influential book on the *Tractatus*, says that "empiricist or idealist preconceptions . . . are a thorough impediment to the understanding of . . . the *Tractatus*."[29] She goes on to say that "there is hardly any epistemology in the *Tractatus*."[30] What Wittgenstein was chiefly concerned with, according to Anscombe, were questions about naming and reference and other matters having to do with language. And these questions, she thinks, are unrelated to any epistemological concerns.[31] This interpretation of the *Tractatus* is utterly insulated from history.

Neutral monism, Wittgenstein's chosen ontology, was designed specifically to solve epistemological problems. So far as language is concerned, what Wittgenstein thought was this: to make an iron-clad case against skepticism what is needed is a theory of meaning that shows that the very nature of language precludes a philosopher from raising questions about (or expressing a belief in) the existence of anything not given in experience. Such a theory is needed, he thought, because philosophers have supposed that they could understand, could make sense of, such unanswerable 'questions' and unverifiable 'beliefs.' Indeed, Russell, in his 1910 essay "Knowledge by Acquaintance and Knowledge by Description," had undertaken to show how this is possible: ". . . among the objects with which we are acquainted are not included physical objects (as opposed to sense-data), nor other people's minds. These things are known to us by what I call 'knowledge by description'. . ."[32] He illustrates this by declaring that although we cannot refer to a table directly, since it is not given in experience, we can still speak of it by means of a definite description of the form "the physical object which causes such and such sense-data." In this way, said Russell, "knowledge by description . . . enables us to pass beyond the limits of our private experience."[34] In the *Tractatus* Wittgenstein undertook to show that neither this nor any other theory of reference could make it possible to speak of (or think of) entities not given in experience.[35] To show this, he devised a theory of language based on the idea that in order for a proposition to have sense it must be connected to the world – to *experience* – by means of unanalyzable names. If language consists, in the last analysis, of elementary propositions which are (as he put it) "configurations" of such names (TLP, 3.21), this will show that, contrary to Russell, one cannot by means of definite descriptions refer to entities that are not given in experience and may not exist.[36] To understand Wittgenstein, then, it is essential to recognize that he meant to show in the *Tractatus* that the only possible language is a phenomenological language and that therefore the epistemological problems posed by philosophical skeptics (since they cannot be formulated in a phenomenological language) are pseudo questions; they are, as he put it, *obvious nonsense*. This is why Wittgenstein could say in the *Tractatus* that "the reason why [philosophical] problems are posed is that the logic of our language is misunderstood" (TLP, p. 3).

So Anscombe's interpretation profoundly misrepresents the *Tractatus*. Worse yet, by failing to recognize Wittgenstein's concern with skepticism and the way this concern dictated his views about language, her interpretation hinders a proper understanding of the *Investigations* and *On Certainty*, both of which, as I will show, presuppose an acceptance of neutral monism.

If one wants to understand Wittgenstein, one must recognize that the fundamental assumption of the *Tractatus* is a metaphysical one, namely, that neutral monism alone provides the means for solving epistemological problems, and that this same premise underlies the *Investigations*, so that the two works are fundamentally alike and their differences relatively unimportant. The common premise of the two books is that Moore and Russell were both wrong about ordinary language, for in everyday life we do not refer to anything that transcends immediate experience. In short, Wittgenstein took the position that philosophical problems can be solved by reductionism. And the difference between the *Tractatus* and the *Investigations*, as the chapters which follow will demonstrate, lies chiefly in the fact that after 1929 he replaced his early version of reductionism with another.

Notes

1. In May 1912 Wittgenstein's friend David Pinset wrote in his diary: "Wittgenstein has only just started reading [in philosophy] and he expresses the most naive surprise that all the philosophers he once worshipped in ignorance are after all stupid and dishonest and make disgusting mistakes."

Quoted by Brian McGuinness in *Wittgenstein, A Life: Young Ludwig 1889–1921* (Berkeley: University of California Press, 1988), p. 104.

2. G. E. M. Anscombe, *An Introduction to Wittgenstein's Tractatus* (London, 1959), pp. 11–12.
3. G. H. von Wright, "Biographical Sketch," op. cit., p. 5.
4. Bertrand Russell, "My Mental Development," in *The Philosophy of Bertrand Russell*, ed. Paul A. Schilpp (New York, 1944), pp. 11–12.
5. Thus, in his 1915 essay "The Ultimate Constituents of Matter" (reprinted in *Mysticism and Logic*, George Allen and Unwin: London, 1951) Russell writes: "Common sense is accustomed to the division of the world into mind and matter" (p. 125), and he goes on to speak of "the dualism of common sense" (p. 126).
6. Russell, in 1912, stated the matter as follows: ". . . the real table, if there is one, is not the same as what we immediately experience by sight or touch or hearing. The real table, if there is one, is not *immediately* known to us at all, but must be an inference from what is immediately known. Hence, two very difficult questions at once arise; namely, (1) Is there a real table at all? (2) If so, what sort of object can it be?" [*The Problems of Philosophy* (London: Oxford University Press, 1912), p. 11].
7. Reprinted in G. E. Moore, *Philosophical Studies* (London: Routledge and Kegan Paul, 1922), pp. 1–30.
8. Reprinted in *Philosophical Studies*, op. cit., pp. 191 and 195. By 1914 Moore and Wittgenstein had become well acquainted (see "An Autobiography" in *The Philosophy of G. E. Moore*, ed. Paul A. Schilpp [Tudor: New York, 1942], p. 33), and there is internal evidence that suggests that various things Wittgenstein later wrote (e.g., PI, §116) were directed at Moore's attack on phenomenalism in "The Status of Sense-data."
9. "The Status of Sense-Data," op. cit., p. 196. In later years Moore was to say that one way in which he differed from philosophical skeptics is that "I am inclined to think that what is 'based on' an analogical or inductive argument, in the sense in which my knowledge or belief that this is a pencil is so, may nevertheless be certain knowledge and *not* merely more or less probable belief" [Four Forms of Scepticism" in *Philosophical Papers* (New York: Macmillan, 1959) pp. 225–226].
10. See my essay "Moore and Skepticism" in *Knowledge and Mind*, eds. Carl Ginet and Sydney Shoemaker (London: Oxford University Press, 1983), pp. 3–25.
11. Published by George Allen and Unwin: London, 1926, pp. 83–93. There can be no doubt that Wittgenstein was familiar with Russell's book, for he makes a number of comments on it in his pre-*Tractatus* notebooks (NB, p. 44)
12. *Our Knowledge of the External World*, op. cit., pp. 88–89.
13. "The Relation of Sense-data to Physics," reprinted in *Mysticism and Logic*, op. cit., p. 155.
14. *Our Knowledge of the External world*, op. cit., p. 74.
15. Op. cit., pp. 145–146.
16. In lectures (see LSD, pp. 12–13, quoted in Chapter 9) Wittgenstein invoked this generalized version of Russell's argument to declare that one is guilty of a *contradiction* if one says both (i) another person's behavior gives us a *clue* to his mental states and (ii) we can't observe the mental states of other people.
17. Quoted from Ramsey's notes by Merrill and Jaakko Hintikka, *Investigating Wittgenstein* (Oxford: Blackwell, 1986), p. 77.

18. The fact that the argument I have stated here is not made explicit in the *Tractatus* was typical of Wittgenstein's general unwillingness to present arguments for his own views. Russell, in a letter dated 28 May, 1912, said of Wittgenstein:

> I told him he ought not simply to *state* what he thinks true, but to give arguments for it, but he said arguments spoil its beauty, and that he would feel as if he was dirtying a flower with muddy hands. I told him I hadn't the heart to say anything against that, and that he had better acquire a slave to state the arguments. I am seriously afraid that no one will see the point of anything he writes, because he won't recommend it by arguments addressed to a different point of view. (Quoted by Brian McGuinness in *Wittgenstein: A Life,* op. cit., p. 104.)

19. A comment is in order here about the term "idealism." In a passage quoted above, Russell says that Bradley, an idealist, argued "that everything that common sense believes in is mere appearance." As thus understood, idealism maintains that tables and chairs, for example, are not real. In *Our Knowledge of the External World* Russell describes idealism as a philosophy that "condemns almost all that makes up our everyday world: things and qualities, relations, space, time, change, causation, activity, the self. All these things, though in some sense facts which qualify reality, are not real as they appear. What is real is one, single, indivisible, timeless whole, called the Absolute" (op. cit., p. 16). Russell also calls this position "universal scepticism" (ibid., pp. 74 and 78). Wittgenstein at some point adopted Russell's usage, in which idealism is identified as a form of skepticism. Thus, in *On Certainty* he writes: "The idealist's question would be something like: 'What right have I not to doubt the existence of my hands?' " (OC, §24). In his 1931 lectures we find him setting up the following contrast: whereas "idealists were right in that we never transcend experience," "realists were right in protesting that chairs do exist" (WL32, p. 80), thus implying that idealists do not allow that chairs exist. Wittgenstein, we might say, came to think that Moore and Russell each had a part of the truth, Moore's being that common sense is philosophically defensible, Russell's being that whatever is philosophically defensible must not transcend immediate experience.

20. These first two sentences were retained in the *Tractatus* at 6.51. In 1930 Wittgenstein said in his conversations with Waismann: ". . . it is only the method of answering a question that tells you what the question was really about. Only when I have answered a question can I know what it was aimed at. (The sense of a proposition is the method of its verification.)" (WVC, p. 79).

21. Op. cit., pp. 77–79.

22. Ibid., p. 242.

23. Moore, despite his rejection of phenomenalism, had said that it has one great advantage over other theories, for "it enables us to see, more clearly than any other view can, how our knowledge of physical propositions can be based on our experience of sensibles" ("The Status of Sense-Data," op. cit., p. 190). Wittgenstein, apparently, found this sufficient recommendation and for the rest of his life took it for granted that some version of phenomenalism must be correct. Even as late as 1948 Wittgenstein praised Berkeley as "a very deep thinker" (see Introduction, this volume), the relevance of this being that Berkeley, while debunking the idea of material things, claimed not to be denying the existence of tables and chairs.

24. At an early stage (see NB, p. 85) he had been willing to embrace solipsism. Russell, in a letter dated 23 April, 1912, wrote of Wittgenstein: "I argued about Matter with him. He thinks it is a trivial problem. He admits that if there is no Matter then no one exists but himself, and be says that doesn't hurt, since physics and astronomy and all the other sciences could still be interpreted so as to be true" (quoted by Brian McGuinness in *Wittgenstein, A Life,* Op. Cit., p. 106). By 1915 Wittgenstein had abandoned solipsism in favor of neutral monism.

25. *Our Knowledge of the External World*, op. cit., pp. 101–104.

26. The term "neutral monism" seems to have first occurred in the literature in Russell's 1914 essay "On the Nature of Acquaintance," reprinted in *Logic and Knowledge*, ed. Robert C. Marsh (London: George Allen and Unwin, 1956), where Russell makes the following three-fold distinction: dualists classify "everything that exists as either mind or matter"; idealists, by contrast, hold that "whatever exists may be called 'mental,' in the sense of having a certain character, known to us by introspection as belonging to our own minds. . . . On the other hand, William James and the American realists have urged that there is no specific character of 'mental' things. . . . These men may be called 'neutral monists,' because, while rejecting the division of the world into mind and matter, they do not say 'all reality is mind,' nor yet 'all reality is matter' " (p. 129).

27. *The Analysis of Sensations*, 5th ed. (New York: Dover, 1959), p. 12.

28. Ralph Barton Perry, one of the leading proponents of this view, put the matter, in part, as follows: "Contrary to common philosophical opinion, my purpose, intention, or desire is least likely to escape you. This element of my mind is revealed even in my gross action, in the motions of my body as a whole. . . . The content of my purpose . . . [is] in your full view, whether you are a historian or a familiar companion" *Present Philosophical Tenencies* (New York: Longmans, Green and Co., 1912), p. 295.

29. *An Introduction to Wittgenstein's Tractatus*, op. cit., pp. 12–13.

30. Ibid., pp. 27.

31. This has become the received view of the *Tractatus*. See, for example, P. M. S. Hacker *Insight and Illusion: Wittgenstein on Philosophy and the Metaphysics of Experience* (Oxford: Oxford University Press, 1971), p. 33. H. O. Mounce ignores epistemological issues altogether in his book *Wittgenstein's Tractatus* (Chicago: University of Chicago Press, 1981).

32. Reprinted in *Mysticism and Logic*, op. cit., p. 214.

33. *The Problems of Philosophy*, op. cit., p. 47.

34. Ibid, p. 59.

35. After returning to philosophy in 1929 Wittgenstein made this quite explicit:

> The verification is not *one* token of the truth, it is *the* sense of the proposition. . . .
> Indeed Russell has already shown by his theory of descriptions, that you can't get a knowlege of things by sneaking up on them from behind and it can only *look* as if we knew more about things than they have shown us openly and honestly. But he has obscured everything again by using the phrase "indirect knowledge" (PR, pp. 200–201).

Although Wittgenstein has Russell's terminology slightly wrong, it is clear that he is criticizing Russell's idea that by means of definite descriptions one can speak of 'transcendent' entities. He also says: "You cannot use language to go beyond the possibility of evidence" (PR, p. 55).

36. In *Philosophical Remarks* he says: "What I once called 'objects,' simples, were simply what I could refer to without running the risk of their possible non-existence. . ." (p. 72). Plainly, if all of language is analyzable into names of such objects, so that one cannot even *allude to* anything not given in experience, then philosophical skepticism cannot arise about *anything*, i.e., the very attempt to pose skeptical problems involves a misinterpretation of our language.

2

Neutral Monism

By 1911, when Wittgenstein arrived in Cambridge, neutral monism was becoming a widely shared view. Among its advocates were Ernst Mach, William James, Karl Pearson, and the American new realists.[1] Russell, too, was greatly interested in neutral monism and discussed it at length in several articles published between 1912 and 1914, although he did not fully embrace the view until 1921. Wittgenstein did not await Russell's approval: by 1916 he had made up his mind that neutral monism provides the way out of philosophical difficulties. This is the single most important fact to be known about Wittgenstein's views, for if one fails to take it into account, one is bound to misunderstand him completely.

The great attraction of neutral monism was that it appeared to offer an escape from the problems generated by dualism. W. T. Stace nicely summarizes the matter as follows:

Neutral monism appears to be inspired by two main motives. The first is to get rid of the psycho-physical dualism which has troubled philosophy since the time of Descartes. The second motive is empiricism. The "stuff" of the neutral monists is never any kind of hidden unperceivable "substance" or *Ding-an-sich*. It is never something which lies *behind* the phenomenal world, out of sight. It always, in every version of it, consists in some sort of directly perceivable entities – for instance, sensations, sense-data, colours, smells, sounds. Thus, if matter is wholly constructed out of any such directly experienceable stuff, there will be nothing in it which will not be empirically verifiable. The same will be true of mind.[2]

By this final remark, that "the same will be true of mind," Stace means to say that neutral monists hold that mental events are also not "something which lies *behind* the phenomenal world."

This, then, is the view that Wittgenstein had embraced by 1916. In the present chapter my aim is to sketch in the main features of this view and to show, by quoting from both the *Tractatus* and his later writings, how Wittgenstein's remarks bear the stamp of neutral monism.

The two most important features of neutral monism were developed by Berkeley (the elimination of matter[3]) and Hume (the elimination of the self as an entity[4]), but the neutral monists made significant additions. Their aim was to dispatch dualism by doing away with (Cartesian) minds as well as matter, which is why the view came to be called *neutral* monism, which distinguishes it from the "mentalistic" monism of idealists such as F. H. Bradley. Accordingly, they sometimes stated their view by saying that the world consists of a neutral stuff, a stuff which, in itself, is neither mental nor physical but which may, in some of its relations, be called "mental" and, in other relations, "physical." This formulation did not interest Wittgenstein, and I will therefore ignore it.[5]

The Elimination of Matter

As we saw in Chapter 1, Mach states his position by saying that "the world consists only of our sensations." Wittgenstein in his pre-*Tractatus* notebooks said something similar: "All experience is world and does not need the subject" (NB, p. 89). This is an explicit affirmation of neutral monism, although Wittgenstein, in his notebooks, calls it "realism" (NB, p. 85) and in the *Tractatus*, "pure realism" (TLP, 5.64).[6]

Mach also states his position by saying: ". . . we do not find the [alleged] gap between bodies and sensations . . . , between what is without and what is within, between the material world and the spiritual world,"[7] and goes on to say: "I see . . . no opposition of physical and psychical, but [see only] simple identity as regards these elements. In the sensory sphere of my consciousness everything is at once physical and psychical."[8] Wittgenstein was endorsing such a view when, in his lectures of 1931–32, he said: "Idealists were right in that we never transcend experience. Mind and matter is a division *in* experience" (WL32, p. 80). He also said: "To talk about the relation of [physical] object and sense-datum is nonsense. They are not two separate things" (WL32, p. 109). In 1938, after much of *Philosophical Investigations* had been written, he repeated this point:

It is not a question here at all whether the name of the physical object signifies one object and the name of the impression signifies another, as if one successively pointed to two different objects and said, "I mean this object, not that one." The picture of the different objects is here used entirely wrongly.

Not, the one name is for the immediate object, the other for something else [that's *not* given in immediate experience]; but rather, the two words are simply used differently (CE, Appendix B, pp. 435–436; my translation).

These passages, and others we will consider presently, show that Wittgenstein joined the neutral monists in dismissing material objects.

Elimination of the Self as an Entity

The most distinctive feature of neutral monism was its insistence that there is no self (or ego) and hence that there is no need for the dualist's distinction between the mental and the physical (or the inner and the outer). In 1914 Russell was not yet prepared to concede this, but he nevertheless recognized the attraction of neutral monism:

In favor of the theory [of neutral monism], we may observe . . . the very notable simplification which it introduces. That the things given in experience should be of two fundamentally different kinds, mental and physical, is far less satisfactory to our intellectual desires than that the dualism should be merely apparent and superficial. Occam's razor, . . . which I should regard as the supreme methodological maxim in philosophizing, prescribes James's [monistic] theory as preferable to dualism if it can possibly be made to account for the facts.[9]

When Russell wrote this passage he thought that neutral monism could not account for all the facts. In particular, he held that a "mental" fact (such as his seeing an image) contains as one of its constituents a "self," which is acquainted with the other constituent of the fact (e.g., an image), and that this makes that other constituent (the image) subjective rather than "neutral." He goes on to acknowledge, however, that this analysis is faced with the difficulty Hume had pointed out:

The strongest objection which can be urged against the above analysis of experience into a dual relation of subject and object is derived from the elusiveness of the subject in introspection. We can easily become aware of our own experiences, but we seem never to become aware of the subject itself. This argument tends, of course, to support neutral monism.[10]

In 1914 Russell did not find this argument compelling and therefore rejected neutral monism and, in consequence, embraced skepticism regarding other minds.

The position Russell was unwilling to adopt in 1914 is that which Mach, in *The Analysis of Sensations*, had formulated as follows:

The primary fact is not the ego, but the elements (sensations). . . . The elements constitute the I. "*I* have the sensation green," signifies that the element green occurs in a given complex of other elements (sensations, memories). When *I* cease to have the sensation green, when *I* die, then the elements no longer occur in the ordinary, familiar association. That is all. Only an ideal mental-economical unity, not a real unity, has ceased to exist. The ego is not a definite, unalterable, sharply-bounded unity.[11]

"The ego," Mach concludes, "must be given up."[12]

In another passage dealing with this topic Mach quotes with approval a passage from Lichtenberg:

In his philosophical notes Lichtenberg says: "We become conscious of certain presentations that are not dependent upon us; of others that we at least think are dependent upon us. Where is the border-line? We know only the existence of our sensations, presentations, and thoughts. We should say *It thinks*, just as we say [of the dawn] *It lightens*. It is going too far to say *Cogito*, if we translate *Cogito* by *I think*. The assumption, or postulation, of the ego is a mere practical necessity." Though the method by which Lichtenberg arrived at this result is somewhat different from ours, we must nevertheless give our full assent to his conclusion.[13]

The elimination of the Cartesian ego seemed essential to the neutral monists because it seemed to them (a) that skeptical questions about the existence of the external world arose precisely from Descartes' *Cogito* and (b) that those questions, once posed, were unanswerable. Although Descartes had said in *The Meditations* that God would not deceive us into thinking that there is an external world, Mach and the other neutral monists were unwilling to invoke a deity in order to avoid skepticism. Yet, they were unwilling to accept skepticism regarding the world dealt with by the sciences. Their way out of this impasse was to reject Descartes' Cogito, and this they accomplished by following Hume's lead in declaring that the *I* is not a genuine entity. For with the Cartesian *I* abolished, there could no longer be a question about what existed 'outside' (or 'beyond') this alleged *I*: if there is no self, there is also nothing 'beyond' it.

Wittgenstein, also intent upon avoiding skepticism, followed Mach's lead in this matter. In a notebook entry dated 7 August 1916 he wrote: "The I is not an object" (NB, p. 80), meaning that the first-person pronoun will not, contrary to Russell, occur in propositions whose logical form has been fully analysed. On 2 September he expanded on this: "Here we can see that solipsism coincides with pure realism, if it is strictly thought out. The I of solipsism shrinks to an extensionless point and what remains is the reality co-ordinated with it" (NB, p. 82). On 9 November, 1916 he explicitly embraced neutral monism: "All experience is world and does not need the subject" (NB, p. 89). In the *Tractatus* Wittgenstein makes these points in a more explicit way: "There is no such thing as the subject that thinks or entertains ideas" (TLP, 5.631). Later, in his conversations with Waismann he said: "The word 'I' belongs to those words that can be eliminated from language" (WVC, p. 49).

In Chapter 5 we will consider in detail Wittgenstein's treatment of this topic, both in the *Tractatus* and in his later work.[14] Suffice it here to say that he was confident that he could dismiss Russell's objection to neutral monism (that a mental fact contains the self as a constituent) and could thereby dismiss the dualist's notion of minds and their private contents. Also, he thought he had seen how to eliminate any epistemological problem about 'other minds,' for there *are* no minds.

There are no Inner and Outer Worlds

Having eliminated the ego, neutral monists thought it important to exhibit the implications of this. One such implication is that the philosophical distinction between an 'inner' and an 'outer' world must be abandoned. Mach stated the matter as follows:

There is no rift between the psychical and the physical, no inside and outside, no "sensation" to which an external "thing" different from sensation, corresponds. There is but one kind of elements, out of which this supposed inside and outside are formed – elements which are themselves inside or outside, according to the aspect in which, for the time being, they are viewed.[15]

Karl Pearson, another of the neutral monists whom Wittgenstein seems to have read and borrowed from, wrote:

There is no better exercise for the mind than the endeavor to reduce the perceptions we have of "external things" to the simple sense impressions by which we know them. The arbitrary distinction between outside and inside ourselves is then clearly seen to be one merely of everyday practical convenience. . . . The distinction between ourselves and the outside world is thus only an arbitrary, if practically convenient, division between one type of sense-impression [color, shape, etc.] and another [e.g., pain]. The group of sense-impressions forming what I term *myself* is only a small subdivision of the vast world of sense-impressions.[16]

Like Mach and Pearson, Wittgenstein was eager to eliminate any distinction between the 'inner' and the 'outer,' as we can see from the following passages:

Thought is a symbolic process. . . . It may involve images and these we think of as being "in the mind." This simile of being "inside" or "outside" the mind is pernicious. It derives from "in the head" when we think of ourselves as looking out from our heads and of thinking as something going on "in our head." But we then forget the picture and go on using language derived from it (WL32, p. 25).

The "inner" and the "outer," a *picture* (Z, §554).[17]

What misleads us here [in thinking about toothache] is the notion of "outside plus the inside" (LSD, p. 10).

"What I show [e.g. a drawing] *reveals* what I see" – in what sense does it do that? The idea is that now [in looking at my drawing] you can so to speak look inside me. Whereas [in truth] I only reveal to you what I see in a game of revealing and hiding which is entirely played with signs of one category [i.e., in a game in which what is revealed and what is hidden are *both* explicable in terms of immediate experience]. . . .
    We are thinking of a game in which there is an inside in the normal sense [e.g., "inside this box"].
    We must get clear about how the metaphor of revealing (outside and inside) is actually applied by us; otherwise we shall be tempted to look for an inside behind that which in our metaphor is the inside. . . .
    You compare it with such a statement as as: "If he had learned to open up, I could now see what's inside." I say yes, but remember what opening up in this case is like [e.g., confessing to secret fears] (NFL, p. 280).

In his last writings on this topic, in 1950, Wittgenstein wrote: "The 'inner' is a delusion" (LW, II, p. 84).

The Elimination of Private Objects

Neutral monists, by eliminating the Ego, meant to dispose of the idea that sense-impressions are "private" – i.e., *belong* to someone. Mach states this explicitly, using "sensations" to mean "sense-impressions":

Whoever cannot get rid of the conception of the Ego as a reality which underlies everything, will also not be able to avoid drawing a fundamental distinction between my sensations and your sensations. . . . From the standpoint which I here take up . . . , I no more draw an essential distinction between my sensations and the sensations of another person, than I regard red or green as belonging to an individual body.[18] Whether it may or may not prove possible to transfer someone else's sensations to me by means of nervous connexions, my view is not affected one way or the other. The most familiar facts provide a sufficient basis for this view.[19]

Wittgenstein's innovation was to extend Mach's pronouncement to include not only sense-impressions but all bodily 'sensations' (pain, tickling, etc.) as well. The Blue Book contains a passage which appears to be a direct commentary on the one just quoted from Mach:

If we are angry with someone for going out on a cold day with a cold in his head, we sometimes say: "I won't feel your cold." And this can mean: "I don't suffer when you catch cold." This is a proposition taught by experience. For we could imagine a, so to speak, wireless connection between the two bodies which made one person feel pain in his head when the other had exposed his to the cold air. One might in this case argue that the pains [I receive from this wireless connection] are mine because they are felt in my head; but suppose I and someone else had a part of our bodies in common, say a hand. Imagine the nerves and tendons of my arm and A's connected to this hand by an operation. Now imagine the hand stung by a wasp. Both of us cry, contort our faces, give the same description of the pain, etc. Now are we to say we have the same pain or different ones? If in such a case you say: "We feel pain in the same place, in the same body, our descriptions tally, but still my pain can't be his," I suppose as a reason you will be inclined to say: "because my pain is my pain and his pain is his pain." And here you are making a grammatical statement about the use of such a phrase as "the same pain." You say that you don't want to apply the phrase, "he has got my pain" or "we both have the same pain," and instead, perhaps, you will apply such a phrase as "his pain is exactly like mine." . . . Of course, if we exclude the phrase "I have his toothache" from our language, we also thereby exclude "I have (or feel) *my* toothache." Another form of our metaphysical statement is this: "A man's sense-data are private to himself." And this way of expressing it is even more misleading because it looks still more like an experiential proposition; the philosopher who says this may well think that he is expressing a kind of scientific truth.

We use the phrase "two books have the same color," but we could perfectly well say: "They can't have the *same* colour, because, after all, this book has its own colour, and the other book has its own colour too." This also would be stating a grammatical rule – a rule, incidentally, not in accordance with our ordinary usage. The reason why one should think of these two different usages at all is this: We compare the case of sense data with that of physical bodies, in which case we make a distinction between: "this is the same chair I saw an hour ago" and "this is not the same chair, but one exactly like the other." Here it makes sense to say, and it is an experiential proposition: "A and B couldn't have seen the same chair, for A was in London and B in Cambridge; they saw two chairs exactly alike." (Here it will be useful if you consider the different criteria for what we call "the identity of these objects." How do we apply the statements: "This is the same day . . .," "This is the same word . . .," "This is the same occasion," etc.?) (BB, pp. 54–55).

It is evident that Wittgenstein meant to dismiss the idea that sensations are private. This is a point he made repeatedly in his later writings and lectures, and in Chapter 6 we will consider this point in greater detail.

Behaviorism

Neither Mach nor Russell had offered a solution to the problem of other minds. Both were prepared to allow that there may be other minds, but neither had explained how one could have knowledge of them. Russell, because he held that the argument from analogy provides no certainty, was a skeptic in this matter. Mach says that "since [a person] does not perceive the sensations of his fellow-men or animals [he] supplies them by analogy,"[20] but Mach fails to address the epistemological problem this view entails. In this respect Mach fails to complete the project of neutral monism, which is to show that everything that exists lies open to view – or, as Stace puts it, nothing is "hidden." The completion of this project fell to the American new realists, especially R. B. Perry, who made a point of declaring that mental activities lie open to view. In a section of his book which is entitled "The Alleged Impossibility of Observing the Contents of Another Mind," he says that the mind is, "like any other thing, . . . open to general [i.e., public] observation."[21] As an illustration of this point he makes the remark (quoted above in note 28 of Chapter 1) that another person's intention or purpose is "in your full view" because his purpose or intention is "revealed . . . in the motions of [his] body." As a further illustration he writes:

There is another way in which you readily follow my mind, namely, through my verbal report. . . . Now it is frequently assumed by the sophisticated that when I thus verbally reveal my mind you do not *directly* know it. You are supposed directly to know only my words. But I cannot understand such a supposition, unless it means simply that you know my mind only *after* and *through* hearing my words.[22]

Perry allows that a person may, on occasion, not wish to divulge his plans or his suspicions and may in this sense keep them "hidden from general observation," but this, he adds, "does not imply any general proposition to the effect that a mind is *essentially* such as to be *absolutely* cut off from observation."[23] Perry's view, then, is that although it may occasionally be *difficult* to know the thoughts, emotions, etc. of another person, there is no general epistemological problem about knowing the mind of another.

Wittgenstein, too, thought that pure realism, having done away with Cartesian minds and their private contents, eliminated the epistemological problem about other minds, for if there are no (Cartesian) minds, then the fact that other people have thoughts and feelings, etc. must *also* be given in experience. This required Wittgenstein to assume that a doubly reductionist account could be given of the thoughts, feelings, etc. of others, i.e., that anything he said about another person's thoughts or feelings could be reduced to propositions about their bodies and that these, in turn, could be reduced to propositions about sense-impressions.

That Wittgenstein had adopted a behavioristic account of other people at the time of the *Tractatus* is evident from Frank Ramsey's notes of his 1923 interview with Wittgenstein regarding the *Tractatus*.[24] Waismann, in his compendium of Wittgenstein's views as they stood in the early 1930s, states Wittgenstein's position as follows:

A proposition cannot say more than is established by means of the method of its verification. If I say "My friend is angry" and establish this in virtue of his displaying certain perceptible behaviour, I only *mean* that he displays that behaviour (WVC, p. 244).

In The Blue Book Wittgenstein put the matter as follows:

. . . the activities of the mind lie open before us. And when we are worried about the nature of thinking, the puzzlement which we wrongly interpret to be one about the nature of a medium [in which thinking occurs] is a puzzlement caused by the mystifying use of our language. This kind of mistake recurs again and again in philosophy. . . . We are most strongly tempted to think that here are things hidden, something we can see from the outside but which we can't look into. And yet nothing of the sort is the case. . . . All the facts that concern us lie open before us. . . . (BB, p. 6).

Wittgenstein's behaviorism will be discussed in detail in Chapter 9.

The Mind–Body Problem

Stace, in the passage quoted at the beginning of this chapter, says that one of the main motives of the neutral monists "is to get rid of the psycho–physical dualism which has troubled philosophy since the time of Descartes." The problem for dualists is that of explaining how thoughts, emotions, sensations, etc. are related to (Cartesian) bodies, and what makes this a problem is that it is difficult to see how something of a mental (immaterial) nature could be related to a material body. Neutral monists maintained that this problem is a bogus one because, contrary to Descartes, the world is *not* composed of two different materials, mind and matter. What did Wittgenstein say about this?

The Blue Book is Wittgenstein's detailed exposition and defense of neutral monism, and in the course of it he undertakes to deal with the mind-body problem. This part of his discussion begins with his comments on the following passage from Mach's *The Analysis of Sensations*:

The philosophical spiritualist [the idealist] is often sensible of the difficulty of imparting the needed solidity to his mind-created world of bodies; the materialist is at a loss when required to endow the world of matter with sensation. The monistic point of view, which reflexion has evolved, is easily clouded by our older and more powerful instinctive notions [i.e., by our dualistic notions of mind and body].[25]

Mach says here that the idealist has difficulty "imparting the needed solidity" to the world, meaning, presumably, that the world would seem to lack solidity if it consists only of sensations (and not matter, too). And it is Mach's claim that neutral monism, by affirming that everything that is perceived is "at once physical and psychical," provides the world its "needed solidity." Wittgenstein begins by explaining Mach's point. He argues that it would be a mistake to think that a world without matter would lack solidity, and he does so by comparing this to the mistake made by popularizing scientists who tell us that "the floor on which we stand is not solid, as it appears to common sense," because wood consists of "particles filling space so thinly that it can almost be called empty" (BB, p. 45). The mistake here, he says, is that, as the word "solidity" is normally used, we contrast a solid floor with one that isn't solid because the wood is rotten, so that "not solid" is so used that it has an anti-thesis, whereas the popularizing scientist is misusing the phrase "lacks solidity" by declaring that *everything* lacks solidity, i.e., even when the wood is *not* rotten. Wittgenstein adds that the truth of the matter is that particle theory in physics is meant precisely "to explain the very phenomenon of solidity." Similarly, if we say that a world consisting of sensations (i.e., a world without matter) would lack solidity, we are again using words "in a typically metaphysical way, namely without an antithesis." I.e., just as it is a mistake to say the floor lacks solidity because it consists of particles, so it is a mistake to say that the table lacks solidity because it consists of sensible qualities, for one of those qualities is the solidity we feel when we handle the table.

At this point (BB, pp. 46–47) Wittgenstein introduces the second part of Mach's claim, namely, that neutral monism enables us to understand how animals and humans can have sensations, i.e., how sensations can be related to *bodies*. Wittgenstein begins by remarking that there are "propositions of which we may say that they describe facts in the material world" and also "propositions describing personal experience." He continues:

At first sight it may appear . . . that here we have [as dualists claim] two kinds of worlds, worlds built of different materials; a mental world and a physical world. The mental world in fact is liable to be imagined as gaseous, or rather, aethereal. But let me remind you here of the queer role which the gaseous and the aethereal play in philosophy – when we perceive that a substantive [e.g., "I"] is not used as what in general we should call the name of an object, and when therefore we can't help saying to ourselves that it is the name of an aethereal object. . . .[26] This is a hint as to how the problem of the two materials, *mind* and *matter*, is going to dissolve (BB, p. 47).

The problem he is referring to here is the mind–body problem (How can a *material* thing have thoughts, sensations, etc.?[27]), and Wittgenstein devotes the remainder of The Blue Book to its dissolution. I will not attempt to summarize all that he says in this regard, but three of his points can be briefly noted.

His first point, which we have already covered, is that we are misled by the substantive term "I" when it is used in, for example, "I am in pain," for in such a proposition it "is not a demonstrative pronoun" (BB, p. 68). Our failure to realize this, he says, "creates the illusion that we use this word to refer to something bodiless, which, however, has its seat in our body. In fact this seems to be the real ego, the one of which it was said, 'Cogito, ergo sum' " (BB, p. 69). In short, the dualist's notion of the mind results from a failure to understand the grammar of "I."

Wittgenstein's second point, by which he dismisses the dualist's notion of matter (i.e., that material things are distinct from sense-impressions), is less easily summarized, but in the course of it says: ". . . don't think that the expression 'physical object' is meant to distinguish one kind of object from another" (BB, p. 51). He is here making the point that he had made earlier in lectures: ". . . there is no fact that this is a physical object over and above the qualities and judgements of sense-data about it" (WL32, p. 81).

Taken together, these two points amount to the following: the idea that the world is composed of two very different materials, mind and matter, is a muddle, because (i) the dualistic conception of mind is a confusion about the grammar of "I," and (ii) the dualistic conception of matter involves the mistake of thinking that a chair, for example, is something over and above sense-data. But how does this provide a solution to the mind–body problem? Wittgenstein's discussion does not make this very clear, but it seems to involve a third point, which he develops early in The Blue Book, a point we have already considered, namely, that "the activities of the mind lie open before us" (BB, p. 6). This, as I have suggested, is a form of behaviorism, and Wittgenstein seems to have thought he could solve the mind–body problem by combining behaviorism with his first two points. He concludes The Blue Book on the following note:

Let us now ask: "Can a human *body* have pain?" One is inclined to say: "How can the body have pain? The body in itself is something dead; a body isn't conscious!". . . . And it is as though we saw that what has pain must be of a different nature from that of a material object; that, in fact, it must be of a mental nature. . . .

On the other hand we can perfectly well adopt the expression "This body feels pain", and we shall then, just as usual, tell it to go to the doctor, to lie down, and even to remember that when the last time it had pains they were over in a day. "But wouldn't this form of expression at least be an indirect one?". . . . One expression is no more direct than the other. . . .

The kernel of our proposition that that which has pain or sees or thinks is of a mental nature is only, that the word "I" in "I have pains" does not denote a particular body. . . . (BB, pp. 73–74).

I will not pause here to assess this argument, but this much is clear: The Blue Book disposes of the mind–body problem in the manner of the neutral monists, i.e., "the problem of the two materials, *mind* and *matter*," is a pseudoproblem because there aren't two such materials.

Opposition to the Causal Theory of Perception

Having dismissed not only matter but also Cartesian minds as repositories of sense-impressions, neutral monists were in a position to reject representative theories of perception, including Locke's causal theory. Thus, Mach writes:

For us . . . the world does not consist of mysterious entities, which by their interaction with another, equally mysterious entity, the ego, produce sensations, which alone are accessible. For us, colors, sounds, spaces, times, . . . are provisionally the ultimate elements, whose given connexion it is our business to investigate. It is precisely in this that the exploration of reality consists.[28]

Mach also says that it is a confusion to think of "experiences . . . as 'effects' of an external world. . . . This conception gives us a tangle of metaphysical difficulties which it seems impossible to unravel."[29] Karl Pearson was equally explicit in rejecting the causal theory of perception, saying: "There is no necessity, nay, there is want of logic, in the statement that behind sense-impressions there are 'things-in-themselves' *producing* sense-impressions."[30]

In his early period Wittgenstein did not state any criticism specifically of the causal theory of perception. Very likely he thought it unnecessary because of his explicitly stated objection to the very idea of causation, e.g., "Belief in the causal nexus is *superstition*" (TLP, 5.1361). Later, however, he stated his opposition to the causal theory in the same way as Russell had stated it (see Chapter 1, this volume) in 1914. In his lectures of 1931–1932 he said:

There is a tendency to make the relation between physical objects and sense-data a contingent relation. Hence such phrases as "caused by," "beyond," "outside." But the world is not composed of sense-data and physical objects. The relation between them is one in language – a necessary relation. If there were a relation of causation, you could ask whether anyone has ever seen a physical object causing a sense-datum. . . . All causal laws are learned by experience. We cannot therefore learn what is the cause of experience. If you give a scientific explanation of what happens, for instance, when you see, you are again describing an experience (WL32, p. 81).

Wittgenstein also said: "It is a fallacy to ask what causes my sense-data . . . ." (WL32, p. 115).

The Distinction between Appearance and Reality

In a clothing store a clerk may have occasion to explain to a customer, "The suit looks black in this artificial light, but take it to the window and you'll see that it *is* navy blue." The clerk does not mean to say: The suit is black, but it will, in chameleon fashion, *turn blue* in other circumstances. To the neutral monist (or any empiricist) the clerk's remark suggests a sort of dualism: how the suit *looks* in artificial light and what color the suit really *is* – despite it's present appearance. It was therefore obligatory for neutral monists to address the matter of "appearance and reality." Thus Mach writes:

A common and popular way of thinking and speaking is to contrast "appearance" with "reality." A pencil held in front of us in the air is seen by us as straight; dip it into water, and we see it crooked. In the latter case we say that the pencil *appears* crooked, but is in *reality* straight. But what justifies us in declaring one fact rather than another to be the reality, degrading the other to the level of appearance? In both cases we have to do with facts which present us with different combinations of the elements, combinations which in the two cases are differently conditioned. Precisely because of its environment the pencil dipped in water is optically crooked; but it is tactually and metrically straight. . . . To be sure, our expectation is deceived when, not paying sufficient attention to the conditions, and substituting for one another different cases of the combination, we fall into the natural error of expecting what we are accustomed to, although the case may be an unusual one. The facts are not to blame for that. In these cases, to speak of "appearance" may have a practical meaning, but cannot have a scientific meaning. Similarly, the question which is often asked, whether the world is real or whether we merely dream it, is devoid of all scientific meaning. Even the wildest dream is a fact as much as any other. If our dreams were more regular, more connected, more stable, they would also have more practical importance for us.[31]

Mach adds: "The expression 'sense-illusion' proves . . . that we have not yet deemed it necessary to incorporate into our ordinary language [the fact] *that the senses represent things neither wrongly nor correctly.*"[32]

In *Our Knowledge of the External World* Russell says something very similar:

The first thing to realize is that there are no such things as "illusions of sense." Objects of sense, even when they occur in dreams, are the most indubitably real objects known to us. What, then, makes us call them unreal in dreams? Merely the unusual nature of their connection with other objects of sense. I dream that

I am in America, but I wake up and find myself in England without those intervening days on the Atlantic which, alas! are inseparably connected with a "real" visit to America. Objects of sense are called "real" when they have the kind of connection with other objects of sense which experience has led us to regard as normal; when they fail in this, they are called "illusions." But what is illusory is only the inferences to which they give rise; in themselves, they are every bit as real as the objects of waking life. And conversely, the sensible objects of waking life must not be expected to have more intrinsic reality than those of dreams. Dreams and waking life, in our first efforts at construction, must be treated with equal respect. . . . [33]

In "The Relation of Sense-Data to Physics" Russell presents a parallel account of hallucinations and more commonplace illusions.[34]

Wittgenstein did not discuss this topic in the *Tractatus*, but the phenomenological language he envisions there contains no provision for propositions of the form "It looks . . . , but it's really _____." In his later years Wittgenstein addressed this topic as follows:

. . . the words "seem," "error," etc. have a certain emotional overtone which doesn't belong to the essence of the phenomena. . . . We talk for instance of an optical illusion and associate this expression with the idea of a mistake, although of course it isn't essential that there should be any mistake; and if appearances were normally more important in our lives than the results of measurement,[35] then language would also show a different attitude to this phenomenon.
There is not – as I used to believe – a primary language as opposed to our ordinary language, the "secondary" one. But one could speak of a primary language as opposed to ours in so far as the former would not permit any way of expressing a preference for certain phenomena over others; it would have to be, so to speak, absolutely *impartial* (PR, p. 84).

In this passage Wittgenstein is saying that the logical form of the facts we perceive is that which is presupposed in the *Tractatus*, i.e., there are not two kinds of perceptual facts: those that are illusory (or *mere* appearance) and those that are not. But does not ordinary language treat matters differently? Wittgenstein writes:

. . . the form of words "the appearance of this tree" incorporates the idea of a necessary connection between what we are calling the appearance and "the existence of a tree." . . . But this connection isn't there [since it is not *necessary* that I encounter resistance when I go to touch what appeared to be a tree].
Idealists would like to reproach language [e.g., the phrase "appearance of a tree"] with presenting what is secondary [e.g., a tree] as primary and what is primary [i.e., appearances] as secondary. But that is only the case with these inessential valuations ("only" an appearance) which are independent of perceptual facts.[36] Apart from that, ordinary language makes no decision as to what is primary or secondary. We have no reason to accept [the objection] that the expression "the appearance of a tree" represents something which is secondary in relation to the expression "tree." The expression "only an image" goes back to the idea that we can't eat the image of an apple (PR, pp. 270–271).

Here Wittgenstein is saying that although ordinary language permits the expression "the appearance of a tree," this should not be taken to mean what it seems (to idealists) to mean, i.e., should not be taken to conflict with Russell's remark that there are no illusions of sense.

In The Blue Book Wittgenstein explains the matter as follows:

Now if I say "I see my hand move," this at first sight seems to presuppose that I agree with the proposition "my hand moves." But if I regard the proposition "I see my hand move" as one of the evidences for the proposition "my hand moves," the truth of the latter is, of course, not presupposed in the truth of the former. One might therefore suggest [as an improvement] the expression "It looks as though my hand were moving" instead of "I see my hand moving." But this expression, although it indicates that my hand may appear to be moving without really moving, might still suggest that after all there must be a hand in order that it should appear to be moving; whereas we can easily imagine cases in which the proposition describing the visual evidence is true and at the same time other evidences make us say that I have no hand. Our ordinary way of expression obscures this. We are handicapped in ordinary language by having to describe, say, a tactile sensation by means of terms for physical objects such as the word "eye," "finger," etc., when what we want to say does not entail the existence of an eye or a finger, etc. We have to use a roundabout description of our sensations. This of course does not mean that ordinary language is insufficient for our special purposes, but that it is . . . sometimes misleading (BB, pp. 51–52).

What we find in these passages is Wittgenstein's attempt to reconcile ordinary language with the neutral monists' view of appearance and reality. As we will see in Chapter 15, he continued to struggle with this problem in *On Certainty*.

Conclusion

I remarked in the Introduction that Wittgenstein held a metaphysical view of the world that was fundamentally opposed to Moore's dualistic realism and the foregoing passages provide some indication of how they differed. In a reference to Moore in The Blue Book (p. 48) Wittgenstein says that "the common-sense philosopher . . . is not the common-sense man, who is as far from realism as from idealism," by which he meant that the plain man is not a (Moorean) realist, in that he does not talk about (or believe in the existence of) things that transcend experience, but is also not an idealist, in that he does not doubt (or deny) the existence of tables, chairs, and other people.[37] In other words, Wittgenstein thought of the common-sense man in just the way that a neutral monist *would* think of him. In this he was in agreement with Hume, who said in the *Treatise* (I, iv, ii) that "however [dualistic] philosophers may distinguish betwixt the objects and perceptions of the senses . . . ; yet this is a distinction which is not comprehended by the generality of mankind, who as they perceive only one being, can never assent to the opinion of a double existence. . . . Those very sensations, which enter by the eye or ear, are with them the true objects; nor can they readily conceive that this pen or paper, which is immediately perceiv'd, represents another, which is different from, but resembling it." Wittgenstein, as we will see, continued to hold this view of what the plain man thinks and says (ordinary language).[38]

Notes

1. In order to understand Wittgenstein one should be familiar with the new realists' manifesto, *The New Realism*, Edwin B. Holt, *et al.* (New York: Macmillan, 1912) and Ralph Barton Perry's *Present Philosophical Tendencies*, op. cit. Wittgenstein was probably made aware of these books by Russell's references to them in his 1914 essay "On the Nature of Acquaintance," op. cit., pp. 140 and 145. Internal evidence suggests that Wittgenstein read portions of the aforementioned books, especially Chapter I of the manifesto and Chapter XII of Perry's book.
2. "Russell's Neutral Monism" in *The Philosophy of Bertrand Russell*, ed. Paul A. Schilpp, op. cit., p. 354.
3. Berkeley puts this in a way that would have appealed to Wittgenstein when he says that it is a mistake to think that all of mankind "believe the existence of Matter or things without the mind. Strictly speaking, to believe that which . . . has no meaning in it, is impossible" (*Principles*, I, §54). As noted in Chapter 1, Wittgenstein told Frank Ramsey that it is "nonsense to believe in anything not given in experience."
4. *Treatise*, I, iv, vi.
5. In *The Analysis of Mind*, Russell says: "The stuff of which the world of our experience is composed is, in my belief, neither mind nor matter, but something more primitive than either" (New York: Macmillan, 1921, p. 10) and goes on in the final chapter to sketch what he calls "that fundamental science which I believe to be the true metaphysic, in which mind and matter alike are seen to be constructed out of a neutral stuff" (p. 287). (Mach also represents his "analysis" as though it were a *scientific* undertaking.) Wittgenstein regarded this as highly misleading because it obscures the logical, or linguistic, character of philosophy (see WL35, pp. 128–129) and makes it appear that philosophers had carried out something like a chemical analysis and discovered one basic stuff. Russell, for example, says that by means "of analysis . . . you can get down in theory, if not in practice, to the ultimate simples of which the world is built" ("The Philosophy of Logical Atomism" in *Logic and Knowledge*, op. cit., p. 270). Wittgenstein thought that this makes it appear that philosophers had discovered something *new*, something hitherto unknown (WL32, p. 35). "Philosophers," he said, "constantly see the method of science before their eyes, and are irresistibly tempted to ask and answer questions in the way science does. This tendency is the real source of metaphysics, and leads the philosopher into complete darkness" (BB, p. 18). It does so because it obscures the fact that philosophical problems "are solved, not by giving new information, but by arranging what we have always known" (PI, §109).
6. In adopting the name "realism," Wittgenstein was following the current fashion, for the name "neutral monism" gained currency somewhat later. R. B. Perry, for example, described Mach's *The Analysis of Sensations* as

"among the classics of modern realism" (*Present Philosophical Tendencies*, op. cit., p. 310). Russell, in *Our Knowledge of the External World*, refers to this view as the "new realism" (op. cit., p. 14). After the publication of the *Tractatus* Wittgenstein did not again use the term "pure realism." It should be noted that his pure realism, which he never abondoned, is to be distinguished from Moore's dualistic "realism," which Wittgenstein invariably disparaged.

7. *The Analysis of Sensations*, op. cit., p. 17.
8. Ibid., p. 44.
9. "On the Nature of Acquaintance," op. cit., pp. 145–146.
10. Ibid., p. 163.
11. Op. cit., pp. 23–24.
12. Ibid., p. 24.
13. Ibid., pp. 28–29.
14. That Wittgenstein continued in his later years to hold the *Tractatus* view that the self is a logical fiction can be seen in many places: WL35, p. 21; BB, p. 63; NFL, pp. 282 and 297; LSD, pp. 32–33 and 137, and PI, §§404–411.
15. Op. cit., p. 310.
16. *The Grammar of Science* (Gloucester, Mass.: Peter Smith, 1957), p. 66. This book was first published in 1892 and was revised in subsequent editions. The third edition, quoted here, was published in 1911.
17. See RPP, II, §§650–651 for an explanation of this passage.
18. This remark of Mach's seems to have greatly influenced Wittgenstein, for he repeatedly used the same comparison, e.g., PR, p. 91, BB, p. 55, and LSD, pp. 4–6.
19. *The Analysis of Sensations*, op. cit., pp. 360–361.
20. Op. cit., p. 34.
21. *Present Philosophical Tendencies*, op. cit., p. 286.
22. Ibid, p. 289.
23. Ibid.
24. These notes are quoted in Merrill and Jaakko Hintikka's book *Investigating Wittgenstein*, op. cit., p. 77.
25. Op. cit., p. 14.
26. Descartes, in the Second Meditation, said he had formerly thought of his soul as "something subtle like air or fire or aether mingled among the grosser parts of my body" *Descartes: Philosophical Writings*, eds. and trans., Elizabeth Anscombe and Peter Geach (Edinburgh: Nelson, 1954), pp. 67–68.
27. Wittgentstein dramatizes the issue by saying that "the problem . . . could be expressed by the question: 'Is it possible for a machine to think?'. . . . The trouble is . . that the sentence 'A machine thinks (perceives, wishes)' seems somehow nonsensical" (BB, p. 47).
28. *The Analysis of Sensations*, op. cit., pp. 29–30.
29. Ibid., p. 35.
30. *The Grammar of Science*, op. cit., p. 68.
31. *The Analysis of Sensations*, op. cit., pp. 10–11.
32. Ibid., p. 10.
33. Op. cit., pp. 92–93.
34. In *Mysticism and Logic*, op. cit., esp. pp. 173–179.
35. On a later page Wittgenstein says: "In visual space there is no measurement" (PR, p. 266), having said that visual space is the *basis* of physical space (PR, p. 100).
36. I have slightly altered the translation of this sentence.

37. For a discussion of this see note 19 in Chapter 1, this volume.
38. This was not an uncommon view. See the discussion of naive realism by R. J. Hirst in *The Encyclopedia of Philosophy* (New York: Macmillan, 1967), ed. Paul Edwards, Vol. 7, in which Hirst reports (and I think correctly) that naive realism "is usually alleged by philosophers to be [the view held by] the plain man" (p. 78). Hirst goes on to say that "the Oxford linguistic analysts," i.e., J. L. Austin and others, who are "strong critics of the sense-datum theory (unlike Moore), . . . reject the traditional naive realism as unfair to the plain man. . ." (ibid., p. 80). Despite Wittgenstein's well-known comtempt for Oxford philosophers (see Norman Malcolm, *Ludwig Wittgenstein: A Memoir*, op. cit., p. 98), it is commonly (but mistakenly) assumed that he agreed with their position on this matter. Malcolm, for instance, attempts to argue for this interpretation in "Wittgenstein's 'Scepticism' in *On Certainty*," *Inquiry* (Vol. 31), esp. p. 292. Malcolm, however, completely misunderstands the passages he quotes from Wittgenstein in defense of this interpretation. See Chapter 10.

3

The 'Objects' of the *Tractatus*

In the *Tractatus* the term "object" plays an important, yet rather obscure, role. It is important because it is said that "objects make up the substance of the world" (TLP, 2.021); they are what the unanalyzable words of language stand for (TLP, 3.203). Yet Wittgenstein does not make as clear as he might have what sort of thing he is thinking of when he speaks of objects. He does say that they must be "simple" (TLP, 2.02), meaning that they do not have nameable parts. He also says: "Objects, the unalterable, and the subsistent are one and the same" (TLP, 2.027). But if Wittgenstein had in mind that these objects belong to some particular metaphysical category, he failed to make this perfectly clear in the *Tractatus*. He does say that "empirical reality is limited by the totality of objects" (TLP, 5.5561). This and other passages (2.0131, 2.0251, and 4.123) suggest that he thought of objects as being phenomenal entities. That this was his actual view is borne out by much that he says elsewhere. Most significant, perhaps, is his remark in his pre-*Tractatus* notebooks that "all experience is the world" (NB, p. 89). Since objects "make up the substance of the world" (2.021), it follows that objects are elements of experience (visual, tactile, etc.). When he explained the *Tractatus* to Frank Ramsey in 1923 he said that ". . . to be given in experience is [the] formal property [that's required] to be a genuine entity."[1] In his conversations with Waismann, in 1929, he explained the *Tractatus* position as follows: "I used to believe that there was the everyday language that we all usually spoke and a primary language that expressed what we really know, namely phenomena" (WVC, p. 45). By this he meant that he used to believe that the analysis of ordinary language would lead, in the end, to elementary propositions, which are about "phenomena." These passages make clear that the world of the *Tractatus* is a phenomenal world.

This interpretation has frequently been rejected by Wittgenstein's commentators, and for this reason it is necessary to consider the three arguments that have been advanced against it. One of these, which will be addressed at the end of this chapter, is that Wittgenstein did not make up his mind about what sort of things his simple objects must be. The second argument is that advanced by G. E. M. Anscombe, who cites the color-exclusion problem mentioned by Wittgenstein at 6.3751 as proof that the simple objects cannot be sense-data.[2] We will consider this argument in due course. The third argument is that Tractarian objects cannot be sense-data because the latter are variable and short-lived. Malcolm puts the matter as follows: "Sense-data are supposed to be 'fleeting': they quickly alter, come and go. The simple objects are not like that: they are enduring and unchanging. . . ."[3]

Sensible Qualities are Tractarian Objects

This third argument contains a grain of truth, for it is certainly true that Tractarian objects cannot be sense-data as these are commonly thought of. But Wittgenstein, as we will see, thought that the usual conception of sense-data – that held by Russell and Moore – is mistaken.

To understand how Wittgenstein thought of Tractarian objects, it is important to understand the role they were meant to play. The relevant remarks about objects are the following:

2.02 Objects are simple.
2.021 Objects make up the substance of the world. This why they cannot be composite.
2.0211 If the world had no substance, then whether a proposition had sense would depend on whether another proposition was true.
2.0212 In that case we could not sketch out a picture of the world (true or false).
2.022 It is obvious that an imagined world, however different it may be from the real one, must have *something* – a form – in common with it.
2.023 Objects are just what constitute this unalterable form.
2.024 Substance is what subsists independently of what is the case.
2.027 Objects, the unalterable, and the subsistent are one and the same.
2.0271 Objects are what is unalterable and subsistent; their configuration is what is changing and unstable.
2.0272 The configuration of objects produces states of affairs.

What these passages tell us is that no matter how the world may change there is no change in the stock of nameable objects. The "unalterability" Wittgenstein speaks of in these passages pertains to the constancy of these objects throughout all possible (or imaginable) worlds.

In these passages, then, we have an echo of Descartes' First Meditation, where, in his attempt to discover what is indubitably real, he concludes that even if he is dreaming and there is no such corporeal world as he has all along supposed, still "it must be admitted that some simple and more universal kinds of things are real, and are as it were the real colours out of which there are formed in our consciousness all our pictures of real and unreal things."[4] He means: these simple, universal kinds of things are things that philosophical skepticism cannot call into doubt. Wittgenstein himself was later to explain: "What I once called 'objects,' simples, were simply what I could refer to without running the risk of their possible non-existence; i.e., that for which there is neither existence nor non-existence, and that means: what we can speak about *no matter what may be the case*" (PR, p. 72). In The Blue Book Wittgenstein repeated and elaborated this explanation:

Talking of the fact as a "complexes of objects" springs from this confusion (cf. *Tractatus Logico-philosophicus*). Supposing we asked: "How can one imagine what does not exist?" The answer seems to be: "If we do, we imagine non-existent combinations of existing elements." A centaur doesn't exist, but a man's head and torso and arms and a horse's legs do exist. "But can't we imagine an object utterly different from any one which exists?" – We should be inclined to answer: "No; the elements, individuals, must exist. If redness, roundness and sweetness did not exist, we could not imagine them" (BB, p. 31).

Here we see that Wittgenstein's project was identical with Descartes', namely, to specify what can survive the arguments of a philosophical skeptic. And this residue, which Wittgenstein called "objects," is comprised, he says, of colors, shapes, tastes and the like. In the early 1930s Wittgenstein was asked by Desmond Lee about the term "objects" in the *Tractatus* and answered: "Objects, etc. is here used for such things as a colour, a point in visual space etc" (WL32, p. 120).

It is important to understand why Wittgenstein avoided the term "sense-datum" in the *Tractatus*. This term was coined by Moore, and presumably Wittgenstein would have thought that he should not appropriate the term if he could not accept Moore's own understanding of it. What, then, was Moore's explanation of the term?

In his 1910–1911 lectures Moore introduced the term as follows: "These things: this patch of whitish colour, and its size and shape I did actually see. And I propose to call these things, the colour and size and shape, *sense-data*. . . ."[5] Moore is here ambiguous on a critical point: Does a particular patch qualify as a sense-datum, or only the color, size, and shape? When Moore later published these lectures, he corrected the ambiguity of this passage in the following footnote: "I should now make, and have for many years made, a sharp distinction between what I have called the 'patch,' on the one hand, and the colour, size and shape, *of* which it is, on the other; and should call, and have called, *only* the patch, *not* its colour, size or shape, a 'sense-datum'."[6] As thus explained, a sense-datum is a substratum of its various properties, and this conception, as we will see, Wittgenstein emphatically rejected.

Russell took a position like Moore's. In 1912, when distinguishing between universals and particulars, he wrote the following:

We shall find it convenient only to speak of things *existing* when they are in time, that is to say, when we can point to some time *at* which they exist (not excluding the possibility of their existing at all times). Thus thoughts and feelings, minds and physical objects *exist*. But universals do not exist in this sense; we shall say that they *subsist* or *have being*, where "being" is opposed to "existence" as being timeless. The world of universals is unchangeable, rigid, exact, delightful to the mathematician, the logician, the builder of metaphysical systems, and all who love perfection more than life. The world of existence is fleeting, vague, without sharp boundaries, without any clear plan or arrangement, but it contains all thoughts and feelings, all data of sense, and all physical objects. . . .

. . . It is obvious . . . that we are acquainted with such universals as white, red, black, sweet, sour, loud, hard, etc., i.e., with qualities which are exemplified in sense-data. When we see a white patch, we are acquainted, in the first instance, with the particular patch; but by seeing many white patches, we easily learn to abstract the whiteness which they all have in common, and in learning to do this we are learning to be acquainted with whiteness. . . . Universals of this sort may be called "sensible qualities."[7]

So for Russell sensible qualities, but not sense-data, are timeless. We can see from this that Wittgenstein's objects could be Russell's universals but not Russell's sense-data.[8] As we have seen, Wittgenstein speaks of his simple objects in the same terms as Russell speaks of universals: Tractarian objects are "unalterable and subsistent."[9]

The answer, then, to the argument that the objects of the *Tractatus* cannot have been sense-data since sense-data are "fleeting," is that Wittgenstein rejected that conception of sense-data. While allowing that the visual world is in constant flux (PR, pp. 80–86), he held that the data of sense are Russell's "timeless" sensible qualities.

There is a further point to be made about this. Wittgenstein speaks of objects as being the "substance" of the world (2.021 and 2.024), which suggests that objects (including colors) are not to be thought of as *properties* of anything, and indeed in his pre-*Tractatus* notebooks he says as much:

Let us suppose that we were to see a circular patch: is the circular form its *property*? Certainly not (NB, p. 65).
That the colours are not properties is shewn by the analysis of physics, by the internal relations in which physics displays the colours.
Apply this to sounds too (NB, p. 82).

It was thus Wittgenstein's position that Russell was wrong to speak, as he does in the passage quoted above, of whiteness being "exemplified in sense-data," i.e., to speak of it as a property of a patch. We could put the point as follows: if we were to think of Tractarian objects as being Russellian sense-data, we would have to think of them as bearers of properties, but Tractarian objects are neither properties nor bearers of properties. In the *Tractatus* this point is made rather obscurely: "In a manner of speaking, objects are colourless" (2.0232). This does not mean that Tractarian objects are like pure water; nor does it mean that they are bare particulars. It means that objects cannot be described, they "can only be *named*" (3.221), i.e., named by a word such as "white" or "sweet."[10]

In the years following the *Tractatus* Wittgenstein frequently criticized the Russellian notion of sense-data, and the nature of these criticisms reveals more clearly his own view.

When Frege and Russell spoke of objects they always had in mind things that are, in language, represented by nouns, that is, say, bodies like chairs. The whole conception of objects is hence very closely connected with the subject–predicate form of propositions. It is clear that where there is no subject–predicate form it is also impossible to speak of objects in this sense. Now I can describe this room in an entirely different way, e.g., by describing the surface of the room analytically by means of an equation and stating the distribution of colours on this surface. In the case of this form of description, single 'objects,' chairs, books, tables, and their spatial positions are not mentioned any more....

... If we say that four elementary colours would suffice, I call such symbols of equal status *elements of representation*. These elements of representation are the 'objects.'

The following question has now [i.e., in the form of description of the room mentioned above] no sense: Are objects something thing-like, something that stands in subject-position, or something property-like, or are they relations, and so forth? (WVC, pp. 41–43).

This passage nicely illustrates how Wittgenstein had thought of the elementary propositions of the *Tractatus*. When he says that he can describe a room using color words and yet avoid the subject–predicate form, he takes this to show (a) that chairs, books, and tables are not part of the essence of the world and (b) that colors, sounds, etc. are not properties. In a logically perfect language colors would not be cast in the role of properties; they would be "objects" in their own right. And thus he says: "The things themselves are perhaps the four basic colours, space, time and other data [*Gegebene*] of the same sort" (PR, p. 169).[11]

It is not difficult, then, to understand why Wittgenstein did not use the term "sense-data" in the *Tractatus*. Yet shortly after returning to philosophy in 1929 he often made use of that term (or others, such as "sense impression"). Thus in *Philosophical Remarks* we find him saying: "The point of talking about sense-data and immediate experience is that we're after a description that has nothing hypothetical about it" (PR, p. 283). Indeed, he even allowed himself to use the word "patch," giving the sentence "I see a light patch in a dark surrounding" to illustrate what he means by "a description of immediate experience" (WL35, p. 67). This raises the question: Did his views change, so that he came to think that colors and shapes, etc. have a substratum (the 'patch'), or did he think that the nouns "sense-datum" and "patch" needn't suggest a substratum?

The latter alternative is plainly the correct answer. The reason for this lay in his idea that grammar is arbitrary in the sense that one 'notation' is just as good as another. He even discusses the word "patch" as an illustration of this point about grammar:

There is a fundamental confusion about questions regarding sense data, the confusing of questions of grammar with those of natural science. For example, Is whiteness circular or is a patch white and circular? What makes the question attractive is that the answer appears to decide between *existence* and *nonexistence* of something, namely a *patch*. We are really just turning our language around here when we ask "Is there a patch or not?" For "Whiteness is circular" and "The patch is white and circular" say the same thing. . . .

. . . the fact that two people say different things is not always a sign of a difference of opinion. The man who says "Here is whiteness which is round" and the man who says "Here is a patch which is white and round" say the same thing. Similarly when one person says that a surface has changed, and another person says it is the same surface which appears different to him. There would only be a difference of opinion if the two statements "The patch is circular" and "Whiteness is circular" belonged to the same game [so that one could say "Either it's _____ or it's . . ."]. . . . And to the question, "Isn't the latter notation more *adequate*, more *direct*?," I would answer No. For one symbolism does not come nearer the truth than the other. (Of course it is all right to ask whether one symbolism is more misleading than another.) (WL35, p. 129).[12]

Wittgenstein is not here condoning the Moore–Russell conception of sense-data. He is sanctioning the use of the word "patch," with the warning that this symbolism may mislead one – as it did Russell and Moore. This warning is also issued in The Blue Book (p. 70) and the *Investigations* (§§400–401).

One of Wittgenstein's principal themes, after 1929, was that grammar – or syntax – is arbitrary: "I want to say that . . . all syntax is arbitrary" (WVC, p. 103).[13] For this reason it no doubt seemed to him unnecessary to avoid the noun "sense-datum" or to reiterate constantly that its use does not commit one to the idea that sensible qualities inhere in a substratum.[14] So he used that noun without always repeating the points made in the passages quoted just above. Moreover, passages written in the last years of his life show that he retained the view that the data of sense are colors, smells, etc. For instance, in 1947 he wrote: "But what are sense-impressions? Something like a smell, a taste, a pain, a noise etc." (RPP, I, §259). Also in 1947 he wrote the following revealing passage:

What holds the bundle of "sense impressions" together is their mutual relationships. That which is 'red' is also 'sweet' and 'hard' and 'cold' and 'sounds' when one strikes it (RPP, I, §896).[15]

Wittgenstein is here denying that sensible qualities are "held together" by a substratum in which they inhere. Just what he intended as his alternative to that idea – namely, "mutual relationships" – is less obvious, but presumably he meant that there are 'in nature' certain regularities among sensible qualities, such as that the color and shape we associate with a lemon are regularly accompanied by a certain taste and that if this were not so, if there were no regularities among sensible qualities, we would not have a concept such as *lemon*.[16] In any case, this passage, written in 1947, makes it plain that the 'objects' of the *Tractatus* were retained in Wittgenstein's later philosophy under the name "sense impressions" or "sense-data" or "the material of experience" (PR, p. 283 and OC, 499), although he had by then given up saying that they are simple and indestructible (see PI, §§46–48 and 55–58).

The Color-Exclusion Problem:

We can now address the second objection that has been raised against the view that sensible qualities are Tractarian objects: the so-called color-exclusion problem. It is an essential feature of the *Tractatus* that elementary propositions are independent of one another, meaning that if "p" and "q" are elementary propositions, then from the truth of "p" one cannot logically infer the truth or falsity of "q" (TLP, 2.062 and 5.1314–5.135), which means that the molecular proposition "p & q" can be neither a tautology nor a contradiction (TLP, 4.211 and 6.3751). And yet, as Wittgenstein himself remarks, "the statement that a point in the visual field has two different colours at the same time is a contradiction" (TLP, 6.3751). It has been argued that this alone proves that Wittgenstein's elementary propositions cannot be sense-datum statements. But this is simply not true. For it was Wittgenstein's view that the contradiction in question arises only because our *ordinary* color words are not fully analyzed terms and that a further analysis of them will yield elementary sense-datum propositions that are independent of one another.

The first point to consider is that Wittgenstein had held in the *Tractatus* that where there is a contradiction it must be possible to show this on a truth table. But such is not the case with "This point is now both red and blue" as it stands. So if this is a contradiction, Wittgenstein cannot have thought that "This point is now red" is a fully analyzed proposition. What, then, did he think its analysis must be? In the *Tractatus* he doesn't say. But in his 1929 article "Some Remarks on Logical Form" he provides a clue to what he had thought:

Take . . . a proposition which asserts the existence of a colour R at a certain time T in a certain place P of our visual field. I will write this proposition "RPT" and abstract for the moment from any consideration of how such a statement is to be further analyzed. "BPT" then, says that the colour B is in the place P at the time T, and it will be clear to most of us here, and to all of us in ordinary life that "RPT & BPT" is some sort of contradiction (and not merely a false proposition). Now if statements of degree were analyzable – as I used to think – we could explain this contradiction by saying that the colour R contains all degrees of R and none of B and that the colour B contains all degrees of B and none of R (RLF, pp. 35–36).

This reference to what he "used to think" is surely a reference to the *Tractatus*, so this passage should show us how he had thought "This point in the visual field is now both red and blue" is to be so analyzed that its contradictory character can be shown on a truth table.

The passage indicates that Wittgenstein had thought of colors as having "degrees." He explains this by saying that a visually given color will have some degree of brightness (RLF, p. 34). So to say simply that a point in the visual field is *red* is not yet to describe it completely, for a complete description would have to say how bright it is. Let us symbolize degrees of a color's brightness by means of subscripts: $r_1, r_2, \ldots r_n$. We can now propose that the English word "red" is not a simple name but that "r_1," "r_2," and so on are. And what the above passage tells us is that in order to produce a fully analyzed version of "This point is red at T and also blue at T," we must recast it in the form Wittgenstein gives there: "R contains all degrees of R and none of B, and B contains all degrees of B and none of R." Assuming for the sake of simplicity that there are only two primary colors, we can do this by rewriting "RPT" as follows:

$$(r_1PT \lor r_2PT \lor \ldots r_nPT) \,\&\, (\sim b_1PT \,\&\, \sim b_2PT \,\&\, \ldots \sim b_nPT)$$

and by also rewriting "BPT" in a similar way:

$$(b_1PT \lor b_2PT \lor \ldots b_nPT) \,\&\, (\sim r_1PT \,\&\, \sim r_2PT \,\&\, \ldots \sim r_nPT).$$

In this way we can produce a formal (truth-table) contradiction by forming the product of these two rewritten propositions.[18]

As the passage quoted above makes clear, at the time of the *Tractatus* Wittgenstein thought that some such analysis is possible. So let us consider this analysis further to see what it tells us about its constituent propositions. Would Wittgenstein have thought that "$r_1PT \,\&\, b_1PT$" is a contradiction? The answer is suggested by a passage in *Philosophical Remarks*, which dates from the same period as his 1929 "Some Remarks on Logical Form." He introduces a discussion of the present topic by saying:

One's first thought is that it's incompatible for two colours to be in *one* place at the same time. The next is that two colours in one place simply combine to make another (PR, p. 105).

The second thought introduced here plainly suggests a way out of the impasse over elementary propositions, namely, that we can represent the color *seen* at a given point – the phenomenally given color (purple, for example) – as a combination of other colors. This suggestion is borne out in *Philosophical Remarks*, where Wittgenstein says:

There appear to be simple colours. Simple as psychological phenomena. What I need is a psychological or rather phenomenological colour theory, not a physical and equally not a physiological one.

Furthermore, it must be a theory in *pure* phenomenology in which mention is only made of what is actually perceptible. . . .

Now, we can recognize colours as mixtures of red, green, blue, yellow, white and black *immediately*. Where this is still always the colour itself, and not pigment, light, process on or in the retina, etc.[19]

We can also see that one colour is redder than another or whiter, etc. (PR, p. 273).

In *Remarks on Colour* he says much the same thing: "We might speak of the colour-impression of a surface, by which we wouldn't mean the colour, but rather the composite of the shades of colour, which produces the impression (e.g.) of a brown surface" (ROC, II, §1). If we take these remarks to shed light on the passage in which he speaks of two colors in one place as combining to make another, and if we take that, in turn, to shed light on the constituent propositions of the foregoing analysis, we can say that "r_1PT & b_1PT," far from being a contradiction, would say that a certain color – which is a combination of r_1 and b_1 – is in the visual field at P at time T. But this, in turn, means that "r_1PT" and "b_1PT" are independent of one another and are therefore candidates for being elementary propositions if only "P" and "T" are further analyzed.[20] And in that case "r_1" and "b_1" would be simple names and what they name would be simple objects.

We can better understand the foregoing account by considering how Wittgenstein would have been thinking of the difference between the ordinary color word "red" and logically proper names, such as "r_1." Why is "RPT & BPT" a contradiction and yet "r_1PT & b_1PT" not? Why, that is, did he think that "This point is now both red and blue" is a contradiction and not our way of saying that the color at P is purple? He would have answered (see RLF, p. 34) that this is not how our ordinary color words are actually used, as is shown by the fact that if I tell you that the paint I am using is red, you wouldn't then ask "Is it blue, too?" – or if you did, I would reply, "I told you: it's red!" By contrast, the logically proper name "r_1" is not used in this way.

This, then, must have been how Wittgenstein had thought of the matter at the time of the *Tractatus*. And not only as regards names of colors but as regards names of other sensible qualities as well. So we may safely allow that sensible qualities are Tractarian objects. The so-called color exclusion problem does not show otherwise.[21]

Examples of Simple Objects

Does the foregoing analysis enable one to pick out actual instances of what Wittgenstein would have counted as simple objects? The analysis uses the symbols "r_1," "b_2," etc., but can we, without further ado, look about us, point to a color, and say that *it* is one of these "simple" colors? Wittgenstein did not think so. Malcolm reports the following conversation:

I asked Wittgenstein whether, when he wrote the *Tractatus*, he had ever decided upon anything as an *example* of a "simple object." His reply was that at that time his thought had been that he was a *logician*; and that it was not his business, as a logician, to try to decide whether this thing or that was a simple thing or a complex thing, that being a purely *empirical* matter.[22]

As a logician, he thought, he could prove that there *must be* simple objects but that is all. This becomes more understandable if we recall that at the time of the *Tractatus* so-called Introspectionist psychologists were conducting laboratory experiments to show that it required highly trained observers to pick out "the simple and primary data of experience." Wittgenstein, who made frequent use of the psychological laboratory at Cambridge in 1912,[23] would surely have been aware of such experiments and no doubt thought it best to leave such matters to psychologists.

Malcolm's report of Wittgenstein's remark about simple objects has frequently been misinterpreted. Although Wittgenstein said only that he could not have given an *example* of a simple object, he is often taken to have meant that he could not have said anything about the metaphysical status of his postulated objects: whether they are sensible qualities or, perhaps, material things. This is *prima facie* an absurd interpretation, for it makes out Wittgenstein to have thought that empirical investigations could decide a philosophical issue. Even so, there are philosophers who insist that at the time of the *Tractatus* Wittgenstein had made no decision as to *what* the simple objects might be.[24]

The evidence cited in support of this reading consists merely in the fact that in 1915 Wittgenstein wrote in his notebooks: "The division of the body into *material points*, as we have it in physics, is nothing more than analysis into *simple components*" (NB, p. 67). This is taken to show that Wittgenstein was prepared to allow that *material* things, rather than sensible qualities, may prove to be the simple things that are named in an ideal language. But there are two obvious difficulties with this interpretation. First of all, as we saw in Chapter 1 (note 24), Wittgenstein told Russell in 1912 that science has no need of *matter*, for even without it "physics and astronomy and all the other sciences could still be interpreted so as to be true." He meant that the sciences can be given a phenomenalistic interpretation. So even if Wittgenstein had allowed that simple objects may be "material points," he would not thereby have allowed that they are different in kind from phenomenal objects. But are the material points that physics speaks of the right kind of thing to be candidates for Tractarian objects? Physics makes use of this concept (mass points) in theoretical calculations (as when a planet is treated as a mass point), but one could not search out actual instances and name them. And yet Wittgenstein's whole purpose in speaking of simple objects is that they are to serve as the things simple names stand for. It is hardly to be wondered at, then, that in the *Tractatus* there is no hint that simple objects might prove to be "material points."

Wittgenstein's Ontology

We can now draw the following conclusions about Wittgenstein's ontology in the *Tractatus*. He held that such things as colors, odors, sounds, and the like comprise the "substance" of the world. Tables and chairs, on the other hand, belong to *"unserer Begriffswelt"* – our conceptual world.[25] In lectures Wittgenstein put the matter as follows: "Idealists were right in that we never transcend experience. Mind and matter is a division in experience. Realists were right in protesting that chairs do exist. They get into trouble because they think that sense-data and physical objects are causally related" (WL32, p. 80). In short, Wittgenstein was a phenomenalist.

In order to understand Wittgenstein's phenomenalism, it is important to bear in mind that he did not arrive at it by way of dualism. Wittgenstein never was a dualist; his first philosophy was idealism (see Chapter 1). The importance of this can be seen by recalling the manner in which Berkeley undertook to dismiss matter. His argument was that sensible qualities provide everything that common sense wants in a chair or an apple and that a material substratum is altogether unnecessary. In dismissing material substance, he was, he insisted, only dismissing something philosophers had dreamed up and that no one else ever talks about. This, no doubt, was Wittgenstein's view as well. Moreover, by embracing neutral monism, which does away with (Cartesian) minds too, he could dismiss the idea that colors, for example, are "in the mind." It would be wrong, then, to depict Wittgenstein's phenomenalism by saying that it left him in a sphere of *private* sense-data, a sphere cut off from 'external' reality. This way of thinking, which is a product of dualism, was utterly foreign to Wittgenstein.

Mach said: ". . . my view [neutral monism] was developed from an earlier idealistic phase," and he went on to say that "of all the approaches to my stand point, the one by way of idealism seems to me the easiest and most natural."[26] He meant: my position can be understood by first appreciating the idealists' elimination of "matter" and by then doing away with Cartesian minds as the repository of sense-impressions. Wittgenstein described his own philosophical development similarly, saying that "idealism leads to realism if it is strictly thought out" (NB, p. 85). For Mach and Wittgenstein there was never a question of whether they had cut themselves off from the plain man's world of chairs and tables. On the contrary, they thought of themselves as rescuing the plain man's world from dualists who, by their causal (or representative) theories of perception, made the real world seem inaccessible.[27]

My reason for emphasizing this point is that David Pears, who is either ignorant of or has simply ignored neutral monism, has, in his recent book, *The False Prison*, employed the imagery and vocabulary of dualism to delineate the issues with which Wittgenstein was contending. Pears, I would say, is attempting to navigate Wittgensteinian waters with a defective compass, so that each turn of his argument leads him further astray. For example, he takes it for granted that sense-data are private, so that any form of reductionism of material things to sense-data is a retreat into a private world. His question then is whether Wittgenstein ever made this retreat into a private world. To avoid an affirmative answer, he endorses the view that Wittgenstein, in the *Tractatus*, left open the possibility that simple objects are material points, which (so Pears assumes) are *not* private. He then invites his readers to choose between two alternatives: either Wittgenstein embraced "classical phenomenalism," and thereby walled himself into a private world, or he rejected phenomenalism and allowed that trees and chairs are public, material objects. But we cannot rightly choose either of these alternatives if we would understand Wittgenstein, for he wanted to maintain that, although trees and chairs are nothing beyond their sensible qualities, they are nevertheless 'public' objects. This is how his neutral monism differed from what Pears calls "classical phenomenalism."

Notes

1. Ramsey's notes are quoted by Merrill and Jaakko Hintikka in *Investigating Wittgenstein*, op. cit., p. 77.
2. *An Introduction to Wittgenstein's Tractatus*, op. cit., pp. 25–27.
3. *Nothing is Hidden*, op. cit., p. 10. James Griffin advances the same argument in *Wittgenstein's Logical Atomism* (Oxford: Oxford University Press, 1964), pp. 149–150.
4. "Meditations on First Philosophy," in *Descartes, Philosophical Writings*, op. cit., p. 63.
5. *Some Main Problems of Philosophy* (New York: Macmillan, 1953), 30.
6. Ibid.
7. Bertrand Russell, *The Problems of Philosophy*, op. cit., pp. 99–101.
8. We know that Wittgenstein had read *The Problems of Philosophy* because Russell states in a letter to Lady Ottoline, dated March 1912, that Wittgenstein had made a criticism of it. See Brian McGuinness, *Wittgenstein, A Life: Young Ludwig 1889–1921*, op. cit., p. 77.
9. This is why, when Wittgenstein later came to criticize the *Tractatus* conception of simple names and simple, indestructible objects, he illustrated that conception by means of color words (PI, §§57–58).
10. In *Philosophical Grammar* Wittgenstein alludes to these passages with the remark "In a certain sense, an object cannot be described" (p. 208) and adds: "So what I am saying means: red can't be described" (p. 209).
11. Here as elsewhere Wittgenstein seems to be echoing Ernst Mach, who says, "The world consists of colors, sounds, temperatures, pressures, spaces, times, and so forth. . . ." *Popular Scientific Lectures*, (Chicago, 1989), p. 209. For evidence of Wittgenstein's familiarity with – and borrowings from – this book, see Henk Visser, "Wittgenstein's Debt to Mach's Popular Scientific Lectures," *Mind*, 1982, pp. 102–105.

12. The style of argument in this passage is not something new at this point in Wittgenstein's career (1935). In 1915 he wrote:

> "Occam's razor" is, *of course*, not an arbitrary rule or one justified by its practical success. What it says is that unnecessary sign-units have no reference.
> It is clear that signs fulfilling the same purpose are logically identical. The purely logical thing just *is* what *all* of these are capable of accomplishing (NB, p. 42).

This passage was retained nearly verbatim in the *Tractatus* at 5.47321.

13. This idea occurs in the *Tractatus* (TLP, 3.34–3.3421) and also in Wittgenstein's later writings, e.g., PI, §§558–569 and LW, I, §326. The idea that syntax (or grammar) is arbitrary, i.e., that very different grammatical forms can be used to say the same thing, is an idea Wittgenstein borrowed from his favorite scientist, Heinrich Hertz, who maintained (see his *Electrical Waves*) that his own electrical theory and those of Maxwell and Helmholtz are equivalent, *despite* their great differences in form, because they all lead to the same predictions. Hertz's way of stating this was to say that in any area of physics several quite different "images" can be equally satisfactory if judged from the standpoint of their empirical application.

14. If one reads the corpus of Wittgenstein's writings and lectures from the pre-*Tractatus* notebooks onward, one is constantly impressed by the fact that as things became "obvious" to him he assumed that they should be obvious to others as well and could be left unsaid. So we find him declaring: "Anything your reader can do for himself, leave to him" (CV, p. 77).

15. For a fuller understanding of this remark, see Waismann's "Theses" (WVC, p. 258) and Wittgenstein's own remarks at WVC, p. 158–159.

16. I assume that in the above passage Wittgenstein put scare quotes around the words "red," "sweet," etc. because he was thinking that there is a certain *range* of sweetness (or sourness) that we find associated with certain other qualities, i.e., that we don't say "That's not an apple" because the taste is somewhat less sweet than we have formerly experienced in conjunction with the color, shape, and size of an apple.

17. In explaining the *Tractatus* to Desmond Lee in 1930 (WL32, p. 119), Wittgenstein said that "This is red" contradicts "This is white" because "red" and "white" are not fully analyzed terms: ". . . the theory of elementary propositions would have to say that [these contradictory propositions] can be further analyzed to give, e.g., r, s, t [for 'This is red'], and v, w, ~t [for 'This is white']," so that "This is red" contains an elementary proposition the negation of which occurs in the analysis of "This is white."

18. This point was worked out some years ago by John Canfield in "Tractatus Objects," *Philosophia*, Vol. 6, No. 1 (March, 1976), pp. 81–99.

19. In his 1946–47 lectures Wittgenstein said: "I can discriminate red and blue in purple, notes in a chord, smells in a perfume" (WL47, p. 77). He also explained (ibid., p. 258) that he was not speaking of mixtures of pigments: ". . . it's the looks that we are talking about. . . . The visual colours are the one's we want." In this connection see Z, §368.

20. In "Some Remarks on Logical Form" Wittgenstein suggests that this further analysis might, as regards P, be carried out by a system of coordinates by whose numbers one could designate areas of the visual field (RLF, p. 33).

21. This is not to say that the view I have just sketched is without its problems.

Wittgenstein alludes to such problems when, in the passage quoted above from *Philosophical Remarks*, he adds a third thought to his first two:

> But third comes the objection: How about the complementary colours? What do red and green make? Black perhaps? But do I then see green in the black colour? – But even apart from that: how about the mixed colour, e.g. mixtures of red and blue? These contain a greater or lesser element of red: what does that mean? . . . Someone might perhaps imagine this being explained by supposing that certain small quantities of red added together would yield a specific degree of red. But in that case what does it mean if we say, for example, that five of these quantities of red are present? It cannot, of course, be a logical product of quantity no. 1 being present, and quantity no. 2 etc., up to 5; for how would these be distinguished from one another? Thus the proposition that 5 degrees of red are present can't be analysed like this (PR, p. 105).

Wittgenstein undertook the search for a new solution to the color exclusion problem in RLF, pp. 36–37, in PR, §§76–86, and in WVC, pp. 63–64. In the last of these passages he says explicitly that his mistake in the *Tractatus* had been to maintain that elementary propositions must be independent of one another, meaning that he should have allowed that "This is red" is an elementary proposition despite the fact that it can be contradicted by "No, it's blue."

22. *Ludwig Wittgenstein: A Memoir*, op. cit., p. 86.
23. David Pinset, in his unpublished diary, reports that he served repeatedly as Wittgenstein's subject in experiments regarding music.
24. See, for example, James Griffin, *Wittgenstein's Logical Atomism*, op. cit., pp. 49–50 and 149–150, and also David Pears, *The False Prison* (Oxford University Press, 1987), Vol. I, pp. 89 and 98, and Vol. II, p. 277.
25. I take the phrase "our conceptual world" from a passage (RPP, II, §672) Wittgenstein wrote in the late 1940s. But in his 1931–1932 lectures he said something similar: "The world we live in is the world of sense-data; but the world we talk about is the world of physical objects" (WL32, p. 82). He did not mean that there are *two* worlds but rather that physical objects are constructs of our language, are part of "our conceptual world."
26. *The Analysis of Sensations*, op. cit., p. 362.
27. Wittgenstein's thinking on this point was the same as that of the new realists, who, in their 1912 manifesto, said that dualists regard it as

> necessary to infer a world of external objects resembling to a greater or less extent the effects, or ideas, which they produce in us. What we perceive is now held [by dualists] to be only a picture of what really exists. . . . The only external world is [on their theory] one that we can never experience. . . . [Yet] the world in which all our interests are centered is the world of experienced objects. Even if, *per impossibile*, we could justify the belief in a world beyond that which we could experience, it would be but a barren achievement, for such a world would contain none of the things that we see and feel. Such a so-called real world would be . . . alien to us . . . (*The New Realism*, op. cit., pp. 4–5).

4

The Essence of the World Can Be Shown but Not Said

In the Preface to the *Tractatus* Wittgenstein wrote: "I . . . believe myself to have found, on all essential points, the final solution of [philosophical] problems" (TLP, p. 5). This, at first sight, is a rather astonishing remark inasmuch as Wittgenstein had at that time given little thought to some of the more perplexing philosophical problems. But Wittgenstein does not say here that he had solved each of these problems. He says that on "all essential points" he has found the final solution. By this he meant that he had shown that philosophical problems are all of the same *kind* and that by coming to understand the kind of problems they are we will be able to work out the details of their individual solutions. What, then, did Wittgenstein show – or think he had shown – about the general character of philosophical problems?

The Nature of Philosophy

We may begin our answer by noticing the sharp distinction Wittgenstein drew between philosophy and science. In his 1913 "Notes on Logic" he wrote: "The word 'philosophy' ought always to designate something over or under, but not beside, the natural sciences. Philosophy gives no pictures of reality, and can neither confirm nor confute scientific investigations" (NB, p. 93). This theme is reiterated in the *Tractatus*, where he says that philosophy "is not one of the natural sciences" (4.111) and then adds: "Philosophy does not result in 'philosophical propositions,' but rather in the clarification of propositions" (4.112).[1] What Wittgenstein is maintaining here could be put as follows. Philosophy differs from science in that the latter seeks to describe the world (or certain aspects of it) and thereby add to our knowledge and understanding of the world, whereas philosophy has nothing at all to say about the world – more particularly, it has nothing to say about what the world happens to be like (because philosophy makes no empirical claims) and it can state no *a priori* truths about the world (because, as can be deduced from a proper theory of language, there can be no synthetic *a priori* propositions).

What grounds did Wittgenstein have for adopting such a revolutionary view of philosophy? Some of the relevant points were stated succinctly by Wittgenstein in his discussions and lectures of the 1930s.

First of all, philosophy is not an empirical discipline: philosophers do not investigate flora or fauna or any other aspect of the world. "It is the essence of philosophy not to depend on experience, and this is what is meant by saying that philosophy is *a priori*" (WL35, p. 97). Moreover, the claims made by traditional philosophers don't look like statements about the world, for they don't say "This is how things are" but rather "This is how things *must* be; things *cannot* be otherwise." ["In the arguments of idealists and realists somewhere there always occur the words 'can,' 'cannot,' 'must.' No attempt is made to prove their doctrines by experience" (WL35, p. 18).] But this, according to Wittgenstein, is sufficient to show that such metaphysical claims cannot be true (or false), cannot be about the world. For if a philosopher says that it *must* be that p, i.e., that not-p is impossible or unimaginable, this means that the proposition "not-p" is not the description of a possible state of affairs and so is not a significant proposition. But that, in turn, means that the proposition "p" lacks a significant negation and so is itself without sense. In his 1930 lectures he explained this as follows:

Any affirmation can be negated: if it has sense to say p it also has sense to say ~p. If you say "The electric lights are burning" when they are not, what you say is wrong (false) but it has meaning. Whereas if you say "Twas brillig and the slithy toves" it has no meaning.

A proposition therefore is any expression which can be significantly negated (WL32, p. 22).

So there cannot be claims or theses which are *a priori* truths and yet say something about the world. Or as Wittgenstein also puts it: "What is essential to the world cannot be *said about* the world; for then it could be otherwise, since any proposition can be negated" (WL32, p. 34).

In his conversations with Waismann, Wittgenstein lays out this argument explicitly. He begins from the premise that every significant proposition has a significant negation (as an example he remarks that when I say "I have no money" this "presupposes the possibility that I do have money"), and he continues:

Now let us take the statement, "An object is not red and green at the same time." Is all I want to say by this that I have not yet seen such an object? Obviously not. What I mean is, "I *cannot* see such an object," "Red and green *cannot* be in the same place." Here I would ask, What does the word "*can*" mean here? The word "can" is obviously a grammatical (logical) concept, not a material one.

Now suppose the statement "An object cannot be both red and green" were a synthetic judgement and the word "cannot" meant logical impossibility. Since a proposition is the negation of its negation, there must also exist the proposition "An object can be red and green." This proposition would also be synthetic. As a synthetic proposition, it has sense, and this means that the state of things represented by it *can obtain*. If "cannot" means *logical* impossibility, we therefore reach the consequence that the impossible [namely, an object's being both red and green] *is* possible.

Here there remains only one way out for [a defender of synthetic *a priori* judgments] – to declare that there is a third [kind of] possibility [i.e., one that is neither empirical nor logical]. To that I would reply that it is indeed possible to make up words [such as "This is uniformly both red and green"], but I cannot associate a thought with them (WVC, pp. 67–68).

So philosophy can say nothing about the world:

The rationalists were right in seeing that philosophy was not empirical, that is, that as soon as it became empirical it became a question for a science of some sort.
   But they were wrong in supposing that there were *a priori* synthetic judgements. . . .
   The empiricists . . . were right in maintaining that . . . synthetic propositions were matters of experience (WL32, pp. 79–80).

But if philosophy can say nothing about the world, what then is the proper task of philosophy?

The Distinction between Logical and Grammatical Form

Wittgenstein's answer is complex. At bottom it depends on the fact that he accepted Russell's distinction between logical and grammatical form: "It was Russell who performed the service of showing that the apparent logical form [i.e., the *grammatical* form] of a proposition need not be its real one" (TLP, 4.0031). Stating this more explicitly, he says:

It is not humanly possible to gather immediately from [everyday language] what the logic of language is. Language disguises the thought. So much so, that from the outward form of the clothing it is impossible to infer the form of the thought beneath it, because the outward form of the clothing is not designed to reveal the form of the body, but for entirely different purposes (TLP, 4.002).

What the *Tractatus* shows, says Wittgenstein, is "that the reason why [philosophical] problems are posed is that the logic of our language is misunderstood" (TLP, p. 3). How can such misunderstandings arise? Because in our everyday language it often happens that the *apparent* logical form of a proposition is not its *actual* logical form. So Wittgenstein, at the time of writing the *Tractatus*, held that all metaphysical problems could be solved and all philosophical disputes ended, by rigorously revealing the logical forms of those sentences of our everyday language that philosophers have regularly misconstrued. Accordingly, "all philosophy is a 'critique of language' " (TLP, 4.0031). Or, as he also put it,

Philosophy aims at the clarification of [the logical form of] thoughts.
   Philosophy is not a body of doctrine but an activity.
   A philosophical work consists essentially of elucidations.
   Philosophy does not result in 'philosophical propositions,' but rather in the clarification of propositions (TLP, 4.112).

Showing What Cannot Be Said

It is important to realize that Wittgenstein, in adopting this position, was not abandoning the traditional philosophical problems. Rather, he was declaring that philosophers must learn to eschew the "material mode of speech" and adopt in its place the "formal mode of speech."[2] What philosophers had formerly tried to *say* they must now undertake to *show* by revealing the logical form of those sentences that are typically misconstrued. In this way they can still perform the task of making clear the essence – the *a priori* structure – of the world, albeit in a more circuitous and less familiar way. The philosopher who does this "will see the world [i.e., the *essence* of the world] aright" (TLP 6.54). Putting the matter more explicitly, he writes:

> ... what belongs to the essence of the world simply *cannot* be said.[3] And philosophy, if it were to say anything, would have to describe the essence of the world.
>   But the essence of language [i.e., *logical* grammar] is a picture of the essence of the world; and philosophy as custodian of grammar can in fact grasp the essence of the world, only not in the propositions of language, but in the rules for this language which exclude nonsensical combinations of signs (PR, p. 85).[4]

So Wittgenstein's position is not that philosophers are to put away their traditional concerns and think about something else instead. Rather, he is saying that traditional philosophical issues can be dealt with only by recasting them as questions about language.[5] Take, for instance, the old question "Do material objects exist even when they are not being perceived?" Wittgenstein is not declaring that philosophers should simply turn their backs on this question. He is saying that although this question, in its traditional form, is nonsense, it can be turned into a genuine question by recasting it in the formal mode: "Is such a proposition as 'There is some money locked in the safe' a categorical proposition, as it appears to be, or is it, as Berkeley claimed, a disguised counterfactual proposition?" And by discovering the answer to *that* question we will grasp something about the essence of the world, and then there will be nothing more for idealists and realists to argue about on this point.

How to Recognize Logical Form

Here, however, we encounter a difficulty. It can be brought to light by asking how one is to recognize the true logical form of a proposition.

Can one do so without first discovering the metaphysical nature (the logical form) of the relevant facts? After all, the true logical form of a proposition is, by definition, that form which mirrors the form of the fact which, if it obtained, would make the proposition true. Suppose, then, that for a given proposition "p" we had several candidates for its logical form, one of them being the grammatical form of the English sentence "p" and the others being the grammatical forms used by several non-Indo-European languages for the sentence that would be used to say the same thing. The question is: How would one determine which, if any, of these candidates exhibits, in its grammar, the true logical form? Can we determine this by somehow investigating language? Or must we determine this by *first* turning our backs on language and somehow discovering the form of the fact itself? And if the latter, how will attention to language help one to discover the form of the fact? Won't philosophers have to go right on, in the same old way, debating their differences over the nature of the facts in question?[6]

These questions go to the very heart of the *Tractatus*, for in the preface Wittgenstein claimed that he had found, in all essentials, the solution to philosophical problems. To make good this claim, however, he would have to show how philosophical disputes over logical form are to be settled. One can see him wrestling with this problem very early in his pre-*Tractatus* notebook, where he says that it is out of the question that "some kind of experience" is required for determining the logical form of this or that proposition (NB, p. 3). What this comes to, in part anyway, is that logic (philosophy) is an *a priori* discipline, not an empirical one. Or, as he was later to say, "In grammar you cannot discover anything. There are no surprises" (WVC, p. 77; compare PI, §126). But must there not be some sort of awareness of the logical form (the essence) of the world that we can draw upon in determining the form of a proposition?

In the *Tractatus* Wittgenstein seems to answer, somewhat enigmatically, in the affirmative:

The "experience" that we need in order to understand logic is not that something or other is the state of things, but that something *is*: that, however, is *not* an experience.
Logic is *prior* to every experience – that something *is so*.
It is prior to the "How?," not prior to the question "What?" (TLP, 5.552).

Here he says that the "experience" we need to understand logic (i.e., to recognize logical form) is not an experience. What did he mean by this paradoxical remark?

During conversations in 1929 Schlick several times pressed Wittgenstein to explain himself on this point. On 30 December he asked how we can "*know* that one syntax is right while another is not." Wittgenstein's response was brief: "there is experience of *that* and experience of *how*" (WVC, p. 65). Three days later Schlick returned to this point, asking, "Is there nothing that can be said in reply to the question, How do I know that such-and-such rules of syntax are valid? How do I know that red and blue cannot be in one place simultaneously? Have we not in this case a kind of empirical knowledge [i.e., a knowledge of the form of a fact]?" (WVC, pp. 76–77). Wittgenstein replied as follows:

Yes and no. It depends on what you mean by empirical. If what you mean by empirical knowledge is not such that it can be expressed by means of a proposition, then this is not empirical knowledge. If it is something different you mean by empirical thinking, then syntax too is empirical. At one point in my *Tractatus* I said: Logic is prior to the question "How?," not prior to the question "What?" Logic [i.e., logical form] depends on this: that something exists (in the sense that there is something), that there are facts [having a logical form]. It is independent of anything's being so. No proposition can describe that there are facts. If you wish, I could just as well say, logic is empirical – if *that* is what you call empirical (WVC, p. 77).[7]

We can see from this that Wittgenstein's position was the following. Anyone who speaks a language is aware of the essence of the world, of the forms of all possible facts (see TLP, 6.33), and therefore there can be no disagreement over logical form in particular cases, *provided* we have rid ourselves of the assumption that the grammatical forms of our native tongue are bound to reflect the essence of the world. [Recall here his insistence that "distrust of grammar is the first requisite of philosophizing" (NB, p. 93).] In other words, his answer to our question is this: in order to decide between the candidates for the logical form of p, it is indeed necessary that we be aware of the logical form of the fact it states, but there is no difficulty in this because everyone is already aware of the form of the fact, and all that is needed for this awareness to come into play in philosophizing is that we set aside the prejudices foisted on us by the grammatical forms of our English (or German, etc.) sentences.

What is the source of the awareness of logical form? Wittgenstein's answer is that it comes from our acquaintance with the simple objects that undergird all language.

2.0123 If I know an object I also know all its possible occurrences in states of affairs.
(Every one of these possibilities must be part of the nature of the object.)
A new possibility cannot be discovered later.
2.01231 If I am to know an object, though I need not know its external properties, I must know all its internal properties.
2.0124 If all objects are given, then at the same time all *possible* states of affairs are also given.
2.0141 The possibility of its occurring in states of affairs is the form of an object.

In answer to our question, then, Wittgenstein could have said: it is only because we are aware of the logical forms of facts that we can *say* anything, can form propositions about the world. So philosophers are aware of logical forms just because they speak a language, and there would be no philosophical questions or disputes were it not for the fact that our everyday language is misleading as to logical form.

At the end of the *Tractatus* Wittgenstein offers the following advice about philosophical method: "The correct method in philosophy would really be the following: to say nothing except what can be said, i.e., propositions of natural science – i.e., something that has nothing to do with philosophy – and then, whenever someone else wanted to say something metaphysical, to demonstrate to him that he had failed to give a meaning to certain signs in his propositions" (TLP, 6.53). This advice, however, is much too vague. How is one to demonstrate to a philosopher that he has failed to give a meaning to certain of the words he uses? Wittgenstein's answer is shown by the kind of example he gives in the following passage:

Most of the propositions and questions to be found in philosophical works are not false but nonsensical. Consequently we cannot give any answer to questions of this kind, but can only establish that they are nonsensical. Most of the propositions and questions of philosophers arise from our failure to understand the logic of our language.

(They belong to the same class as the question whether the good is more or less identical than the beautiful.) (TLP, 4.003).

Wittgenstein gives a similar example in the course of discussing his claim that "logic must look after itself," for he goes on to say:

The reason "Socrates is identical" means nothing is that there is no property called "identical." The proposition is nonsensical because we have failed to make an arbitrary determination [i.e., because we haven't named any property "identical"], and not because the symbol, in itself, would be illegitimate (TLP, 5.473).

Wittgenstein is not suggesting that philosophers make *silly* mistakes, that their problems arise as the result of their making simple grammatical mistakes in their native tongues. His point is that philosophical mistakes are in a certain respect *like* the mistake one would be making if one thought one could say (assert) "Socrates is identical." The similarity is that the way to demonstrate to a philosopher that he is mistaken is similar to the way we would explain why "Socrates is identical" is meaningless, namely, by pointing out that (a) he is using a familiar word (or phrase), (b) that he is not using it according to its usual grammatical rules, and (c) that he has not assigned the word a new meaning.[8]

Let us agree that, taken together, (a), (b), and (c) are a prescription for philosophical disaster. The question remains: when philosophers disagree (as Berkeley and Moore did) about the logical form of a proposition such as "There is money locked in this safe," how is it to be determined which of them is guilty of the errors in (b) and (c)?

The answer must lie somewhere in the *Tractatus*, even if it is not very obvious, and it lies, I suggest, in what was argued in Chapter 3, namely, that the 'objects' of the *Tractatus* are 'sensible qualities.' Wittgenstein, taking this for granted, took it to be obvious that desks and chairs are *not* what Moore took them to be. In short, he was an empiricist, and he therefore took it for granted that philosophical disputes about logical form are to be decided always in favor of empiricism. To put the matter differently, his way of thinking about philosophical disputes was not philosophically unbiased; on the contrary, his *only* way of thinking of them was to take it for granted both that empiricism is right and that philosophers of a contrary opinion, such as Moore, can be brought around to empiricism by being shown the ineptitudes in their contrary opinion.

So what Wittgenstein took to be the essence of the world [for example, he adopted Hume's view of causation (TLP, 5.135–5.1361)] is simply one philosophical theory (empiricism) among others, no less subject to criticism than any other. But because it never occurred to him to challenge the empiricists' notion of 'experience,' he imagined that, instead of embracing a *debatable* philosophical theory, he was, in every instance, aware of the form of the facts in question, of the essence of the world. (Since sensible qualities "make up the substance of the world" (TLP, 2.021), he thought: Berkeley must be right about the nature of material things, Hume must be right about causation, and so on.) Wittgenstein's reliance on empiricist assumptions will become more evident in later chapters when we consider his treatment of such topics as solipsism, other minds, causation, and the past.

As we consider his treatment of these topics it will be important to bear in mind the following points. (i) Wittgenstein held that traditional metaphysical problems must be restated in the formal mode, as questions about language. (ii) In answering those questions by commenting on the 'grammar' of various words, he meant to be showing something about the essence of the world, not merely something about language.[9] (iii) Once a question has been recast in the formal mode, the answer Wittgenstein gives is dictated by his empiricist assumptions. (iv) Because of his views about language and philosophy, he regularly criticized other philosophers in the following ways: (a) he criticized Moorean realists for failing to distrust the grammar of ordinary language; (b) he criticized empiricists (e.g., solipsists) for stating their views in the material mode; and (c) he reprimanded empiricists who, by failing to realize that grammar is arbitrary, attack ordinary language because of its grammar (e.g., PI, §402).[10]

Notes

1. In the *Investigations* he alludes to the *Tractatus* on this point: "It was true to say that our considerations could not be scientific ones" (PI, §109).

2. These terms are Carnap's rather than Wittgenstein's, but the idea had come to Wittgenstein first and he was annoyed that Carnap should have failed to acknowledge the priority. In a letter to Moritz Schlick, dated August 8, 1932, he wrote: "You know very well yourself that Carnap is not taking any step beyond me when he is for the formal and against the "material mode of speech" [*inhaltliche Redeweise*]. And I cannot imagine that Carnap should have misunderstood so completely the last propositions of the *Tractatus* – and hence the basic ideas of the entire book [as not to know that, too]." Published in *Wittgenstein: Sein Leben in Bildern und Texten*, eds. Michael Nedo and Michelle Ranchetti (Shurkamp: Frankfort am Main, 1983), pp. 254–255.

3. In lectures he said: "Whenever we try to talk about the essence of the world [i.e., try to state an a priori matter in the material mode of speech] we talk nonsense" (WL32, p. 110). The importance Wittgenstein attached to this is shown by a remark he made in a letter to Russell, dated 19 August, 1919: "The main point is the theory of what can be expressed by propositions – i.e., by language – (and, which comes to the same, what can be *thought*) and what cannot be expressed by propositions, but only shown; which, I believe, is the cardinal problem of philosophy" [*Letters to Russell, Keynes and Moore*, ed. G. H. von Wright (Blackwell, 1974), p. 71].

4. In the *Tractatus* he had written:

What finds its reflection in language, language cannot represent.

What expresses *itself* in language, *we* cannot express by means of language.

Propositions *show* the logical form of reality.

They display it (TLP, 4.121).

He goes on to say: "What *can* be shown, cannot be said" (TLP, 4.1212). Some years later, in lectures, he said: "Nonsense is produced by trying to express in a proposition something which belongs to the grammar of our language" (WL35, p. 18).

5. In later years he was to write: "Philosophical investigations: conceptual investigations. The essential thing about metaphysics: that the difference between factual and conceptual investigations is not clear to it. A metaphysical question is always in appearance a factual one, although the problem is a conceptual one" (RPP, I, §949).

6. Irving Copi advances such an argument in "Language Analysis and Metaphysical Inquiry" reprinted in *The Linguistic Turn*, ed. Richard Rorty (Chicago University Press: Chicago, 1967), pp. 127–131.

7. See also WVC, p. 217. In his 1929 paper "Some Remarks on Logical Form" Wittgenstein, addressing the question put to him by Schlick, wrote:

Now we can only substitute a clear symbolism for the unprecise one by inspecting the phenomena which we want to describe [by means of the clear symbolism], thus trying to understand their logical multiplicity. That is to say, we can only arrive at a correct analysis by, what might be called, the logical investigation of the phenomena themselves, i.e. in a certain sense *a posteriori*, and not by conjecturing about *a priori* possibilities (RLF, p. 32).

8. This way of stating the matter is found also in *Philosophical Remarks*, pp. 55–56. See also RPP, I, §§548–550.

9. This idea can be seen in the *Investigations* when he says: "*Essence* is

expressed by grammar" (PI, §371). In his 1946–47 lectures Wittgenstein said: "Grammatical characteristics must characterize *what* it is that we talk about, as opposed to what is said about them" (WL47, p. 293).

10. In his 1946–47 lectures Wittgenstein said that it is a "typical philosophical utterance" to object to the grammar of ordinary language by saying: "We *ought* to say so-and-so" (WL47, p. 44).

5

What the Solipsist Means is Quite Correct

In his pre-*Tractatus* notebooks Wittgenstein wrote: "This is the way I have travelled: Idealism singles men out from the world as unique, solipsism singles me alone out, and at last I see that I too belong with the rest of the world, and so on the one side *nothing* is left over, and on the other side, as unique, *the world*. In this way idealism leads to realism if it is strictly thought out" (NB, p. 85). In this chapter and the next we will be concerned with understanding Wittgenstein's intellectual travels: his transition from idealism to solipsism to a position beyond solipsism, which he calls "realism." This final position, which we have already identified as neutral monism, will be discussed in Chapter 6. Here we will be concerned with his treatment of solipsism.

As I remarked in Chapter 1, Wittgenstein's early concerns were epistemological: he was eager to defeat the philosophical claim that there are many things one *cannot* know. This, very likely, was his reason for moving from idealism to solipsism. Idealism, in arguing that 'material things' are nothing but bundles of sense-impressions, undercuts skepticism regarding the existence of material things. And yet, because it allows that there may be 'other minds,' which are *not* given in one's experience, idealism leaves open the door to skepticism regarding other *people*. If another person – a friend or neighbor – is to be thought of as another *mind*, and is thus to be thought of as something that is *not* given in experience, then whether one *has* a friend or neighbor must remain unknowable. Wittgenstein found this unacceptable and undertook to defeat such skepticism.

From Idealism to Solipsism

One way to do so was to embrace solipsism, and for a time Wittgenstein found solipsism an attractive alternative to skepticism. For the solipsist, unlike the skeptic, does not say: "While it *may* be the case that I have friends and neighbors, I cannot *know* that I do." Rather, the solipsist says that there is no such thing to *be* known, nothing of the sort to *wish* to know. He says: "I alone exist" or "Reality and immediate experience are one and the same" or "My own experiences are all that is real."[1] As we have seen, Wittgenstein regarded philosophical skepticism as nonsense, for it appears to pose a genuine question and then declares it unanswerable, and for this reason he took solipsism to be an improvement over skepticism. The solipsist, he thought, has the good sense not to allow even *the possibility* that there is something beyond immediate experience.[2]

Yet there is something unsatisfactory about the way in which the solipsist states his position. When he says "I alone exist" or "Nothing is real but my own experiences," he employs the material mode of speech, and in doing so he *seems* to leave open the possibility that there are other minds and material things. For these claims of his seem to have genuine negations, e.g., "I am *not* the only one that exists," and any such negation, if it is a genuine proposition must, in Wittgenstein's view, have a chance of being true. (It's falsity can't be ruled out *a priori*.) Thus, the solipsist, because he employs the material mode of speech, leaves himself open to attempted rejoinders by philosophers who imagine that they can at least *think of* something – friends and neighbors – beyond immediate experience. Worse yet, the solipsist's way of stating his claim seems to put him in conflict with much of our everyday language, for even a solipsist, when not engaged in philosophy, will say such things as "It fell on his foot, not mine"; "I sat on a chair, and the others stood around me"; and "My sister has blue eyes." Surely there is something peculiar in his occasionally saying such things while yet, when philosophizing, declaring that he alone exists. Indeed, since he will sometimes say such a thing as "I know my father is older than my mother," he seems to *know* that other people exist and so seems to know that solipsism isn't true. What are we to think of this?

During lectures Wittgenstein emphatically dismissed the attempts of a philosopher such as Moore to seize on such oddities in order to discredit solipsism.

No philosopher lacks common sense in ordinary life. So philosophers should not attempt to present the idealistic or solipsistic positions, for example, as though they were absurd – by pointing out to a person who puts forward these positions that he does not really wonder whether the beef is real or whether it is an idea in his mind, whether his wife is real or whether only he is real. Of course he does not, and it is not a proper objection. You must not try to avoid a philosophical problem by appealing to common sense; instead, present it as it arises with most power. You must allow yourself to be dragged into the mire, and get out of it. Philosophy can be said to consist of three activities: to see the commonsense answer, to get yourself so deeply into the problem that the commonsense answer is unbearable, and to get from that situation back to the commonsense answer. But the commonsense answer in itself is no solution; everyone knows it. One must not in philosophy attempt to short-circuit problems (WL35, pp. 108–109).

What are the three stages in the present case?

The first stage, seeing the commonsense answer, amounts to seeing that in ordinary language we say such things as "My sister has blue eyes" and "My father suffered greatly." The second stage, finding the common sense answer unbearable, is explained by Wittgenstein in The Blue Book as follows:

... I am told: "If you pity someone for having pains, surely you must at least *believe* that he has pains." But how can I even *believe* this? How can these words make sense to me? How can I even have come by the idea of another's experience if there is no possibility of any evidence for it? (BB, p. 46).

Several paragraphs later he makes the same point while commenting on the idea that it is a *hypothesis* (or belief) that others, too, have personal experiences:

But is it an hypothesis at all? For how can I even make the hypothesis if it transcends all possible experience? How could such a hypothesis be backed by meaning? (Is it not like paper money, not backed by gold?) It doesn't help if anyone tells us that, although we don't know whether the other person has pains, we certainly believe it when, for instance, we pity him. Certainly we shouldn't pity him if we didn't believe that he had pains; but is this a philosophical, a metaphysical belief? Does a realist pity me more than an idealist or a solipsist? – In fact, the solipsist asks: "How *can* we believe that the other has pains; what does it mean to believe this? How can the expression of such a supposition make sense?" (BB, p. 48).

Wittgenstein goes on to comment that the trouble with the common-sense philosopher, the realist, "is always that he does not solve but skip[s] the difficulties which his adversaries see" (ibid.). The difficulty, as Wittgenstein sees it, is that while ordinary language *seems* to allow for speaking of things beyond immediate experience, it is not really *possible* to speak of (or think of) anything not given in immediate experience. And this is the difficulty he also credits the solipsist with seeing.[3]

What, then, is the third stage? How does Wittgenstein propose to get back to common sense, i.e., get back the possibility of saying such things as "My sister has blue eyes" and "My father suffered greatly"?[4]

The answer must begin with the matters discussed in the preceding chapter, namely, the idea that philosophers must avoid the material mode of speech. The solipsist is guilty of trying to *say* something that can only be shown, and to avoid the appearance of absurdity he must restate his position in the formal mode. Once this is done, Wittgenstein thought, the correctness of solipsism can be seen. This is what he was getting at in the following passages of the *Tractatus*:

5.61 Logic pervades the world: the limits of the world are also its limits.
    So we cannot say in logic [i.e., as an *a priori* truth], "The world has this in it, and this, but not that."
    For that [i.e., saying that such-and-such does not exist] would appear to presuppose that we were excluding certain possibilities, and this cannot be the case, since it would require that logic should go beyond the limits of the world [i.e., that language should be able to describe a situation that transcends experience, e.g., that there are other minds]. . . .

We cannot think what we cannot think; so what we cannot think we cannot *say* either.

5.62 This remark provides the key to the problem, how much truth there is in solipsism.

For what the solipsist *means* is quite correct; only it cannot be *said* [in the material mode], but makes itself manifest.

That the world is *my* world is manifest in this: that the limits of *language* (of that language which alone I understand) signify the limits of *my* world.[5]

These passages require a bit of deciphering, but the key lies in the fact that the topic here is solipsism.

To see what he is getting at, we can restate 5.61 as an explicit comment on solipsism. It then comes to the following. The world consists of nothing more than (contains no possibilities other than) can be represented in language. So the solipsist's use of the material mode, in saying such a thing as "I alone exist" or "Only my experiences are real," is unacceptable, because such sentences appear to have genuine negations, i.e., appear to allow that it is *possible* (conceivable) that there is something beyond immediate experience. (If I thought myself to be the sole survivor of a terrible plague, I might write in my diary "I alone exist," but I could also add: "Oh, I wish it weren't so," and this would be a genuine thought: it is conceivable that others should have survived as well.) But the point of embracing solipsism would be that it avoids skepticism by declaring that it is *impossible* that something exists beyond immediate experience. And since solipsism is an *a priori* thesis (i.e., the solipsist does not arrive at his position by taking a head count), this impossibility is a *logical* impossibility. So what solipsism properly *means* is that one cannot so much as *think of* (conceive of) anything beyond immediate experience. This is why Wittgenstein goes on to say, in 5.62, that "what the solipsist *means* is quite correct." What the solipsist means is *not*: "While one can conceive of material things and other minds, they do not *in fact* exist," but rather: "The very idea of 'things outside (or beyond) immediate experience' is a delusion, for language is grounded in names being given to objects in immediate experience, and therefore only such objects can, in the last analysis, be spoken of (conceived of)."[6]

It is clear that solipsism, formulated in the formal mode, cannot relevantly be replied to by saying, "But, as you surely know, there are many thousands of people in London alone and many more elsewhere." Such a rejoinder could seem relevant only so long as the solipsist is taken to be saying something akin to the diary entry by a survivor of a plague: "I alone exist." But what are we to think of the fact that the solipsist, when not engaged in philosophy, will say such things as "The rock fell on his foot, not mine" and "My sister has blue eyes" and "His pain is worse than mine, so attend to him first"? Is he not, in saying such things, speaking of things beyond his immediate experience?

Wittgenstein's answer would have to be that such propositions only *seem* to be about something beyond experience, i.e., that their grammatical form is misleading. That is, having endorsed what the solipsist *means*, and having said, too, that "all the propositions of our everyday language . . . are in perfect logical order" (TLP, 5.5563), Wittgenstein's position must be that it is possible to reconcile whatever he says in everyday language with his sophisticated version of solipsism. In Chapter 3 we saw that he believed that such a thing as a table could be defined in terms of sensible qualities, and the same would hold, of course, for human bodies. This being so, he could allow that there are in immediate experience many human bodies, and it is in reference to *these* that one can say such things as "My sister has blue eyes" and "It fell on his foot, not mine."[7] So propositions such as these describe what is given in experience and can be reconciled with solipsism. This helps us to understand Wittgenstein's dismissal of the commonsense philosopher who represents solipsism as an absurdity. For the solipsist does not have to think it invariably untrue to say, "My sister has blue eyes"; he need only propose an analysis of that proposition that can be reconciled with solipsism.

The problem does not end here, however, for even if solipsism can accommodate such a proposition by taking it to refer to a body (rather than to a mind or soul), how can it accommodate propositions containing psychological terms, such as "I am thinking," "I believe it will rain," and so on? It is tempting to regard *these* sentences – sentences of the form "A thinks that p," "A believes that p" – in the way that Descartes did, i.e., to take the pronoun in "I think" as referring to an immaterial soul or self. But in that case, how are other people to be accommodated?

Wittgenstein addresses this problem by declaring that the grammatical form of such sentences is misleading and that once they are set out in their true logical form they can be seen not to refer to a unitary self at all. In his pre-*Tractatus* notebooks he put this by saying: "The I is not an object" (NB, p. 80), meaning that in a fully analyzed version of the sentences in question there will be nothing corresponding to the first-person pronoun. In the *Tractatus* he allows himself, at one point, to put this matter in the material mode: "There is no such thing as the subject that thinks or entertains ideas" (TLP, 5.631), but in another passage he avoids the material mode, saying of the sentences in question:

It is clear, however, that "A believes that *p*", "A has the thought *p*", and "A says *p*" are of the form "p says *p*": and this does not involve a correlation of a fact with an object [a self], but rather the correlation of facts by means of the correlation of their objects (TLP, 5.542).

This shows too that there is no such thing as the soul – the subject, etc. – as it is conceived in the superficial psychology of the present day. A composite soul would of course no longer be a soul (TLP, 5.5421).

Here Wittgenstein is saying that once we realize that the true logical form of the sentences in question does not involve a subject we will also

see the form of the facts in question, will see the essence of the world.[8]
And yet he here again resorts to the material mode to *say* what is shown,
for he says: "This shows that there is no such thing as the soul." It is this
sort of thing that, at the end of the *Tractatus*, he declares to be nonsensical (TLP, 6.54).

In later years he was more careful to avoid saying what (in his own
view) cannot be said. For instance, in lectures he made a similar point
about logical form in the following way:

The function "x has toothache" has various values, Smith, Jones, etc. But not
I. I is in a class by itself. The word "I" does not refer to a possessor in sentences
about having an experience, unlike its use in "I have a cigar" [where it refers
to a body]. We could have a language from which "I" is omitted from sentences
describing a personal experience (WL35, p. 21).

Wittgenstein also put this point by saying: "Instead of saying 'I think' or
'I have an ache' one might say 'It thinks' (like 'It rains'), and in place of
'I have an ache,' 'There is an ache here'" (Ibid.).[9] In these versions
Wittgenstein avoids the material mode altogether.

In *Philosophical Remarks* we find him saying:

One of the most misleading representational techniques in our language is the
use of the word "I," particularly when it is used in representing immediate
experience, as in "I can see a red patch."
    It would be instructive to replace this way of speaking by another in which
immediate experience would be represented without using the personal pronoun; for then we'd be able to see that the previous representation wasn't
essential to the facts. Not that the representation would be in any sense more
correct than the old one, but it would serve to show clearly what was logically
essential in the representation (PR, p. 88).

The obvious question to ask at this point is this: What was it that led
Wittgenstein to embrace this analysis?

Wittgenstein's Grounds for This Analysis

Why did Wittgenstein think that "I" is superfluous in the cases in
question here? In the *Tractatus* he reaches this conclusion in the following group of remarks:

5.632 The subject does not belong to the world: rather, it is a limit of the world.
5.633 Where *in* the world is a metaphysical subject to be found?
    You will say that this is exactly like the case of the eye and the visual field. But
really you do *not* see the eye.
    And nothing *in the visual field* allows you to infer that it is seen by an eye.
5.6331 The form of the visual field is surely not like this

Eye →

5.634 This is connected with the fact that no part of our experience is at the
same time *a priori*.

Whatever we see could be other than it is.
Whatever we can describe at all could be other than it is.
There is no *a priori* order of things.
5.64 Here it can be seen that solipsism, when its implications are followed out
   strictly, coincides with pure realism. The self of solipsism shrinks to a point
   without extension, and there remains the reality coordinated with it.

The gist of this argument can be stated roughly as follows: if there were
a *necessary* connection between, say, the visual field and something that
sees, then that something would have to be referred to in a fully analyzed version of "I see a red square," but since there is no such connection, the first-person pronoun in that proposition is superfluous and
would have no role to play in a proposition whose logical form mirrors
the form of the fact.

There are two related points to consider in this argument. One is the
contention that the visual field has no necessary connection with anything else. The other, which I will turn to first, is a more general version
of this, namely, the contention that there are no necessary connections
in the world (no *a priori* order of things), since whatever we observe (and
can describe) could be otherwise. This comes to: given any statement of
fact, i.e., any description of how things stand in the world, its negation
must also describe a thinkable, possible, state of affairs. This is Wittgenstein's general point about significant propositions: their negations
must also be significant. Thus, he is saying that even if it happens to be
the case that I *always* see with eyes, still it is conceivable that I should
sometimes see, instead, with my hand and conceivable, too, that I
should see although I have no body. The fact that something has always
been the case should not, Wittgenstein is saying, mislead us into thinking that matters couldn't have been otherwise.[10] So, although we have
never yet found a case in which a person has thoughts but no brain, it
is conceivable that this correlation will break down in the future and
even that it should never have existed at all. Thus Wittgenstein says:
"Similarly, we can talk of a toothache without there being any teeth, or
of thinking without there being a head involved" (WL35, p. 23).

In the passages quoted above from the *Tractatus* he brings this general
point to bear on the question about the logical form of such propositions
as "I am thinking," "I believe that . . . ," "I see . . . ," and similar cases.
He asks: Where in the world is a subject (of thinking, seeing, etc.) to be
found? Here we may recall Hume, who declared that whenever he
looked into himself he always came upon some particular impression
but never a subject. We can grasp Wittgenstein's argument by entertaining the following rejoinder to Hume: Whenever I see or hear something, I find that if I look downward there is a body of such-and-such
a description, so *that* is the subject I speak of when I say "I see . . ." or
"I hear . . . ." Against this Wittgenstein argues as follows.[11] Granted,

there is this constancy in your life, but suppose it were otherwise; suppose that each time you turned your gaze downward you saw something different: a table, a carpet, etc. Would you still think that each time you said "I see" you refer to a subject, I? If not, then surely that body you usually see when you turn your gaze downward is not such a subject either, for it is no more an essential element in your seeing than would be, for a example, an overly loyal dog that you always noticed when you looked down.[12] The point is that if one were to say, "I hear a siren," and then looked down and did *not* see one's body, one would not think: So, it was wrong of me to say, "I hear a siren." Therefore, the truth of "I hear . . ." does not depend on one's having a body. (". . . our body is not at all essential for the occurrence of our experience" (PG, p. 147).) So the pronoun in "I see," "I hear," etc. could, without loss, be eliminated from our language.

Wittgenstein's Continued Allegiance to the Foregoing Analysis

This, then, is Wittgenstein's argument, and it is important to realize that he continued to hold this view in his post-*Tractatus* years. For instance, in *Philosophical Remarks*, he put this point by saying: "Visual space has essentially no owner" (PR, p. 100). Similarly, he wrote:

The experience of feeling pain is not that a person "I" has something.
I distinguish an intensity, a location, etc. in the pain, but not an owner (PR, p. 94).

In 1932 lectures, he said:

. . . the description of a sensation does not contain a reference to either a person or a sense organ. Ask yourself, How do I, the person, come in? How, for example, does a person come into the description of a visual sensation? If we describe the visual field, no person necessarily comes into it. We can say the visual field has certain internal properties, but its being *mine* is not essential to its description. That is, it is not an intrinsic property of a visual sensation, or a pain, to belong to someone. There will be no such thing as *my* image or someone else's (WL35, p. 22).[13]

In The Blue Book, in a lengthy discussion of solipsism, Wittgenstein put the matter as follows:

Now let us ask ourselves what sort of identity of personality it is we are referring to when we say "when anything is seen, it is always I who see." What is it I want all these cases of seeing to have in common? As an answer I have to confess to myself that it is not my bodily appearance. I don't always see part of my body when I see. And it isn't essential that my body, if seen amongst the things I see, should always look the same. In fact I don't mind how much it changes. And I feel the same way about all the properties of my body, the characteristics of my behaviour, and even about my memories. When I think about it a little longer I see that what I wished to say was: "Always when anything is seen, something is seen." I.e., that of which I said it continued during all the experiences of seeing was not any particular entity "I," but the experience of seeing itself (BB, p. 63).

Wittgenstein goes on to formulate his conclusion as follows: "To say, 'I have pain' is no more a statement *about* a particular person than moaning is" (BB, p. 67) and "In 'I have pain,' 'I' is not a demonstrative pronoun" (BB, p. 68). In 1948 Wittgenstein was still making this point: in a comparison of "It looks . . . to me" and "It looks . . . to you," he declared that when we say the former "a person does not occur as perceiving subject" (RPP, II, §317; Z, §424).

In the *Investigations* (§§404–411) Wittgenstein maintains the same position. He makes his point most explicitly in the following passage:

> When I say "I am in pain," I do not point to a person who is in pain, since in a certain sense I have no idea *who* is. And this can be given a justification. For the main point is: I did not say such-and-such a person was in pain, but "I am . . . ." Now in saying this I don't name any person. Just as I don't name anyone when I *groan* with pain. Though someone else sees who is in pain from the groaning.
> What does it mean to know *who* is in pain? It means, for example, to know which man in this room is in pain: for instance, that it is the one who is sitting over there, or the one who is standing in that corner, the tall one over there with the fair hair, and so on. What am I getting at? At the fact that there is a great variety of criteria for personal "*identity*."
> Now which of them determines my saying that "*I*" am in pain? None (PI, §404).

Here Wittgenstein is once again arguing that the grammatical form of "I am in pain" is misleading, for it suggests that there is a *subject* of pain, a self or ego or person who *has* a headache or a toothache.

Wittgenstein's Argument Against a Cartesian Ego

So far we have considered only one argument for this view, namely, the argument that the pronoun in "I see . . ." or "I am in pain" does not refer to one's *body*, because one's body could always change or vanish. But this argument does not address the Cartesian view that in such cases "I" stands for one's mind, not one's body. In the years following the *Tractatus* Wittgenstein saw the need to address this point and did so as follows:

> Now the idea that the real I lives in my body is connected with the peculiar grammar of the word "I," and the misunderstandings this grammar is liable to give rise to. There are two different cases in the use of the word "I" (or "my") which I might call "the use as object" and "the use as subject." Examples of the first kind of use are these: "My arm is broken," "I have grown six inches," "I have a bump on my forehead," "The wind blows my hair about." Examples of the second kind are: "*I* see so-and-so," "*I* try to lift my arm," "*I* think it will rain," "*I* have a toothache." One can point to the difference between these two

categories by saying: The cases of the first category involve the recognition of a particular person. . . . On the other hand, there is no question of recognizing a person when I say I have toothache. To ask "Are you sure that it's *you* who have pains?" would be nonsensical. . . .

The word "I" does not mean the same as "L.W." [which is the name of a body] even if I am L.W., nor does it mean the same as the expression "the person who is now speaking." But that doesn't mean that "L.W." and "I" mean different things [i.e., doesn't mean that they designate two different entities, one a body, the other something non-bodily]. All it means is that these words are different instruments in our language. . . .

We feel then that in the cases in which "I" is used as subject, we don't use it because we recognize a particular person by his bodily characteristics; and this creates the illusion that we use this word to refer to something bodiless, which, however, has its seat in our body. In fact *this* seems to be the real ego, the one of which it was said, "Cogito, ergo sum." "Is there then no mind, but only a body?" Answer: The word "mind" has meaning, i.e., it has a use in our language; but saying this doesn't yet say what kind of use we make of it (BB, pp. 66–70).[14]

In his 1946–47 lectures he said: "The blunder is to think the word 'Self' means something in the way that 'body' stands for the body; . . . [that it] stands for something inside the body. If you consider substituting a signal for 'I suffer' you see that the first mistake is to take 'I' as *standing* for something" (WL47, p. 47).

Solipsism and Ordinary Language

At the end of Chapter 4 I remarked that one sort of criticism Wittgenstein made of other philosophers, including empiricists, was that they fail to realize that grammar is arbitrary. Because they fail to realize this, they are sometimes led to attack our ordinary way of speaking. We have seen an example of this in the passage, quoted by Mach with approval, in which Lichtenberg declares that, instead of saying "I think," we *should* say "It thinks" (like "It's raining"). Wittgenstein was alluding to this when he said:

The solipsist wishes to say, "I should like to put, instead of the notation 'I have real toothache' 'There is toothache'." What the solipsist wants is not a notation in which the ego has a monopoly, but one in which the ego vanishes (WL35, p. 22).

While Wittgenstein was sympathetic with this desire for a different notation, he also thought it misguided:

One symbolism is just as good as the next. The word "I" is one symbol among others having a *practical* use, and could be discarded when not necessary for practical speech. . . .

Whenever we feel [as Lichtenberg did] that our language is inadequate to describe a situation, at bottom there will be a misunderstanding of a simple sort (WL35, p. 63).

In the *Investigations* Wittgenstein is making the same point when he writes:

"It is true I say 'Now I am having such-and-such an image,' but the words 'I am having' are merely a sign to someone *else*; the description of the image is a *complete* account of the imagined world." You mean: the words "I am having" are like "Now hear this! . . . ."[15] You are inclined to say it should really have been expressed differently. Perhaps simply by making a sign with one's hand and then giving a description. When as in this case, we disapprove of the expressions of ordinary language (which are after all performing their office), we have got a picture in our heads which conflicts with the picture of our ordinary mode of expression [*der gewohnlichen Ausdrucksweise*]. Whereas we are tempted to say that our mode of expression does not describe the facts as they really are. As if, for example the proposition "he has pains" could be false in some other way than by that man's *not* having pains. As if the form of expression were saying something false even when the proposition *faute de mieux* asserted something true.

For *this* is what disputes between Idealists, Solipsists and Realists look like. The one party [e.g., Lichtenberg] attack the normal form of expression as if they were attacking a statement [of fact]; the others defend it, as if they were stating facts recognized by every reasonable human being (PI, §402).

It would be a mistake to read this passage as an rejection of solipsism, of what the solipsist *means*. What is rejected here is merely one way of formulating solipsism, namely, as an attack on our ordinary mode of expression.

Did Wittgenstein Remain a Solipsist?

Here it may be asked: Is the position Wittgenstein finally settled on significantly different from solipsism? Let us review the main points in what he says about solipsism. The classical solipsist says, "I alone exist." In the *Tractatus* Wittgenstein made the following two comments on this: (i) ". . . what the solipsist *means* is quite correct; only it cannot be *said*, but makes itself manifest," and (ii) ". . . solipsism, when its implications are followed out strictly, coincides with pure realism." The first of these comments is an objection to stating solipsism in the material mode by saying "I alone exist," which makes it look as though the solipsist arrived at his position by taking a head count and thus invites irrelevant criticisms of the sort Moore was prone to make. At the same time Wittgenstein is saying that what the solipsist *means* is quite correct and that this shows itself in language. The second of the above comments brings out what Wittgenstein held to be correct, namely, that in a description of one's sensations the word "I" is not a demonstrative pronoun and is not essential to the representation of the fact. This is how solipsism, when its implications are followed out strictly, coincides with pure realism (neutral monism).

Now, is this position significantly different from solipsism? The answer depends on what one regards as a significant difference in philosophy. One might say that Wittgenstein's pure realism is only a sophisticated version of solipsism, which he arrived at, as he said, by thinking out properly the implications of solipsism. Accordingly, John Canfield aptly remarks that "what might be called the thesis of selfless solipsism lies at the heart of the *Tractatus*."[16] On the other hand, had Wittgenstein himself been asked (after 1915) if he was a solipsist, he would have emphasized differences, saying that solipsism is a metaphysical view, an attempt to *say* something (instead of *showing* something) about the essence of the world, and is thus a piece of nonsense.[17] He might also have pointed out that classical solipsism, since it employs the formulation "I alone exist," has no way of accommodating such ordinary sentences as "It fell on his foot, not mine" and "My sister has blue eyes." Finally, he might have emphasized that the classical solipsist fails to understand the grammar of the words "I" and "my" when used in speaking of experiences and in consequence says such things as "I alone exist" and "Only my experiences are real." Yet granted these differences between his own philosophical position and that of the classical solipsist, he held that reality consists of phenomenal objects, so that, considered ontologically, material objects and other people can be nothing more than that. This is the view Wittgenstein held from 1916 until his death.

One formulation of solipsism is this: It is not possible to transcend immediate experience, even in thought. In his 1931–32 lectures Wittgenstein stated this idea in the material mode: "Idealists were right in that we never transcend experience" (WL32, p. 80). In later years he did not abandon this idea, but he did reformulate it in the formal mode. Thus, in a passage he preserved for *Zettel* he says: "It is only apparently possible 'to transcend any possible experience'; even these words only seem to make sense, because they are arranged on the analogy of significant expressions" (Z, §260). Wittgenstein's fundamental view did not change, but he adopted a new way of stating it.

Notes

1. Moore, reporting on Wittgenstein's lectures of the early 1930s, writes: "As regards Solipsism and Idealism he said that he himself had been often tempted to say 'All that is real is the experience of the present moment' or 'All that is certain is the experience of the present moment'; and that anyone who is at all tempted to hold Idealism or Solipsism knows the temptation to say 'The only reality is the present moment' or 'The only reality is *my* present experience' " (G. E. Moore, "Wittgenstein's Lectures in 1930–33," reprinted in *Philosophical Papers*, op. cit., p. 311).
2. Referring to the solipsist, Wittgenstein remarks that ". . . he would say that it is *inconceivable* that experiences other than his own were real" (BB, p. 59). See also WL35, p. 22.

3. Very often the solipsist Wittgenstein refers to in his writings and lectures is his own earlier self, which is why he credits the solipsist with his own adjunct views about meaning. In Chapter 1 I explained why Wittgenstein dismissed the Russellian view that one can refer to (and believe in) something not given in experience.

4. For Wittgenstein this was the great question of philosophy. In lectures he said: "The solipsist flutters and flutters in the flyglass, strikes against the walls, flutters, flutters further. How can he be brought to rest?" (LSD, p. 300). In the *Investigations* he repeated the image: "What is your aim in philosophy? To shew the fly the way out of the fly-bottle" (§309). The question he should have, but failed to, ask is this: How did the fly get *into* the fly-bottle?

5. In speaking of "that language which alone I understand," Wittgenstein did not mean to allow that there might be a language (or languages) that he does *not* understand. In MS 109, p. 196, he writes: "A language that I don't understand is no language. [*Ein Sprache die ich nicht verstehe ist keine Sprache.*]" (Quoted and translated in Merrill B. and Jaakko Hintikka, *Investigating Wittgenstein*, op. cit., p. 21.)

6. In his pre-*Tractatus* notebooks Wittgenstein addressed the question whether there could be something that is not given in experience and so cannot be expressed by a proposition. He answers: "In that case this could not be expressed by means of *language*; and it is also impossible for us to *ask* about it" (NB, p. 51). See *Philosophical Remarks*, p. 80 for a more adequate statement of this position.

7. As for the pronoun "I" in "I sat on the floor," Wittgenstein must have had such an example in mind when he wrote: " 'I' clearly refers to my body, for *I* am in this room; and 'I' is essentially something that is in a place, and in a place belonging to the same space as the one the other bodies are in too" (PR, p. 86). In the *Tractatus* and also later on he said that in some uses of "I" it refers to nothing at all, as when one says, "I have a toothache" (see WL35, p. 21 and BB, p. 66–67).

8. There is, of course, a problem left over here. For the complexity of the *p* that says that p is, on Wittgenstein's account, a thought, and a thought, he held, is comprised of psychical elements. (Answering a query from Russell in 1919 he wrote: " 'Does a Gedanke consist of words?' No! But of psychical constituents that have the same sort of relation to reality as words. What those constituents are I don't know" (NB, p. 130).) That being so, how can Wittgenstein adopt a reductionist account of other people? Granted that if he does not need a soul for the first-person case of "A thinks that p," he also doesn't need a soul for third-person cases, but if "psychical constituents" are required for the first-person case, are they not required also for making "He is thinking it over" true? But if so, a reductionist account of others' thoughts is out of the question. In the *Tractatus* Wittgenstein does not explicitly deal with this problem, but he seems to have held that in third-person cases the verbs "to think," "to believe," etc. require a different explanation from that given for first-person cases, viz, a behavioristic explanation (see WL35, p. 17).

9. See also NFL, pp. 282 and 297, and LSD, pp. 32–33 and 137.

10. Moore, in his account of these lectures, reports: "In this connection [regarding the word "I"] he gave the warning 'Don't be prejudiced by anything which *is* a fact, but which *might* be otherwise.' And he seemed to be quite definite on a point which seems to me certainly true, viz. that I might see without physical eyes, and even without having a body at all; that the

connection between seeing and physical eyes is merely a fact learnt by
experience, not a necessity at all. . . ." ("Wittgenstein's Lectures in 1930–
1933," op. cit., p. 306).

11. This argument is more fully spelled out by Wittgenstein in his later writings and lectures, e.g., PR, pp. 100–103; WL35, p. 23 and 62; BB, pp.
59–67, esp. p. 63; and NFL, pp. 298–300.

12. In notes that he made for lectures in 1936 Wittgenstein presented the
matter as I have here:

> I am tempted to say: "It seems at least a fact of experience that at the
> source of *the visual field* there is mostly a small man with grey flannel
> trousers, in fact L.W." Someone might answer to this: It is true you
> almost always wear grey flannel trousers and often look at them. . . .
>
> On the other hand, if I describe the visual appearance of my body
> around the geometrical eye, this is on the same level as saying that in the
> middle of the visual field there is in general a brown table and at the
> edges a white wall (as I generally sit in my room). . . (NFL, pp. 298–299).

This is perhaps the point of his remark in his pre-*Tractatus* notebooks: "The
human body, however, my body in particular, is a part of the world among
others, among animals, plants, stones, etc., etc. Whoever realizes this will
not want to procure a pre-eminent place for his own body or for the human
body" (NB, p. 82); and later: "A stone, the body of a beast, the body of a
man, my body, all stand on the same level" (NB, p. 84).

13. Here we see Wittgenstein dismissing the idea that sensations are private:
it is not an intrinsic property of a visual sensation, or a pain, to belong to
someone. We will consider this in detail in the next chapter.

14. See also WL35, p. 60 and 62; NFL, p. 300 and 308 and PI, §36.

15. I have changed the translation from "I say!" to "Now Hear this!" since
Wittgenstein deliberately used here a German phrase (*Jetzt Achtung!*),
which does not contain the personal pronoun.

16. "Tractatus Objects," op. cit., p. 82.

17. In his lectures of 1932–1933 he said: "The solipsist who says 'Only my
experiences are real' is saying that it is *inconceivable* that experiences other
than his own are real. This is absurd if taken to be a statement of fact"
(WL35, p. 22), i.e., absurd if stated in the material mode. His point here is
similar to the following: "From the very outset 'Realism,' 'Idealism,' etc. are
names which belong to metaphysics. That is, they indicate that their adherents believe they can say something definite [as opposed to *showing*
something] about the essence of the world" (PR, p. 86).

6

Pure Realism and the Elimination
of Private Objects

In Chapter 2 we saw that a principal tenet of neutral monism is its rejection of the dualist's idea that there are "inner" and "outer" worlds. In consequence, it refuses to allow that anything is subjective or private. As W. T. Stace points out, "In a pure neutral monism there should, of course, be nothing which is purely subjective."[1] This element of neutral monism was evident in the writings of the American realists as early as 1912, when R. B. Perry wrote:

Most philosophers assume that it is essentially characteristic of a mind to be accessible only to itself. This proposition is rarely supported by evidence; it is commonly held to be sufficient to call attention to it. . . . As [one] writer expresses it, "That the mind of each human being forms a region inaccessible to all save its possessor, is one of the commonplaces of reflection."

. . . I believe this presupposition . . . to be the greatest present obstacle to the clear and conclusive definition of mind. . . .[2]

Perry goes on to argue that "the notion of the privacy of mental contents" is the product of fallacious reasoning.[3]

In this chapter we will consider how Wittgenstein came to adopt and defend this aspect of neutral monism.

Formulating the Problem

Wittgenstein's way of understanding the problem was shaped by an objection to neutral monism that Russell had raised in his 1914 essay "On the Nature of Acquaintance." Russell begins by referring to Perry's *Present Philosophical Tendencies* and agrees with Perry that "the same thing may enter into two different people's experience, and . . . therefore one mind's objects are not necessarily cut off from the direct observation of another mind."[4] He then makes three points. First, even if two minds are acquainted with the object O, it does not follow (unless neutral monism is assumed) that the one person *knows* that the other person is acquainted with O. (To illustrate this he says: ". . . suppose I am thinking 3 + 3 = 6. I can know directly that I am thinking this, but no other man can.") Second, if neutral monism *is* assumed, the assumption must be this: a mind is (as Hume claimed) simply constituted by the objects that are its "contents." Given this assumption, says Russell, two minds "must be accessible to each other's direct observation." This second point comes to the following. Neutral monists must hold that "I am thinking 3 + 3 = 6" is a misleading form of words and that when it is properly analysed the words "I am thinking" will be eliminated, so that only "3 + 3 = 6" remains. Since two people can equally well know that 3 + 3 = 6, any mind can know what another other knows – if, that is, everything there *is* to know is like "3 + 3 = 6." Russell's third point is that there are many things to be known that are *not* like "3 + 3 = 6." He spells this out as follows:

Neutral monists have done a service to philosophy in pointing out that the same object may be experienced by two minds. This certainly applies . . . to all experiencing of universals and abstracts [such as numbers]; it applies also, though I think only as a theoretic possibility, to the things of sense [i.e., sense-data]. But there remain a large number of things which only one mind can experience. First and foremost, an experiencing, as opposed to the mere object experienced, seems . . . to be only capable of being experienced by one person. I can know by immediate experience what I am seeing at this moment; but another person, though it is theoretically possible for him to see the same object, cannot, as a matter of empirical fact, know by immediate experience that I am seeing it. Exactly the same is true of other mental facts, such as judging, feeling, desiring, willing. All these can only be experienced by one person.[5]

In order to maintain this as an objection to the neutral monists' claim that nothing is subjective (or private), it is necessary, Russell admits, to assume that there is a thinking, knowing subject. And here, as we saw in Chapter 2, Russell concedes the difficulty pointed out by Hume: there is no subject – no unitary self – given in experience. This, he acknowledges, tends to support neutral monism. But in 1914, as we saw, Russell was not yet willing to abandon the self, and accordingly he goes on, in the essay under consideration, to maintain that neutral monism cannot eliminate subjectivity because *his* thinking that 3 + 3 = 6 (or *his* seeing a patch of red) is a private episode, since it involves a subject (or self).

For Wittgenstein, then, the challenge was to show that Russell's objection to neutral monism can be overcome, and we have already seen how he went about this in the *Tractatus*. In Chapter 3 we saw that Tractarian objects are universals, not Moorean sense-data (patches), and in Chapter 5 we saw that he proposed to analyze "A has the thought *p*" as " 'P' says *p*," so that the 'thinking subject' disappears in the analysis. By means of these two steps he intended to show that everything there is to know is relevantly like Russell's example "3 + 3 = 6." In addition, in order to address Russell's claim that one person cannot *know* that another person is thinking or seeing something, Wittgenstein took the additional step of embracing behaviorism. At the time of the *Tractatus*, then, he had proposed a way of dealing with Russell's objection to neutral monism.

In order to appreciate fully the way in which Wittgenstein understood this philosophical development, it will be useful to review his account (NB, p. 85) of his philosophical journey, which was quoted at the beginning of the preceding chapter. He says that he initially embraced idealism, which "singles men out from the world as unique"; he then turned to solipsism, which "singles me alone out," and finally, he says, "I see that I too belong to the world." He sums up the journey by saying: "In this way idealism leads to realism if it is strictly thought out." In order properly to identify this final destination, let us trace in greater detail the path by which he arrived at it.

Idealism rejects material substance while retaining spiritual substance (minds), and in this way it singles men out as unique. But whereas, by rejecting material substance, idealism proposes to avoid skepticism regarding the "external world," it invites skepticism regarding "other minds." This skepticism, in turn, invites solipsism: if I alone exist, then there can be no problem of other minds. But now the question becomes: What is this I, this self, that alone exists. On the Cartesian view the answer is: an immaterial substance that thinks, feels, sees, etc. This was Berkeley's view, too, and in the third of his Three Dialogues we find the following exchange. Philonous, conceding that he no more has an idea of mind or spirit than he has of material substance, goes on to say:

I do nevertheless know that I, who am a spirit or thinking substance, exist as certainly as I know my ideas exist. Farther, I know what I mean by the terms *I* and *myself*; and I know this immediately or intuitively, though I do not perceive it as I perceive a triangle, a colour, or a sound. The Mind, Spirit, or Soul is that indivisible unextended thing which thinks, acts, and perceives.

Dissatisfied with this, Hylas remarks: ". . . you acknowledge you have, properly speaking, no *idea* of your own soul," and then, following a lame response from Philonous, declares:

. . . to me it seems that, according to your own way of thinking, and in consequence of your own principles, it should follow that *you* are only a system of floating ideas, without any substance to support them. Words are not to be used without a meaning. And, as there is no more meaning in *spiritual Substance* than in *material Substance*, the one is to be exploded as well as the other.

That the self is but "a system of floating ideas" was not, of course, Berkeley's own view, but it became Hume's and is a half-way point to Wittgenstein's pure realism.

The following passages from his pre-*Tractatus* notebooks show how his position developed:

Isn't the thinking subject in the last resort mere superstition?
 Where in the world is a metaphysical subject to be found?
 You say that it is just as it is for the eye and the visual field. But you do *not* actually see the eye.
 And I think that nothing in the visual field would enable one to infer that it is seen from an eye.

The thinking subject is surely mere illusion (NB, p. 80).

He goes on to say:

Here we can see that solipsism coincides with pure realism, if it is strictly thought out.

The I of solipsism shrinks to an extensionless point and what remains is the reality co-ordinated with it (NB, p. 82; cf. TLP 5.64).

This, as we have seen, is the conclusion of Wittgenstein's journey. As an idealist he had held that there are numerous minds, his own being one among many; as a solipsist he had held that there was but one mind, and at last he gave up that mind as well. So now *the world* is identical with what he had earlier thought of as the *contents* of his mind. We might say that his pure realism consists of his turning his mind inside out, so that what were formerly to be thought of as *private* objects are no longer so. Even at this early date, then, Wittgenstein would have thought it a mistake to say: "I alone know what I mean by 'red,' because others can't see what I call 'red'." And the same goes, of course, for a word such as "pain": this is not the name of something private. Employing a simile he was to use later on (PI, §293), we might put the matter as follows: there can be no beetle in the box, i.e., no private mental content, *because there is no box.*

This is the point of Wittgenstein's remark that when "the I of solipsism" is abolished, "what remains is the reality coordinated with it." He meant: the reality – the *world* – that remains (and this includes thoughts, emotions, sensations, sense-impressions, etc.) is not in some private domain. Put differently, the world is, in the words Berkeley attributes to Hylas, "a system of floating [i.e., unattached] ideas." In the notes he made for his 1936 lectures Wittgenstein made this explicit. Discussing the idea that sensations are private, i.e., *belong* to someone, he said: "But here solipsism teaches us a lesson: It [solipsism] is that thought which is *on the way* to destroy this error. For if the *world* is idea it isn't any person's idea" (NFL, p. 297). This is how solipsism, when strictly thought out, leads to pure realism: it does away with everything *private* or subjective.

What is it that prevents one from recognizing this straightaway? Here as elsewhere Wittgenstein's answer is that language is to blame. Language, he claims, sets "traps" for us; it "is an immense network of easily accessible wrong turnings" (CV, p. 18). Accordingly, in his post-*Tractatus* writings and lectures he undertook to call attention to the wrong turnings that lead philosophers to think that there are "private" as well as "public" objects.

Perspective and the Privacy of Visual Sense-Data

One of the ways in which philosophers have arrived at this view is by thinking that visual sense-data are private because no two people, at a given moment, see a table or a book from the same perspective. Russell thought of the matter as follows:

We are all in the habit of judging as to the 'real' shapes of things, and we do this so unreflectingly that we come to think we actually see the real shapes. But, in fact, as we all have to learn if we try to draw, a given thing looks different in shape from every different point of view. If our table is 'really' rectangular, it will look, from almost all points of view, as if it had two acute angles and two obtuse angles. If opposite sides are parallel, they will look as if they converge to a point away from the spectator; if they are of equal length, they will look as if the nearer side were longer. All these things are not commonly noticed in looking at a table, because experience has taught us to construct the 'real' shape from the apparent shape, and the 'real' shape is what interests us as practical men.[6]

Having represented the matter in this way, Russell adds that "what we call different appearances of the same thing to different observers are each in a space private to the observer concerned."[7]

If one thinks about these two passages in the way Wittgenstein would have, one must conclude that there is something amiss in Russell's thinking. For Russell's point that the 'real' table (the rectangular one) is *constructed* from appearances is a point that should hold for all other 'external' objects, *including the several people looking at the table 'from different angles.'* That is, Russell ought to hold that these observers are *also* constructs. Were he to do so, however, he could not say, as he does, that there are several appearances of the table, each of which is "in a space private to the observer concerned." For in order to say *that*, he would have to be thinking that the dualistic picture is correct, i.e., that there are two *equally real* kinds of spaces involved: the (physical) space that is common to the table and the spectators, in which they stand in various spatial relations to one another, and also the (private) visual spaces, each of which is directly perceived by only one of the spectators. But Russell cannot have it both ways. He must choose between saying (i) that 'physical space' is a construction with visual space as its base or (ii) that physical and visual space are equally real. Suppose he chooses the latter. In that case he will be confronted with the skeptic's question: How do you *know* that there are, in physical space, tables and other people? Since this question is unanswerable, Russell could not mount a sound argument which (a) assumes that other minds exist and (b) concludes that there *are* private visual spaces. Suppose, then, that he chooses the other alternative, namely, that 'physical space' is a construction with visual space as its basis. Since visual space (a) has no owner and (b) is the only real (nonconstructed) space, visual perception cannot be thought to involve anything private (subjective). For even though someone may, *in the idiom of physical space*, speak of one person seeing an appearance of the table which the person on his left does not see, this (because it *is* a construction) is a manner of speaking that ought not to be taken literally by philosophers, i.e., ought not to taken to show anything about the essence of the world (about the essential nature of space).

This is what Wittgenstein is arguing for in *Philosophical Remarks* when he says that "visual space has essentially no owner" (p. 100) and then explains this as follows:

Let's assume that, with all the others, I can always see one particular object in visual space – viz. my nose. Someone else naturally doesn't see this object in the same way. Doesn't that mean, then, that the visual space I'm talking about *belongs to me*? And so is subjective? No. It has only been construed subjectively here, and an objective space opposed to it, which is, however, only a construction with visual space as its basis. In the – secondary – language of 'objective' – physical – space, visual space is called subjective (PR, p. 100).

Wittgenstein is saying that 'objective' (or 'physical') space is a construct – a logical fiction, and that it is only in terms of that fiction that visual space gets represented as 'subjective.' What he means is something like this. When one employs the language of 'physical' space (as one has a perfect right to do), one can say that several people are standing around a table and looking at it from different angles. And having said *that*, one can go on to report that one of them describes the appearance of the table in one way, while another describes it another way, but if one realizes that in speaking this way one is employing a logical fiction, one will also realize that one cannot *conclude* anything from these two descriptions, for it is always a mistake to draw conclusions from a misleading form of words. And having realized *that*, one will realize that when one speaks in a *non*-misleading way, one will not say, with Russell, that there are several minds, each with its own private sense-datum of the table. So the idea that sense-data are private is a confusion that results from (a) the fact that in ordinary language we employ the idiom of 'physical space' and (b) the misguided tendency philosophers have to regard this idiom as revealing the essence of the world. This is an example, then, of what Wittgenstein meant when he wrote: "The worst philosophical errors always arise when we try to apply our ordinary – physical – language in the areas of the immediately given" (PR, p. 88). This, he thought, is the mistake a philosopher is making when he says that sense-data are private.

The Idioms of Possession

Wittgenstein found himself again and again encountering features of ordinary language which seem to suggest that there are many minds, each with its own stock of thoughts, sensations, and so on. It was therefore necessary that he show that each of these features of our language is misleading, that our grammar disguises what is actually being said.

One such feature is the pronoun "I" in such a sentence as "I have a toothache," and in the preceding chapter we saw that Wittgenstein maintained that this use of "I" is an "idling" – or inessential – feature of our language. But what about the verb in this sentence? Doesn't "have" suggest possession and hence a possessor? Does not our language here conflict with Wittgenstein's pure realism, according to which pains, thoughts, sense-impressions, and the like have no 'owner'? And what about our use of the possessive pronouns in such sentences as "His toothache is worse than mine" and "My headache is better now"? Aren't these pronouns similarly at odds with Wittgenstein's pure realism? Do they not entitle us to say such things as "I have my pains and you have yours" and "I can't feel your sensations, so I can't know what you mean by 'pain' "?

These are among the features of ordinary language that Wittgenstein noticed, and he discussed them frequently in his later writings and lectures. His solution was always the same: ordinary language is mis-leading. Thus, we find him saying:

The logic of our language is so difficult to grasp at this point: our language employs the phrases "my pain" and "his pain," and also the expressions "I have (or feel) a pain" and "He has (or feels) a pain." . . .
The phenomenon of feeling toothache I am familiar with is represented in the idioms of ordinary language by "I *have* a pain in such-and-such a tooth." Not by an expression of the kind "In this place there is a feeling of pain." The *whole* field of this experience is described in this language by expressions of the form "I have. . . ." Propositions of the form "N has toothache" are reserved for a totally different field. So we shouldn't be surprised when for propositions of the form "N has toothache," there is nothing left that links with experience in the same way as in the first case (PR, pp. 94–95).

The difficulty lies in the grammar of "*having* toothache" (WL35, p. 18).

In "I have toothache" the expression of pain is brought to the same form as a description "I have 5 shillings" (NFL, p. 302).

In The Blue Book Wittgenstein indicates how he thinks this feature of our language leads us into confusion:

Now the answer of the common-sense philosopher . . . is that surely there is no difficulty in the idea of supposing, thinking, imagining that someone else has what I have. But the trouble with the realist [e.g., Moore] is always that he does not solve but skip[s] the difficulties which his adversaries see, though they too don't succeed in solving them. The realist answer, for us, just brings out the difficulty; for who argues like this overlooks the difference between different usages of the words "to have," "to imagine." "A has a gold tooth" means that the tooth is in A's mouth. This may account for the fact that I am not able to see it. Now the case of his toothache, of which I say that I am not able to feel it because it is in his mouth, is not analogous to the case of the gold tooth. It is the apparent analogy, and again the lack of analogy, between these cases which causes our trouble. And it is this troublesome feature in our grammar which the realist does not notice (BB, pp. 48–49).

In the *Investigations* Wittgenstein indicates how one is to escape the trap our grammar sets for us by allowing us to say both "I have a toothache" and "I have a gold tooth."

"But when I imagine something, or even actually *see* objects, I *have* something which my neighbor has not." I understand you. You want to look about you and say: "At any rate only I have THIS." What are these words for? They serve no purpose. Can one not add: "There is here no question of a 'seeing' – and therefore none of a 'having' – nor of a subject, nor therefore of 'I' either"? Might I not ask: In what sense do you *have* what you are talking about and saying that only you have it? Do you possess it? . . . Must you not really say that no one has it? And this too is clear: if as a matter of logic you exclude other people's having something, it loses its sense to say that you have it (PI, §398).[8]

In this passage, which recapitulates Wittgenstein's intellectual journey from idealism to solipsism to pure realism, he is indicating how he means to eliminate the private object: There is here no question of a "seeing" – and therefore none of a "having" – nor of a subject, nor therefore of "I" either. That being so, the private object is a grammatical fiction. Or as Wittgenstein puts it: "The 'private experience' is a degenerate construction of our grammar. . . . And this grammatical monster now fools us; when we wish to do away with it, it seems as though we denied the existence of an experience, say, toothache" (NFL, p. 314).

Perhaps Wittgenstein's most explicit way of making this point is that which we find in his lectures of 1946–47. He begins by remarking that we are inclined to say that we cannot know whether others feel pain, but we *assume* they do. He then says:

Nothing is easier than to imagine a people who do not make the assumption that "another man, when he has pain, has what we have." In German, English, French, the expression for "I have" is used in the sense that something [e.g., a gold tooth] has a particular relation to my body. There is no reason why people should express pain by the auxiliary "I have." Suppose, for example, the utterance of pain in the first person were expressed by something like a groan. . . . [And] suppose "He has pain" could be expressed in terms of pain-behaviour. . . .
Suppose this people [who do not use "I have pain" and "He has pain"] had no idea that "another person feels what I feel." . . . [T]hey will not be inclined to have such a philosophy [i.e., dualism] as we have. Problems about the ego may not occur. . . . They have not some of our pictures (WL47, pp. 178–179; see also pp. 50–54).

Wittgenstein's point here is that the philosophical picture of pain as something "inner" or "private" is merely the result of our being taken in by a superficial, inessential feature of our language.

"Same" and "Exactly Alike"

We speak of my toothache and your toothache, which suggests that my toothache is one thing and yours is another. And that, in turn, suggests that we do not – indeed, *cannot* – have the *same* pain but, at most, have pains exactly alike. But this makes it look as though pains are the private contents of our several minds. Accordingly, Wittgenstein undertook to show that such reasoning involves a confusion about "same" and "exactly alike."

This is what he is getting at in *Philosophical Remarks* when he writes:

If the word 'toothache' has the same meaning in both cases, then we must be able to compare the toothaches of the two people; and if their intensities, etc. coincide, they're the same. Just as two suits have the *same* colour, if they match one another in brightness, saturation, etc.

Equally, it's nonsense to say two people can't have the same sense datum, if by "sense datum" what is *primary* is really intended (PR, p. 91).[9]

As we saw in Chapter 2, the point Wittgenstein is getting at here had already been stated as follows by Mach: "From the standpoint which I here take up . . . , I no more draw an essential distinction between my sensations and the sensations of another person, than I regard red or green as belonging to an individual body."[10] Wittgenstein, in his later writings and lectures, repeated this point in a variety of ways. One of his most detailed discussions is found in his 1936 lectures, where his argument runs, in part, as follows:

One is inclined to say I can't know whether another person can have this impression. There's a tendency to say also that it makes no *sense* to say another person might have this impression.

Supposing I said "Only this chair *can* be green" – this means it has no sense to say of another chair [that] it is green.

We say the same colour can be in different places. But someone might say it is really not the *same* colour – though it looks like it. Then he is trying to give to a colour the same kind of identity which we give to a physical object. We have a criterion for what we call the identity of a physical object.[11] We can imagine also someone saying a colour can't travel.

But then why say "This *chair* is green"? why not just say "there is green"?

If we say "Green can't be in two places," this would mean we are going to use a word differently from the way in which we use it now. And then we can't go on to say "This chair is green" and use "green" as we do now use it.

Thus (to the question about "I *have*") if I have an impression which I call "alpha," then I can't say "I see alpha" without being redundant.

The proposition that "Only I can see" or "Only I can have this sense datum" is not a statement of a fact of experience, an empirical generalization. It means: to say that he and I have the same sense datum is senseless. *Therefore* I can't use the expression that I *have* it. . . .

Can another person have my toothache? You could say "Yes of course: the same intensity, same throbbing etc." I might object, "That means exactly alike, but not the same." Then you answer, "Aha, by 'my toothache' you mean an identity like that of a physical object." Then if I say he can't have the same toothache, that is now a proposition of grammar.

People say he and I can't have the same pain, because he has his pain and I have my pain. But then we should not talk of "his pain" and "my pain" – or rather of "*having* my pain"; we should say only "There is my toothache" (LSD, pp. 4–6).

Wittgenstein is making the same point when, in the *Investigations*, he writes:

"Another person can't have my pains." Which are *my* pains? What counts as a criterion of identity here? Consider what makes it possible in the case of physical objects to speak of "two exactly the same," for example, to say "This chair is not the one you saw here yesterday, but is exactly the same as it."

In so far as it makes *sense* to say that my pain is the same as his, it is also possible for us both to have the same pain. (And it would also be imaginable for two people to feel pain in the same – not just the corresponding – place. That might be the case with Siamese twins, for instance.)

I have seen a person in a discussion on this subject strike himself on the breast and say: "But surely another person can't have THIS pain!" The answer to this is that one does not define a criterion of identity by emphatic stressing of the word "this." Rather, what the emphasis does is to suggest the case in which we are conversant with such a criterion of identity, but have to be reminded of it (PI, §253).

Let us see if we can formulate more precisely what Wittgenstein is getting at in these remarks.

Three steps seem to be involved in his argument. The first is to point out that when someone says that no two people can have the *same* pain, he does not intend to be stating a fact of experience and must, therefore, be taken to be formulating (in an obscure way) a grammatical rule which excludes from the language such a sentence as "Jack and Jill have the same pain." The second step is to point out that a rule which excludes such a sentence as "Jack and Jill have the same pain" must also exclude "Jack and Jill do *not* have the same pain," since there could be no occasion for saying the latter if there is none for saying the former. The third and final step is to point out that if one excludes "They do *not* have the same pain," one thereby excludes also "Jack and Jill have pains that are exactly alike," for the phrase "exactly alike" has a use only where the *facts* of the situation warrant our saying "It's not the same one" (or "It's a different one"). Wittgenstein is getting at this third point when he says that we fall into a confusion here because we

compare the case of sense data [or pains] with that of physical bodies, in which case we make a distinction between: "this is the same chair I saw an hour ago" and "this is not the same chair, but one exactly like the other." Here it makes sense to say, and is an experiential proposition: "A and B couldn't have seen the same chair, for A was in London and B in Cambridge; they saw two chairs exactly alike" (BB, p. 55).

When we say that sensations are private, what we really want, says Wittgenstein, is a new notation, one in which the form of words "We have the same pain" is excluded and is *replaced* by "We have pains exactly alike."[12] But the trouble is that in this new notation the phrase "pains exactly alike" is to be used *instead of*, rather than in *contrast with*, "same pain," and consequently "exactly alike" can't mean what it does in "Two chairs exactly alike" and *therefore* doesn't do what we wanted it to do. So when we try to explain our idea that sensations are private, we find that we can't do so: the rule of grammar we want to lay down does not amount to what we, at first, thought it would.

That Wittgenstein is mounting an argument *against* the idea that sensations are private is obscured in the *Investigations* because it is easy to misconstrue §248, where he says: "The proposition 'Sensations are private' is comparable to: 'One plays patience by oneself'." This is sometimes taken to be an endorsement of "Sensations are private."[13] That this was not Wittgenstein's intention is made clear in The Blue Book. Commenting on the statement "One can't know whether others have pain," which he held to be *untrue* (see BB, p. 24 and PI, §246), he said that this statement "is not comparable, though always falsely compared, with such a one as 'it is impossible for a human being to swim across the Atlantic'; but it *is* analogous to a statement like 'there is no goal in an endurance race'" (BB, p. 54). He meant that they are analogous in being disguised rules, *not* that they are analogous in both being *correct*. He makes the same point regarding "Two people can't have the same pain," declaring it to be a *grammatical* statement. He adds: "Another form of our metaphysical statement is this: 'A man's sense data are private to himself.' And this way of expressing it is even more misleading because it looks still more like an experiential proposition; the philosopher who says this may well think that he is expressing a kind of scientific truth" (BB, p. 55).

His point, then, in §248 of the *Investigations* is that "Sensations are private," like "One plays patience by oneself," does not *look like* a rule we have invented, although that is what it is. What may mislead one here is that "One plays patience by oneself" states a *correct* rule, and so one might think Wittgenstein meant to suggest that "Sensations are private" *also* gives a correct rule. In fact, however, his view is just the opposite. As we have seen, he meant us to realize that we are confused when we think of sensations as private, i.e., to realize that the rule we want to lay down regarding "pains exactly alike" can't be worked out.

In criticizing the idea that sensations are private, Wittgenstein is defending his pure realism against the idea that there are numerous minds (or selves), each with its own pains, sense-data, and so on. His criticism is that when we think of pains, visual experiences, etc. as being private objects, we are trying to use words such as "pain," "sense-datum," etc. as if their grammar were, in certain respects, like that of the word "chair," where we can speak of two being exactly alike, but when we try to make this grammar fit, we find we cannot do so. We are to conclude, then, that we are in a muddle in thinking that sensations are private.

A Problem About The Term "Sense-Datum"

Here it will be useful to pick up a thread from Chapter 3, where we found Wittgenstein insisting that sensible qualities are not *properties*. For this reason he declared that Moore and Russell were causing confusion when they spoke of seeing colored *patches* and spoke of seeing, for example, a green *sense-datum*. This way of speaking of visual experience Wittgenstein called "objectification," which he explained as follows:

I want to go on to the question as to the nature of sense data.

The word "sense datum" really means the same as "appearance." But the term introduces a particular way of looking at appearance. We might call it *"objectification."* If "personification" means, e.g., using the word "time" as though it were the name of a person, then objectification is talking of it as though it were a thing. . . .

I might say, for example: "This suit seemed to me dirty, but it was not dirty." Suppose I then said: "The *appearance* of the suit *is* dirty." In the first case I would be ready to say "I was wrong." The other seems to be connected with "I was right."

Suppose I say, "If this coat appeared grey, then something must have been grey." This is objectification. We assimilate the grammar of appearance to the grammar of physical objects (LSD, pp. 25–26).

Wittgenstein also explained this as follows:

This is connected with the point that: "When something seems to me green, then something *is* green." First of all we have [in our language] sentences such as "The table is green"; or it may be, "The table seems green to me." If in this latter case you say "then there is *something* [a sense-datum] which is really green" – this is a change of mode of expression, so that we no longer have the idea of *seeming* but of *being* (LSD, p. 137).

One sort of confusion this leads to, according to Wittgenstein, is that it suggests that when we perceive things, there are, in addition to colors, odors, flavors, etc., also entities of *another* sort – entities which philosophers had discovered, namely, the sense-data that are the bearers of these properties. In The Blue Book Wittgenstein alludes to this:

Philosophers say it as a philosophical opinion or conviction that there are sense data. But to say that I believe that there are sense data comes to saying that I *believe* that an object may appear to be before our eyes even when it isn't. Now when one uses the word "sense datum," one should be clear about the peculiarity of its grammar. For the idea in introducing this expression was to model expressions referring to 'appearance' after expressions referring to 'reality' . . . . Queerly enough, the introduction of this new phraseology has deluded people into thinking that they had discovered new entities, new elements of the structure of the world. . . (BB, p. 70).

He means that philosophers have been deluded into thinking that in addition to sensible qualities there are *other* entities which are the bearers of these properties.

In the *Investigations* Wittgenstein reiterates this point. He does so by first introducing the phrase "the visual room" and then remarking that one may be tempted "to use the same form of expression about it [the visual room] as about the material room" in which one sits (PI, §398). He continues:

The "visual room" seemed like a discovery, but what its discoverer really found was a new way of speaking, a new comparison; it might even be called a new sensation (PI, §400).
    You have a new conception and interpret it as seeing a new object. You interpret a grammatical movement made by yourself as a quasi-physical phenomenon which you are observing (PI, §401).

Wittgenstein's point here is that if, instead of introducing the noun "sense-datum," Russell and Moore had followed Berkeley in speaking of sensible qualities, they would not have created the impression that they had discovered new entities: the substratum of sensible qualities.
    There is a second sort of confusion that Wittgenstein alleges to have arisen from the introduction of the term "sense-datum."

I want to talk about the view that perhaps sense data alone are real.
    Objectification leads people to compare an 'appearance' with a *picture*. The idea is that we not only look at a chair, but also *look at* (not merely see) something else. . . .
    The question of the reality of sense data comes first with the idea of our senses *cheating* us. The suggestion that we never see the real thing: we only get pictures which are more or less correct.[14]
    The next step was: dissatisfaction with this simile – we seem to have pictures which we compare with nothing.
    We then go on to say: The picture is the only thing which is real, nothing else exists.
    Thus we first objectify, and then go on to talk of existence and non-existence [of physical objects] (LSD, p. 27).

This is Wittgenstein's diagnosis of how philosophers come to think that sense-data are representative of 'external things' and of how, in consequence, they fall prey to skepticism. When philosophers objectify sense-data, they create the impression that they have discovered something new and make it appear that sense-data block our view of such things as tables and chairs, so that "we never see the real thing."
    In the *Investigations* Wittgenstein opposes this view in the following way:

The fluctuation in grammar between criteria and symptoms makes it look as if there were nothing at all but symptoms. We say, for example: "Experience teaches that there is rain when the barometer falls, but it also teaches that there is rain when we have such-and-such sensations of wet and cold, or such-and-such visual impressions." In defence of this one says that these sense-impressions can deceive us. But here one fails to reflect that the fact that the false appearance is precisely one of rain is founded on a definition [of "It's raining"] (§354).

His point is the following. A falling barometer is a *symptom* of rain, i.e., we learn this from experience. But it is a mistake to say that experience "also teaches that there is rain when we have such-and-such sensations of wet and cold, or such-and-such visual impressions," for *this* we do not learn from *experience* but from learning the word "rain," i.e., we learn the "convention" (PI, §355) that "rain" is used to describe certain sensations of wet and cold and also certain visual impressions, i.e., those sensations are not *evidence* of rain; they are what we *mean* by "rain." This is Wittgenstein's point when he writes: "What is common to sense-experiences? – The answer that they acquaint us with the outer world is partly wrong and partly right. It is right inasmuch as it is supposed to point to a *logical* criterion" (RPP, I, §702).

In the next chapter we will consider in greater detail Wittgenstein's view of the relation of sense-data and physical objects.

Notes

1. "Russell's Neutral Monism," op. cit., p. 362.
2. *Present Philosophical Tendencies*, op. cit., p. 286.
3. Ibid., pp. 286–295.
4. Op. cit., p. 155.
5. Ibid., pp. 161–162.
6. *The Problems of Philosophy*, op. cit., pp. 10–11.
7. "The Relation of Sense-Data to Physics," Op. Cit., p. 154.
8. At three places in this passage I have changed the translation from the idiomatic "have got" to "have."
9. A few pages later he poses the question: "Suppose my visual field consisted of two red circles of the same size on a blue background: what occurs twice here and what once?" He answers: "Here we have *one* colour, but two positions" (PR, p. 122), i.e., not *two* colors exactly alike.
10. *The Analysis of Sensations*, op. cit., pp. 360–361.
11. ". . . the grammar of words of which we say that they stand for physical objects is characterized by the way in which we use the phrase 'the *same* so-and-so', or 'the *identical* so-and-so', where 'so-and-so' designates the physical object" (BB, p. 63).
12. In his 1936 lectures Wittgenstein said: "To say 'sense data are private' would give a rule of grammar: you must not say 'I have the same sense datum as he,' and also you must not say 'I have a different sense datum from him' " (LSD, p. 9). In the notes he made for those lectures he wrote: " 'The sense datum is private' is a rule of grammar, it forbids the use of such expressions as 'They saw the same sense datum' . . ." (NFL, p. 317).
13. It is common to find philosophers taking Wittgenstein to mean that "Sensations are private" is some sort of "*a priori* truth." See, for example, Alan Donagan, "Wittgenstein on Sensation" in *Wittgenstein: The Philosophical Investigations*, ed. George Pitcher (Notre Dame: University of Notre Dame Press, 1968), p. 335.
14. See the passage quoted in Chapter 3, note 27, in which the American realists say that, according to dualists, what we see is "only a picture of what really exists."

II

The Metaphysics of Wittgenstein's Later Philosophy

7

Wittgenstein's Phenomenalism

Wittgenstein's ideas about the relation of sense-data and material objects are not easily discovered and are even less easily explained. There are several reasons for this, the most important of which is that his ideas underwent a change between the time of the *Tractatus* and his later work. This change in his thinking has been widely misunderstood. The received view is that Wittgenstein at some point ceased to hold a phenomenalist view of material things. In this chapter we will see that this interpretation is wrong. The change that took place in his thinking had nothing to do with allowing the existence of objects he had formerly dismissed in a reductionist fashion. His change of mind consisted merely in the adoption of a new form of phenomenalism. To understand this, we must begin with the *Tractatus* view of the matter.

The *Tractatus* Version of Phenomenalism

Nowhere in the *Tractatus* does Wittgenstein explicitly discuss the relation of sense-data and material things. It is nevertheless possible to determine what his view was at that time. As we have seen, he held that phenomenal entities comprise "the substance of the world," while also holding that ordinary language is "in perfect logical order" (TLP, 5.5563). From this we may infer that he thought of material things as being, in some sense, reducible to sense-data – to colors, shapes, etc. Moreover, it was this reductionist view that enabled him to dismiss skepticism as nonsense, for the question "Are there material things beyond my sense-data?" cannot arise for a philosopher taking a reductionist view of material things. We can say, then, that the elementary propositions of the *Tractatus* are to be thought of as sense-datum propositions and that Wittgenstein thought of our ordinary propositions about tables and chairs as being in some way built up from these. We can be more specific. He thought of the relation between the two types of propositions as being analytic: an ordinary proposition about a chair, say, is a truth-function of propositions about sense-data, so that when certain propositions about sense-data are true, this implies that a proposition about a chair is true. In this way "There's a chair in the corner" is itself really a proposition about sense-data.

Wittgenstein would no doubt have been prepared to add: If this is not how we are initially inclined to think of such a proposition, that is because its truth–functional connection with sense-datum propositions is not made explicit in ordinary language. Indeed, it would be extremely difficult to spell out this connection in detail, for it would have to be immensely complex. This is one reason Wittgenstein says in the *Tractatus*:

Man possesses the ability to construct languages capable of expressing every sense, without having any idea how each word has meaning or what its meaning is – just as people speak without knowing how the individual sounds are produced.
 Everyday language is part of the human organism and is no less complicated than it.
 It is not humanly possible to gather immediately from it what the logic of language is. . . .
 The tacit conventions on which the understanding of everyday language depends are enormously complicated (TLP, 4.002).[1]

One of these complicated conventions is that which connects the word "chair" with sensible qualities.[2]

In the above passage Wittgenstein speaks of such conventions as being "tacit," meaning that they are not in evidence in ordinary language. This means, of course, that Wittgenstein himself had no direct evidence that there *are* such conventions. Rather, he simply thought that they *must* be there, that it must be possible to make explicit a truth–functional connection that holds between "There's a chair in the corner" and propositions about colors and shapes and tactile sensations.

Wittgenstein's Later Version of Phenomenalism

I said above that Wittgenstein's views about this changed in his post-*Tractatus* years but that the change did not involve his abandoning phenomenalism. Thus, in his lectures of 1931–32 Wittgenstein said that "there is no fact that this is a physical object over and above the qualities and judgements of sense-data about it" and went on to say that "the world is not composed of sense-data and physical objects" (WL32, p. 81). He also said that "to talk about the relation of object and sense-datum is nonsense. They are not two separate things" (ibid., p. 109). In The Blue Book (1933–1934) he warns: "And now don't think that the expression 'physical object' is meant to distinguish one kind of object from another" (BB, p. 51) and a few pages later adds that "it confuses everything" to say that "a sense-datum is a different kind of object from a physical object" (p. 64). In 1938, in notes he made for his own use, Wittgenstein wrote:

It is not a question here at all whether names of physical objects signify one thing and names of sense impressions another, as if one successively pointed to two different objects and said "I mean this object, not that one." The picture of the different objects is here used entirely wrongly.

Not, the one is the name for the immediate object, the other for something else; but rather the two words are used differently (CE, Appendix B, pp. 435–436, my translation).

It is significant that this passage was written in 1938, several years after much of the *Investigations* had been written.

Plainly, then, Wittgenstein continued to embrace some form of phenomenalism, but it differed from the *Tractatus* version of phenomenalism. It was to emphasize this difference that Wittgenstein said in The Blue Book that "it can never be our job to reduce anything to anything.... Philosophy is 'purely descriptive'" (BB, p. 18). This is not a rejection of phenomenalism, broadly understood; rather, in dismissing reductionism, Wittgenstein meant only to say that "There's a chair" does not belong to a calculus whose rules determine its truth or falsity for every imaginable situation. In the *Investigations* he states this point as follows:

Does it *follow* from the sense-impressions which I get that there is a chair over there? – How can a *proposition* follow from sense-impressions? Well, does it follow from the propositions which describe the sense-impressions? No (PI, §486).

This negative answer distinguishes his later from his earlier version of phenomenalism, for it means that "There is a chair over there" is not completely analyzable into propositions which describe sense-impressions, for if it *were* so analyzable, "There is a chair over there" *would* follow from the propositions which describe sense-impressions.

How did Wittgenstein come to change his mind on this point? There appear to have been two considerations that forced him to abandon the *Tractatus* view.

Wittgenstein's Primary Reason For Abandoning The *Tractatus* View

A most important reason for Wittgenstein's change of mind was his realization that his view of perception at the time of the *Tractatus* was thoroughly artificial. This realization came to him, apparently, as the result of reading Wolfgang Kohler's *Gestalt Psychology*, which was first published in 1929.[3] Although Wittgenstein was later to criticize some aspects of Kohler's view, it appears that Kohler's attack on introspectionist psychology led Wittgenstein to abandon the Tractarian view of objects and the analysis of perception.[4]

Kohler's views will be discussed in detail in Chapter 10, and therefore I will here give only a brief summary of his gestalt theory of perception. In stating what is at issue between himself and the introspectionists, Kohler makes the following three points: (i) We ordinarily speak of seeing such things as books and chairs, but introspectionists insist that, while this manner of speaking may be harmless in everyday life, it is not suitable for psychology, where one must learn to see "the simple and primary data of experience." (ii) To do this, one must, according to the introspectionists, put aside the learning that leads us to speak of seeing objects, for "pure seeing has nothing to do with such knowledge. As psychologists, we have the task [according to introspectionists] of separating all these acquired meanings from the seen material *per se*, which consists of simple sensations. . . . [A]mong the genuine sensory data there can be nothing like objects. Objects exist for us only when sensory experience has become thoroughly imbued with meaning."[5] (iii) But the introspectionists are wrong in maintaining that "the simple and primary data of experience" include only sensible qualities, for the *organization* of these into things (books, apples, etc.) is primary, too. Kohler states this last point as follows:

There is, in the first place, what is now generally called the *organization* of sensory experience. The term refers to the fact that sensory fields have in a way their own social psychology. Such fields appear neither as uniformly coherent continua nor as patterns of mutually indifferent elements. What we actually perceive are, first of all, specific entities such as things, figures, etc., and also groups [such as constellations of stars or groups of pencil strokes] of which these entities are members.[6]

I will not rehearse here Kohler's argument for adopting this view, but this much is clear: his account is plainly at odds with the *Tractatus*, according to which the *real* entities in experience (what we really see, hear, etc.) are simple qualities (colors, sounds, etc.).

How was Wittgenstein influenced by Kohler? Near the end of *Philosophical Remarks* we find the following passage (probably written in the spring of 1930), which sounds very much like the sort of thing Kohler says:

Nowadays the danger that lies in trying to see things as simpler than they really are is often greatly exaggerated. But this danger does actually exist to the highest degree in the phenomenological investigation of sense impressions. These are always taken to be *much* simpler than they are.

If I see that a figure possesses an organization which previously I hadn't noticed, I now see a different figure. Thus I can see | | | | | | as a special case of | | | | | | or of | | | | | | or of | | | | | | etc. This merely shows that that which we see isn't as simple as it seems.

Understanding a Gregorian mode doesn't mean getting used to the sequence of notes in the sense in which I can get used to a smell and after a while cease to find it unpleasant. No, it means hearing something new, which I hadn't heard before, much in the same way – in fact it's a complete analogy – as it would be if I were suddenly able to see 10 strokes | | | | | | | | | |, which I had hitherto only been able to see as twice five strokes, as a characteristic whole. Or suddenly seeing the picture of a cube as 3-dimensional when I had previously only been able to see it as a flat pattern (PR, p. 281).

Wittgenstein says here that in "the phenomenological investigation of sense-impressions" there is a great danger in "trying to see things as simpler than they are." By joining Kohler in warning of this danger, Wittgenstein was rejecting his earlier idea that the real entities in experience are "simple objects" (colors, etc.). In his *Tractatus* period he had held that one's visual impressions could be described by propositions that specify the color of every part of one's visual field at a given moment.[7] In §48 of the *Investigations* he suggests how he had thought of this by presenting a group of nine colored squares. And the "danger" he is warning of in the above passage is that of thinking that visual impressions are like *that*.

In *Philosophical Grammar* he alludes to this matter as follows:

... think of the problem of the exact reproduction or description of what is seen in the visual field; of the description of the perpetual flux of phenomena; also of "how many raindrops do you see, if you look at the rain?" (PG, p. 175).

In lectures he was more explicit about the nature of this problem:

One often has the experience of trying to give an account of what one actually sees in looking about one, say, the changing sky, and of feeling that there aren't enough words to describe it. One then tends to become fundamentally dissatisfied with language. We are comparing the case with something it cannot be compared with. It is like saying of falling raindrops, "Our vision is so inadequate that we cannot say how many raindrops we saw, though surely we did see a specific number." The fact is that it makes no sense to talk of the number of drops we saw. There is similar nonsense in saying "It passed too quickly for me to see. It might have gone more slowly." But too quick for what? Surely it did not go too quickly for you to see what you did see. What could be meant by "*It* might have gone more slowly?" (WL35, p. 63).

To understand the way in which Wittgenstein thought of this, consider the following situation. You are looking down a long hallway and suddenly see, in the distance, a number of people dash across the hall from a room on the left and into a room on the right. Suppose, further, that they are evacuating a chemistry lab in which toxic fumes have been accidentally released. In that case someone might ask you: "Did you see if all twelve people got out of the lab?" or "How many people did you see run across the hall?" It is likely that, if there were more than six or seven, you would be unable to answer with confidence. But is there a problem here, as Wittgenstein thought, about whether you *did* see some definite number of people? Surely, it would be easy enough to find out how many you saw by going to the room they dashed into and counting them. But Wittgenstein, being a phenomenalist, could not think of the matter in this way. His idea is that when you saw people dashing across the hall, you had a sequence of visual impressions, and then the question arises: Were there, at a given moment, a definite number of people (human figures) in your visual field? But how could such a question be definitively answered? One cannot, as it were, retrieve the visual impression and make it hold still in order to count the human figures in it. So it would seem that the phenomenalist has to say: It makes no sense to speak of the number of human figures that were seen. And yet the phenomenalist would want to say that *something* was seen, for one *can* say: "I saw some people dash across the hall." But how is one to describe that visual impression in greater detail? Here we have nothing like the arrangement of nine colored squares in §48 of the *Investigations*. So there is an absurdity in the *Tractatus* requirement that "I saw some people dash across the hall" be analyzable into propositions composed of simple names.

It was apparently Wittgenstein's encounter with this problem that led him to abandon his earlier analytic version of phenomenalism. When, in the above-quoted passage, he joined Kohler in warning of the danger of "trying to see things as simpler than they really are," he meant: it is a mistake to think that there ought to be a way to describe one's constantly changing visual field as one can describe an arrangement of nine colored squares printed on a page. He meant, in other words, that it is a mistake to think of this as he had in the *Tractatus*. This is what he is getting at in the following bit of dialogue with his own earlier self:

". . . [W]hy, take just visual experience! Your gaze wanders almost incessantly, how could you describe it?" And yet I do describe it! "But that is only a quite crude description, it gives only the coarsest features of your experience." But isn't this just what I *call* description of my experience? How then do I arrive at the concept of a kind of description that I cannot possibly give? (RPP, I, §1079).

Imagine looking at flowing water. The picture presented by the surface keeps on changing. Lights and darks everywhere appear and disappear. What would I call an 'exact description' of this visual picture? There's nothing I would call that. If someone says it can't be described, one can reply: You don't know what it would be right to call a description. For you would not acknowledge the most exact photograph as an *exact* representation of your experience. There is no such thing as exactness in this language-game. (As, that is, there is no king in draughts.) (RPP, I, §1080).[8]

In these two passages, written in 1947, Wittgenstein is merely reiterating the point he had become convinced of in 1930, namely, that there can be no *pure* phenomenological language. Thus, in *Philosophical Remarks* he says: "I do not now have phenomenological language . . .in mind as my goal" (p. 51).

His earlier view had been that we use such words as "table" and "chair" and "rain" because it is more convenient than giving phenomenological descriptions, but he came around to Kohler's view that the use of this 'coarser' language is no mere convenience but (in many cases) the only possible language for describing experience (see PR, p. 51 and RPP, I, §1070). In his 1946 lectures he put the matter as follows:

There is a philosophical question as to what one *really sees*. Does one really see depth, or physical objects, or sadness, or a face, etc.? There is a temptation to say that all of this is 'interpretation,' 'hypothesis,' etc., and that what one *really* sees is a flat surface of coloured patches.

But if I am required to describe what I see, I do it with physical-object expressions: e.g. "I see the top of a tan table; on it is an ink bottle towards the right end," etc. I would not be able to describe it by referring only to coloured patches. . . .

We have the idea of an *ideal* model or an *ideal* description of what one sees at any time. But no such ideal description exists. There are numerous sorts of things which we call "descriptions" of what we see. They are all *rough*. And "rough" here does *not* mean "approximation." We have the mistaken idea that there is a certain exact description of what one sees at any given moment.[9]

Wittgenstein says in this passage: "if I am required to describe what I see, I do it with physical-object expressions." One must be careful not to misunderstand this, as I believe many philosophers have. One must not, I mean, take what he says here to show that he had abandoned phenomenalism. What he was saying, rather, was that it is *by means of* physical-object expressions that one describes sense-impressions.

This is a point that he made repeatedly. In a discussion in The Blue Book (pp. 51–52) of "It looks as though my hand were moving," he says that "we are handicapped in ordinary language by having to describe . . . a sensation by means of terms for physical objects. . . . We have to use a roundabout description of our sensations." He adds that in saying this he does "not mean that ordinary language is insufficient for our special purposes, but that it is . . . sometimes misleading" (ibid.). The sentence "It looks as though my hand were moving" is misleading, he explains, because "what we want to say does not entail the existence" of a hand. (See also BB, p. 47.) His point, then, is that "It looks as though my hand were moving" is, as he puts it, a "roundabout description of our sensations." In notes that he made for his own use in 1938, we can see him trying to make peace with ordinary language when he debates this matter with himself as follows:

"You speak of the thing [e.g., the hand], but want actually to speak of the sense impression." I want to speak as I do speak, and you can say that I speak of sense impressions. Only realize that talk about sense impressions does not look the way you imagine [i.e., as imagined in the *Tractatus*]. . . .

"If I speak of this tree, I naturally want to speak in some way of appearances. So let me therefore speak directly of appearances and not by the detour of [talking about] the tree." But that [complaint about having to use the word "tree" *instead* of talking about appearances] is as if one had before one's mind a number of views of the tree and used the word "tree" as a kind of abbreviated mode of expression [and so could replace the abbreviation with the unabridged version].

"But what interests me when I talk about a physical object is what I see and hear, taste, smell and feel. Therefore, the sense-impressions are what interest me; so surely I can speak *just* of them." If that is so, then I *speak* 'of sense impressions' by speaking of physical objects (CE, Appendix B, pp. 435–437; my translation).

He obviously ends this debate by concluding that, when one speaks of a tree or a hand, one *is* speaking (in the only way one *can*) of sense-impressions. In the late 1940s he reiterated this point, saying: "We learn to describe objects, and thereby, in another sense, our sensations" (RPP, I, §1082). By this he meant to say: Although we use such (philosophically misleading) words as "hand" and "tree," when we do so we are speaking (in a roundabout way) of our sensations. "Certainly it's clear," he says, "that the description of impressions has the form of the description of '*external*' objects" (RPP, I, §1092).

What we can see from these passages is that Wittgenstein continued to embrace phenomenalism, while yet wanting to abandon the analytic version of it he had held in the *Tractatus*.

A Second Reason For Abandoning the *Tractatus* View of Analysis

There is a second, and concurrent, reason why Wittgenstein abandoned the *Tractatus* view. He had maintained there that the propositions of ordinary language are connected to reality by elementary propositions, meaning that propositions about tables and chairs are analytically related to these elementary propositions. In his 1929 paper "Some Remarks on Logical Form" he still held this view: "If we try to analyse any given propositions [of ordinary language] we shall find in general that they are logical sums, products or other truth-functions of simpler propositions" (RLF, p. 32). But he soon came to think that the propositions of ordinary language are not related to reality by this *formal* connection with sense-datum propositions. This is not to say that there is *no* connection between ordinary propositions and reality, but it is to say that the connection, whatever it is, is not mediated by a formal (truth-functional) connection *hidden* in the meaning of our propositions. In *Philosophical Grammar* Wittgenstein explains his change of mind as follows:

Can a logical product be hidden in a proposition? And if so, how does one tell, and what methods do we have of bringing the hidden element of a proposition to light? If we haven't yet got a method, then we can't speak of something being hidden or possibly hidden. And if we do have a method of discovery then the only way in which something like a logical product can be hidden in a proposition is the way in which a quotient like 753/3 is hidden until the division has been carried out. . . .

My notion in the *Tractatus Logico-Philosophicus* was wrong: 1) because I wasn't clear about the sense of the words "a logical product is *hidden* in a sentence" (and suchlike), 2) because I too thought that logical analysis had to bring to light what was hidden (as chemical and physical analysis does) (PG, p. 210).

Amplifying this, Wittgenstein writes:

... if we're to say that a proposition isn't an elementary proposition unless its complete analysis shows that it isn't built out of other propositions by truth-functions, we are presupposing that we have an idea of what such an 'analysis' would be. Formerly, I myself spoke of a 'complete analysis,' and I used to believe that philosophy had to give a definitive dissection of propositions so as to set out clearly all their connections and remove all possibilities of mis-understanding. I spoke as if there was a calculus in which such a dissection would be possible. I vaguely had in mind something like the definition that Russell had given for the definite article, and I used to think that in a similar way one would be able to use visual impressions etc. to define the concept say of a sphere, and thus exhibit once for all the connections between the concepts and lay bare the source of all misunderstandings, etc. At the root of all this there was a false and idealized picture of the use of language.... [I]t is not a definition of the concept of a physical sphere that we need; instead we must describe a language game related to our own, or rather a whole series of related language games, and it will be in these that such definitions may occur. Such a contrast destroys grammatical prejudices and makes it possible for us to see the use of a word as it really is, instead of *inventing* the use for the word (PG, pp. 211–212).[10]

How could a "grammatical prejudice" be destroyed by *inventing* a lan-guage-game that differs from, but is related to, our own?

What Wittgenstein had in mind can be seen in a passage he wrote some years later:

We can *imagine* a game in which "Such and such a body is there" is shorthand for "I have had such and such impressions." But to take this as the general rule is to simplify our language – [to] construct a game which is not the one played. Not just a simplification, a falsification, and there is hardly any similarity be-tween the game described ... and the game actually played.

But what tempts one to do this sort of thing? There is a tendency to say [and in the *Tractatus* Wittgenstein did say] that everything must be "well grounded." The game we play with the word "sofa" must be well grounded: and we imagine there is unshakable evidence [for there being a sofa over there] in what our senses tell us (CE, Appendix B, p. 440).

This passage explains very clearly the difference between the *Tractatus* and Wittgenstein's later view. His idea in the *Tractatus* had been that if he were to have such-and-such sense-impressions, he would *know* that there is a chair over there, i.e., that he would have (as he puts it here) "unshakable evidence" for this. And the evidence, he thought, would be unshakable because the proposition "There's a chair over there" *follows logically* from propositions describing his sense-impressions. In *Investiga-tions* §486, as we saw above, Wittgenstein rejected this idea: he came to think that no matter how good a look he might get, it *could* turn out that there *is* no chair over there.

What changed Wittgenstein's mind about this? Evidently, it dawned on him at some point that the course of his sense-data could fail to run true to form, i.e., that something completely unheard of could occur that would make him doubt whether there is a chair over there *despite* his having taken a long, careful look. Possibly, the following passage from Pearson's *The Grammar of Science* suggested this to him:

> ... the *real* table lies ... in the permanent association of a certain group of sense-impressions. ...
>
> Let us return for a moment to our old friend the blackboard. In the first place we have size and shape, then colour and temperature, and lastly, properties like hardness, strength, weight, etc. Clearly the blackboard consists for us in the permanent association of these properties. ... [I]f the hardness and weight were to vanish, we might *see* the ghost of a blackboard, but we should soon convince ourselves that it was not the "reality" we had termed blackboard.[11]

Pearson means: if I found that I couldn't touch it, I'd say, "There's no blackboard here."

Wittgenstein, in his conversations with Waismann, spoke of a similar case: ". . . there is surely no logical necessity why by verifying one proposition a different one should also be verified. I can e.g. very well imagine that, although I see this hyacinth over there, I shall have no tactile perceptions when I want to touch it . . ." (WVC, p. 161). What is one to *say* in such a case: Was there a *hyacinth* there or wasn't there? In The Blue Book Wittgenstein gives his answer: "We could easily imagine cases in which the visual evidence was true and at the same time other evidences make us say that I have no hand" (BB, p. 52). Waismann, in his summary of Wittgenstein's views, writes:

> Does the following question make sense? How many aspects [i.e., sense-impressions] is it necessary to have seen before the existence of an object is safely established? No, it does not. No number of aspects can prove that hypothesis [e.g., that there's a chair over there]. Whether we accept the hypothesis or reject it – that depends entirely on what the hypothesis will accomplish.
>
> And that is how we in fact behave. What should I do, for example, if this book dissolved into nothing as soon as I had a close look at it. Or if I had visual images without the corresponding tactile perceptions? I should say, "*There was no book there*; I only *believed* I was seeing one" (WVC, p. 259).

In *Philosophical Grammar* Wittgenstein speaks of the *Tractatus* as describing "a calculus to which, misled as I was by a false notion of reduction, I thought that the *whole* use of propositions must be reducible" (PG, p. 211, my italics). In saying that he had thought the *whole* use must be reducible, he meant that he had thought that the rules of the calculus leave nothing undecided. Had Wittgenstein later been asked *why* he had thought that nothing is left undecided, he would presumably have answered that he simply had not thought of unheard-of events like those described in the above passages, i.e., had not thought of those abnormal situations in which we wouldn't know what to say.

In the *Investigations* he states his new position as follows: "It is only in normal cases that the use of a word is clearly prescribed; we know, are in no doubt, what to say in this or that case. The more abnormal the case, the more doubtful it becomes what we are to say" (PI, § 142). To illustrate this point, Wittgenstein asks us to consider the following:

I say "There is a chair." What if I go up to it, meaning to fetch it, and it suddenly disappears from sight? "So it wasn't a chair, but some kind of illusion." But in a few moments we see it again and are able to touch it and so on. "So the chair was there after all and its disappearance was some kind of illusion." But suppose that after a time it disappears again – or seems to disappear. What are we to say now? Have you rules ready for such cases – rules saying whether one may use the word "chair" to include this kind of thing? But do we miss them when we use the word "chair"; and are we to say that we do not really attach any meaning to this word, because we are not equipped with rules for every possible application of it? (PI, §80).

The *Tractatus* view was that in our use of ordinary language we are "operating a calculus according to definite rules" (PI, §81), and this meant that "There is a chair" *follows* from various sense-datum propositions. In opposing that view, Wittgenstein now asks us to consider a case in which something unheard of occurs in the stream of sense-impressions. And we are asked whether, in truth, we know what to say in such a situation. If the *Tractatus* view were correct, we *would* know, and Wittgenstein is counting on his readers to admit that they don't know – and thus to acknowledge that the *Tractatus* view was in error. This is what he getting at when he says: "It is the same [mistake] when one tries to define the concept of a material object in terms of 'what is really seen.' What we have rather to do is *accept* the everyday language-game, and to note *false* accounts of the matter *as* false" (PI, p. 200).[12] He means that the *false* account is the *Tractatus* account, according to which there is an *analytic* relation between "There is a chair over there" and propositions that describe sense-impressions.

The Search for an Empiricist Theory of Knowledge

We could describe Wittgenstein's change of mind by saying that he came to think that there is a looser, less formal, connection than the *Tractatus* allowed between sense-impressions and propositions about tables and chairs. Thus, he says that a proposition of the sort in question here "has a connection with reality which is, as it were, looser than that of verification" and that it "has a different formal relation to reality from that of verification" (PR, pp. 284 and 285). He also says that such propositions are "coupled with reality with varying degrees of freedom" (PR, p. 282).

What exactly is this "looser" connection? As we will see, no single answer can be given, for on this question Wittgenstein vacillated greatly and, I believe, never found an answer that satisfied him. To trace his thoughts on this matter, it is useful to begin with a passage from his earliest conversations with Waismann, where we find him still thinking along the lines of the *Tractatus*.

> If I say, for example, "Up there on the cupboard there is a book," how do I set about verifying it? Is it sufficient if I glance at it, or if I look at it from different sides, or if I take it into my hands, touch it, open it, turn over its leaves, and so forth? There are two conceptions here. One of them says that however I set about it, I shall never be able to verify the proposition completely. A proposition [of this kind] always keeps a back-door open, as it were. Whatever we do, we are never sure that we were not mistaken.
>
> The other conception, *the one I want to hold*, says, "No, if I can never verify the sense of a proposition completely, then I cannot have meant anything by the proposition either. Then the proposition signifies nothing whatsoever."
>
> In order to determine the sense of a proposition, I should have to know a very specific procedure for when to count the proposition as verified (WVC, p. 47, emphasis added).

This is an excerpt from a conversation on 22 December 1929, very shortly after Wittgenstein returned to philosophy, and so it is not surprising that the conception Wittgenstein here says he *wants* to hold is that found in the *Tractatus*. It is the view that such a proposition as "There is a book on top of the cupboard" follows from a set of propositions about sense-data. During the course of his conversations with Waismann Wittgenstein abandoned this view. Thus, in a conversation on 22 March 1930, he declared that propositions of the sort in question "never count as proved" (WVC, p. 100) and later said: "If I were to describe the grammar of an hypothesis [such as "There's a chair"], I would say that it follows from no single [sense-datum] proposition and from no set of single propositions. It will – in a sense – never be verified" (WVC, p. 211).

But if the linguistic (grammatical) relation between "There's a chair" and reality (sense-impressions) is not truth-functional, what relation did Wittgenstein think there is?

The first thing to understand is the terminology Wittgenstein adopted for explaining his new conception: his distinction between "propositions" and "hypotheses." A passage from a 1931 lecture explains this distinction:

> A proposition is a judgement about sense data, a reading of one's sense data; for example "This is red." No further verification is needed. . . . A hypothesis is an expression of the form "This man is ill," "The sun will rise tomorrow" or "This is a chair." It is confirmed or rejected, when its meaning is clear, by empirical science (WL32, p. 66).[13]

Wittgenstein also said that " 'propositions' about physical objects and most of the things we talk about in ordinary life are always really hypotheses" (WL32, p. 53).

What is a hypothesis, as the term is meant here? Wittgenstein explains: "A hypothesis goes beyond immediate [i.e., present] experience. A proposition does not" (WL32, p. 110). He also says: "A hypothesis is a law by which we can construct propositions. The use of a hypothesis is to make inferences about the future," i.e., about future sense-data (WL32, p. 83). This means that in saying "There's a chair," one is predicting that future experience will be of a certain sort, e.g., that I *will* feel resistance if I go to touch the chair and that it won't suddenly vanish.

What is essential to an hypothesis is, I believe, that it arouses an expectation by admitting of future confirmation. That is, it is of the essence of an hypothesis that its confirmation is never complete" (PR, p. 285).

Why does Wittgenstein say here that one cannot completely confirm (or verify) "This is a chair"? On the face of it, this seems odd, for although I might, in certain cases, have to look twice to make sure that there is a chair in the corner (in case, for instance, I am in a dimly lit loft with lots of old furniture piled haphazardly), it would seem that beyond a certain point the matter is settled, there is nothing further to investigate. But Wittgenstein was not here thinking of 'normal' situations. Rather, he was thinking, as his neutral monism requires (see Chapter 2, above), that the distinction between appearance and reality is a distinction *within* the course of one's sense impressions. What is real, on this view, is what meets certain expectations. So long as we continue to have sense impressions that meet our expectations, we will stick to saying that there's a chair in the corner. But this could all change at any moment, Wittgenstein was thinking, as his example of the "chair" that disappears and reappears (PI, §80) is meant to illustrate. Wittgenstein, in other words, was thinking that one's sense impressions could at any moment confound one by taking an uncanny turn, and this is why he says: "If I were to describe the grammar of an hypothesis, I would say that it follows from no single [sense-datum] proposition and from no set of single propositions" (WVC, p. 211). He also speaks of a hypothesis as being "a law for forming expectations" (PR, p. 285), and says that "physical statements refer to the future *ad infinitum*. They never count as proved; we always reserve the right to drop or alter them, in contrast with a real statement [such as 'This is red'], whose truth is not subject to alteration" (WVC, p. 100).[14]

This, then, is the view that Wittgenstein adopted once he had abandoned the *Tractatus* view in the early 1930s, and even as late as 1947 he continued to hold this view (see Chapter 15, note 1, this volume). It is a view he was to reconsider in the final months of his life.

He was forced to reconsider it when he asked himself how he could accommodate the fact that we say, for example, "I *know* it's a tree." For if, as Wittgenstein held, propositions about such things as trees and houses can never be completely verified, i.e., if some uncanny experience could prove them false (or questionable), then it would seem that we can never properly claim to *know* that we are seeing a tree or a house. Hence, the view Wittgenstein adopted in the 1930s seems to lead straight to skepticism.

In the last year and half of his life Wittgenstein addressed this problem in a series of notes now published under the title *On Certainty*.[15] How, he asked himself, can we show that "we *know* truths, not only about sense-data, but also about things" (OC, §426).

In Chapter 15 we will consider in detail his various attempts to solve this problem. Here I will mention one of his proposed solutions. In the 1930s Wittgenstein had maintained that " 'propositions' about physical objects . . . are always really hypotheses" (WL32, p. 53). Here he allows for no exceptions, and one of his proposed solutions in *On Certainty* is to allow that there *are* exceptions: not *all* propositions about physical objects are hypotheses. This is what he is getting at when he says: "Our 'empirical propositions' do not form a homogeneous mass" (OC, §213). He means: not all of our empirical propositions are hypotheses, not all are falsifiable by future experience. This becomes apparent when he says that "it is wrong to say that the 'hypothesis' that this is a bit of paper would be confirmed or disconfirmed by later experience" (OC, §60). Similarly, with reference to Moore's example, "Here is a hand," he says that it "can't be called a hypothesis" and contrasts it in this respect with a proposition about a planet, which *would* be a hypothesis (OC, §52). He is saying the same thing when he remarks that Moore could be interpreted as saying quite *rightly* that "a proposition saying that here is a physical object may have the same logical status as one saying that here is a red patch" (OC, §53). By adopting this new account Wittgenstein was hoping to show that one could say "I know that's a tree" and would not have to retract it if some uncanny experience occurs later on.

In Chapter 15 we will consider further this solution to his problem and also three other solutions he proposes in *On Certainty*. Each of these, as we will see, is meant to address the question: Given that the course of one's sense-impressions could suddenly take an uncanny turn, i.e., given that what we take to be a chair could suddenly and unaccountably vanish, how can we claim to know, for example, that there's a chair in the corner? Wittgenstein, in other words, was attempting to solve a problem that arises only for philosophers who embrace some form of phenomenalism.

Notes

1. It is perhaps noteworthy that Moore, in his 1914 essay "The Status of Sense-data," remarked that the phenomenalist's counterfactual version of

what we all normally *mean* in saying that something existed at a time when it wasn't perceived would be "immensely complicated" – so complicated, he added, that "I cannot come anywhere near to stating exactly what it would be" (op. cit., p. 190).

2. Early in his pre-*Tractatus* notebooks Wittgenstein wrote: "A proposition like 'this chair is brown' seems to say something enormously complicated. . . ." (NB, p. 5). He goes on to say that in its completely analyzed form "it would have to be infinitely long." Seven months later he changed his mind, saying that "the chain of definitions must some time come to an end" and that although the completely analyzed version of the proposition will be "more complicated" than the original, "the reference of our propositions is not infinitely long" (NB, p. 46). "Language," he adds, "is part of our organism and no less complicated than it" (NB, p. 48). It is significant that this last remark, which is retained nearly verbatim in the *Tractatus* at 4.002, was originally connected with the thought that names of material things are names of complexes. This idea was still in Wittgenstein's thinking in 1929, when he wrote in MS 107 (p. 1) that visual space "can be described immediately (though we are far from knowing a mode of expression which does describe it). The usual physical language is related to it in a *very* complicated way instinctively known to us." (Quoted and translated in Hintikka, *Investigating Wittgenstein*, op. cit., p. 163.) See also WL47, pp. 52, 178, and 293.

3. I will quote from the Mentor edition (New York, 1947).

4. There is strong evidence that Wittgenstein read Kohler's book in early 1930. (i) In *Philosophical Remarks*, which was written during the period February 1929 to May 1930 (see Editor's Note, PR, p. 347) there is a passage near the end (p. 281, quoted below) which contains what appears to be a reference to Kohler and which goes on to state a position very much like Kohler's own. (ii) During this period one also finds Wittgenstein discussing (PG, pp. 174–180) one of Kohler's favorite examples: the expressions of a human face. (iii) In his 1931–1932 lectures Wittgenstein borrowed a striking metaphor from Kohler's book. He said: "The world we live in is the world of sense-data" (WL32, p. 82). Kohler said that "the world we actually live in" is the world of immediate experience (p. 51).

5. Op. cit., pp. 43.

6. Ibid., p. 71.

7. This was still his view in December of 1929. During his conversations with Waismann he spoke of "describing the surface of the room analytically by means of an equation and stating the distribution of colours on this surface" (WVC, p. 41), meaning that *this* is the logical form of the elementary propositions into which our everyday language must be analyzable.

8. See also RPP, I, §§1081–1085.

9. From Norman Malcolm, *Ludwig Wittgenstein: A Memoir*, op. cit., pp. 49–50. This passage is Malcolm's summary of remarks made by Wittgenstein during his 1946 lectures.

10. People have argued that Wittgenstein could not have remained a phenomenalist in his later years because in the *Investigations* (§§60–64) he rejected the Tractarian idea of analysis. But the above passage, which was written no later than 1933, dismisses the Tractarian idea of analysis, and yet Wittgenstein plainly remained a phenomenalist well beyond this date. Even in PI, §91 he speaks of the statements "we make about phenomena."

11. Op. cit., p. 69.

12. Wittgenstein also says: ". . . like the relation: physical object–sense-impres-

sion. Here we have two different language-games and a complicated relation between them. If you try to reduce their relation to a *simple* formula you go wrong" (PI, p. 180). The simple "formula" is that of the *Tractatus*. It was also Russell's "formula." In "The Relation of Sense-data to Physics" Russell says: "The 'thing' of common sense may in fact be identified with the whole class of its appearances. . . ." (*Mysticism and Logic*, op. cit., p. 154). The "simple formula" says that a proposition such as "This is my hand" can be completely verified because it is equivalent to a *fixed number* of sense-datum propositions. This was rejected by Wittgenstein as early as 1931 (see WVC, pp. 210 and 254).

13. Although Wittgenstein continued to use "hypothesis" in this way (see, for example, OC §§52, 60, 87, 190–191, and 203), he soon discontinued using "proposition" in this narrow sense.

14. This required Wittgenstein to alter his views about verification and the sense of a proposition (in the broader meaning of "proposition"). In the passage quoted above from his 1929 conversation he said that in order for a proposition to have sense, there must be "a very specific procedure for when to count the proposition as verified," for otherwise it "signifies nothing whatsoever." As this account could not hold for an hypothesis, in Wittgenstein's sense, he was now obliged to declare that "all that's required for our propositions (about reality) to have a sense, is that our experience *in some sense or other* either tends to agree with them or tends not to agree with them. That is, immediate experience need confirm only something about them, *some* facet of them" (PR, p. 282).

15. In the Preface of *On Certainty* the editors report: "In the middle of 1949 [Wittgenstein] visited the United States at the invitation of Norman Malcolm. . . . Malcolm acted as a goad to his interest in Moore's 'defence of common sense,' that is to say his claim to *know* a number of propositions for sure, such as 'Here is one hand, and here is another'. . ." (OC, p. vi).

8

A New Philosophical Method

As we saw in the preceding chapter Wittgenstein did not, in his later years, abandon phenomenalism. What he abandoned was only the *Tractatus* view that the propositions of ordinary language are truth-functionally constructed from more elementary propositions. But this change required a modification of Wittgenstein's ideas about philosophical method. While he continued to think that philosophical problems arise from misunderstandings of the 'logic' of our language, he could no longer think that such misunderstandings can be corrected by logical analysis. The idea of analysis is the idea that a philosopher can dissect our ordinary propositions into those sense-datum propositions from which they are truth-functionally constructed and can thereby show, for example, that Moore was wrong to oppose Berkeley's account of propositions about material objects. But with analysis now out of the question, the discovery of a new method became an urgent matter for Wittgenstein.

The discovery was not long in coming. Drury reports that Wittgenstein said to him in 1930: "I know that my method is right."[1] And Moore, in his account of Wittgenstein's lectures of 1930–1933, reports him as saying that his particular results did not matter as much as the fact that "a method had been found."[2] What was this new method?

The New Method Utilized Much That Was Not New

To begin with, there was much in it that was not new. In his later as well as in his earlier period he depended on the following ideas, which we surveyed in Chapter 4: (a) philosophy, being an *a priori* discipline (not a science), can *say* nothing about the world, since any significant proposition must have a significant negation; (b) philosophical problems must be stated in the formal mode; (c) by answering questions so formulated philosophy can show something about the essence of the world; (d) philosophical problems arise from our misunderstanding the logic of our language; (e) such misunderstandings occur because our language contains grammatical forms ("forms of words") that mislead us as to the essence of the world; and so (f) the job of philosophy is nothing more than the job of clarifying those propositions of ordinary language which, by their grammar, generate philosophical problems. In addition to carrying over these ideas from the *Tractatus*, Wittgenstein also carried over, as we have seen, his original ontology, his pure realism. What, then, were the differences between the two periods?

To identify these differences, we need to notice two things about the *Tractatus*. The first is that, while it declared that the job of philosophy is to settle philosophical problems by analyzing propositions of our everyday language into sense-datum propositions, Wittgenstein was well aware that he had not the faintest idea of how to carry out an actual analysis. We are at present, he said, "unable to give the composition of elementary propositions" (TLP, 5.55). Thus, although he declared that "all the propositions of our everyday language, just as they stand, are in perfect logical order" (TLP, 5.5563), he had no idea how to show this in any particular case. The cases in which this needs showing are those in which the propositions of everyday language seem to conflict with his ontology. For instance, when we talk about the thoughts and feelings of other people, we seem to be talking about something that is not given in experience. Yet according to the *Tractatus*, we must be able to dispel this impression by carrying out a doubly reductive analysis of such statements: first, an analysis in which the other person's thoughts and feelings are reduced to bodily movements or states and, second, an analysis of those bodily movements or states into sense-data. Yet Wittgenstein could not have begun to carry out either part of this analysis. The truth about the *Tractatus*, then, is this: although it argues that certain conditions would have to be met by anything that counts as a language, it fails to demonstrate that the propositions of everyday language actually fulfill those conditions. If they were found *not* to be analyzable in the anticipated way, Wittgenstein would have had to conclude that they do not describe possible states of affairs and so say nothing at all.

By 1930 Wittgenstein had become dissatisfied with this situation and spoke of it as follows:

The following is a question I constantly discuss with Moore: Can only logical analysis explain what we mean by the propositions of ordinary language? Moore is inclined to think so. Are people therefore ignorant of what they mean when they say "Today the sky is clearer than yesterday"? Do we have to wait for logical analysis here? What a hellish idea! Only philosophy is supposed to explain to me what I mean by my propositions and whether I mean anything by them (WVC, pp. 129–130).

It is clear from this that Wittgenstein had come to think that it is *not* logical analysis that shows what one means by a proposition.

Wittgenstein's new method was intended to remedy the aforementioned predicament. It would have to show that what one says in everyday life can be reconciled with neutral monism, and it would have to show this without translating what we say into some *other* language – an explicitly phenomenological language – which we do not actually have. Wittgenstein was explaining this in 1931 when he said:

> ... I used to believe ... that it is the task of logical analysis to discover the elementary propositions. ... Only in recent years have I broken away from that mistake. ... The truth of the matter is that we have already got everything, and we have got it actually *present*; we need not wait for anything. We make our moves in the realm of the grammar of our ordinary language, and this grammar is already there (WVC, pp. 182–183).

What Wittgenstein had in mind here he explained more thoroughly in the opening paragraphs of *Philosophical Remarks*:

> A proposition is completely logically analyzed if its grammar is made completely clear: no matter what idiom it may be written or expressed in [i.e., even if it is in the idiom of ordinary language].
>
> I do not now have phenomenological language, or 'primary language' as I used to call it, in mind as my goal. I no longer hold it to be necessary. All that is possible and necessary is to separate what is essential from what is inessential in *our* language.
>
> That is, if we so to speak describe the class of languages which serve their purpose, then in so doing we have shown what is essential to them and given an immediate representation of immediate experience.
>
> Each time I say that, instead of such and such a representation [in ordinary language], you could also use this other one, we take a further step towards the goal of grasping the essence of what is represented.
>
> A recognition of what is essential and what inessential in our language if it is to represent, a recognition of which parts of our language are wheels turning idly, amounts to constructing a phenomenological language (PR, p. 51).

This passage shows more clearly than any other he ever wrote the difference between the *Tractatus* and all of his later work, and because I will have occasion to refer to it later on, I will refer to this passage as Wittgenstein's "Methodological Reassessment."

A New Way of Showing Ordinary Language to be a Phenomenological Language

One must take careful note of what his Methodological Reassessment contains. Most important, perhaps, is the fact that the term "phenomenological language" is used here in two senses. When, in the second paragraph, he says, "I do not now have phenomenological language ... in mind as my goal," he means an *explicit* phenomenological language, i.e., one that would contain names of sensible qualities but not words such as "table," "chair," and "Mr. Smith." But in the last paragraph, where he says that his new method "amounts to constructing a phenomenological language," he has something else in mind, namely, that our ordinary language is a phenomenological language *despite* the fact that it contains words such as "table" and "chair." To understand this, it is important to bear in mind that in the *Tractatus* Wittgenstein maintained that ordinary language is a phenomenological language in two senses: (i) in the sense that the propositions of ordinary language do not, contrary to Moore, refer to entities that transcend sense-data, and (ii) in the sense that the propositions of ordinary language are truth-functions of (can be analyzed into) propositions which are explicitly phenomenological. In his Methodological Reassessment he is saying that ordinary language is a phenomenological language but only in sense (i). And his new philosophical method is a method of showing, in particular instances, that ordinary language *is* a phenomenological language in this sense. This is what he means when he says in his Methodological Reassessment that it is a method that brings about "a recognition of what is essential and what inessential in our language if it is to represent, a recognition of which parts of our language are wheels turning idly."[3] By this he meant that his new method is a way of showing which features of ordinary language mislead philosophers such as Moore into thinking that in speaking ordinary language one is constantly speaking of entities that transcend immediate experience.

How does he propose to show that some feature of our language *is* a misleading form of words? In his Methodological Reassessment he explains this rather cryptically by saying: "Each time I say that, instead of such and such a representation [in ordinary language], you could also use this other one, we take a further step towards the goal of grasping the essence of what is represented." By this he meant that his new method consists in showing that whereas we presently use such-and-such a misleading form of words, we could, without losing anything, use a different form of words – one that would contain no suggestion that one is speaking of something that is not given in immediate experience. We saw an example of this method in Chapter 5, namely, Wittgenstein's claim that instead of saying "I am in pain" one could say "There is pain" and that, since we would lose nothing by this substitution, this new form of words shows that the fact which we presently describe by using the pronoun "I" does *not* have a self (or ego) as one of its constituents.

We will presently consider a second example of Wittgenstein's use of this method. Before doing so, however, we must take note of the second difference between the *Tractatus* and his Methodological Reassessment. In explaining what he means by separating "what is essential from what is inessential in *our* language," he says that the way to do this is to "describe the class of languages which serve their purpose," and by this latter phrase he means "languages which serve the *same* purpose." His discussion of "I" is a case in point, for his claim is that both "I am in pain" and "There is pain" would *serve the same purpose*. At the time of the *Tractatus*, instead of speaking of the *purpose* of words, he would have spoken of logical *form*. Indeed, in dealing with the first-person pronoun, he had said that the proposition "I believe that p" is "of the *form* 'p says p' " (TLP, 5.542). This idea of logical form is not to be found in his Methodological Reassessment, and in its place we find him speaking of the *purpose* words serve. The difference is important, for here we see him introducing the "use" theory of meaning, which plays so large a role in his later work.

The Use Theory of Meaning

In the *Tractatus* he had placed great emphasis on the idea of logical form, this being distinct from grammatical form. It is the logical form of a proposition, he said, that enables it to be a picture of a possible state of affairs. Sentences having different *grammatical* forms – perhaps sentences from different languages – can be used to say the same thing, but if they can be used to *say* the same thing, they have the same *logical* form. The very idea of logical form, then, belongs with the idea that our ordinary sentences are only the surface beneath which lie the elementary propositions that do the real work of language. So when Wittgenstein came to think that the things we commonly say are not undergirded by elementary propositions, he was obliged to dispense with the distinction between logical and grammatical form. But in doing so, he could not conclude that they are one and the same, i.e., that the grammatical form of an ordinary sentence *is* its logical form, for it remained his view that it is the grammatical form of many things we say that misrepresents the nature of the facts. So there would seem to be no place at all in his post-*Tractatus* views for his original idea of logical form. And this is what he himself concluded: "In the *Tractatus Logico-Philosophicus* I said something like: it [the pictorial character of a proposition] is an agreement of *form*. But that is an error" (PG, p. 212, emphasis added). This is why he says in his Methodological Reassessment that a proposition can count as fully analyzed "no matter what idiom" it is written in, i.e., regardless of its form. And it is this same point that he is getting at when he says that grammar is "arbitrary."

We have encountered his view about the arbitrariness of grammar in earlier chapters, but it bears repeating here. Wittgenstein says that it is a mistake to think that of two notations having the same use one is "more *adequate*, more *direct*" than the other. This is so because "one symbolism does not come nearer the truth than the other." He adds, significantly: "Of course it is all right to ask whether one symbolism is more misleading than another" (WL35, p. 129). So Wittgenstein's position is that even if the grammatical form of a sentence is misleading, that does not make it less adequate than some other sentence whose form is not misleading, *even though it cannot be analysed into elementary propositions that reveal its logical form*. He also said: "One symbolism is just as good as the next" (WL35, p. 63). They are equally good because form is irrelevant, i.e., contrary to the *Tractatus*, form does not determine meaning.

What, then, does determine meaning? Wittgenstein's answer is: The *use* of words. This, then, is where his 'use' theory of meaning comes in. To see its point, we have to realize that he is not in this context concerned with what we ordinarily call "meaning." He is concerned, rather, with the fact that we all commonly say things which at least *appear* to conflict with his ontology, neutral monism. In the *Tractatus* he undertook to explain how such propositions could still have a sense, could still picture the world, by holding that they have a hidden logical form. He now needed a different explanation, and the explanation he adopted is one that had long been popular with philosophers who found their ontologies at odds with what we all commonly say: a theory which says that because our sentences serve the practical ends of speech they are all right despite the fact that they seem to misrepresent the matters they deal with.

Berkeley was the first to advance this theory in a general way,[4] and it will be useful to consider how he invokes it to reconcile ordinary language with his view of causation. As we will see in Chapter 11, Berkeley, in his *Principles of Human Knowledge*, gives an account of causation according to which, when I extend my hands toward the fire to warm them, it is not the fire that warms them but rather, at the right moment, God "excites in me a sensation of warmth." More generally, his theory is that the objects of our perception have no causal powers. Yet we *say* that the fire warmed my hands, that the fire in the hearth warmed the room very quickly, and so on. So it would seem that Berkeley's theory is in conflict with what we all commonly say. In recognition of this, Berkeley entertained the following objection to his theory:

... it will ... be demanded [of me] whether it does not seem absurd [for a philosopher] to take away natural causes [e.g., the fire in the hearth], and to ascribe everything to the immediate operation of spirits? We must no longer say upon these principles that fire heats, or that water cools, but [must say instead] that a spirit heats [the room], and so forth. Would not a man be deservedly laughed at, who should talk after this manner?

In reply Berkeley concedes that a man who talked in that manner would be deserving of ridicule, but he denies that his theory requires us to talk in this absurd way. For, he says,

... in such things we ought to think with the learned, and speak with the vulgar. They who ... are convinced of the truth of the Copernican system do nevertheless say "the sun rises," "the sun sets," or "comes to the meridian"; and if they affected a contrary style in common talk it would without doubt appear very ridiculous. A little reflection on what is said will make it manifest that the common use of language would receive no manner of alteration or disturbance from the admission of our tenets [regarding causation].

In the ordinary affairs of life, any phrases may be retained, so long as they excite in us proper sentiments, or dispositions to act in such a manner as is necessary for our well-being, how false soever they may be if taken in a strict and speculative sense.[5]

Berkeley says here that there are forms of expression in our language that will mislead us if we take them in a "strict sense," i.e., take them to mean what they seem to mean. But how else, we might ask, *can* we take (what at least appear to be) causal verbs in our language, as when someone orders us to "warm up the room with a big fire"? Berkeley's answer would be that sentences of this sort serve us well because (as he puts it) they excite in us proper sentiments or dispositions to act. If someone says to me, "Warm up the room with a fire in the hearth," he only wants me to start a fire; he doesn't additionally want me to think that the fire has in it an "active principle" for raising the room temperature. He will get the result he wants if I build a fire and then God (not the fire) does the rest. So despite the fact that our form of expression lends itself to philosophical misunderstanding, it is nevertheless eminently practical, and that is all that is required of the words and phrases of ordinary language. If they perform their office, they do not merit the disdain of philosophers.

This, it must be added, is a particular application of Berkeley's more general point about language, namely, that

... the communicating of ideas marked by words is not the chief and only end of language, as is commonly supposed. There are other ends, as the raising of some passion, the exciting to or deterring from an action, the putting the mind in some particular disposition; to which the former [i.e., putting an image in one's hearer's mind] is in many cases barely subservient, and sometimes entirely omitted, when these [i.e., passions, actions, etc.] can be obtained without it, as I think does not unfrequently happen in the familiar use of language. ... If anyone shall join ever so little reflection of his own to what has been said, I believe that it will evidently appear to him that general names are often used in propriety of language without the speaker's designing them for marks of ideas in his own, which he would have them raise in the mind of the hearer.[6]

Berkeley is here rejecting Locke's account of the 'chief and only end of language'[7] and is replacing it with a use theory of meaning.

This theory differs markedly from the *Tractatus* theory in that it says that there need not be any 'fit' between language and the world because the purpose of language can be simply to get someone to act or refrain from acting. In such a theory logical form plays no part. That is why a form of words, despite being *philosophically* misleading, is perfectly all right so long as it serves the practical ends of speech.

This is the theory Wittgenstein adopted as the principal part of his new philosophical method. His agreement with Berkeley is evident in two respects. First of all, he agrees in rejecting the Lockean view of language: "We fail to get away from the idea that using a sentence involves imagining something for every word" (PI, §449; see also §317 and §363). Second, he agrees with Berkeley's emphasis on the *use* we make of words: "Look at the sentence as an instrument, and at its sense as its employment" (PI, §421). "Language," he says, "is an instrument. Its concepts are instruments" (PI, §569). His agreement with Berkeley on both these points comes out when he remarks:

What we call *"descriptions"* are instruments for particular uses. Think of a machine-drawing, a cross-section, an elevation with measurements, which an engineer has before him. Thinking of a description as a word-picture of the facts has something misleading about it: one tends to think only of such pictures as hang on our walls: which seem simply to portray how a thing looks, what it is like. (These pictures are as it were idle.) (PI, §291).

His view in the *Tractatus* had been that propositions are like the pictures that hang on our walls: they merely portray how a thing looks. His new idea was that propositions are more like the drawings made by a machinist or an architect: they tell us what we are to *do*.

In the above passages we can see Wittgenstein abandoning the *Tractatus* idea that language pictures the world, an idea that had required him to posit a logical form hidden beneath the sentences of ordinary language. With his new theory of language he could declare, by contrast:

Every sign *by itself* seems dead. *What* gives it life? – In use it is *alive* (PI, §423).

If it is asked: "How do sentences manage to represent?" – the answer might be: "Don't you know? You certainly see it, when you use them." For nothing is concealed.

How do sentences do it? – Don't you know? For nothing [i.e., no logical form] is hidden (PI, §435).

As I said above, the role of this 'use' (or instrument) theory of language is not to answer questions we might pose about the meaning of something in the ordinary sense of "meaning."[8] Rather, it is meant to explain how the things we commonly say can mean something very different from what they appear to mean. Which is to say, the theory is intended to explain how something which *seems* to conflict with a philosopher's favored ontology can be reconciled with that ontology. Wittgenstein, as I have said, needed such a theory after 1929 because, while his ontology conflicts with many of the things we all commonly say, he had dispensed with the means provided in the *Tractatus* for reconciling such conflicts.

Counterfactual Analysis

By considering the way Wittgenstein dealt with one such conflict, we can see what his new philosophical method amounts to. The problem I will introduce for purposes of illustration is the dispute between (Moorean) realists and idealists over whether things continue to exist unperceived. Wittgenstein discussed this many times, sometimes making one point and sometimes another, and it requires some care to recognize what point he is making in any particular passage. An obvious place to begin is to recall that this issue had formerly been debated in the material mode and was thus made to look like a factual issue: Do things exist when unperceived or do they not? Wittgenstein is remarking on this when he says: "From the very outset 'Realism,' 'Idealism,' etc. are names which belong to metaphysics. That is, they indicate that their adherents believe they can say [rather than show] something about the essence of the world" (PR, p. 86). We can expect Wittgenstein to insist that the dispute between realists and idealists can be set out clearly only in the formal mode, that they are really engaged in a dispute about grammar. For instance, in The Blue Book he says:

... it is particularly difficult to discover that an assertion which the meta-physician makes expresses discontentment with our grammar when the words of this assertion can also be used to state a fact of [possible] experience. . . . When [a philosopher] says: "this tree doesn't exist when nobody sees it," this might mean "this tree vanishes [i.e., is never seen again] when we turn our backs to it" (BB, pp. 56–57).

In the *Investigations* he puts the matter as follows:

For *this* is what disputes between Idealists, Solipsists and Realists look like. The one party attack the normal form of expression as if they were attacking a statement [of fact]; the others defend it, as if they were stating facts recognized by every reasonable human being (PI, §402).

In both of these passages Wittgenstein represents the idealist as attacking the grammar of ordinary language (e.g., "The money is locked in the safe") but doing so indirectly and misleadingly by employing the material mode ("The money doesn't exist when nobody sees it").

This is a point that deserves particular attention. Wittgenstein is here representing the idealist as a philosopher who, unlike Berkeley, has failed to realize that the form of a proposition is irrelevant to its meaning (or sense). Accordingly, Wittgenstein depicts the idealist as one who thinks that the present indicative mood of such a sentence as "The money is locked in the safe" disqualifies it from possibly being true. Commenting on a similar case, Wittgenstein says:

When as in this case, we disapprove of the expressions of ordinary language (which are after all performing their office), we have got a picture in our heads which conflicts with the picture of our ordinary way of speaking. Whereas we are tempted to say that our way of speaking does not describe the facts as they really are. . . . As if the form of expression were saying something false even when the proposition *faute de mieux* asserted something true (PI, §402).

These remarks are meant to bring out the oddity of the idea that the grammar of our ordinary propositions renders them somehow unfit. For the statement that the money is locked in the safe could hardly be untrue unless the money is *not* in the safe. And this means that the money I put into the safe *is* in the safe unless, for example, someone removed it. Pointing this out to the idealist will not relieve his dissatisfaction, as Wittgenstein readily acknowledges:

> If, for instance, you ask, "Does the box still exist when I'm not looking at it?," the only right answer would be "Of course, unless someone has taken it away or destroyed it." Naturally, a philosopher [an idealist] would be dissatisfied with this answer, but it would quite rightly reduce his way of formulating the question [i.e., in the material mode] *ad absurdum* (PR, p. 88).

Why will a philosopher remain dissatisfied? Because he will be left with the question: How *can* one say that the money *is* in the safe, i.e., that it presently exists unperceived, when money is nothing but sense-impressions, which *cannot* exist unperceived?

Wittgenstein's answer is to say that in cases of this kind the present indicative mood of our sentences is misleading and inessential, for what we really mean can be brought out by means of a counterfactual conditional:

> We can actually *transform* a statement about a pencil into a statement about appearances of a pencil – even when no one is there: "If someone *were* there, he would see ... etc.' One is often tempted: always to use the picture of someone seeing the pencil and then to talk of "a pencil somewhere else" as a pencil seen by someone (LSD, p. 28).

This is clearly a comment on Berkeley's remark: "The table I write on I say exists, that is, I see and feel it: and if I were out of my study I should say it existed; meaning thereby that if I was in my study I might perceive it, or that some other spirit actually does perceive it" (*Principles*, I, 3).[9] Wittgenstein is agreeing with the analysis Berkeley first offers ("If I were there, I would see it") and is rejecting the second of Berkeley's suggestions, namely, that when we speak of something which *we* don't perceive, we mean that "some other spirit" does.[10]

To identify more precisely the point of Wittgenstein's "transformation," it will be useful to consider a passage from The Blue Book. Having remarked that a philosopher who finds something "queer about the grammar of our words" may (misleadingly) express his discontent in the material mode by declaring, "This tree doesn't exist when nobody sees it" (BB, pp. 56–57), Wittgenstein goes on to comment as follows:

> I shall try to elucidate the problem discussed by realists, idealists, and solipsists by showing you a problem closely related to it. It is this: "Can we have unconscious thoughts, unconscious feelings, etc.?" The idea of there being unconscious thoughts has revolted many people. Others again have said that these [people] were wrong in supposing that there could only be conscious thoughts, and that psychoanalysis had discovered unconscious ones. The objectors to unconscious thoughts did not see that they were not objecting to the newly discovered psychological reactions, but to the way in which they were described. The psychoanalysts on the other hand were misled by their own way of expression into thinking that they had done more than discover new psycho-

logical reactions; that they had, in a sense, discovered conscious thoughts that were unconscious. The first could have stated their objection by saying "We don't wish to use the phrase 'unconscious thoughts'; we wish to reserve the word 'thought' for what you call 'conscious thoughts'." They state their case wrongly when they say: "There can only be conscious thoughts and no unconscious ones." For if they don't wish to talk of "unconscious thought" they should not use the phrase "conscious thought," either (BB, pp. 57–58).

To see how Wittgenstein intends this to illuminate the dispute between realists and idealists, we need to work out his intended parallels.

Plainly the phrase "unconscious thoughts" is introduced here as the analogue for those 'forms of words' which idealists attack and realists defend, e.g., "There is money locked in this safe." Further, we are meant to think that the realist is like those psychoanalysts who imagine that they have discovered something more than the observable behavioral reactions of their patients, who think that unconscious thoughts are "conscious thoughts that are unconscious." The realist, then, in defending the grammatical form of such sentences, is portrayed by Wittgenstein as guilty of an absurdity, namely, the absurdity of thinking that there is *more* to the money in the safe than the sense-impressions someone had before it was locked away and will have once the safe is opened.[11] The idealist, on the other hand, is portrayed as wanting (quite rightly) to oppose this absurdity but as opposing it in the wrong way, namely, by stating his objection in the material mode. What the idealist *ought* to say, according to Wittgenstein, is (i) that our normal form of expression is misleading and (ii) that the sentence "There is money locked in this safe" is to be construed, not as the realist does, but as meaning "If one *were* to open the safe, one *would* see. . . ." This, then, is the point of Wittgenstein's "transformation." It is meant to show what we are really saying when we say that there is money locked in the safe.

Here, then, we have an example of Wittgenstein's new philosophical method. In his Methodological Reassessment he says he can separate "what is essential from what is inessential in *our* language" by describing "the class of languages which serve their purpose," i.e., which have the *same use*. In the present case he proposes to settle the issue between realists and idealists, not by analyzing "There's money locked in the safe" into elementary propositions, but by declaring that this sentence has the *same use* as the counterfactual sentence "If you were to open the safe, you would see money." His aim is to show that ordinary language does not contain forms of words that refer to unperceived entities. What are we to think of this?

An Evaluation of Wittgenstein's New Method

At first sight it may seem as though there is nothing peculiar in Wittgenstein's 'transformation,' for there are situations in which we use counterfactual conditionals in a way that may sound like what Wittgenstein is suggesting. For instance, on a dark night I might say to someone: "If there were more light, you could see the boat dock." Or I might say to someone who is eager to see a certain painting, "If you had gone to The Walker Art Center today, you would have seen it." In both these cases we have a counterfactual conditional with the verb "to see" in the second clause. So Wittgenstein's 'transformation,' considered simply as a sentence, has nothing odd about it. And yet if we consider more carefully the cases in which we say such things, we find that they do not give us what Wittgenstein wants, for the whole point of his 'transformation' is to eliminate the present indicative verb in such sentences as "My desk is in my study" or "There is some money locked in this safe," but no such elimination occurs in the foregoing examples, for in the first of them I might add, pointing into the darkness, "It [the dock] is down there at the end of the path," and in the second I might add, "It [the painting] is hanging in the north gallery." Here the present indicative is retained. A phenomenalist, no doubt, would reply that these 'categorical propositions,' e.g., "It [the dock] is down there at the end of path," need to be recast as counterfactuals. But anyone with an ear for dialogue will find this absurd. When I say, "It's down there at the end of the path," I say this to explain my first remark, that if there were more light you could see it. Similarly, when, in the second example, I say, "It [the painting] is hanging in the north gallery," I say this as an explanation of my remark that if you had gone to the Walker today, you would have seen the painting. (One might say that if, in ordinary dialogue, one form of words explains another, it is the categorical form that explains the counterfactual form, not the other way about, as phenomenalists would have it.) And if we were to try to recast my categorical remarks in these examples into counterfactual form, it is not at all clear what they could mean, what role they could play in an actual piece of dialogue. They certainly could no longer play their normal explanatory role. The recasting would make them merely redundant, so that the dialogue would appear utterly wacky.[12]

So contrary to what one might at first think, what we say in such cases in the counterfactual form (or subjunctive mood) is *not* what Wittgenstein had in mind for his transformation. When phenomenalists propose the transformation "If you were in my study, you would see . . . ," we mustn't think that this could be expanded with the explanation, "for that is where I now keep my desk." What Wittgenstein and Berkeley had in mind, in fact, is something more like what we find in examples of a very different sort. I am thinking of the way in which we talk about such things as afterimages and double images (seeing double). We might tell someone who is just learning about afterimages: "If you look at a light bulb and then close your eyes, you will see a green afterimage."

In this case we are telling someone that a certain thing will happen if he looks at a light bulb and then closes his eyes. We are telling him how to *produce* an after image. And if he tries and fails and suggests that we've been kidding him, we might say to him: "If you'd looked at the light bulb longer, you would have seen an afterimage. Try again." This counterfactual is more the sort of thing Wittgenstein had in mind, for in this case, unlike that of the painting at the Walker, we would *not* go on to suggest that an afterimage was there all along. A similar example is that in which we explain to someone: "If you press on your eyeball, you will see a double image of this pencil." Here I am telling someone how to produce a double image. And if we told someone, using a counterfactual form, "If *your* eyeball were displaced, you too would see a double image," we would not be explaining a way for him to get to see something that is already there to be seen. In this respect these two counterfactuals resemble the sort of counterfactual Wittgenstein wanted for his transformation.

Wittgenstein, as I said, is maintaining that a counterfactual form of words shows *what* we are saying when we say such a thing as "There's money locked in that safe." His account may sound plausible until we bethink ourselves that when we do say something like "If there were more light, you could see the boat dock," we stand prepared to add, by way of explanation, "It's right down there at the end of the path." Wittgenstein, of course, can't allow this in his 'transformation.' *His* conditional has to be construed on analogy with saying, "If your eyeball were displaced, you would see a double image," for in this case we are explaining how a double image is produced and not explaining a means by which you can see something that is already there to be seen. But just because we must construe Wittgenstein's conditional in this way, it loses whatever plausibility it may seem to have had prior to our realizing how we are meant to take it.

Along with Berkeley, Wittgenstein has invented, as we might put it, a bastard form of conditional by conflating the two types of examples mentioned above. From the one sort of example he takes the word "desk" (or "money," etc.) and from the other he borrows the fact that we are not speaking of something that is already there to be seen.[13] The result, he thinks, brings out the meaning of – preserves what is essential in – what we say when we say, "There is money locked in this safe." Why does he think this? The answer is that he thinks we *must* mean this if we aren't talking nonsense. Another philosopher might have said: In truth we *are* saying something nonsensical in these cases, for we *should* mean (but don't mean) what the bastard conditional means. Wittgenstein rejected this attitude, saying: "How strange if logic were concerned with an 'ideal' language and not with *ours*. . . . (It would be odd if the human race had been speaking all this time without ever putting together a genuine proposition.)" (PR, p. 52). For Wittgenstein the problem is that there is much in what we commonly say that *looks* like nonsense to an empiricist, as when we say that there is money locked in the safe. And yet, it is hard to swallow the conclusion that people have seldom, if ever, actually *said* anything because the grammatical form of their sentences renders them nonsensical.

Let us try to reconstruct how Wittgenstein might have thought about this issue. I imagine that he might have put it to himself somewhat as follows:

The situation, at the very least, is that people go about their lives in a more or less successful way. They are faced with numerous practical matters which they deal with in a fashion that lets life continue. And in the course of this they make sounds with their mouths and make marks on paper.[14] Sometimes they hum tunes as they work, but the sounds we call "language" are not merely incidental to their lives in the way that humming is incidental to the carpenter's sawing. For a person who can speak can *get something accomplished* by making sounds. For example, if he is hungry, he can go to a place that serves food and, by making certain sounds, get the server to produce before him the food he wants to eat. In this, and in hundreds of other ways, making sounds or marks plays a vital role in human life. So isn't there something odd in declaring that all these people who use sounds and marks in ways that are essential to their lives are not really *saying* anything – that they are not, for example, *ordering food* when they utter the sentence "Two fried eggs, please, and a cup of coffee"? Indeed, what would ordering food *be* if not what people have been doing all along? Surely, then, it is the height of absurdity to declare that ordinary language is mostly nonsense! The *most* one can say is that much of ordinary language *looks* like nonsense, that it contains forms of words that *suggest* something nonsensical. But the right conclusion to draw here is that these apparently nonsensical forms of words are perfectly meaningful. And that being so, we must also conclude that what makes a form of words meaningful is its function in people's lives. What counts is the *use* that is made of a sentence. And yet we must be able to show that those forms of words that *appear* nonsensical do not mean what they appear to mean. We must be able to show, for example, that "There is money locked in this safe" does not express an irreducibly present indicative proposition, for if it did so, it would be as nonsensical as asking "Where is your headache, now that it's gone?" The point is that people can *say* something by using this apparently nonsensical form of words: they can direct someone to where he will find some money. That alone is what matters in language. And so our motto should be: "Look at sentences as instruments and at their sense as their employment" (see PI, §421).

It was reasoning of this sort, I suggest, that led Wittgenstein to embrace Berkeley's "use" theory of meaning.

What this theory says, in effect, is this: Don't pay attention to the grammar of sentences that appear to conflict with neutral monism; pay attention, instead, to their *use*, i.e., to the role they play in our activities. Accordingly, he complained: "If I had to say what is the main mistake made by philosophers of the present generation, including Moore, I would say that it is that when language is looked at, what is looked at is a form of words and not the use made of the form of words" (LC, p. 2). What we are meant to discover by looking at the 'use' of words is that problematical sentences do *not* mention 'unobservable' entities (or states). And if we concede this, we will, according to Wittgenstein, be conceding that the problem sentences can be reconciled with his neutral monism – conceding, that is, that those sentences refer only to sense-data. But this conclusion of his begs a very large question. For one could hold that when we say, e.g., "The pot boiled over while no one was watching," we are speaking neither of sense-data (as Wittgenstein thought) nor of something unobservable on the far side of sense-data (as Russell and Moore thought). To do so, of course, one would have to dismiss entirely the idea of sense-impressions, and this is an option Wittgenstein never considered. Because it never dawned on him that he might have gotten off on entirely the wrong foot by accepting un-critically the idea of sense-impressions, he became caught up in a false dilemma, namely, either we are speaking nonsense whenever we say things that conflict with phenomenalism or much of what we say is said in misleading forms of words, in which case we don't mean what we appear to mean. His new philosophical method, then, is a way of embra-cing the second of these alternatives. In 1915 he had written, using Russell's terminology: "My method is not to sift the hard from the soft, but to see the hardness of the soft" (NB, p. 44). This comes to: My method, unlike Russell's, is not to determine *which* of our ordinary propositions can be reconciled with empiricism, but to show that they can *all* be reconciled. In his later years this remained, in outline, his method. What changed were only the details.

Bringing Words Back to Their Everyday Use

In the *Investigations* Wittgenstein says: "What *we* do is to bring words back from their metaphysical to their everyday use" (PI, §116). From the example we have been considering, we can see that what he re-garded as the "everyday use" was instead an empiricist's version of the everyday use.[15] This is why we also find him saying, in 1940: "Sometimes an expression has to be withdrawn from language, in order to disinfect it, and then it can be put back into circulation" (CV, p. 39). In Chapter

5 we saw an example of this in Wittgenstein's treatment of the pronoun "I": rather than taking an unbiased look at the matter, he offers an account of the use of this word that he can reconcile with his empiricism. Another example of his 'disinfecting' words is found in his discussion of the word "can't" in "An iron nail can't scratch glass." Being an empiricist, he regarded it as a muddle to think that there are necessities or impossibilities in nature (see Chapter 12, this volume), and so he declared that "we could write this [sentence] in the form 'experience teaches that an iron nail *doesn't* scratch glass,' thus doing away with the 'can't'" (BB, p. 49). In this chapter we have found an additional example of such disinfecting: because of its present indicative verb, he 'transforms' such a sentence as "There is money locked in the safe" into a peculiar counterfactual conditional. We find him offering a similar transformation when, in a discussion of what it is to *expect* someone to come (although his coming doesn't occupy our thoughts), he says: "Here 'I am expecting him' would mean 'I should be surprised if he didn't come'" (PI, §577). By means of this transformation (or substitution) Wittgenstein means to convince us (see Chapter 17, this volume) that the sentence "I am expecting him" is a misleading form of words because it makes expectation look like a (nonphenomenal) *state*.

What can we learn from the way in which Wittgenstein proceeds in these cases? In the *Investigations* he says: "Philosophy may in no way impugn [*antasten*] the actual use of language; it can in the end only describe it" (PI, §124). But this is not what Wittgenstein does, as he himself elsewhere acknowledges. In a passage written in the late 1940s, one that echoes his Methodological Reassessment in *Philosophical Remarks*, he says: "How far do we investigate the use of words? – Don't we also judge it? Don't we also say that this feature is essential, that one inessential?" (RPP, I, §666). As we have seen, his way of determining what is 'inessential' is to consider whether some feature of language – some 'form of words' – conflicts with his empiricist ontology. This, then, is one part of his new philosophical method. The other part is to avoid impugning as nonsense the 'inessential feature' – the 'misleading form of words' by declaring, with Berkeley, that grammar is arbitrary and that words are instruments. This second part of his method could not, of course, come into play without the first part, for only by means of the first part can one pick out the (allegedly) 'misleading forms of words.' One can employ Wittgenstein's method, then, only if one is has accepted his ontology.

Notes

1. M. O'C. Drury, "Conversations with Wittgenstein," op. cit., p. 110.
2. "Wittgenstein's Lectures in 1930–1933," op. cit., p. 322.

3. In a conversation with Waismann that is contemporaneous with his Methodological Reassessment, he explained that when he speaks of wheels that turn idly in our language, he is speaking of words or phrases in our language that lack "a phenomenological meaning" (WVC, p. 65).
4. Augustine and Leibniz had invoked the theory in particular cases but had not advanced it as a general theory of meaning. Following Berkeley, Thomas Reid invoked the theory in his defense of "common sense" against Hume.
5. *Principles*, Part I, Secs. 51 and 52.
6. Ibid., Introduction, Sec. 20.
7. Locke had maintained that "the chief end of language" is that "men learn names, and use them in talk with others, only that they may be understood: which is then only done when by use or consent the sound I make by the organs of speech excites in another man's mind who hears it, the idea I apply it to in mine when I speak it" (*An Essay Concerning Human Understanding*, III, iii, 3).
8. In lectures Wittgenstein said: "The point of examining the way a word is used is not at all to provide another method of giving its meaning. When we ask on what occasions people use a word . . . and in reply try to describe its use, we do so only insofar as it seems helpful in getting rid of certain philosophical troubles" (WL35, p. 97).
9. Berkeley, in a later section (§45), imagines the following objection being raised by someone who has not grasped his explanation of "exist":

> . . . it will be objected that from the foregoing principles it follows [that] things are every moment annihilated and created anew. The objects of sense exist only when they are perceived: the trees therefore are in the garden, or the chairs in the parlour, no longer than while there is somebody by to perceive them. Upon shutting my eyes all the furniture in the room is reduced to nothing, and barely upon opening them it is again created.

In reply to this objection Berkeley refers his reader back to the passage quoted above, in which he explains that if he were out of his study he would say that his table exists, *meaning* thereby that if he were in his study he would perceive it. Berkeley's point is that no one would raise the above objection if they were mindful of the actual *meaning* of the word "exist." Wittgenstein, in his conversations with Waismann, also addressed the above objection, which he states as follows: "If I turn away the stove is gone. (Things do not exist during the intervals between perceptions.)" Wittgenstein's reply is: "If 'existence' is taken in the empirical (not in the metaphysical) sense, this statement [i.e., 'Things do not exist during the intervals between perceptions'] is a wheel turning idly. Our language is in order, once we have understood its syntax [e.g., understood that 'exists' requires Berkeley's counterfactual analysis] and recognized the wheels that turn idly" (WVC, p. 48). In the present case, the "wheel that turns idly," i.e. that *does not engage with experience*, is the metaphysical use of "exist" in the statement "The stove ceases to exist when I shut my eyes and is created anew when I open them." Wittgenstein distinguishes in this passage between the 'empirical' and the 'metaphysical' sense of "existence," and it is plain that he regarded the 'empirical sense,' which can be elucidated by a counterfactual analysis, as the everyday use of the word. That he retained this idea in later years is evidenced by the fact that in PI, §116 he includes "existence" ["*Sein*," which Anscombe translates as "being"] among the words of which he says: "What *we* do is to bring words back from their metaphysical to their everyday use."

10. In *Our Knowledge of the External World* (op. cit., p. 88) Russell proposes a counterfactual analysis like Berkeley's and then says: "If we are to avoid non-sensible objects, this [counterfactual analysis] must be taken as the whole of our meaning," adding: "I think it may be laid down quite generally that, *in so far as* physics and common sense is verifiable, it must be capable of interpretation in terms of actual sense-data alone." Russell is saying here: when the plain man says "The money is locked in the safe," all that can be *salvaged* from this is what can be captured in a counterfactual analysis, for the plain man actually means something different, namely, that the money exists in an occurrent sense of "exist" despite not being perceived. This is what Wittgenstein is opposing.

11. The point Wittgenstein was wanting to make here is the same that he makes by means of his "white rabbit" examples (WL35, p. 26 and WL32, p. 111).

12. Philosophers who are driven by theory and have no ear for language will find this to be no objection. They will insist that these ordinary categorical propositions *must* be recast as counterfactuals. At that point one would need to ask them about the metaphysical theory that has driven them to this view. We could then expect to be told that sense-data are what we really perceive and that sense-data cannot exist unperceived.

13. A passage Wittgenstein wrote in the late 1940s explains his attitude toward this procedure: "My difficulty is altogether like that of a man who is inventing a new calculus (say the differential calculus) and is looking for a symbolism" (RPP, I, §134). In his 1946–47 lectures he said: "I am doing a sort of mathematics – mathematics at the stage that precedes calculation [i.e., at the stage when new concepts are introduced]. . . . I want to substitute a new sort of description – not that the old one is bad, but to remove misconceptions" (WL47, p. 68). This is his 'new method.'

14. Wittgenstein often characterized talking and writing in these ways. For example, we find him saying:

> . . . a criterion for people talking is that they make articulated noises. For instance, if you see me and Watson at the South Pole making noises at each other, everyone would say we were talking, not making music, etc.
>
> Similarly if I see a person with a piece of paper making marks in a certain sort of way, I may say, "He is calculating," and I expect him to use it in a certain way (LFM, p. 203).

15. This is what prompted Frank Ebersole to remark that Wittgenstein "does not – in truth – ever follow his own advice." *Meaning and Saying: Essays in the Philosophy of Language* (Washington, D.C.: University Press of America, 1979), p. ix. In one way Ebersole is right about this and in another not. Wittgenstein did not, it is true, bring words back to their everyday use, but then he understood his own 'advice' as an empiricist *would* understand it – and so, of course, he did follow his own advice.

9

Wittgenstein's Behaviorism

In the Preface of *Philosophical Investigations* Wittgenstein says that he wanted it published together with the *Tractatus* because his new thoughts "could be seen in the right light only by contrast with and against the background of my old way of thinking" (PI, p. x). Nowhere is this more relevant than in his later treatment of the problem of other minds: to understand his later thoughts, one must begin by seeing what he found defective in his earlier ones. In the *Tractatus* Wittgenstein did not discuss the problem of other minds, but we can nevertheless see that that book implicitly proposes a solution to the problem. To see what this solution is, we must begin by understanding the problem itself.

The Problem of Other Minds

The problem is about how, if at all, skepticism regarding the minds of others is to be overcome. That the problem should arise at all is owing to the plausibility of dualism, the idea that a person is comprised of a mind and a body. A dualist is obliged to think that when we speak of the thoughts and feelings of others we are making a leap – inferential or otherwise – from something we perceive (the body) to something we don't perceive (the other person's thoughts or feelings). This leads to the question: What grounds, if any, can be given for this leap? The argument from analogy seems to provide the only hope here: I notice that there is a correlation between the various states of my mind and the behavior of my body and then, upon noticing similar behavior in other bodies, I infer that the same correlation holds for them. This is the view taken by Berkeley:

It is evident that, when the mind perceives an idea not immediately and of itself, it must be by the means of some other idea. Thus, for instance, the passions which are in the mind of another are of themselves to me invisible. I may nevertheless perceive them by sight; though not immediately, yet by means of the colours they produce in the countenance. We often see shame or fear in the looks of a man, by perceiving the changes in his countenance to red or pale (*A New Theory of Vision*, §9).

Berkeley goes on to say that there is no "necessary connexion . . . between the redness of a blush and shame" (ibid., §23) and then explains the matter by saying that although shame and anger are themselves invisible; they are nevertheless let in by the eye along with colours and alterations of countenance which are the immediate object of vision, and which signify [the passions in another's mind] for no other reason than barely because they have been observed [in oneself] to accompany them. Without which experience we should no more have taken blushing for a sign of shame than of gladness (ibid., §65).

In the third dialogue between Hylas and Philonous Berkeley states the matter as follows:

It is granted that we have neither an immediate evidence nor a demonstrative knowledge of the existence of other finite spirits, but it will not thence follow that such spirits are on a foot with material substances . . . [for] we see signs and effects indicating distinct finite agents like ourselves, and see no sign or symptom whatever that leads to a rational belief [in the existence] of Matter.

Berkeley is saying: one knows what is in another's mind by means of *symptoms* of their mental states, and these symptoms have for us the significance they do because in our own case we have found them to be regularly accompanied by such-and-such mental states.

As examples of such symptoms Berkeley mentions blushing, but if he had expanded this point, he would, I assume, have come around, as philosophers always do, to talking about the "bodily behavior" we observing in others. This is the usual way of stating the argument from analogy, so that inferences to the minds of others are said to be based on the behavior of bodies. But it is essential to realize that this 'behavior' is *not* to be described by terms such as "blushing," "writhing," "wincing," "moaning," "laughing," "confessing," "arguing," and so on, for a description in terms such as these would beg the question of whether there is a mind engaged here. So the 'behavior' must be describable in the same terms in which we would describe something that does *not* think or feel. For this reason philosophers have introduced special terms, such as "bodily movements" or "colorless movements,"[1] as the general name for the 'behavior' in question, including making 'sounds' by means of the mouth. The problem for the dualist, then, is that of explaining how it would be possible to infer thoughts and feelings from bodily movements. He cannot, of course, regard the inference as deductive, since dualists would refuse to *define* mentalistic words in terms of bodily movements. (As Berkeley says, there is no *necessary* connection here.) So the dualist resorts to the argument from analogy, but that means he has but one case, his own, to serve as grounds for the inference. And that makes the grounds entirely insufficient. The dualist, therefore, has no way of dealing with skepticism about other minds. To avoid such skepticism, then, one must find a way of dismissing mind–body dualism. How is one to do that?

Behaviorism and the *Tractatus*

The usual solution has been to adopt a nondualistic ontology. This is what the behaviorist does. He dismisses Cartesian minds but retains Cartesian bodies and their movements and then proposes to define mentalistic words in terms of bodily movements. In this way he avoids the burden of having to show how it is possible to make inferences from observed bodily movements to unobservable thoughts and feelings in the minds of others. He may encounter other difficulties, but his ontology enables him to declare that the sort of skepticism that plagues the dualist is a pseudoproblem. This dismissal of skepticism would have made behaviorism attractive to Wittgenstein, for he had declared philosophical skepticism to be "obviously nonsensical" (TLP, 6.51). As we have already seen, however, to avoid skepticism regarding the 'external world,' Wittgenstein had opted for a reductionist account of material objects, and this left him with an ontology of sense-data. But sense-data, as typically conceived of, are themselves 'in the mind' and so would seem to be irreconcilable with behaviorism, which aims to eliminate things 'in the mind.'

We have already seen how Wittgenstein avoided this difficulty: he traveled from idealism to solipsism and finally to pure realism, i.e., neutral monism, which rejects the idea that sense-data are 'in the mind.' The ontology of the *Tractatus*, then, is nondualistic: it rejects both unknowable 'external' objects and 'inner' (or 'private') contents of the mind. This ontology enabled Wittgenstein to combine phenomenalism and behaviorism, i.e., to hold that the thoughts and feelings of others are definable in terms of their bodily behavior and that their bodies are definable in terms of sense-data.

This, then, was the solution offered in the *Tractatus*, and by taking this as our starting point we can discover the changes he introduced in his later years.

Behaviorism and Wittgenstein's Later Views

The first thing to be said is that he did not, in his later years, revert to some form of dualism and the argument from analogy (see BB, p. 24 and Z, §537). From that viewpoint bodily movements and mental states are only contingently connected, and Wittgenstein continued to hold that one could not, on such a view, account for knowledge of what others think and feel. Thus in his 1936 lectures he said:

On the one hand we are inclined to say that your behaviour is [for us] the only *clue* to whether you see or not.

On the other hand [we are] inclined to say: Whether you see or not is independent of [i.e., is not *necessarily* connected with] your behaviour.

I say there is a contradiction here.

Suppose you say, "The eye turns yellow when the liver is out of order." This we know from the correlation of two experiences. And here the clue is [logically] independent of the sense of the proposition "the liver is out of order." But we can say it is a clue because we have the correlation of the two experiences.

But in the other case we have not the two experiences to correlate. And if (a) the two are [logically] independent, and if (b) we have ex hypothesi no experience correlating them, how could we say one was a clue to the other?

In the case of a new disease, "flu," we might say "having flu is simply defined by his having fever etc." But in our [philosophical] case we say he might be blind and behave as if he were not blind. And you might say this shows that *seeing* and *behaving* are independent.

But this does not follow (LSD, pp. 12–13).

The point he makes here about seeing can be generalized: Wittgenstein continued to hold that knowledge of the 'mental' life of others requires that their 'mental' life have a noncontingent connection with behavior: the *sense* of the proposition "He is in pain" is not (logically) independent of what we regard as showing us that he is in pain. He makes the same point in the following passage:

"Of course the psychologist reports the words, the behaviour, of the subject, but surely only as signs of mental processes." That is correct. If the words and the behaviour are, for example, learned by heart, they do not interest the psychologist. And yet the expression "as signs of mental processes" is misleading, because we are accustomed to speak of the colour of the face as a sign of fever [where the fever can be discovered directly by feeling the person's brow]. And now each bad analogy gets explained by another bad one, so that in the end only weariness releases us from these ineptitudes (RPP, I, §292).

Here again Wittgenstein is rejecting the idea that in observing another's behavior we see only 'signs' – *symptoms* – that they are worried, in pain, angry, etc. But he would have rejected this also at the time of the *Tractatus*. So what changed in his view of this matter?

At the time of the *Tractatus* he would have said that the mentalistic terms of ordinary language are *defined* in terms of bodily behavior. This means that the rules governing mentalistic terms specify both necessary and sufficient conditions for their use and that therefore I can never be in doubt whether someone is worried or in pain if I have closely observed his bodily movements. There are two parts to the *Tractatus* view. One is the idea that to know that someone is angry or in pain we need to know only about his behavior (bodily movements). The second part is that in our language there are rules laid down which specify the necessary and sufficient conditions for someone's being angry or afraid, etc., so that the behaviorism of the *Tractatus* is what we might call "analytic behaviorism." In his later years Wittgenstein criticized both these ideas.

His criticism of the first part of the *Tractatus* view comes out in a remark he made in his 1930 lectures:

Behaviourism must be able to distinguish between real toothache and simulated toothache, between a man who is pretending to have toothache and a man who really has it. If I see you reading I can only say that you have certain symbols before you and do something. But I must be able to distinguish between reading and not reading (WL32, p. 46).

It is of greatest significance that Wittgenstein says here that *behaviorism* must distinguish between such cases, for this makes it plain that he thought of himself as simply modifying (or improving) behaviorism. A modification is needed, he thought, for if being in pain just *is* behaving in such-and-such a way, then behaviorism is committed to the absurdity that an actor who acts the part of a man with toothache *is* in pain. To avoid this absurdity, Wittgenstein adopted the view that bodily behavior is not *by itself* a sufficient condition for a person's being in pain (or being angry or sad, etc.), for we must also take into account the *circumstances* of the behavior – whether, for example, he is pretending to be in pain so as to avoid an unpleasant chore.

Wittgenstein makes this explicit when he says: "If someone behaves in such-and-such a way *under such-and-such circumstances*, we say that he is sad" (Z, §526). He also says: "I observe pain in another man if I watch his behaviour, e.g. holding his cheek and groaning *in certain circumstances*" (WL47, p. 35). I have italicized the phrases in these quotations that distinguish Wittgenstein's later view from his earlier one.

There are various ways he drives home this point against the *Tractatus* version of behaviorism. For instance, he writes:

"But you will surely admit that there is a difference between pain-behaviour with pain and pain-behaviour without pain?" Admit it? What greater difference could there be? (PI, §304).[2]

The difference Wittgenstein allows here is not the sort of difference a dualist would allow but only a difference in the circumstances surrounding the pain-behavior, a difference he had failed to allow for in the *Tractatus*. Accordingly, when making this same point in lectures he said: " 'Toothache is not a behaviour' – this is a grammatical sentence" (LSD, p. 10), meaning that Tractarian behaviorism, which defines "toothache" in terms of behavior *alone*, gives the wrong account of the grammar of that word. He is saying: I will agree that toothache is not *just* behavior if you will agree that the 'something more' that's relevant to the distinction we make in saying "He isn't pretending; he's really in pain" is only a matter of the circumstances surrounding the behavior, i.e., if you will agree that this distinction does not depend on there being, in the case of another person's genuine pain, something *behind* his behavior. Wittgenstein makes this explicit when he writes:

"But aren't you saying that all that happens is that he moans, and that there is nothing behind it?" I am saying that there is nothing *behind* the moaning (NFL, p. 302).

In his notes Wittgenstein said, in opposition to Tractarian behaviorism, that we get the function of our concepts wrong "if we say that the genuine expression [of pain, etc.] is a particular behaviour and nothing besides," but he added, in opposition to the dualist, that it is "misleading to describe the genuine expression [of pain, etc.] as a *sum* of the expression and something else" (NFL, p. 303). These two remarks come to this: while there is a difference between genuine pain behavior and shamming (or acting), it does not consist in there being something *behind* the genuine behavior; rather, in the one case the man who moans goes off to the dentist (or takes an aspirin), while in the other the man is an actor on stage and exhibits no pain behavior once the curtain falls.

I said above that the change that came about in Wittgenstein's thinking involved two parts. The second part can be identified by considering the question: Did Wittgenstein come to think that one can *deduce* that another is in pain from a description of his behavior together with an account of his circumstances? The answer is that this was *not* what he thought. In his later years, although he speaks of there being *criteria* for applying such terms as "toothache" and "angry" to other people, he explicitly denies that such terms are used "according to strict rules" (BB, p. 25). As we saw in Chapter 7, Wittgenstein had decided in the 1930s that propositions about 'material objects' are related to reality in a "looser" way than he had earlier supposed, and he adopted the same view of propositions about the thoughts and feelings of others. [In the *Investigations* (p. 180) he explicitly compares the two cases.] This is his point in The Blue Book where, in the course of discussing "He has toothache," Wittgenstein says that "in general we don't use language according to strict rules – it hasn't been taught us by means of strict rules, either." He adds: "We are unable clearly to circumscribe the concepts we use; not because we don't know their real definition, but because there is no real 'definition' to them" (BB, p. 25; see also Z, §§439–440). These remarks are aimed at the analytic aspect of Tractarian behaviorism, and his point is that a truth-functional analysis of "She has toothache" will not do. So although he continued to think that the connection that holds between another's having a toothache and her behavior (and circumstances) is not *contingent*, he came to think that it is not *analytic*. He explicitly dismissed the idea that our ordinary concepts of "pain," "sadness," etc. are comprised, in part, of a list of circumstances such that if certain behavior occurs in one or another of them, it then *follows deductively* that the person is in pain, is sad, or whatever. He declared it a mistake to think that there could be such a list – a *logically definitive* list – of circumstances (Z, §440 and LW, I, §§966–973). He states this point by saying that our language game employs "elastic," rather than "rigid," concepts (LW, I, §246).

Wittgenstein was making this same point against analytical behaviorism when he wrote:

I can be as *certain* of someone else's sensations as of any fact. But this does not make the propositions "He is much depressed," "25 × 25 = 625" and "I am sixty years old" into similar instruments. The explanation suggests itself that the certainty is of a different *kind*. This seems to point to a psychological difference. But the difference is logical (PI, p. 224).

This comes to: Although I can be as certain that another is in pain as that I am sixty years old, this doesn't mean that "He's in pain" can be *deduced* from a description of the other person's behavior and circumstances as "I'm sixty" could be *deduced* by someone who knows both today's date and the date of my birth. Wittgenstein also says: "I can't give criteria which put the presence of the sensation beyond doubt; that is to say: there are no such criteria" (RPP, I, §137).

Why are there no such criteria? He is explaining this point when he remarks that "one human being can be a complete enigma to another," adding that this is what we find when we "come into a strange country with entirely strange traditions" (PI, p. 223). This example plays the same role in his thinking as that of his 'disappearing chair' (PI, §80), namely, to show that our language is "not everywhere bounded by rules" (PI, §84). This is not a concession to skepticism, but a way of saying that skepticism ignores the fact that the language game of attributing thoughts, emotions, sensations, etc. to other people can be played *despite* the fact that analytic behaviorism is misguided.

Why did Wittgenstein think that this behavioristic 'language game' *can* be played? On this point he declared that language rests on instinct, rather than reasoning, and to illustrate this he says: "Being sure that someone is in pain, doubting whether he is, and so on, are so many natural, instinctive, kinds of behaviour towards other human beings, and our language is merely an auxiliary to, and further extension of, this relation. Our language-game is an extension of primitive behaviour" (Z, §545). This amounts to saying: Strange though it may seem, this is what we do. I will not pursue this aspect of Wittgenstein's thinking, for it should be evident that prior to giving this sort of explanation he had already taken several wrong turns.

A Possible Misunderstanding

As a first attempt at understanding Wittgenstein's later version of behaviorism, let us consider whether it could be summarized as follows.

In order rightly to say that a person is in pain, we must take into account something more than his or her behavior, namely, the circumstances (or context) of the behavior. It is one thing if the person is an actor playing the part of a man with toothache and who exhibits no pain behavior when off stage. In that situation his pain behavior will elicit no pity for him. It is quite another thing if the person has been hit by a car and now lies groaning and writhing on the ground. Even here, of course, we may be in doubt if the collision was not very great or we know that this man has committed insurance fraud. But these are special circumstances. If it were a child that was hit and now lies groaning and holding his head, we would surely not be in doubt about its suffering. And in fact many cases are like this: we see a person exhibiting pain behavior and are in no doubt that he's in pain.

Does this summary provide an accurate account of Wittgenstein's thinking? While it points in the right direction, this summary is highly misleading, for it fails to make clear that Wittgenstein was merely proposing a modified version of behaviorism, i.e., that he retained Cartesian 'bodies' and their 'behavior.' That he intended merely to modify (or improve on) behaviorism comes out in his remark about the need for *behaviorism* to allow for cases of pretending, and it comes out in many other ways as well.

The most obvious point to be made here is that we already know that Wittgenstein was a phenomenalist, i.e., that his 'pure realism' is an ontology in which there is nothing over and above (or beyond) sense-data. Accordingly, when he speaks of other people, he understands himself to bespeaking of what we might call "sense-data people."[3] Now sense-data, plainly enough, are *not* the sort of thing that have, as it were, unperceived dimensions, that could have more to them than is given in experience. But that means that when Wittgenstein speaks of 'other people' *what* he is speaking of are nothing more than is given in experience. So there *can* be nothing more (ontologically) than the observed 'behavior' of these sense-data people. This he makes plain in many ways, as when he says (see above) that "there is nothing *behind* the moaning." This is what the foregoing summary fails to make clear.

To see that my proposed summary of Wittgenstein's mature view is misleading, we need to see that he remained a behaviorist. One way to do so is to notice how he used the word "body." Another is to notice how he used (and explained) the term "behavior." Let us take these in order.

Wittgenstein's Metaphysical Use of "Body"

A number of passages in the *Investigations* make it plain that Wittgenstein dealt with the mind–body problem by subtracting from dualism that queer entity, the Cartesian mind, and by uncritically retaining that other queer entity, the Cartesian body.[4] Thus, we find him saying: "Only of what behaves like a human being can one say that it *has* pains. For one has to say it of a body, or, if you like, of a soul which some body *has*. And how can a body *have* a soul?" (PI, §283). He continues:

But isn't it absurd to say of a *body* that it has pain? And why does one feel an absurdity in that? In what sense is it true that my hand does not feel pain, but I in my hand?

What sort of issue is: Is it the *body* that feels pain? How is it to be decided? What makes it plausible to say that it is *not* the body? Well, something like this: if someone has a pain in his hand, then the hand does not say so (unless it writes it) and one does not comfort the hand, but the sufferer: one looks into his face (PI, §286).

So Wittgenstein is maintaining that when we say, for example, "She is in great pain," we are saying this of a *body* although not of a *part* of the body. This comes out most clearly when he entertains the question "Can a human *body* have pain?" and comments that we are inclined to think that by looking into the nature of pain we can see that "it lies in its nature that a material object can't have it" (BB, p. 73). To combat this idea he declares that

We can perfectly well adopt the expression "this body feels pain" [in place of "She is in pain"], and we shall then, just as usual, tell it to go to the doctor, to lie down, and even to remember that the last time it had pains they were over in a day (ibid.).

This is an example of Wittgenstein employing his new method: substituting for an "ordinary form of expression" some other form of words which he deemed to be less misleading. In the present case his point is that when we say, "She is in great pain," what we refer to by "she" is a *body*.

He does not, of course, think that just *any* body will do, not even just any *human* body. He remarks:

One says to oneself: How could one so much as get the idea of ascribing a *sensation* to a *thing*? One might as well ascribe it to a number! And now look at a wriggling fly and at once those difficulties vanish and pain seems able to get a foothold here, where before [when thinking of a stone] everything was, so to speak, too smooth for it.

And so, too, a corpse seems to us inaccessible to pain. Our attitude to what is alive and to what is dead, is not the same. All our reactions are different. If anyone says: "That cannot simply come from the fact that a living thing moves about in such-and-such a way and a dead one not," then I want to intimate to him that this is a case of the transition 'from quantity to quality' (PI, §284).

This last remark comes to: The attitude we take towards living things is not an attitude we would take towards something like a wind-up toy, which behaves *somewhat* like a person or an animal; for such attitudes – e.g., pity – are prompted in us only by something that exhibits the *full range* of human (or animal) behavior (see RPP, II, §§622–629). And Wittgenstein regards this as being simply a fact about *us* (see Z, §§537–545 and also Z, §§378–388, and §§528–529). So he thinks that we simply react instinctively to bodies that move about in certain ways and that make certain sounds. Accordingly, he can say: "If one sees the behaviour of a living being, one sees its soul" (PI, §357), and also: "The human body is the best picture of the human soul" (PI, p. 178). We also find him saying that when a person makes a decision, he "says something [and his body acts accordingly" (WL47, p. 36). It never dawned on Wittgenstein that the 'bodies' he is here alluding to are *just* as peculiar as those Cartesian 'minds' he denounces as a muddle and that therefore behaviorism, too, is a muddle.

Wittgenstein's Metaphysical Use of "Behavior"

Let us turn now to the question of what Wittgenstein means by "behavior." I said above that someone who approaches the problem of other minds from the direction Wittgenstein did must be careful about how he uses the word "behavior": he must not count as behavior such familiar things as smiling, frowning, crying, moaning, arguing, and so on, for to speak *as we normally do* of someone smiling, frowning, etc. would beg the philosophical question whether what we are speaking of is a living person with a 'mental life.' (A skeptic could say: *if* I had to grant that I observe people laughing, crying, talking, and so on, then of course I would grant that they have a mental life like my own, but I will *not* grant that I observe people laughing, crying, etc.) Rather, a philosopher who approaches the problem as Wittgenstein did must, when he uses the term "behavior," mean something highly metaphysical, something pertaining to the 'bodies' that remain when behaviorists dismiss Cartesian 'minds.' As noted earlier, philosophers have introduced a special, metaphysical, term to denominate this 'behavior' – the term "bodily movements." Wittgenstein, unfortunately, was not rigorous in sticking to this terminology. He often used familiar words, such as "moaning" and, for a more general term, "behavior." Yet I think there can be no question but that he used such words to mean what other behaviorists have meant by "bodily movements," namely, something pertaining to (Cartesian) 'bodies.' For instance, he used the phrase "bodily behaviour" (BB, p. 53) and did so precisely to emphasize that he was speaking of a 'body.' He also used "movement" in this way, as when he says that writing is "a voluntary movement" (Z, §586) and when he asks: "What makes [a child's] movements in play into voluntary movements?" (Z, §587). Occasionally he put matters in a plainly behaviorist fashion, as when he said:

This much is certain: He can predict some of his bodily movements [*Bewegungen seines Korpers*] that I can't. And if I do predict his actions I do so in a different way (LW, I, §232).

Voluntary movements are certain movements with their normal *surroundings* of intention, learning, trying, acting. Movements, of which it makes sense to say that they are sometimes voluntary, sometimes involuntary, are movements in a special surrounding (RPP, I, §776; cf. Z, §577).

Had Wittgenstein consistently employ the behavioristic terms "bodily behavior" and "movements," he might have spared his readers considerable misunderstanding. Instead, when discussing the problem of other minds, he took the liberty of using ordinary words, such as "moan" and "cry out," while thinking that moaning and crying out are *bodily behavior*.

It might seem that in doing this he is cheating, begging the philosophical question. It might seem, that is, that a philosophical skeptic would be within his rights to reply to Wittgenstein: If I were to grant you that we observe others crying and moaning, then I'd have to agree that there is no room for skepticism here, but I do *not* grant this, for I can observe nothing but another's bodily movements. But Wittgenstein would be vulnerable to such a reply only if he were not prepared to offer a reductionist account of such familiar words as "moaning" and "crying out" – and, of course, a reductionist account of the term "behavior" when used as a more general term for moaning, crying out, talking, etc. Wittgenstein was aware of this and accordingly offered the required reductionist account:

... the word "behaviour," as I am using it, is altogether misleading, for it includes in its meaning the external circumstances – of the behaviour in a narrower sense (RPP, I, §314).

This passage is crucial for understanding Wittgenstein's philosophy of mind. For what he means here by "behaviour in a narrower sense" is "movements of a body," and he is saying that *generally* when he speaks of "behavior" (as when he speaks of "pain behavior") – and also when he speaks of "moaning," "crying," 'talking," and so on – he means to be speaking of bodily movements taken together with their circumstances.[5] So he is here conceding that when he uses the term "behavior" (or "moaning," "crying out," and so on), he is taking for granted his behavioristic solution to the problem of other minds.[6] In other words, he is saying here that, faced with the skeptic's reply that I formulated above, he would have to respond as follows: "I will grant that I may *seem* to be begging the question, but the fact of the matter is that when I speak of another person's pain behavior or of his moaning or talking, I stand ready to allow that these are nothing more than movements of a body together with certain sorts of circumstances." We can say, then, that Wittgenstein's use of such words as "behave," "cry," etc. does not beg the philosophical question, for he intends that these words should be understood in a special, behavioristic way. At the same time, however, we can say two other things. First, we can say that since, in our ordinary use of such words, we are *not* speaking metaphysically of 'bodies' and their 'movements,' Wittgenstein's appropriation of our vocabulary for his metaphysical purposes is highly misleading.[7] Second, we can say that in Wittgenstein's world there are no smiles or frowns, no crying or complaints, for there are only 'bodies' that move in various ways and make noises.[8]

Why did Wittgenstein use terms such as "behavior," "moaning," "laughing," "talking," and so on in a misleading way, i.e., in a way that fails to make explicit that his own understanding of such terms is thoroughly metaphysical? There are several points to bear in mind here. First of all, he had made up his mind, as we saw in Chapter 8, that it would be absurd for a philosopher to maintain that perhaps the things the plain man says are perfectly senseless. Accordingly, he proceeds on the premise that the proper job of philosophy is to make clear what plain men *are* saying when they say things that seem, on their face, to be philosophically insupportable. But because he also took it for granted that there is nothing dubious in the idea of sense impressions, and because he thought it impossible to defend any argument for the existence of 'transcendent entities,' he was obliged to undertake a reconciliation of ordinary language with a monistic ontology that equates reality with a world of sense impressions. And that, in turn, meant that, when he came to the things we say about other people, he was obliged to adopt a doubly reductionist view, i.e., a phenomenological version of behaviorism. He realized, of course, that this committed him to quite an extraordinary account of the plain man's meaning, but because he also accepted Berkeley's 'use' theory of meaning, he did not think that his doubly reductionist account credits plain men with a reasoned philosophical view (or analysis) of what they all regularly say. In this way, then, Wittgenstein could readily adopt Berkeley's slogan that philosophers "ought to think with the learned and speak with the vulgar."[9] And this is what he is doing in allowing himself to use such familiar words as "moaning," "crying out," "talking," etc., while at the same time thinking (with 'the learned') that these terms require a behavioristic explanation. In other words, although he allows himself to put matters in an extremely misleading way, his own philosophical principles made him believe he was doing what is only right. The next chapter will provide additional grounds for this interpretation.

Was Wittgenstein a Behaviorist in Disguise?

I quoted Wittgenstein above as saying that "there is nothing *behind* the moaning." Because he here allows himself to use the material mode of speech, we might think that he holds that other people are never *really* in pain, i.e., that other people are never *in fact* in pain (but only pretending). This would be a misunderstanding. Wittgenstein writes: "To say that others have no pain, presupposes [because it is in the material mode] that it makes sense to say they do have pains" (PR, p. 95). This is the point he is also making in the *Investigations* when he writes: "As if, for example, the proposition "he has pains" could be *false* in some other way than by the man's *not* having pains" (PI, §402, first emphasis added). He makes his meaning explicit when he says:

... I might seem to be denying that he has toothache. But I am not saying he really hasn't got it. Of course he has it: it isn't that he behaves as if he had it but really doesn't. For we have criteria for his really having it as against his simulating it (WL35, p. 17).

If someone had tried to state Wittgenstein's behaviorism in the material mode by saying that he thought the pains of other people are not real, he might have replied: No, they *are* real but only in the way that the pains of others *can* be real, namely, that they sometimes exhibit pain behavior without the surroundings of pretence behavior.

In the *Investigations* Wittgenstein imagines someone asking him: "Are you not really a behaviourist in disguise? Aren't you at bottom really saying that everything except human behaviour is a fiction?" He answers: "If I do speak of a fiction, then it is of a *grammatical* fiction" (PI, §307). What Wittgenstein regards as a 'grammatical fiction' is the dualist's interpretation of a word such as "thinking" or "toothache," for the dualist maintains that the thoughts and pains of others are entities of which one can have no first-hand knowledge. Why, then, does Wittgenstein dismiss the suggestion that he is a behaviorist? He does so because he here takes behaviorism to be a philosophical view that is stated in the material mode, one that tries to *say* something about the world. That is, he takes the behaviorist to be making the factual claim that there *are* no thoughts, feelings, images, etc., that thoughts and feelings and so on are *fictions* in the sense that unicorns are. This comes out in his remark: "Finitism and behaviourism are quite similar trends. Both say, but surely, all we have here is. . . . Both *deny the existence of something*, both with a view to escaping from a confusion" (RFM, p. 142, emphasis added).

Historically speaking, of course, Wittgenstein is right to characterize behaviorism in this way. The classical statement of behaviorism is J. B. Watson's *Behaviorism*, published in 1924, where we find the author saying:

... the behaviorist began his own formulation of the problem of psychology by sweeping aside all mediaeval conceptions. He dropped from his scientific vocabulary all subjective terms such as sensation, perception, image, desire, purpose, and even thinking and emotion as they were subjectively defined.

The behaviorist asks: why don't we make what we can *observe* the real field of psychology? . . . . Now what can we observe? We can observe *behavior - what the organism does or says*. And let us point out at once: that *saying* is doing - that is, *behaving*. Speaking overtly or to ourselves (thinking) is just as objective a type of behavior as baseball.[10]

... one is inclined to say: "Why, yes, it is worth while [sic] to study human behavior in this way, but the study of behavior is not the whole of psychology. It leaves out too much. Don't I have sensations, perceptions, conceptions? Do I not forget things and remember things, imagine things, have visual images and auditory images of things I once have seen and heard? ... Behaviorism is trying to rob us of everything we have believed in since earliest childhood."

Having been brought up on introspective psychology, as most of us have, you naturally ask these questions and you will find it hard to put away the old terminology and begin to formulate your psychological life in terms of behaviorism.... Let me hasten to add that if the behaviorist were to ask you what you mean by the subjective terms you have been in the habit of using he could soon make you tongue-tied with contradictions. He could even convince you that you do not know what you mean by them....

This is the fundamental starting point of behaviorism.[11]

Watson seems to be saying that thinking, intending, desire, and so on are no more real than fairies and witches. Plainly, Wittgenstein would not have wanted to identify himself with a view that is stated in *this* way. Watson, while plainly advocating here a philosophical view, presents it as though he were saying something about the world, and in fact he goes on to declare that "behaviorism is a true natural science."[12] In Wittgenstein's view this is doubly confused: a philosophical idea is being represented as denying the existence of something and is then, in turn, being represented as a science. Plainly, Watson means to say: there *are* no such things as those we take ourselves to be speaking of when we speak of thoughts and feelings and remembering and desire. So when Wittgenstein has his interlocutor ask whether he isn't a behaviorist in disguise, he then turns this question into: Aren't you saying that everything but human behavior is a *fiction*? This makes it easy for Wittgenstein to parry the question, for of course he regards it as illegitimate for a philosopher to make existential claims, to say that something is a *fiction*. (This comes out in his saying: "And now it looks as if we had denied mental processes. And naturally we don't want to deny them" (PI, §308). In PI, §305 he asks: "What gives the impression that we want to deny anything?" and in §306: "Why should I deny that there is a mental process?") Even so, in responding to the charge that he is a behaviorist in disguise, he does not say, "I am no behaviorist." He says only that he is making a *grammatical* point, namely, that 'thinking' is not used as the dualist imagines it is: "In order to get clear about the meaning of the word 'think' we watch ourselves while we think; what we observe will be what the word means! But this concept is not used like that" (PI, §316). In short, he wants to replace material mode statements of the sort made by classical behaviorists with statements about words. But this does not mean that Wittgenstein is not a philosophical (or logical) behaviorist. And of course he cannot help but be a behaviorist of *that* sort, for his ontology commits him to it.

"Inner Processes" and Outward Criteria

The following passage in *Philosophical Investigations* has led some philosophers to think that Wittgenstein rejected behaviorism: "An 'inner process' stands in need of outward criteria" (§580). If one ignores the inverted commas, one may take this passage to show that Wittgenstein unquestionably allowed that there are inner processes, which is something no behaviorist would allow. But the inverted commas are there, and one needs to know the reason. The reason, as we saw in Chapter 2, is that Wittgenstein rejected the very idea that mental activities or events are 'inner' activities or events. (His rejection of the 'inner' was not confined to some early stage in his thinking, for in 1950 he wrote: "The 'inner' is a delusion" (LW II, p. 84).) Indeed, the whole point of his saying that an 'inner process' stands in need of outward *criteria* is this: when you realize that there are outward *criteria* for doing a sum in one's head, for example, or for being in pain, you will see that these are *not* 'inner' activities or events. What Wittgenstein means by his term "criteria" comes out in his remark: "The inner is tied up with the outer logically, not merely empirically" (LW II, p. 64). Let us ask: How can x be "tied up" *logically* with y, i.e., how can it be a matter of *logic* that if x occurs y occurs? Plainly, x and y cannot be separate states of affairs, as they would be if they were empirically related. Rather, x and y are related as, in a game of poker, holding a hand of five hearts is related to holding a flush. But this means that if certain bodily movements are, in *these* circumstances, the *criteria* for a person's being in pain, then his being in pain is not something *other than* those bodily movements (in these circumstances), and hence is not something 'inner' or nonbehavioral.

Notes

1. The latter term is used by the behaviorist C. L. Hull, *Principles of Behaviour* (New York, 1943), p. 25.
2. I have altered the translation of this passage. The German reads: ". . . Schmerzbenehmen mit Schmerzen und Schmerzbenehmen ohne Schmerzen." Anscombe has translated this: "pain-behaviour *accompanied* by pain and pain-behaviour without any pain" (my italics). Plainly, the word "accompanied" gives altogether the wrong impression, suggesting as it does that Wittgenstein is prepared to allow that the behavior, if it is not pretense, can be *accompanied* by something, the pain.
3. Alluding to his reaction to another person's pain behavior, he says: "My relation to the appearances [*Erscheinung*] here is part of my concept [of pain]" (Z, §543), i.e., other people are to be thought of as *Erscheinungen*. In *On Certainty* he says: "What if something *really unheard-of* happened? If I, say, saw . . . trees gradually changed into men and men into trees" (OC, §513). How could he have thought he might see men change in trees?

When he speaks of "men" here he is thinking of those patterns of colors and shapes that he thinks we call "men." That is why he can think of them 'changing into trees,' as in a cartoon film men could change into trees. And it is 'men' *as thus construed* that figure in his examples of other people being in pain, being angry, etc. So the philosophical problem, as he understood it, is this: How can those patterns of colors and shapes – those *Erscheinungen* – that we speak of as our friends and neighbors be said to have toothaches, be angry, etc.?

4. For criticisms of the Cartesian notion of 'bodies,' see Douglas C. Long, "The Philosophical Concept of a Human Body," *Philosophical Review*, July, 1964, pp. 321–337, and "The Bodies of Persons," *The Journal of Philosophy*, May, 1974, pp. 291–301. In my essay, "Human Beings," in *Studies in the Philosophy of Wittgenstein*, ed. Peter Winch (London: Routledge & Kegan Paul, 1969) I, too, criticized the Cartesian/behaviorist notion of bodies but wrongly supposed that Wittgenstein would concur in my criticisms.

5. "Take the various psychological phenomena: thinking, pain, anger, joy, wish, fear, intention, memory, etc., and compare the behaviour corresponding to each. But what does behaviour include here? Only the play of facial expressions and the gestures? Or also the surrounding, so to speak the occasion of this expression?" (RPP, I, §129).

6. This becomes apparent also when Wittgenstein allows himself to strip away, in thought, the surrounding and is then left with bodily movements:

> If only *one* person had, *once*, made a bodily movement [*Korperbewegung*] – could the question exist, whether it was voluntary or involuntary? (RPP, I, §897).

> . . . what is activity? *Prima facie* bodily movement. But not any movement – not if the chair gives way, nor the beating of the heart. It must be voluntary movement (WL47, p. 35; see also p. 156).

7. Wittgenstein did not initiate this practice. Russell, in the course of explaining his skepticism regarding other minds, says: "From the expression of a man's face we judge as to what he is feeling: we say we *see* that he is angry, when in fact we only see a frown" (*Our Knowledge of the External World*, op. cit., p. 76). Several pages later he says that "the belief in other people's minds . . . is psychologically derivative from our perception of their bodies" (p. 79). Plainly, then, he is treating the word "frown" as though it could be used to describe something (a body) even if it has no mental life at all.

8. Recall here Wittgenstein's remark (quoted in note 14 of the preceding chapter) that "a criterion for people talking is that they make articulated noises." He adds: "Similarly if I see a person with a piece of paper making marks in a certain sort of way, I may say, 'He is calculating' " (LFM, p. 203). This is plainly a behavioristic characterization of talking and writing. We find the same idea in the *Investigations*, where he characterizes saying something as making "a noise" (PI, §363). And in his lectures of 1946–47 he said: "But consider what happens in giving a report. You make a noise" (WL47, p. 261; see also pp. 55 and 180).

9. *Principles*, Part I, Sec. 51.

10. Chicago: University of Chicago Press, 1959, pp. 5–6.

11. Ibid., pp. 9–10.

12. Ibid., p. 19.

10

Wittgenstein and Kohler

In the preceding chapter I promised to provide additional grounds for my claim that Wittgenstein remained a behaviorist in his later years even though his choice of words occasionally suggests otherwise, as when he says that we see another person smile or hear him moan. One might expect a behaviorist to avoid words such as "smile" and "moan" and even to insist that, while we see other bodies move in certain ways, we do not see other people frown or grimace, and to insist also that, while we may hear other bodies make sounds, we don't hear people cry out or answer questions. Wittgenstein, I have suggested, thought that he needn't adhere to such strictures, i.e., that he could reconcile his version of behaviorism with the ways we normally talk about other people ("I saw him smile"), and we will now consider one of his reasons for thinking this. At the same time we will consider a related problem about his phenomenalism, namely, his unapologetic way of using such nouns as "table" and "book" in his philosophical discussions. One might expect a phenomenalist to purge his philosophical remarks of such words, and the fact that Wittgenstein did not do so may suggest that he was not a phenomenalist at all. In this chapter we will find reason to think otherwise.

During the last years of his life Wittgenstein devoted considerable time to investigating the use of the phrase "seeing . . . as . . . ." Some of what he wrote on this topic appears in Part II, Sec. xi, of the *Investigations*, although he says little there to explain the importance he attached to this subject. A partial explanation is offered in his notes:

What is the philosophical importance of this phenomenon [of seeing as]? Is it really so much odder than everyday visual experiences? Does it cast an unexpected light on them? In the description of it, [the] problems about the concept of seeing come to a head (LW, I, §172).

What problems about the concept of seeing did Wittgenstein have in mind?

He had especially in mind problems concerning 'the external world' and 'other minds.' He thought his investigation of "seeing as" would shed light on two categories of propositions philosophers have found problematic: those in which we speak of seeing such things as chairs and apples and those in which we say such things as "I saw him smile" and "I saw the fear in her face." What has made these seem problematic is the idea that if we were fastidious about saying what we actually *see*, we would speak only of seeing sensible qualities, such as colors and shapes. That this is *not* how we ordinarily speak would seem, then, to require an explanation. In the *Tractatus* Wittgenstein took the view that our ordinary way of speaking in such cases is misleading, i.e., that what one really sees are only colors variously arrayed in one's visual field. But, as we saw in Chapter 7, his reading of Wolfgang Kohler in 1930 led him to renounce this view. In Part I of the *Investigations*, however, he said nothing about this. So in 1947, when he returned to investigate this matter, he was addressing an issue that had been on his agenda for almost two decades. But how can an investigation of "seeing as" shed light on "seeing an apple" and "seeing her smile"? And more importantly, what did Wittgenstein find problematic here?

To answer these questions it will be necessary to consider in greater detail Kohler's views, for much of what Wittgenstein wrote on this topic was meant as a commentary on Kohler's book *Gestalt Psychology*.[1] This is important because Kohler discusses in great detail the two categories of problematic propositions mentioned above.

Kohler's Views

It must be said at the outset that Kohler declares himself to be a mind–body dualist. The physical world, he says, is "behind" or "beyond"[2] our "direct experience." If we know anything about that world, we do so "by a process of inference," for it "does not appear in immediate experience."[3] Furthermore, Kohler says that, as a scientist, he is obliged to accept the causal theory of perception.[4] And, as one might expect, Kohler declares that our experiences are "private"[5]: "one person cannot observe another person's experience."[6] All of this Wittgenstein would have found naive and unacceptable, but it was not on these points that he was concerned to dispute Kohler's views. As we will see, his concern was focused on Kohler's way of characterizing certain sorts of perceptions. Before we turn to this, however, let us consider those aspects of Kohler's views that Wittgenstein would have found congenial.

Although Kohler maintains that mind–body dualism is the philosophically correct view to take, he nevertheless insists that this is not how the plain man thinks of the world: "... in common life we pay no attention to the philosophical premises which lead to this [dualistic] conviction. First of all, in common life we are Naive Realists. It does not occur to us to regard the things around us as mere perceptual counterparts of physical things. This also holds for the particular objects which we call other persons."[7] "The world we actually live in," says Kohler, is the world of immediate experience.[8] "Most people," he says, "live permanently in a world such as this, which for them is *the* world. . . ."[9] And this holds as well for the thoughts and feelings of other people. "From the point of view of naive phenomenology," we needn't *infer* that a child throwing a tantrum is in a rage, for we do not think of his rage as private, as "something that happens in another world."[10] Wittgenstein would surely have found this account, which accords with his own neutral monism, to be a welcome corrective to Moore's dualistic account of the 'common-sense view of the world.'[11]

The foregoing remarks by Kohler give us an indication of how he proposes to deal with the problem of other minds, which he poses as follows: "How does it come to pass that we ascribe to others experiences, more or less like those which we have ourselves?"[12] He begins by rejecting the philosophical view that we do this by employing the argument from analogy and comments: ". . . it seems that the [philosopher's] theory has little support in observation. In common life people simply do not proceed in this fashion, while at the same time they seem to understand their fellow men pretty well."[13] Here is a further point of similarity with Wittgenstein, who remarks: ". . . as you don't in fact make any such 1in-ference, we can abandon the justification by analogy" (Z, §537).

Kohler's own solution to the problem of other minds depends on a distinction he makes between the human body as a part of the perceptual world and as a physical object:

On the one hand, our body is given to us as a particular thing in sensory experience. On the other hand, this particular sensory experience is caused by physical events in the physical object which we call our organism. Only the body as a part of sensory experience is directly accessible to us. About the organism, just as about other physical things, we know merely by a process of inference or construction.[14]

The mistake that lies behind the argument from analogy, says Kohler, is that philosophers, having embraced Descartes' distinction between the physical body and the immaterial soul, forget that we *do not* perceive the physical body. This leads dualists to think that "the facts of behavior are physical facts and can, *qua* physical facts, have nothing in common with mental processes," so that an inference is required from the former to the latter, e.g., from a child's behavior to its being in a rage.[15] But we can see this to be wrong, says Kohler, by considering a simple example:

. . . if in a friendly-looking face we try to separate the friendliness from the characteristics of the face as such, we find the task quite difficult. So long as we consider the face as a whole, rather than as a mosaic of colored spots, the friendliness seems to remain an intrinsic characteristic of the face [i.e., not something inferred].[16]

To understand this, says Kohler, we need to realize that

the problem of social understanding does not directly refer to behavior in [the physical] sense. It refers in the first place to perceptual facts which one person experiences in contact with other persons; for, both the bodies and the behavior of such other persons are given to the first person only as percepts and changes of percepts. It follows that [dualistic] theses about the nature of the physical world and its relation to mental processes have no place in a first discussion of our problem. Obviously, our first question must be how behavior as *perceived* can help a person to understand other persons.[17]

It is not only dualists who neglect this simple truth, says Kohler, for behaviorists have heretofore neglected it as well. Because they reject dualism, they think of psychology as studying the behavior of *physical bodies*. For this reason, says Kohler, behaviorism of the standard variety must be dismissed: "If we listen to Behaviorists we may have the impression that to them the physical and physiological worlds as such are directly known, and that in their, the Behaviorists', case knowing has nothing to do with direct experience. . . . Naturally, with this I find it frightfully difficult to become a Behaviorist."[18]

In order to understand the example of seeing the friendliness of a face, and other examples like it, it is necessary, says Kohler, to bear in mind that what we perceive of others are *perceptual* bodies, for that will allow us "to defend a certain form of Behaviorism."[19] He explains this new form of behaviorism as follows:

If, on an evening, I think of the contacts with other people which I have had during the day, I find that for the most part it has not been particularly difficult to understand these people. And yet I feel sure that during these contacts I have hardly been occupied with their inner experiences *per se*. Now that I think of it, I can of course try and deliberately evoke pictures of the way in which Mr. X and Mrs. Y probably have felt on this or that occasion. I can also make this attempt when I am actually together with these persons. But during the effort I soon realize that this is an entirely unfamiliar procedure; plainly, I seldom do anything of the kind in normal social life. . . . Apparently, I always forget to take the final step by which we are supposed [by philosophers] to enter other people's inner life.

Our analysis refers to understanding as it occurs under ordinary circumstances. . . . The facts of social life which we are considering occur in the absence of any theoretical concepts. To a theorist, who sharply distinguishes between perceptual data and facts of subjective ['inner'] experience in others, a step from the former to the latter may seem to be entirely necessary if men are to understand each other. But in common life we pay no attention to the philosophical premises which lead to this conviction. First of all, in common life we are Naive Realists. It does not occur to us to regard the things around us as mere perceptual counterparts of physical things. This also holds for the particular objects which we call other persons. As a consequence, all characteristics which things and persons owe to perceptual organization are commonly taken as characteristics of these [perceptual] things and persons as such. But we also ignore a second [philosophical] distinction: we draw no sharp dividing line between subjective phenomena in the narrower sense of the term [i.e., as being 'inner'] and such perceptual facts as constitute human bodies. . . . [W]e take it as a matter of course that directions [of attention], tensions, efforts, excitements, and so forth, of other persons appear in or on their [perceptual] bodies.

This, it seems, is the reason why in the social contacts of common life the final step from perceptual facts to the mental processes of others is seldom taken.

From the point of view of naive phenomenology, it need not be taken. If I refer to the calmness of a man before me, I refer to a fact which I perceive. . . . Similarly, if the man "gets excited," . . . the perceptual event *is*, or *contains*, what I call the man's excitement. I do not ask myself [as a dualist must ask] whether something that belongs to a different world accompanies the impressive display [of behavior].[20]

Kohler goes on to say that, when we are aware of other people's "hesitation," "restlessness," "determination," "depression," "avoiding," "reaching," and so forth, such terms "refer to events in perceptual space."[21]

This is the "form of Behaviorism" Kohler embraces. It is an account of the way in which the plain man, who harbors no dualistic theories, perceives and understands other people. It is not, in other words, intended to be an account of what people actually *are*, for as I have said, Kohler, *qua* scientist, dismisses standard behaviorism and defends dualism. As remarked above, his reason for dismissing standard behaviorism is that it regards the 'physical organism' rather than the 'perceptual body' as the object of perception and that it thereby leaves out the very thing that can have those characteristics, such as anger, which in common social life we attribute to people. And it was precisely to include the perceptual body that Kohler embraced dualism. There are, of course, other alternatives here, none of which Kohler considers. One of these is neutral monism, for a neutral monist, in rejecting dualism, will declare that Kohler's version of behaviorism is a correct account, *not only* of the plain man's understanding of other people, but of what people actually *are*. Or, putting the matter in Wittgensteinian terms, we might say that a neutral monist would think that Kohler's version of behaviorism can be made sound by recasting it in the formal mode, by treating it as an analysis of such terms as "anger," "fear," and so on. This, as we have seen, was Wittgenstein's view.[22]

What I have wanted to call attention to in emphasizing the points of agreement between Kohler and Wittgenstein is that Wittgenstein found in Kohler an account of 'common sense' that, in important ways, fit his own view. But let us turn now to those aspects of Kohler's theory of perception that Wittgenstein found unacceptable and deserving of criticism.

How Wittgenstein and Kohler Differed

Kohler's theory consists of two main parts, one having to do with *what* we perceive, the other with *how* we perceive. In what follows we will be chiefly concerned with the first of these. Kohler states as follows his basic idea regarding *what* we perceive:

There is, in the first place, what is now generally called the *organization* of sensory experience. The term refers to the fact that sensory fields have in a way their own social psychology. Such fields appear neither as uniformly coherent continua nor as patterns of mutually indifferent elements. What we actually perceive are, first of all, specific entities such as things, figures, etc., and also groups [such as constellations of stars] of which these entities are members.[23]

To understand what Kohler is getting at here, it is necessary to realize that he presents his view as a corrective to the Introspectionist psychology that was prevalent in the early part of this century. He describes as follows what he finds objectionable in Introspectionism:

The very moment we try to observe experience in an impartial fashion we are bound to hear objections from the Introspectionist. If I say that before me on my desk I see a book, the criticism will be raised that nobody can see a book. If I lift the book, I shall be inclined to say that I feel its weight as something external to my fingers and roughly in the place in which the book is also seen. These statements, my critic would remark, are typical of the language of un-trained observers. He would add that for the practical purposes of common life such statements may be entirely satisfactory, but that none the less they differ widely from the descriptions which a trained psychologist would have to give. For instance, the statements imply that the terms "book" and "desk" refer to objects or things. In correct psychological discussion such terms are not admissible according to the Introspectionist. For if observation is to give us the simple and primary data of experience, we must learn to make the all-important distinction between *sensations* and *perceptions*, between the bare sensory material as such and the host of other ingredients with which this material has become imbued by processes of learning. One cannot see a book, the Introspectionist tells us, since this term involves knowledge about a certain class of objects to which the present specimen belongs, about the use of such objects, and so forth. Pure seeing has nothing to do with such knowledge. As psychologists, we have the task of separating all these acquired meanings from the seen material *per se*, which consists of simple sensations. . . . [A]mong the genuine sensory data there can be nothing like objects. Objects exist for us only when sensory experience has become thoroughly imbued with mean-ing.[24]

Stated baldly, Kohler's view of *what* we perceive differs from that of the Introspectionists in this way: while they hold that "the primary data of experience" include only sensible qualities, he holds that the organiza-tion of these into units or things (books, apples, people, etc.) is primary, too.

In stating his case against the Introspectionists, Kohler argues, in part, as follows:

In most visual fields the contents of particular areas "belong together" as circumscribed units from which their surroundings are excluded. . . .
   On the desk before me I find a number of circumscribed units or things: a piece of paper, a pencil, an eraser, a cigarette, and so forth. What is included in a thing becomes a unit, and this unit is segregated from its surroundings. In order to satisfy myself that this is more than a verbal [i.e. a *learned*] affair, I may try to form other units in which parts of the visual thing and parts of its environment are put together. In some cases such an attempt will end in complete failure. In others, in which I am more successful, the result is so

strange that, as a result, the original organization appears only the more convincing as a visual fact. . . .

. . . To be sure, the piece of paper, the pencil, and so forth are well-known objects. I will also grant without hesitation that their uses and their names are known to me from numerous contacts in previous life. Much of the meaning which the objects now have unquestionably comes from this source. But from these facts there is a large step to the statement that papers, pencils, and so forth, would not be segregated units without that previously acquired knowledge. How is it to be proved that before I acquired this knowledge the visual field contained no such units? When I see a green object, I can immediately tell the name of the color. I also know that green is used as a signal on streets and as a symbol of hope. But from this I do not conclude [as the Introspectionist's view would seem to require] that the color green as such can be derived from such knowledge. Rather, I know that, as an independently existent sensory fact, it has acquired secondary meanings. . . . In exactly the same fashion, Gestalt psychology holds, sensory units [such as books and desks] have acquired names, have become richly symbolic, and are now known to have certain practical uses, while nevertheless they have existed as units before any of these further facts were added. Gestalt psychology claims that it is precisely the original [i.e., unlearned] segregation of circumscribed wholes which makes it possible for the sensory world to appear so utterly imbued with meaning to the adult; for, in its gradual entrance into the sensory field, meaning follows the lines drawn by natural organization; it usually enters into segregated wholes.[25]

Wittgenstein was no doubt alluding to these passages when he wrote: "It is – contrary to Kohler – precisely a *meaning* that I see" (RPP, I, §869). Just what Wittgenstein meant by this we will consider presently. But at least this much is clear: he means to dispute Kohler's claim that our sensory field has a "natural organization" consisting of such things as apples, books, and trees.

This does not mean that Wittgenstein joins the Introspectionists in denying that we can see such a thing as a book or a smile. On the contrary, he speaks out repeatedly against the Introspectionist's claim. For example, he writes:

. . . one would like to say: We surely can't 'see' the expression, the shy behaviour, *in the same sense* as we see movement, shapes and colours. What is there in this? . . . Well, one does say, that one sees both the dog's movement and its joy. If one shuts one's eyes one can see neither the one nor the other. But if one says of someone who could accurately reproduce the movement of the dog in some fashion in pictures, that he saw all there was to *see, he* would not have to recognize the dog's joy. So if the ideal representation of what is seen is the photographically (metrically) exact reproduction in a picture, then one might want to say: "I see the movement, and somehow *notice* the joy."

But remember the meaning in which we learn to use the word "see." We certainly say we see this human being, this flower, while our optical picture – the colours and shapes – is continually altering, and within the widest limits at that. Now that just is how we do use the word "see." (Don't think you can find a better use for it – a phenomenalogical one!) (RPP, I, §1070).

There are many other passages in which Wittgenstein sides with Kohler against the Introspectionists. For example, he writes:

One may note an alteration in a face and describe it by saying that the face assumed a harder expression – and yet not be able to describe the alteration in spatial terms. . . . (RPP, I, §919).

One may also say: "He made *this* face" or "His face altered like *this*," imitating it – and again one can't describe it in any other way. (There just are many more language-games than are dreamt of in the philosophy of Carnap and others.) (RPP, I, §920).[26]

And as for our saying that we saw the glance she threw at him, Wittgenstein remarks: ". . .if someone wanted to correct me and say I don't really *see* [the glance], I should hold this to be a piece of stupidity" (RPP, I, §1101).

But if Wittgenstein allows that we can *see* a book or a glance, how does he differ from Kohler?

To see how they differ, we must recall that Kohler declares that our field of vision has a "natural organization," meaning that it is by nature, rather than learning, that we see a book or a smile. Another way in which Kohler puts this point is to say:

. . . experience as such exhibits an order *which is itself experienced*. For instance, at this moment I have before me three white dots on a black surface, one in the middle of the field and the others in symmetrical positions on both sides of the former. This . . . order . . . is concrete and belongs to the very facts of experience. . . . [O]ne dot is seen between two others; and this relation is just as much a part of the experience as the white of the dots is.[27]

What is significant in this passage is Kohler's insistence that the order among the dots "is just as much a part of the experience as the white of the dots." And more importantly, he extends this characterization to a great many other things. For instance, he extends it to the aspects that we see when we see a drawn figure now one way and now another.[28] (This is what Wittgenstein most directly and obviously criticizes in Part II of the *Investigations*.) Kohler also extends this characterization to seeing emotions in other people: another's anger or embarrassment, he says, "is a perceptual fact."[29] What are Wittgenstein's views about this?

Whereas Kohler insists that trees and smiles are on the same footing with colors, Wittgenstein maintains that they are not. Indeed, he credits the Introspectionist with an insight about this:

And if someone says "I don't really see the eye's glance, but only shapes and colours," is he contradicting the naif form of expression? Is he saying that the man was going beyond his rights, who said he saw my glance all right, that he saw this man's eye staring, gazing into vacancy, etc.? Certainly not. So what was the purist [i.e., the Introspectionist] trying to do?

Does he want to say it's more correct to use a different word here instead of 'seeing'? I believe he only wants to draw attention to a division between concepts (RPP, I, §1102).

This last remark provides the key to understanding Wittgenstein's criticism of Kohler.

Kohler notices that the verb "to see" takes a variety of direct objects but maintains that these 'objects' all have the same status. Wittgenstein criticizes this idea in several ways. For instance, in a passage that begins with a paraphrase of Kohler, he writes:

"When you get away from your physiological prejudices, you'll find nothing queer in the fact that the glance of the eye can be seen." Certainly I too say that I see the glance that you throw someone else. And if someone wanted to correct me and say I don't really *see* it, I should [along with Kohler] hold this to be piece of stupidity.

On the other hand I have not *conceded* anything with my way of putting it, and I contradict anyone [e.g., Kohler] who tells me I see the eye's glance 'just as' I see its form and colour.

For 'naive language', that's to say our naif, normal, way of expressing ourselves, does *not* contain any theory [about the objects] of seeing – it shews you, not any theory, but only a *concept* of seeing (RPP, I, §1101).[30]

Wittgenstein is saying: while it's true that in our language we can say both "I see some red here" and "I see how he's looking at her," this should not be taken to imply the Gestalt theory that these direct objects have the same status. Or as Wittgenstein also puts it, the fact that I say that I saw fear in a child's face, "is not to deny the difference between two concepts of what is perceived" (RPP, I, §1066–1068). Wittgenstein continues:

Naturally the question isn't: "Is it right to say 'I *see* his sly wink.' " What should be right or wrong about that, beyond the use of the English language? Nor are we going to say [with Kohler] "The naif person is quite right to say he *saw* the facial expression"! (RPP, I, §1069).

Why does Wittgenstein think we should disagree with Kohler here? Because, he says, Kohler has in mind something more than simply the fact that it is proper English to say "I see his sly wink":

But really the one who insists on the *correctness* of our normal way of talking seems to be saying: everything is contained in the visual impression; that the *subjective eye* equally has shape, colour, movement, expression and glance (external direction). [Kohler wants to say] that one does not detect the glance, so to speak, *somewhere else*. But that doesn't mean 'elsewhere than in the eye [that glances]'; it means 'elsewhere than in the visual picture.' But how would it be for it to be otherwise? Perhaps so that I said: "In this eye I see such and such shapes, colours, movements, that means it's looking friendly at present," i.e., as if I were making an inference.[31] So [since we make no inference here] one might say [as Kohler does]: The place of the *perceived* glance is the *subjective* eye, the visual picture of the eye itself (RPP, I, §1102).

Commenting on this idea, Wittgenstein writes:

First and foremost, I can very well imagine someone who, while he sees a face extremely accurately, and can, e.g., make an accurate portrait of it, yet doesn't recognize its smiling expression as a smile. I should find it absurd to say that his subjective visual object just wasn't smiling, although it has all the colours and form that mine has (RPP, I, §1103).

Kohler's mistake, according to Wittgenstein, is that he treats "I see some red here" and "I see his sly smile" as being alike in a particular way: he takes the former as a paradigm and assimilates the latter to it. But if this assimilation is a mistake, what is the difference between the two cases?

This is the place to recall Wittgenstein's rather odd remark (quoted above) that, contrary to Kohler, it is precisely a *meaning* that I see. What is the word "meaning" doing here? Presumably Wittgenstein is taking it from Kohler's remarks. In particular, Kohler describes the Introspectionist's position as the claim that (aside from sensible qualities) *what* we see is a result of sensory experience becoming "imbued with meaning," as when

the sign + fairly looks its meaning of the operation of adding, especially if it is seen between numbers; and yet it might as well have been chosen as a symbol for the operation of dividing. If for a moment we hesitate to accept this last statement, we do so [according to the Introspectionist] only because the connection of a particular meaning with this simple figure has been impressed upon us ever since we went to school.[32]

Kohler does not dispute this example. Rather, he concedes to the Introspectionist that our seeing the meaning of the sign + is *not* a primary fact of experience, but he then declares this case to be different from those that interest him, such as seeing a chair or seeing someone's smile.[33] He denies, that is, that these latter "phenomena" are products of learning. He makes the same point by saying that seeing a pencil or a piece of paper is not a merely "verbal affair."[34]

It is evidently to these passages that Wittgenstein is referring when he declares (RPP, I, §869) that, contrary to Kohler, what we see (in seeing a pencil, for example) is a *meaning*. He means to say that this *is* a verbal affair, a matter of acquired meaning. Support for this interpretation can be found by comparing another of Kohler's remarks with one of Wittgenstein's. Kohler at one point distinguishes his view from the Introspectionist's by saying that the *objects* we see belong to "the world we actually live in."[35] Perhaps Wittgenstein was picking up this phrase from Kohler when, in his 1932 lectures, he said: "The world we live in is the world of sense-data; but the world we talk about is the world of physical objects" (WL32, p. 82). He might have put the second half of this by saying: "... the world of physical objects (contrary to Kohler) is the world of meanings." If this is so, then his remark that it is precisely a *meaning* that we see can be taken as a way of reiterating his earlier thought that the world of physical objects is in some sense a product of our language. This is also why in the late 1940s Wittgenstein could speak of "our conceptual world" (RPP, II, §672).[36]

We will get a better sense of how Wittgenstein understood this matter if we take notice of the way in which he responds to some other remarks of Kohler's. The latter writes:

So far we have considered ourselves and things exclusively as visual experiences. But the situation remains the same if we consider other experiences as
well. Things and their properties may be experienced by touch instead of
visually. Also, things are felt to be warm or cold; they smell; are heavy; and emit
sounds. All these experiences are localized in one perceptual space. . . . More
particularly, all have a location in relation to visual facts. Thus a voice may be
heard as outside the window; a room as a visual scene may seem to contain the
smell of a cigarette; and the cold surface of the glass in my hand is felt where
the object is seen.[37]

Kohler goes on to remark that several explanations have been given for
"the fact that all sensory experiences appear in a common space." One
is that this case is similar to binocular vision, where "we know that the
co-operation of the two eyes in giving us one field of vision is at least in
part a matter of inherited factors." A second proffered explanation is
that "the experiences of the various sense modalities are localized in a
common space because we have learned in early childhood how they
must be spatially correlated." A third explanation, which fits the views
of Gestalt psychology, is that "in very early childhood the experiences of
the various sense modalities may have been more or less adequately
united in one space for *dynamic* reasons."[38]

Wittgenstein makes several comments on these possible explanations.
The third alternative, which Kohler favors, is that we *see* an apple *as* a
thing, i.e., that this is not something that has to be learned but is,
instead, an achievement of dynamic factors in the nervous system. Wittgenstein dismisses this suggestion:

Can I, e.g., say: I see the chair as *object*, as *unit*? In the same way as I say I see
now the black cross on a white ground, and now the white cross on a black
ground?
    If someone asks me "What have you there in front of you?" I shall of course
answer "A chair"; so I shall treat it as a unit. But can one now say I *see* it *as a
unit*? (RPP, I, §423).

Wittgenstein does not answer his own question here, but I think we can
infer his answer from two passages that occur shortly before this one:

. . . I take it as the typical game of "seeing something as something" when
someone says "Now I see it as this, now as that." When, that is, he is acquainted
with *several* aspects, and that independently of his making any application of
what he sees (RPP, I, §411, emphasis added).
    Would a child understand what it means to see the table 'as a table'? It learns:
"This is a table, that's a bench" etc., and it completely masters a language-game
without any hints of there being an aspect [one among several] involved in the
business (RPP, I, §412).

Of course the question "Does he see the table as a table?" is not the same
as "Does he see the table as a unit?" But Wittgenstein's point would seem
to apply to the latter in this way: unless Kohler could show how we *could*
see a table *otherwise* than as a unit, there's no sense to the idea that we

do *see* the table *as* a unit. I take it, then, that Wittgenstein would dismiss the alternative favored by Kohler for explaining how we perceive different qualities – e.g., color and odor – in a common space.

Even so, it is significant that Wittgenstein says in RPP, I, §423 that in identifying something as a chair, i.e., in using this singular noun, we "treat it as a unit." What could Wittgenstein be thinking of? Presumably he means that when we *see* a chair, we sometimes also walk over and take hold of it, and sometimes we say, "Do you see that chair? Please bring it here" and "See that clock over there? Its ticking annoys me." In these ways we speak of seeing and touching (or seeing and hearing) the *same thing*. (We do not think of a clock as being like, say, the human figures on a movie screen with a sound track, where we know that the two-dimensional figures we see on the screen aren't making the sounds we hear; i.e., we put our ear to the clock to hear it ticking but would not put our ear to the screen to hear better the voices of the actors.) This is what seems to need explaining, and Wittgenstein offers the following explanation:

What holds the bundle of 'sense-impressions' together is their mutual relationships. That which is 'red' is also 'sweet' and 'hard' and 'cold' and 'sounds' when one strikes it (RPP, I, §896).

Wittgenstein seems to be following Hume here in maintaining that there are certain regularities among sensible qualities, such as that a certain color and shape regularly go together and are accompanied by a certain taste and that if this were not so, if there were no regularities but only chaos among sensible qualities, we would not have a concept such as *lemon*.[39] What he has in mind here is revealed in his remark: "I can e.g. very well imagine that, although I see this hyacinth over there, I shall have no tactile perceptions when I want to touch it. . . ." (WVC, p. 161). So he is saying that if this sort of thing were to happen with some frequency we would not say and do the things we presently say and do, e.g., we wouldn't say, "Do you see that lemon over there? Please bring it here."

Presumably this is an example of one of the things he had in mind when he wrote:

It is very hard to imagine concepts other than our own because we never become aware of certain very general facts of nature. It doesn't occur to us to imagine them differently from what they are. But if we do, then even concepts which are different from the ones we're used to no longer seem unnatural to us (LW, I, §209; cf. PI, p. 230).

Wittgenstein, I take it, would say that it is a general fact of nature that certain colors and shapes go regularly with certain tactile sensations (e.g., resistance and weight) and that if these regularities had not existed we would not have such concepts as *chair* and *book*.[40]

In his notes on Kohler Wittgenstein wrote:

Isn't what Kohler says roughly: "One couldn't *take* something for this or that, if one couldn't *see* it as this or that?" Does a child start by seeing something this way or that, before it learns to take it for this or that? Does it first learn to answer the question "How do you see that?" and only later "What *is* that?" (RPP, I, §977).[41]

Can one say it must be capable of grasping the chair as a whole, in order to be able to recognize it as a thing? – Do I grasp that chair visually as a thing, and which of my reactions shews this? Which of a man's reactions shew that he recognizes something as a thing, and which, that he *sees* something as a whole, thingishly? (RPP, I, §978).

Wittgenstein would presumably say that if a man is shown a drawing of a schematic cube and indicates what he sees there by pointing to a three dimensional cube, we can say that he sees the drawing *as* a cube. To the question "Which of a man's reactions shew that he recognizes (or grasps) something as a thing?" Wittgenstein would presumably have responded as follows: a man may walk up to a tree that he sees and lean against it; when he approaches a chair that he sees, he will not try to walk through it; when he is hungry, he may search out an apple and bite into it, and so on. And these 'reactions,' Wittgenstein was thinking, are a consequence of the regularities among sensible qualities.

In Waismann's "Theses," which is a report of Wittgenstein's views, the chapter entitled "Objects" contains the following passage:

... the concept of an object is connected with *induction*.

Induction appears in the form of hypotheses [such as "That's an apple"]. ...

The concept of an object involves an hypothesis, for we assume as an hypothesis that the particular aspects we perceive are connected in a law-governed manner [i.e., that there are certain *regularities* among sensible qualities]. ...

The language of everyday life uses a system of hypotheses [about future experience]. It does so by means of using nouns [such as "apple" and "book"]. '

Aspects [of objects] are spatially and temporally connected.

An object is the way aspects are connected. ...

The hypothesis of an object connects facts of *different kinds*.

The word 'table' makes us think, not only of the connection between different visual images, but also of the connection between those and tactile sensations. An object is something that connects all those facts.

An hypothesis is designed to comprise *more* than the reproduction of *one* kind of experience. When we have a particular experience (see the visual image of a table, for instance) we, on the basis of an hypothesis, expect to be to able to have particular experiences of a different kind (tactile sensations) (WVC, pp. 255, 256, and 258).

This gives us a partial summary of Wittgenstein's view in 1930 as to the logical grammar of "That's an apple" and "There's a ball in the corner." From what we have seen in this chapter, it would appear that he never abandoned this view. In his lectures of 1946–47 he said that we have a "form" – presumably a logical form, namely, certain nouns – for "connecting up experiences with one another; we populate a space with sense-impressions. This is quite correct, because there is a relation between sense-impressions of two completely different spaces [i.e., visual space and tactile space]. Our impressions hang together" (WL47, p. 197). This is an almost perfect rendering of the position summarized by Waismann. At the end of Chapter 7 I indicated that in *On Certainty* he considered some modifications of this position, suggesting that perhaps not *all* of our empirical propositions are 'hypotheses.' But the very fact that he continued to use the word "hypothesis" (OC, §§52, 60, 87, 191, and 399; Z, §211, and elsewhere) to characterize the logical grammar of many of our 'empirical propositions' tells us that he retained the kernel of his 1930's view.

Summary of Wittgenstein's View

Let us review the principal points covered in this chapter. On the question "Do we *see* objects, such as books and apples?" we have found Wittgenstein's position to include the following: (i) it would be a piece of stupidity for someone to correct us when in an ordinary context we say that we see a book, for this just is how we use the word "see"; (ii) but Kohler, when he insists on the correctness of our saying such things, was making the mistake of assimilating "I see a book" to "I see some red here"; (iii) when the Introspectionist declares that we do not see such things as books and apples, he is not contradicting the ordinary use of "see" but is merely calling attention to a conceptual difference between the two sorts of objects of perception, and moreover, on this point the Introspectionist is right; (iv) yet the Introspectionist goes wrong when he wishes for an ideal, phenomenological language for describing sensations, for there is no description that he would acknowledge as living up to the 'ideal' he has in mind; (v) even so, we do describe our sense impressions, but we do so by means of 'physical object' words, as when we say "I see a waterfall over there" or "I feel a bug on my back," i.e., these are not 'crude' descriptions, which we could hope to replace with more 'accurate' ones, for this is what we mean by "describing our sense impressions"; and finally (vi) the fact that we employ 'physical object' words does not, contrary to Moore, show that we *believe in* (or *infer*) the existence of objects 'beyond' or 'behind' our sense impressions; rather, we employ such words as a consequence of our experiencing regularities among sensible qualities and do not infer the existence of a substratum in which they inhere.

We could give a parallel summary of Wittgenstein's views regarding the question whether we see another person's fear or anger: (i) we say, for example, "I could see how angry he was" and "I saw the fear in his face," and if someone were to correct me when I say such things in an ordinary context, this would be a piece of stupidity, for this just is how we use the word "see"; (ii) but Kohler, when he insists on the correctness of our saying such things was making the mistake of assimilating "I see him smile" to "I see some red here"; (iii) when the Introspectionist declares that we do not see such things as anger and fear, he is not contradicting the ordinary use of "see" but is merely calling attention to a conceptual difference between the two sorts of objects of perception, and moreover, the Introspectionist is right in this; (iv) yet the Introspectionist goes wrong when he wishes for an ideal, phenomenological language for describing the behavior of other people, for there is no description that he would acknowledge as living up to the "ideal" he has in mind; (v) even so, we do describe our sense impressions, but we do so by means of such words and phrases as "smile," "frown," "the fear in his face," "his sly wink," etc.; and finally (vi) the fact that we employ such language does not, contrary to Moore, show that we *believe in* (or *infer*) the existence of 'private objects' *behind* other people's behavior.[42]

With these summaries in mind, we can now come to the point of this chapter. As I remarked at the outset, my aim here is to explain how Wittgenstein, if he remained a phenomenalist and a behaviorist in his later years, could have allowed himself, when philosophizing, to give examples in which he uses such ordinary nouns as "apple" and "book" and examples in which he speaks, in our ordinary way, of seeing another person frown or hearing him cry out. Should he not have, when philosophizing, spoken only of colored patches and the like? Bertrand Russell once wrote:

I say "I sit at my table," but I ought to say: "One of a certain string of events causally connected in the sort of way that makes the whole series what is called 'a person' has a certain spatial relation to one of another string of events causally connected with each other in a different way and having the spatial configuration of the sort denoted by the word 'table'." I do not say so because life is too short; but that is what I should say if I were a true philosopher.[43]

Wittgenstein makes no such apology for constantly using our familiar words ("apple") and phrases ("see him frown," "hear her cry out," etc.) instead of speaking of colors and shapes and seeing bodily movements. We have now found an explanation for this: he did not think that these ordinary words and phrases are in conflict with phenomenalism and behaviorism. Indeed, he thought that it would be a mistake for a philosopher to try to get beyond our ordinary words and phrases to a purely phenomenalistic description of experience. So Wittgenstein believed he had license to conduct his philosophizing with the words and phrases of everyday life, and most of his examples are couched in such terms. This is one reason it is difficult to recognize that he remained both a phenomenalist and a behaviorist.

Notes

1. Op. cit.
2. Ibid., pp. 8 and 16.
3. Ibid., p. 9.
4. Ibid., p. 17.
5. Ibid., p. 21.
6. Ibid., p. 23.
7. Ibid., p. 142.
8. Ibid., p. 51.
9. Ibid., p. 7.
10. Ibid., p. 143.
11. Wittgenstein declares that "the common-sense man" does not embrace Moore's "realism" (BB, p. 48). This matter was discussed above in Chapter 2, esp. note 38.
12. Op. cit., p. 128.
13. Ibid., p. 130.
14. Ibid., p. 9.
15. Ibid., p. 131.
16. Ibid.
17. Ibid., pp. 131–132.
18. *Ibid*, p. 19.
19. Ibid., p. 141.
20. Ibid., pp. 141–143.
21. Ibid., p. 143.
22. A related point is that Kohler qualifies his behaviorism in the following way:

> Most people begin to conceal themselves early in life; and this holds particularly for their emotional life and their motivations. Actors, pianists, singers, and lecturers seldom look the stage fright which not a few of them nevertheless feel. To be sure, calmness which has merely been acquired as a social cover may sometimes fail to convince, just because it involves an effort. But it is undoubtedly true that innumerable passing events in the inner life of a person remain entirely hidden while he is in company (ibid., p. 145).

This of course agrees with, and was perhaps the source of, Wittgenstein's remark: "Behaviourism must be able to distinguish between real toothache and simulated toothache, between a man who is pretending to have toothache and a man who really has it" (WL32, p. 46).
23. Ibid., p. 71.
24. Ibid., p. 43.
25. Ibid., pp. 80–82.
26. See also RPP, I, §§287, 695, 953, 1072, 1079–1080 and PI, p. 200.
27. Ibid., pp. 38–39.
28. Ibid., Chapters V and VI.
29. Ibid., p. 143.
30. The sentence in quotation marks which begins this passage is an allusion to Kohler's claim that psychologists have held a theory of the nervous system (he calls it "the machine theory") which has forced them to hold false views about what can be perceived.
31. I have used the phrase "making an inference" where the printed text uses "drawing a conclusion." Compare what Wittgenstein says elsewhere:

"We *see* emotion." As opposed to what? We do not see facial contortions and make inferences from them (like a doctor framing a diagnosis) to joy, grief, boredom. We describe a face immediately as sad, radiant, bored, even when we are unable to give any other description of the feature (Z, §225; this is a developed version of RPP, II, §570).

32. Ibid., pp. 43–44.
33. Ibid., pp. 52–53.
34. Ibid., p. 81.
35. Ibid., p. 51.
36. This view of language and the world is also found in Waismann's essay "Verifiability," reprinted in *Logic and Language* (First Series), ed. A. G. N. Flew (Oxford: Blackwell, 1955), esp. pp. 140–141. A valuable criticism of this idea is found in Frank Ebersole, *Language and Perception* (Washington, D.C.: University Press of America, 1979), Chapter 2. Wittgenstein may have first encountered this view in William James's *Some Problems of Philosophy* (Reynolds & Son: New York, 1911) where, in Chapter Four, James maintains that the "world of common-sense 'things' " is the product of our substituting "a conceptual order" for the "perceptual order" in which our experience originally comes. It is by means of our concepts, he says, that we hear a song or see a bird.
37. Op. cit., pp. 127–128.
38. Ibid., p. 128.
39. Hume, taking the example of a sweet and fragrant fig, says that "we incorporate and conjoin these qualities with such as are color'd and tangible." We do so, he explains, because "the taste and smell of any fruit are inseparable from its other qualities of colour and tangibility. . . . [T]hey are always co-existent. Nor are they only co-existent in general, but also co-temporary in their appearance in the mind" (*Treatise*, I, iv, v).
40. In The Blue Book he gives a similar account of people's names, saying that our use of "the same person" and of personal names is based on the fact that our bodies and characteristic habits "only change slowly and within a narrow range." "We are," he adds, "inclined to use personal names in the way we do, only as a consequence of these facts. This can best be seen by imagining unreal cases which show us what different 'geometries' we would be inclined to use if facts were different" (BB, p. 61). One of the 'cases' he goes on to consider ("if facts were different") is that in which "people's shape, size and characteristics of behaviour periodically undergo a complete change" (ibid., p. 62). Elsewhere he entertains a variety of cases involving such a "complete change," e.g., a case in which "one of you suddenly grew a lion's head and began to roar" (EL, p. 10). In *On Certainty* he asks us to consider a case in which "trees gradually change into men and men into tree" (OC, §513).
41. Wittgenstein's way of characterizing Kohler's view in this passage is reminiscent of something he had written in his pre-*Tractatus* notebooks:

Can we regard a part of space as a thing? In a certain sense we obviously always do this when we talk of spatial things.

For it seems . . . that the matter is not settled by getting rid of [ordinary] names by means of definitions: complex spatial objects, for example, seem to me in some sense to be essentially things – I as it were *see them as* things. . . . Spatial complex objects – for example – really, so it seems, do appear as things (NB, pp. 47–48, emphasis added).

42. These summaries do not contain anything that looks like a justification for Wittgenstein's alternative to Kohler. What stands in need of justification is Wittgenstein's claim that, contrary to Kohler, the direct object of the verb "to see" in "I see some red here" and "I see a ball" (or "I see his frown") are different kinds of concepts, i.e., that it is a mistake to regard the first of these ("red") as a paradigm to which we may assimilate the others. Insofar as Wittgenstein offers a justification for this claim he does so only indirectly, by criticizing Kohler's account of what we see in seeing an aspect. (Kohler maintains that seeing an aspect is comparable to seeing a color.) Wittgenstein's reason for adopting this indirect strategy is that he was willing to concede that it is extremely tempting to think that when, for example, we see the duck–rabbit figure now as a duck and now as a rabbit, our *visual picture* changes. And Kohler claims not only that, in experiencing a change of aspect, our visual picture does change but also that this experience provides direct evidence of the correctness of his general view that 'organization' is a perceptual fact in the same sense as seeing a speck of red (ibid., p. 108). This, then, is why Wittgenstein, in order to undermine Kohler's account of seeing a ball (or a frown) sets about criticizing Kohler's account of seeing an aspect. I have not discussed his criticisms of Kohler on this point because that would lead us very far from the topic of this chapter. For an explication of this part of Wittgenstein's view, see John Hunter, "Wittgenstein on Seeing and Seeing As," *Philosophical Investigations*, Spring, 1981, pp. 33–49. But even though Wittgenstein is right in his criticism of Kohler's view of 'seeing as,' it does not follow that Wittgenstein was right about, for example, seeing a ball.

43. Bertrand Russell, *Philosophy* (Norton, New York, 1927), pp. 243–244.

III

Causation and Science in a Phenomenal World

11

Hume on Causation

In this chapter and the two that follow we must go to the heart of empiricism: the Humean view of causation. This is not simply one topic among others, for the empiricist view of causation brings in its wake some fantastical ideas about language and the proper conduct of philosophy. In particular, it burdens us with the idea of "logical possibility," which leads, as we will see in Chapter 14, to a peculiar view of the way in which philosophy is to construct and deal with examples. To understand this matter fully, we must investigate its source – or its modern source – in Hume.

What Was Hume Talking About?

What lesson, exactly, are we supposed to learn from Hume's discussion of causality? G. E. M. Anscombe states the lesson as follows:

> . . . [Hume] made us see that given any particular cause – or 'total causal situation' for that matter – and its effect, there is not in general any contradiction in supposing the one to occur and the other not to occur. That is to say, we would know what was being described – what it would be like for it to be true – if it were reported for example that a kettle of water was put, and kept, directly on a hot fire, but the water did not heat up.[1]

Hume, I am sure, would have found this a tidy summary of his views on causation, but there is something peculiar about it nonetheless. Anscombe plainly thinks that Hume's point can be illustrated by examples involving such things as fire and kettles of water. But is this true? Did Hume, in his discussion of causation, talk about anything at all like fire and kettles of water? He did, of course, sometimes resort to *words* of this sort. He uses the noun "fire" several times, and in the *Enquiry* he uses the nouns "tree" and "sun," saying that we can conceive that trees will leaf out and blossom in the dead of winter and that the sun will not rise tomorrow. Evidently, Anscombe, like so many others, assumes she can rely on Hume's words here. This assumption has caused enormous confusion in modern philosophy. For Hume is not talking about fire and trees and the sun. He is talking about something he calls "qualities," a fact which he does not at all hide from us. Of course he thinks that anyone who talks about fire and trees and the sun is *thereby* talking about 'qualities.' What else, he might have asked, *is* there to talk about? For it was in the early pages of the *Treatise* that Hume did away with 'material substance' and the 'external world,' so that long before he got around to the topic of causation he had nothing left to talk about but 'qualities.' But what are these so-called 'qualities'? And how do they figure in his discussion of causation?

Hume's Dependence on Berkeley

From the beginning of the *Treatise* it is plain that Hume has followed Berkeley in abandoning Locke's causal theory of perception. It is also plain that he went about this in the same way: like Berkeley, he did away with the causal (or material) end of Locke's theory and retained the alleged effects. And what were these effects? 'Sensible qualities,' of course: blue and sweet and hard and cold. This is the world we are left with, then, when Locke's causal theory is abandoned in the manner of Berkeley and Hume.[2] This has obvious consequences as regards causation. For in this world of 'sensible qualities' is there anything that could be thought to *cause* anything? Is there anything that could knock something down or knock it across the room? Is there anything here that could break windows or cause illness or death? Can sensible qualities cause tooth decay or skin rashes? Can they make dents? Berkeley's answer is stated clearly in the *Principles*:

All our ideas, sensations, notions, or the things which we perceive . . . are visibly inactive: there is nothing of power or agency included in them. So that one . . . cannot produce or make any alteration in another. . . . A little attention will discover to us that the very being of an idea implies passiveness and inertness in it; insomuch that it is impossible for an idea [i.e., a sensible quality] to do anything or, strictly speaking, to be the cause of anything . . . (Part I, Sec. 25).

Berkeley says here that an idea is inert and can cause nothing. How are we to understand that?

When I try to think of examples, one that comes to mind is that sadness is often caused by thoughts or memories. When a parent's mind is flooded with memories of her kidnapped child, this makes her sad and even depressed. So I can't think that Berkeley's point can be generalized to cases of this sort. But then Berkeley had something else in mind. When he says that "it is impossible for an idea to do anything," he is thinking chiefly of the 'sensible qualities' that are supposedly left over when the material end of Locke's causal theory has been discarded. So he is saying that it is impossible for blue or yellow or cold or sweet to do anything. But how are we to understand this? Don't we all know that in autumn cold weather causes the leaves to turn yellow and that the sourness of the grapefruit we eat makes the milk taste peculiar? Doesn't this show that such qualities have causal powers?

If we approach the matter in this way, we won't get far with Berkeley.

But then it must be acknowledged here that when we warn someone that the grapefruit he is eating will make his milk taste peculiar we are not thinking of ourselves as the inhabitants of that world of 'sensible qualities' Berkeley and Hume retained after dismissing the material end of Locke's causal theory. When we warn someone about the effect of eating grapefruit, we are speaking of grapefruit, and of course it is the acidity of the grapefruit that makes milk taste peculiar. But suppose now that, with Berkeley, we make the metaphysical move of doing away with the grapefruit while retaining the sourness. Can this sourness, stripped of everything material, i.e., the acidity, still *do* something?

I don't really know what to think of this question, for I don't understand the supposition behind it. I don't know how to retain the sourness of grapefruit when I have no grapefruit to eat. Perhaps if I were a dualist I could make something of this. I would think that the sourness is 'in my mind' and so is something in its own right, quite apart from the grapefruit on my plate. Locke, of course, was a dualist and thought of the matter in this way. (Sourness, he said, is a secondary quality.) And that was Berkeley's starting point. He took it to be obvious that sourness is something in its own right, and when he subsequently convinced himself that no distinction could be made between primary and secondary qualities, he concluded that all sensible qualities are something in their own right. So when he came to the question I posed above about whether sourness, stripped of everything material, can *do* anything, he was entertaining a very peculiar question. The closest I can come to understanding it is to put to myself the question: If I were to follow Berkeley in doing away with the grapefruit, including its acidity, and if I were to do away also with everything else material, including taste buds, would I still think I could use causal language in talking of sourness? When I put it to myself this way, I'm inclined to think that Berkeley has a point here. When the qualities of things are transformed into 'sensible qualities' by stripping them of everything material, this seems to have consequences for the language of causal powers.

This becomes more obvious if we approach the whole matter from a different angle. We regularly talk about things being pushed and pulled and knocked about by other things. We say that the avalanche pushed the house off its foundation, that the cat knocked the vase off the table, that the wave capsized the boat, and so on. This is causal language that even a child understands. But let us see what happens to this in the following thought experiment. Suppose we imagine ourselves to be like the prisoners in Plato's Allegory of the Cave. We sit facing a wall on which shadows are moving. In Plato's story these shadows are cast by objects carried along the parapet behind the prisoners, objects illuminated by a fire at the rear. Plato's version can serve us here as an analogue for Locke's causal theory of perception: while we see only shadows, these are caused by something we don't see. Now let us further suppose that the objects casting the shadows are manipulated in such a way as to produce the following movement of their shadows: whenever a round shadow approaches a square one and they touch, the square one moves off at a speed proportionate to their sizes and to the velocity of the round shadow. Shadows, of course, are not the sort of things that can knock each other about. So if we confine ourselves to what we observe of the shadows on the wall before us, we do not have what is needed for causal explanations, no matter how regular the pattern of the shadows' movements: if we ask what made the square shadow move to the right, we can't answer that its movement was caused by some other shadow. Of course these movements are not inexplicable as the story now stands, for we still have the fire at the rear and the people carrying the objects to and fro. So we can say the square shadow moved to the right because the object casting the shadow was moved in that direction. But suppose now that we introduce the analogue for Berkeley's treatment of Locke: we eliminate from the story the fire and the objects casting the shadows, while retaining the shadows themselves. We are then left with *uncast* shadows moving in various ways on the wall before us. I don't propose that we try to understand this story of uncast shadows. Rather, I want only to call attention to the fact that in this Berkelean version we find ourselves observing movements that have been rendered inexplicable. While the pattern of movements may be as regular as you please, this does not warrant any talk of one shadow knocking another one to the left or pushing another to the right. The movement of (actual) shadows can be explained in terms of the movements of the objects that cast them. But having now dispensed with such objects, we are left with phenomena uncaused by anything at all. So in this Berkelean version we find ourselves with what we might call an acausal world of shadow movements.

I have introduced this story to help myself understand Berkeley's claim that his 'sensible qualities' are powerless and 'inert.' In saying this, of course, Berkeley is not reporting the results of experimentation. Rather, he has told himself a story that affords no foothold for our causal language, for such verbs as "push" and "knock down," and "cause." Before one embraces Berkeley's story, one can ask such questions as "What knocked the vase off the table?", "What caused this rash?" "What was the cause of his death?", "What made this dent in the table?", and so on. And typically we are able to answer that the cat knocked the vase off, poison ivy caused the rash, a blow to the head killed him, a platter falling on the table made the dent, and so on. Berkeley's story has no place for such questions and answers. His ontology of 'sensible qualities' has the consequence of banishing causal language from the world. Can sweet cause a rash? Can sour kill? Could red in conjunction with sweet and round and hard knock things about? An apple, if it fell from a tree, might knock something about, but in Berkeley's story we no more have apples than we have grapefruit. And it doesn't change matters even if Berkeley wants to rechristen some collection of 'qualities' an "apple": he still hasn't got in his story the *kind* of thing that can knock other things about. He has left himself, then, with an acausal world.

It seems, however, that Berkeley was uneasy about this strange conclusion to his story, and so, to mitigate the strangeness, he introduced two measures to patch things up a bit. The first measure he introduced is one for which we may drum up some sympathy by recalling that in our Berkelean version of Plato's allegory we said that the shadows were moving about in regular patterns, but we introduced nothing to explain this. How could we have allowed such regularities in our story? Why weren't the shadows moving in a perfectly random, chaotic fashion? Or, for that matter, why were they moving at all?

Berkeley was faced with a similar question. If his acausal world is to be neither thoroughly chaotic nor utterly static, isn't something needed to make it otherwise? At this juncture in his metaphysical storytelling, Berkeley was evidently put in mind of the story that the world has a creator, and this, he thought, gave him a way to explain how changes come about in his world of 'inert sensible qualities':

We perceive a continual succession of ideas; some are anew excited, others are changed or totally disappear. There is, therefore, *some* cause of these ideas . . . which produces and changes them. That this cause cannot be any quality . . . is clear from the preceding section. It must therefore be a *substance*; but it has been shown that there is no corporeal or material substance: it remains therefore that the cause of ideas is an incorporeal active substance or Spirit (ibid., Part I, Sec. 26).

In this way Berkeley hoped to get some sort of causality back into his story, but of course he does not mean to put it back into the world of 'sensible qualities.' Within *that* world causal language is permanently off limits. Taken by itself, it is an acausal world. And even by putting God into the story, Berkeley doesn't give us back our ordinary causal language, for it would seem to be perfectly pointless to ask "What caused this?" or "What caused that?" if the answer must always be the same: "God did it." So putting God into the story is not enough to remove its strangeness. To give us back our causal language, Berkeley had to resort to a second measure.

We have already taken notice of this measure, for as we observed in Chapter 8, Berkeley introduced a 'use' theory of meaning as a way of accommodating our causal language. He says that since this language serves a practical function in our lives, we are entitled to use it even though, when considered strictly or taken literally, it is highly misleading as to the nature of things. That is to say, the question "What caused this?" would, if taken strictly, always have to be answered by saying, "God did it," but we are entitled to say "The fire warmed the room" or "A plate fell on the table and made the dent," so long as we don't take ourselves to be assigning causes – so long, that is, as we don't mean to be *explaining* anything. On a Berkelean view, when we say that the falling plate made the dent, we only mean to say, "If you don't want dents in the table, don't let plates fall on it," which is consistent with: "Because God will put dents there."

We may sum up this second measure of Berkeley's by saying that while his use theory of language is meant to give us back our ordinary causal language, it does not really do so. What it does is to allow that we may speak of 'inert' qualities (or collections thereof) in *causal* terms only so long as we don't mean what we say. (This is parallel, of course, to his explanation of what we are saying when we say, for example, "The pot boiled over while no one was watching." He allows us to say this so long as we are *really* saying something else.) But this, of course, is the best that Berkeley can do, given his ontology. For if he allowed that we are speaking 'strictly' when we ask and answer causal questions about dents and rashes and so on, he would have to conclude that we are asking and answering questions that make no sense at all. He would have to say that such a question as "What caused this rash?" is like asking "How tall is red?" On Berkeley's view, then, causal language (in the strict sense), if it has any application at all, has application only to God. Or, to put the matter differently, Berkeley's view has the following implication: a philosopher who accepts his way of dealing with Locke will be making a great mistake if he says both (a) that he wants to figure out what causation is (or what it means to speak of one thing causing another) and (b) that he will figure this out by considering familiar examples in which we speak of one thing causing another, as when we speak of poison ivy causing a rash. He will be making a mistake, in Berkeley's view, because the observable world does not contain anything to which causal language pertains. This is where empiricism leads us when it is consistently followed out.

I have emphasized this point because many empiricists have failed to follow their story where it properly leads. They have tried to keep causal language in their story, even though their story is essentially Berkeley's. Hume was the first to err in this way, and it will be useful to see how he fell into this mistake.

Hume's Account of Causation

To understand Hume, we have to go back to the first stage of Berkeley's attempt to remove the strangeness from his story, namely, to his accounting for the 'regularities' among sensible qualities by bringing God into the picture. In the *Treatise* Hume flatly dismissed this move:

As to those impressions which arise from the senses, their ultimate cause is, in my opinion, perfectly inexplicable by human reason, and 'twill always be impossible to decide with certainty, whether they arise immediately from the object, or are produc'd by the creative power of the mind, or are derived from the author of our being (I, III, V).

In short, Hume concludes that, contrary to Berkeley, we can never know what, if anything, causes our sense impressions. He concludes, in other words, that when a philosopher comes to think about causation, he must begin from the realization that the known world consists only of Berkeley's 'inert sensible qualities.' So if he had had his wits about him, Hume would have ended his discussion of causation at this point, declaring that, since we live in an acausal world, we cannot rightly speak of one thing causing another. Instead, Hume's discussion takes a peculiar turn here. He undertakes to figure out what causation is, what it *means* to say that one thing caused another, and he does so by considering familiar examples in which we use causal language. But such a procedure, as I said above, can only be a great mistake, given that Hume has embraced Berkeley's world of 'inert' sensible qualities. The result is quite predictable: Hume proceeds to invent an *ersatz* meaning for causal language, a meaning that he explains in terms of 'constant conjunctions' and 'expectations.'[3]

Hume's Ersatz Causation

I am not suggesting, of course, that Hume realized he was inventing an ersatz meaning. On the contrary, he imagined that he was explaining what we actually mean in saying that one thing caused another. He makes this plain when he writes:

Thus upon the whole we may infer, that when we [i.e., philosophers] talk of any being, whether of a superior or inferior nature, as endow'd with a power or force, proportion'd to any effect; when we speak of a necessary connexion betwixt objects, and suppose that this connexion depends upon an efficacy or energy with which these objects are endow'd; in all these expressions, *so apply'd*, we have really no distinct meaning, and make use only of common words, without any clear and determinate ideas. But as 'tis more probable, that these expressions here lose their true meaning by being *wrongly apply'd*, than that they never have any meaning; 'twill be proper to bestow another consideration on this subject, to see if possibly we can discover the nature and origin of those ideas we annex to them (*Treatise*, I, III, xiv).

What Hume goes on to do in his further 'consideration' is to explain what he thinks we actually mean in saying that one thing causes another. His explanation, of course, is bound to fail because he has accepted, by way of preamble, Berkeley's story about the sensible world being a

world of 'inert' qualities. In *such* a world nothing causes (or does) anything. Whatever happens, happens causelessly. There is nothing here
that could break a window or cause illness or death.

In a way, of course, Hume is perfectly aware of this, for he stresses
that, even in those cases in which we (quite rightly) say that something
has caused something else, there is no 'connexion' between the (so-
called) cause and the (so-called) effect. What this means is that in the
event itself there is nothing to distinguish it from a mere coincidence.
(Whatever 'connexion' there is in such cases, he says, lies in our expectations.) So Hume is in agreement with Berkeley that, *ontologically
speaking*, there are no causal episodes in the observable world. Where he
differs from Berkeley is only in this: whereas Berkeley (rightly) concludes from the foregoing that a doctor who cites drowning as the cause
of a man's death cannot be assigning a *cause* of death (in the strict sense),
Hume (wrongly) concludes that since we do use the word "cause" in
speaking of events in a world of qualities, the actual *meaning* of the word
"cause" does not include that there be any 'connexion' between the
(so-called) cause and the (so-called) effect.

Let us be clear about what exactly this means. Hume typically uses the
word "connexion" in stating his views, but this is an evasion, a way of
disguising the paradoxical character of what he is saying. When he says
that there is no *connexion* between the cause and the effect, he is disguising the fact that his claim amounts to the following: when a tree
branch blowing in the wind breaks a window, the branch does not really
break it; when a bolt of lightning splits a tree, the lightning does not
really split it; when a spark from a campfire ignites some nearby grass,
the spark does not really ignite it; and so on. Had Hume been perfectly
explicit, he would have stated his view in this paradoxical way. Instead,
he chose a formulation that is not so obviously paradoxical: there is no
connection between a cause and its effect. It is to his credit, however, that
he acknowledges that "of all the paradoxes, which I have had, or shall
hereafter have occasion to advance in the course of this treatise, the
present one is the most violent" (*Treatise*, I, III, xiv).[4]

It was Hume's intention to explain what we all *mean* when we give
causal explanations. He tells us that the meaning of our causal explanations is such that they can be appropriate (or true) *despite* the fact that
there is no 'connexion' between the cause and the effect. But when we
notice that his word "connexion" is only a camouflage term for such
familiar verbs as "knock down," "break," "ignite," and "cause," his paradox becomes an obvious contradiction. He is really saying: when one
thing causes another, the one does not cause the other, e.g., when a
swinging tree branch breaks a window, the impact of the branch doesn't
break it.

How did Hume fall into this mistake? Part of the explanation, surely, is that he was simply not mindful of the route by which he had arrived at the idea that we live in a world of 'sensible qualities,' a route which involves banishing the sorts of objects that *can* knock each other about, break windows, and so on. Had he thought this matter through with care, he would have had to conclude with Berkeley that causal language, if taken 'strictly,' can have no place in speaking of events in the world. Hume is guilty, then, of failing to follow the argument where it properly leads.

In a passage quoted above Hume declares that it is "more probable, that [causal terms] lose their true meaning by being *wrongly apply'd* [i.e., by being used to mean that some power or energy in involved], than that they never have any meaning." Hume, of course, provides no reason for accepting this, but it evidently struck him as reasonable, and so he set about trying to explain what we can mean by assigning causes in an acausal world. And the best he could do then was to conclude that causation involves only constant conjunctions and expectations. A great many philosophers have failed to see just how peculiar this account of causation is. Some have even supposed that Hume's account is plausible whether we are speaking of material things or 'inert sensible qualities.' For this reason we must now proceed to examine the details of Hume's argument with an eye to whether it has any plausibility when considered apart from his empiricist ontology.

The Flaw in Hume's Ersatz Concept of Causation

The difficulty in Hume's account lies in his notion of constant conjunction. To see this we must turn to the beginning of his discussion, in the *Treatise*, of "the idea of causation." A part of what is involved in this idea, he says, is that the cause precedes the effect and that the two are spatially contiguous. This is only *part* of what is involved since we ordinarily distinguish causation from coincidence. If I sneeze in the vicinity of a lighted candle and it then goes out, it may not have been my sneeze, but a draft through a nearby window, that put out the flame. So something more is involved than contiguity and succession. But the trouble is, says Hume, that when one goes looking for this additional element in the objects themselves, one cannot find it there. What one finds is only the contiguity and succession. To illustrate this point, he asks us to consider a case of 'impulse,' i.e., a case in which we would say that one thing knocked something else down or knocked it across the table.

Having thus discover'd or suppos'd the two relations of *contiguity* and *succession* to be essential to causes and effects, I find I am stopt short, and can proceed no farther in considering a single instance of cause and effect. Motion in one body is regarded upon impulse as the cause of motion in another. When we consider these objects with the utmost attention, we find only that the one body approaches the other; and that the motion of it precedes that of the other, but without any sensible interval. 'Tis in vain to rack ourselves with *farther* thought and reflexion upon this subject. We can go no *father* in considering this particular instance (*Treatise*, I, III, ii).

To understand this passage, it is essential to realize that Hume meant to be describing a case we would normally describe in causal terms, i.e., in which we would say that the one object *knocked* the other across the floor or across the billiard table. That is, we are not to think that Hume meant to describe here a mere coincidence – one in which the movement of the second object was produced by, say, an unexpected breeze or by a magnet concealed beneath the table.

And yet, given Hume's intention here, his description is decidedly peculiar. For he says that the first object "approaches" the second and that the second object then begins to move. What does this mean? It sounds as though he is describing shadows. If one were describing the behavior of two shadows on the wall – say, the shadows people make with their hands to entertain children, one might say that the one approached the other and that the other then began to move. One would give such a description – a merely *sequential* description, as we might put it – because the objects are shadows, and causal language has no place here. (It has no place, of course, because the motion of a shadow results from the motion of the object casting the shadow.) Now if we could take Hume to be thinking of shadows, as his choice of words suggests, we could understand why he says that careful scrutiny of the two objects will reveal no connection between the arrival of the one and the motion of the other, since all we have among the shadows themselves is a mere succession of events. But we said above that Hume did not intend to be describing anything like a mere coincidence, in which the true cause lies elsewhere. He meant to be describing a case in which we would normally use causal language, a case in which we would say that the one object knocked the other across the table or pushed it along the floor. He could have been thinking of an avalanche in which we see the snow push a small house off its foundations or of a wave capsizing a boat. And he is saying that no matter how closely you study the event, you won't see the avalanche *do* anything to the house or see the wave *do* anything to the boat. What we *really* see, he wants to say, are two unconnected events: the one thing approaches the other and then the other begins to move.[5] But what warrant does he have for such a description of what we really see?

The answer is obvious enough, namely, that Hume is not here talking about billiard balls or avalanches of snow or waves on the ocean. He is talking about Berkeley's 'inert sensible qualities.' In Hume's world there is nothing else to talk about. And given that he thinks that we, too, when talking about billiard balls and avalanches, are talking only of 'inert sensible qualities,' he naturally thinks we are bound to accept his sequential description of the case in question. So we might concede to Hume that, given his ontology, he has so far told the right story, since in a world such as his there *can* only be sequences of events. The trouble is that he didn't stop at this point and declare that all causal accounts are misguided and ought to be abolished. He should have said that science is a great mistake, that one cannot sensibly hope to find the cause of scurvy or cancer or sun spots or anything else.

This, of course, is what all those empiricists who followed Hume should have said, too. Yet very few did. Wittgenstein, as we will see, was something of an exception, for he came at least very close to declaring science to be a sham. Most empiricists, unfortunately, made the great mistake of trying to reconcile science with empiricism and thereby made a shambles of the philosophy of science.[6] What they did was to follow Hume blindly in his assumption that he could figure out what causation is *despite* the ontology he is taking for granted. They thought that if we pile up *enough* conjunctions, i.e., enough to make a *constant* conjunction, then we can speak of regularities and laws, and that *that* is sufficient to make science viable. What they failed to see is that one cannot get even so far as finding a *single* conjunction, if by "conjunction" one means anything like what Hume meant. For Hume's 'conjunctions' are supposed to occur in an acausal world of 'sensible qualities.'

Sequential Descriptions

Here one may think that my argument has gone too far or has missed its mark. For one may take it to be obvious that we observe conjunctions of the sort illustrated by Hume's example. Is it not quite common, in fact, to give sequential descriptions of events even when we are speaking of physical objects and not of shadows or sense-data? Don't we sometimes say that this happened and then that happened, rather than saying that the one thing caused the other? And isn't this what scientists do, too, when they begin to study some hitherto uninvestigated subject matter? Don't they begin by compiling correlations?

There are, of course, cases in which we give sequential descriptions of what we have seen. But to understand whether this fact supports a Humean view of causation, we must consider whether such descriptions meet Humean requirements. Let us recall how Hume is thinking of his example of 'impulse.' When he says that the one object "approaches" the other and that the other then moves away, he thinks he is giving a more fitting description of what we actually see in the objects than the description we would normally give. We would normally say such things as "The wave struck the boat broadside and rolled it over," or "The wave capsized the boat," or "The avalanche struck the house with such force that it knocked it off its foundations." Hume thinks that in such cases, if we want to describe the objects themselves, we should say something like "The wave came up to the boat, and then the boat rolled over," or "The wall of snow came up to the house, and then the house began moving." But this is *not* because he means to be presenting an example of coincidence, one in which the actual cause of the motion of the second object was something other than its collision with the first. On the contrary, it is essential to Hume's argument that he be discussing here cases in which we are fully justified in the causal account we give, cases in which we haven't overlooked the actual cause. And yet, Hume prefers these sequential descriptions, as I said, because he thinks they are more fitting descriptions of what we actually *see*. But is he right about this?

There are, of course, cases in which, wanting to say exactly what we have seen, we say that such-and-such happened and then so-and-so happened. For example, if I were to witness a performance by someone who claimed to be able to perform amazing feats, and if I were suspicious of his claimed powers and suspected him of being an unscrupulous magician, then in later reporting what I saw (reporting it, perhaps, to a magician friend of mine), I might very well say that the performer did such-and-such and then so-and-so happened. This is not how the performer himself would describe what he had done. He would claim, for instance, to have lit a match (or caused it to light) by concentrating on it.

But I, rather than naively repeating his claim, say to my friend, "He held the match at arm's length, between his thumb and forefinger; he closed his eyes and screwed up his face, and then the match lit." Why do I choose this way of describing what I saw? Because I don't think he could have caused the match to light by concentrating on it. Consider also a case in which I might say, "Just as the wave reached the boat, the boat capsized." Perhaps I have been accused of piloting my boat negligently, thereby causing another boat to capsize. I am being sued, and I say to my lawyer, "I did pass near that boat, and it's true that just as my wake reached it, the boat capsized. But my wake was not large enough to cause the boat to capsize. Of *that* I'm quite sure. I suspect that the people aboard the boat, who were fishing at the time, all leaned over the starboard side at once and that that's why the boat capsized. My wake was barely a ripple." Here I say, "Just as my wake reached it, the boat capsized." But I say this in the course of protesting that my wake did *not* cause the boat to capsize. I might also say this, of course, if I were *uncertain* whether my wake was the cause. I might say, "It's true that the boat capsized just as my wake reached it, but I'm not at all certain that the wake *caused* the boat to capsize. The boat was too large for that."

And, finally, there is the sort of case in which we undertake research in order to discover the cause of something and record the results of tests in sequential descriptions, such as "In the six cases so far investigated, when citrus fruit was added to their diet, the subjects were cured of scurvy." When our research succeeds in identifying the cause in such a case, we do not persist in giving sequential descriptions but say instead, for example, "Scurvy is caused by a dietary deficiency" or, after further research, "Scurvy is caused by a deficiency of vitamin C." If, when we were confident that our research had identified the cause in such a case, we encountered someone who still spoke of the matter in sequential terms, we would think either that he was ignorant of what our research had established or that he believed our research methods were defective and that some unnoticed concomitant factor was the real cause. The point is that sequential descriptions in such cases cease to be appropriate once the research is successfully completed.

Sequential descriptions, then, are appropriate only when either (i) we believe that we are dealing with mere coincidence rather than cause and effect, i.e., where we believe that the actual cause was something *other than* anything mentioned (e.g., the boat's wake) in our sequential description; or (ii) when we are unsure of the cause; or (iii) we are engaged in research designed to identify the cause of something but haven't yet completed the research.

The relevance of this to the objection we are considering is that a Humean view of causation requires that sequential descriptions be appropriate even when the episode being described is a plainly causal one, i.e., is known *not* to be a mere coincidence. A Humean must think that sequential descriptions are somehow more fitting, more apt, than causal descriptions of such episodes. But this, as we have just seen, is not true. On the contrary, sequential descriptions are *in*appropriate in precisely the cases in which Hume wants to speak of there being a mere "conjunction," a mere sequence of events. Hume failed to notice this point, but in his case we can perhaps excuse this oversight on the grounds that he supposed himself to be talking about an acausal world of inert sensible qualities. No such excuse can be made for philosophers who do not share Hume's ontology. If we are speaking of a world of physical objects, a Humean account of causation in terms of 'constant conjunctions' has no plausibility at all.

This can be made more apparent by considering again the passage in which Hume gives the example of colliding objects. He presents the example as one in which "motion in one body is regarded upon impulse as the cause of motion in the other." By this he presumably means that he is speaking of a case in which the impact really does set the other in motion. In other words, he is telling us that the case he is thinking of is *not* one of the following: the second body is attached to a string by which it is pulled away just as the first body arrives; the second body is made of steel and is drawn away by a strong magnet just as the first body arrives; the second body is on a slope, held there by a third body, which is removed just as the first body arrives, etc. But this is not all that he is telling us. For the fact that he speaks here of *bodies* suggests that he also means to be excluding a case in which a shadow approaches another shadow, whereupon the second one begins to move. This much, then, is built into Hume's own example. And yet Hume goes on to say: "When we consider these objects with utmost attention, we find only that the one body approaches the other; and that the motion of it precedes that of the other, without any sensible interval." By this he means that, if one looks closely at these objects as they collide, one does not find some third factor – some factor in addition to contiguity and succession – that entitles us to pass beyond a merely sequential description to a description such as "It knocked the other one into the corner pocket." But this is strange indeed. For why should Hume think that, if there *is* some third factor warranting our causal description, it ought to be revealed by looking more closely at the objects at the moment of impact. I mean, he has already told us, if only by implication, that we are dealing here with something like billiard balls, not *shadows*. And isn't this the relevant factor? I mean, if Hume were describing an actual demonstration and it were perfectly clear that the colliding objects are billiard balls, he would hardly think it relevant to look closely at the balls as they collide in order to discover *there* why the second one moved. Given that he would not be looking for a string or a magnet by which the second ball was pulled away, what would he be looking *for*? In short, what Hume failed to notice is that he has already specified the additional factor – the factor entitling us to pass beyond a merely sequential description – when he describes his example as one involving *bodies*. We know, of course, what Hume thinks of bodies: he thinks they are bundles of 'inert sensible qualities,' and this no doubt is why he does not attach any significance to the fact that he describes his example as one involving bodies (rather than shadows or patches of light projected onto a screen). But philosophers who do not share Hume's ontology cannot be similarly indifferent to this. On the contrary, we can only think that it is because we are dealing with billiard balls or the like that we are entitled to say such a thing as "The wave struck the boat broadside and rolled it over."

Necessity and Impossibility

When Hume sets out to examine the idea of causation, he says that that idea involves somehow the idea of a *necessary* connection, and it is this necessity, he says, that he fails to discover when he attends to the objects themselves. Such attention, he says, reveals contiguity and succession but nothing of necessity between the supposed cause and its effect. What this comes to, I suppose, is the claim that observed regularities never reveal necessities in nature. What are we to make of this claim?

Let us put the matter this way: If we wanted to discover whether there is a necessary connection between Xs and Ys, isn't the way to go about this simply to make tests with Xs and Ys and observe what happens? This is, after all, what scientists often say they do.[7] Hume, of course, would say that in making such tests we do *not* discover any necessary connection in the objects themselves; we discover no more than constant conjunctions. Why does he think this?

Consider first what Hume means in saying that such tests never reveal a necessary connection between Xs and Ys. He means simply that such tests can never show us that an observed regularity between Xs and Ys *must* continue to hold in the future. To put it another way, Hume is saying: *if* by such tests we could discover that when certain things happen certain other things are *bound* to ensue, *then* such tests would reveal necessary connections, but in fact such tests *cannot* reveal this sort of thing, i.e., cannot reveal that an observed regularity won't cease (break down) in the future. But what makes Hume think *this*?

The answer once again is that Hume imagines himself to be residing in a world of 'inert sensible qualities.' In such a world whatever happens just happens. Nothing causes it to happen; nothing brings it about. If Xs and Ys have been found to have been *constantly* conjoined, this is no more than a long lucky run. And lucky runs, however long they may be, have nothing inevitable about them. So as a new day dawns and we once more run the test with Xs and Ys, there is no reason to think we will get the same result as before. If we get a different result, we will have on our hands 'a change in the course of nature.' And this, once again, will be something that just happens, something that happens causelessly.

Hume, of course, imagines that he is giving an account of our ordinary idea of causation. He believes that only philosophers, not ordinary folk, think that there is necessity in nature. Here there are two questions to ask. First, is he right about this? Second, if not, where did he go wrong?

A few examples will show that he is not right about this, for we obviously do speak of necessities in nature – and of impossibilities, as well. Let us consider a few examples. A child is climbing a tall tree and is warned by his mother, "You're bound to get hurt if you fall from up there." Similarly, we might warn someone with fair skin, "You are bound to get a sunburn if you don't cover up on a day like this." Also, if a child cleaning his goldfish bowl has put the fish in a small dish of water, we might warn him, "You shouldn't leave them in that dish very long. They are bound to die if you do." And doctors, of course, regularly say that a patient has a terminal illness or a fatal injury.[8] In short, we regularly say things that Hume takes no account of. He imagines that it is only philosophers who think that, given certain conditions, certain other things are bound to ensue. Similarly, he disregards the fact that we regularly declare certain things to be impossible. For example, suppose that someone finds printed in the newspaper the following diet for people wanting to lose weight: "Fruit and dry toast for breakfast, a light salad for lunch, and for dinner a piece of broiled meat, a vegetable, and a loaf of bread." If she knows something about nutrition, she is likely to say: "This must be a misprint. They must mean a *slice* of bread. One *couldn't* lose weight eating a *loaf* of bread each day, along with the rest of the menu." Another example: I have been working on my car and have disconnected the battery to clean the terminals. Later I forget this and try to start the engine, whereupon my friend exclaims, "Well, you *can't* start it with the battery disconnected!" Or consider this: I have tried, without success, to grow azaleas in my yard and consult a friend about my failure. As soon as she sees that I have planted the azaleas in an area below the high tide line she explains: "Azaleas can't survive in this salty soil; they aren't salt tolerant." Again, a neighborhood child wants to breed her cat with my tom cat, and I tell her she may do so, but when I look closely at her cat, I tell her: "Your cat is a male. A male cat can't breed with another a male cat." Finally, I am reading a fairy tale to my child who interrupts to ask, "Could that really happen, Daddy? Could a prince turn into a frog?" I reply, "No, that couldn't happen. Tadpoles turn into frogs, but people can't turn into frogs."

Had Hume noticed that we regularly say such things, he would have found this perplexing and in need of explanation. Indeed, he would have declared that we can't really mean what we say in such cases. Why? Part of the explanation is that he could find no impressions that would give rise to the ideas of necessity and impossibility in nature. There was, of course another option here, for it was open to him to regard such examples as showing that he was wrong about 'the origin of ideas.' But he had another reason for ignoring examples of the sort I have just given. Early in the *Treatise*, long before he comes to the topic of causation, he says:"Tis an established maxim in metaphysics, *That whatever the mind clearly conceives includes the idea of possible existence*, or in other words, *that nothing we imagine is absolutely impossible*" (I, II, ii). Hume does not tell us how he thinks this can be established, but it is clear that he takes this idea for granted throughout the *Treatise*, as when we find him saying, "Anything may produce anything." How are we to take this? Does Hume mean to say that two male cats can produce offspring? And does he think that a child's *imagining* two male cats producing offspring is enough to show that such a thing is not absolutely impossible?[9]

The answer, of course, is that Hume isn't talking about things like cats – not real flesh and blood cats. Rather, he is talking about a world of 'inert sensible qualities.' For it is also very early in the *Treatise* that he makes clear that he follows Berkeley in dismissing Locke's causal theory of perception by dispensing with the material, causal end and retaining the supposed effects, sensible qualities. And given this ontology, Hume is obliged from the outset to think that anything that occurs in the world has no discernible why or wherefore. Whatever happens, just happens. And if something astonishing and inexplicable should occur, then that too just happens. There is no *limit* on what *can* happen, since sensible qualities *always* come into being and pass away causelessly.[10]

So it is Hume's ontology that leads him to see something fishy in the idea of necessities and impossibilities in nature. Accordingly, if we do not share his ontological views, we have no reason to think that there is anything peculiar, anything we should want to explain away, in the quite ordinary examples given above.

Conclusion

In the passage I quoted at the beginning of this chapter, Anscombe says that Hume has "made us see that given any particular cause – or 'total causal situation' for that matter – and its effect, there is not in general any contradiction in supposing the one to occur and the other not to occur." And she explains this by saying that "we would know what was being described – what it would be like for it to be true – if it were reported for example that a kettle of water was put, and kept, directly on a hot fire, but the water did not heat up." She thinks, in other words, that Hume has made us see that this world is an indeterministic world (even if a very *regular* one). I have argued that Hume has shown no such thing. At most he has shown that if we accept his ontology, we will then think what Anscombe thinks. But he has not shown that we would know what was being described if we were told that a kettle – an ordinary kettle – of water did not heat up when kept over a hot flame in the usual way. When it comes to kettles of water and hot flames, we do not think as Hume does about his sensible qualities. I mean, if someone came to us reporting a case such as Anscombe describes, we would either not take it seriously or would regard it as incomplete. Perhaps we would challenge it, saying, "How could *that* happen?" We might respond to the report as we do when we hear from naive people that while in India they saw the famous Indian rope trick performed, i.e., saw a man climb a rope that was not suspended from above. People do indeed *imagine* that they have seen such things happen, but that is only because they are easily fooled. Those of us who have our wits about us do not think such things *could* happen. This is not because we believe in the law of induction or expect the future to resemble the past. (Only someone who shares Hume's ontological views could give that explanation.) It is rather because we know quite a lot about how the world works. And how do we know such a thing? We gain such knowledge from our experience of the world. Or to put it in Humean terms, our observations and the tests we perform do indeed reveal necessary connections. And why shouldn't they if our world is not Hume's world of 'inert sensible qualities'? Why, that is, should it be surprising that we know from our observations of real flesh and blood human beings that if a man falls unimpeded to the pavement from a very great height – say, from the top of a ten story building – he is bound to be badly injured or killed? If we thought that Hume's world is a possible world and that we may, for all we know, reside in such a world, then we should have to declare that we do not really know such things. But there is no reason to allow that Hume's phenomenal world is a possible world. Put differently, Humeans have assumed that the burden of proof rests on anyone who would (with the vulgar) speak of necessities and impossibilities in nature. I have tried to show that the burden of proof rests on the shoulders of those who say that there are no necessities or impossibilities in nature and, furthermore, that Humeans cannot meet this challenge, that they have seemed to meet it only by begging the question, i.e., only by assuming that we live in an acausal world.

Notes

1. "Causality and Determination" in G. E. M. Anscombe, *Metaphysics and the Philosophy of Mind* (Oxford, 1981), p. 134.
2. There is a very different way of dealing with the causal theory. See Frank Ebersole's essay, "The Causal Theory of Perception," in his *Language and Perception*, op. cit., pp. 113–164.
3. In recent years several philosophers have undertaken to argue that Hume was a "causal realist," i.e., that he believed in objective necessary connections. This interpretation of Hume has been resoundingly refuted by Kenneth P. Winkler in "The New Hume," *The Philosophical Review*, October, 1991, pp. 541–579.
4. Another aspect of the paradox is that Hume is obliged to acknowledge that on his view "anything may produce anything" (*Treatise*, I, III, xv).
5. He says: "All events seem entirely loose and separate. One event follows another; but we never can observe any tie between them. They seem *conjoined*, but never *connected*. . . ." (*Enquiry*, Sec. VII, Part II).
6. For a useful account of these shambles, see Rom Harré, *The Principles of Scientific Thinking* (University of Chicago Press: Chicago, 1970), esp. Chapter Four.
7. For instance, physicists discussing the second law of thermodynamics will say *both* that this law "is a generalization of experience" and that it states, or implies, that when two bodies with a temperature differential are in contact, the flow of energy *must* be (*can only* be) from the warmer to the cooler body. See, for example, David Halliday and Robert Resnick, *Fundamentals of Physics* (John Wiley and Sons, Inc.: New York, 1981), second

edition, pp. 404–405. This is why physicists can declare that a certain sort of perpetual motion machine is impossible.

8. My dictionary defines a fatal injury as one that is "destined inevitably to cause death."

9. I here refer the reader to a delightful article on Hume by Jose Benardete, "Is there a Problem about Logical Possibility?" *Mind*, July, 1962, pp. 342–352. Although Benardete does not get to the bottom of the issue, i.e., does not explain the *source* of Hume's error, he does a nice job of sharpening the issue by showing that Hume's view of possibilities is in sharp conflict with our usual way of thinking.

10. Hume declares that we can "conceive any object to be non-existent this moment and existent the next, without conjoining to it the distinct idea of a cause or productive principle" and further declares that since we can conceive of such a causeless occurrence, such an occurrence is possible (*Treatise*, I, III, iii).

12

Wittgenstein's Humean View of Causation

A proper grasp of Wittgenstein's view of causation is essential for understanding many of his other philosophical views. Without such a grasp one cannot understand, for example, his 'machine-as-symbol' argument and so cannot understand what he says about following a rule and about the impossibility of a private language. Given what we have so far discovered about Wittgenstein's ontology, it is not difficult to anticipate his view of causation. As we saw in the preceding chapter, the idea that the world we perceive is an indeterministic world has its origin in the way Berkeley dismissed Locke's causal theory of perception: he dismissed Locke's material causes and retained the supposed effects, sensible qualities. This left him with a world in which nothing causes anything. Wittgenstein, as we have seen, also rejected Locke's causal theory in this manner, and accordingly we can expect to find that he thought we live in a world of uncaused sense-data. The *Tractatus* spells out very clearly the implications of this.

The Tractatus Account of Causation and Science

Wittgenstein states his basic idea with characteristic brevity: "Belief in the causal nexus is superstition" (TLP, 5.1361). He also says: "There is no compulsion making one thing happen because another has happened. The only necessity that exists is *logical* necessity" (TLP, 6.37)., i.e., there is no *causal* necessity. If we see someone falling to the pavement from a very great height, we think he is bound to be badly injured or killed, but Wittgenstein is saying that nothing is *bound to* happen: the man could walk away unhurt. Putting the same point, Wittgenstein says that "outside logic everything is accidental" (TLP, 6.3), "all that happens and is the case is accidental" (TLP, 6.41). This means that whatever happens, happens causelessly. It also means that regardless of what we have so far found to happen, it needn't happen like that in the future, e.g., if we put, and keep, a kettle of water directly on a hot fire, we may find (to our great surprise) that it turns to ice. Although this would be an astonishing event, it would, in an important respect, be no different from instances in which the water became hot, for whatever happens to the water is, as Wittgenstein puts it, accidental; i.e., even in the normal case all that happens is a *sequence* of events: the kettle is placed above the flame and then it heats up. There is no causal connection between the flame and the increased temperature of the water. Accordingly, there is, as Hume put it, no contradiction in supposing that tomorrow, or in the next minute, the course of nature (i.e., the regularities among our sense-data) will change. Wittgenstein himself put this as follows:

The so-called law of induction [i.e., that past regularities will continue into the future] cannot possibly be a law of logic, since it is obviously a proposition with sense [and so could prove to be false]. Nor, therefore, can it be an *a priori* law (TLP, 6.31).

He elaborates this point by saying:

It is clear that there are no grounds for believing that the simplest eventuality will in fact be realized (TLP, 6.3631).
    It is an hypothesis that the sun will rise tomorrow: and this means that we do not *know* whether it will rise (TLP, 6.36311).

Here we find Wittgenstein following Hume's practice of speaking of the sun – or rather, using the phrase "the sun" – while yet thinking that the world is comprised solely of sensible qualities. This makes these remarks somewhat misleading, but his point remains clear enough: it is conceivable that at any moment chaos – the breakdown of past regularities – could reign among our sense-impressions. Or, as Wittgenstein also puts it,

There is no possible way of making an inference from the existence of one situation [such as a man falling to the pavement from a great height] to the existence of another, entirely different situation [such as his being injured or killed] (TLP, 5.135).
    There is no causal nexus to justify such an inference (TLP, 5.136).
    We *cannot* infer the events of the future from those of the present (TLP, 5.1361).

Wittgenstein draws from this three implications regarding science. The first of these, which he regards as too obvious to bother stating, is that science is an inductive procedure. The second implication he states as follows:

The procedure of induction consists in accepting as true the *simplest* law that can be reconciled with our experiences (TLP, 6.363).
    This procedure, however, has no logical justification but only a psychological one (TLP, 6.3631).

He means: scientific laws are general propositions (of the simplest form we can manage) that hold for all *past* sense-data, but they cannot be shown to hold for *future* sense-data, although we expect them to.
    Having said this, Wittgenstein goes on to the third implication regarding science:

The whole modern conception of the world is founded on the illusion that the so-called laws of nature are the explanations of natural phenomena (TLP, 6.371).

Thus people today stop at the laws of nature, treating them as something inviolable, just as God and fate were treated in past ages.

And in fact both are right and both wrong: though the view of the ancients is clearer in so far as they have a clear and acknowledged terminus, while the modern system tries to make it look as if *everything* were explained (TLP, 6.372).[1]

Wittgenstein's attitude toward scientific explanation is, quite obviously, a proper consequence of his ontology. For once sense-data have been cut loose from material things, there can be no accounting for the regularities they exhibit. That there *are* such regularities is itself a mere accident, a wondrous, inexplicable happenstance. So explaining that so-and-so happened *because* such-and-such happened is as muddle-headed as anything could be. If, for example, we think that we can explain a man's death by saying that he ingested arsenic, and think that our explanation is sound because arsenic is known to be a poison, we are guilty of thinking that the correlation of arsenic and death bespeaks a causal nexus, that deaths have been *brought about* by arsenic. So Wittgenstein would say that a man's death cannot be *explained*; at most it can be fitted into a pattern of past regularities.

An important consequence of the foregoing is that "the only impossibility that exists is *logical* impossibility" (TLP, 6.375). This means that nothing is *physically* impossible and that therefore anything that is *logically* possible could actually occur. Accordingly, Wittgenstein says: "What can be described can also happen" (TLP, 6.362). Wittgenstein is saying that *any* purported description could be true, provided it contains no logical flaw, such as a contradiction. We can see the ramifications of this by considering a famous passage from the annals of phenomenalism:

What if something were to happen? . . . It can happen any time, perhaps right now. . . . For example, the father of a family might go out for a walk, and, across the street, he'll see something like a red rag, blown towards him by the wind. And when the rag has gotten close to him he'll see that it is a side of rotten meat, grimy with dust, dragging itself along by crawling, skipping, a piece of writhing flesh rolling in the gutter, spasmodically shooting out spurts of blood. Or a mother might look at her child's cheek and ask him: "What's that – a pimple?" and see the flesh puff out a little, split, open, and at the bottom of the split an eye, a laughing eye might appear. . . . And someone else might feel something scratching in his mouth. He goes to the mirror, opens his mouth: and his tongue is an enormous, live centipede, rubbing its legs together and scraping his palate.[2]

What Sartre means to be describing here – what we might call "metaphysical nightmares" – are things we would normally regard as being impossible, as we would many of the episodes that we find in fairy tales.

If a child who is being read a fairy tale were to ask, "Could straw really be spun into gold?" or "Could a prince turn into a frog?" we would assure him that such things *could not* happen. There are many things we would all regard as impossible, and yet Sartre says that such things "can happen any time, perhaps right now." And that is what Wittgenstein, too, is saying when he declares that "what can be described can also happen." His phrase "what can be described" is meant to cover anything we might find in a fairy tale or in the telling of a dream.[3] This is why he declares that nothing is impossible unless it is *logically* impossible. Because he finds no logical impossibility in such a sentence as "The man turned into a tree," he is prepared to allow that this could actually happen.

In Chapter 14 we will consider in greater detail this idea of logical possibility. Here it is sufficient to recognize that in the *Tractatus* Wittgenstein was declaring that metaphysical nightmares, such as those Sartre describes, could actually occur.

Did Wittgenstein's Views Change?

As I remarked in the Introduction, it is commonly held that after 1929 Wittgenstein dismissed the views he had set forth in the *Tractatus* and went on to create a revolutionary new philosophy. If this were true, we should expect to find him rejecting the Humean view of the world, i.e., dismissing the idea that metaphysical nightmares could actually occur. But is this what we find?

A pair of passages near the beginning of the *Tractatus* capture the Humean view of the world in a particularly striking way:

1.2 The world disintegrates [*zerfällt*] into facts.[4]
1.21 Each item can be the case or not the case while everything else remains the same.

Wittgenstein is saying here that in order for a state of affairs to come into being, no *other* state of affairs is required, i.e., states of affairs come into being *ex nihilo*. Also, in saying that such-and-such can *not* be the case while everything else remains the same, he is making a point which he was later to illustrate by saying, "I can, e.g., very well imagine that, although I see this hyacinth over there, I shall have no tactile perceptions when I want to touch it" (WVC, p. 161). In this instance, he means, everything else has remained the same, but this time the usual tactile perceptions do not occur. In his later writings Wittgenstein very often employed examples of this sort, as when he asks in the *Investigations*: "What kind of reason have I to assume that my finger will feel a resistance when it touches the table?" (PI, §478). He is taking it for granted here that he might walk up to a table and discover that his hand passes right through it.[5] Another of his examples is that he might put his hand in a fire and not get burned.

> If a man struggles against having his hand put in the fire, you can ask "Why does he struggle against it when he hasn't been burnt yet?"...
>
> If he says he "is likely" to be burnt, this seems to be a new suggestion. The reason why it's likely is [he might say] that he has been burnt a thousand times before. But we can omit the "likely"; for whatever reason he gives, he still may be burnt or not (WL32, p. 87).

He means that his past experience with fire gives him no *reason* to think, even, that it is *likely* that he will again be burned.

In the *Investigations* Wittgenstein again employs this example:

> The character of the belief in the uniformity of nature can perhaps be seen most clearly in the case in which we fear what we expect. Nothing could induce me to put my hand into a flame – although after all it is *only in the past* that I have burnt myself (PI, §472).
>
> The belief that fire will burn me is of the same kind as the fear that it will burn me (PI, §473).

In saying that we *expect* fire to burn us, that we *fear* that fire will burn us, and that we *believe* fire will burn us, he is thinking that the next time we stumble into a fire we may find that it does *not* burn us – not because we are wearing some sort of protective covering, but because fire (as Hume would say) has suddenly ceased to be 'conjoined with its usual attendant.'[6] Considered apart from the idea that we inhabit a world of uncaused sense-impressions, none of this would seem the least bit intelligible. For the belief (or expectation or fear) that he is thinking of is not like the following: Billy, age five, stays well back from the bonfire for fear that (or in the belief that) he will get burned if he goes a step closer. Billy's belief is a belief about how *close* one can safely get to a fire, and of course Billy may be overly cautious. Wittgenstein, by contrast, is saying that we have the belief (fear, expectation) that *fire* will burn us. Plainly, he thinks that one day we might encounter a fire that *won't* burn us. If one wonders how fire could be divided up in this way, i.e., separated from its capacity to singe things, cause blisters, etc., one must recall that Wittgenstein, like Hume, regards 'material things,' including flames, as 'bundles of sense-impressions' (RPP, I, §896), these impressions being only contingently related to one another. Wittgenstein's idea, then, is that just as I might feel no resistance when I go to put my hand on the table, so I might feel no heat or pain and get no blisters when I put my hand in a flame and hold it there. In both cases familiar visual qualities are present but the tactile qualities that have accompanied them in the past are absent.

Wittgenstein's remark that the world *disintegrates* into facts echoes Hume's remark that "all events seem entirely loose and separate.... They seem *conjoined*, but never *connected*."[7] The Humean-Wittgensteinian world is, one might say, a fractured world, a world in which events are bereft of any causal connections with one another. It is a world in which whatever happens 'just happens.' It is also a world in which planning and taking precautions provide no assurance of a safe or satisfactory outcome. Suppose, for example, that I take the precaution of building a boiler with walls thicker than safety engineers require. Wittgenstein says: "Now, can't a boiler produced in this way explode? Oh, yes" (PI, §466)[8] Had Wittgenstein been asked *how* such a thing *could* happen, he would have dismissed the question, for as he understands the world, an explosion, like any other event, 'just happens.' As he says in a passage quoted above, "There is no compulsion making one thing happen because another has happened," i.e., when something happens, it is not because something else has brought it about.

The passages I have quoted from *Philosophical Investigations* (§§466, 472–473, and 478) show that, contrary to received opinion, Wittgenstein did not, in his later years, turn his back on the *Tractatus* and reject the Humean view of the world. In the remainder of this chapter we will explore several consequences of Wittgenstein's embracing this view of the world.

Wittgenstein and Ordinary Language

Berkeley and Hume, having recognized that we commonly say things that conflict – or appear to conflict – with their claim that there are no causes in nature, tried, in their different ways, to show that the conflict is merely apparent. Wittgenstein was faced with the same problem, for he agreed with Berkeley and Hume that there is no causation in nature. But did he, like they, attempt to reconcile this with what we all think and say? In the *Tractatus* he says that "all the propositions of our everyday language, just as they stand, are in perfect logical order" (5.5563), so he presumably thought that there is no conflict between our use of causal language and his Humean view of the world – thought, that is, that a reductionist account of our causal language could be worked out. Yet he made no attempt in the *Tractatus* to show how this could be done. What does one find in his later work? Surprisingly, he says nothing at all about the fact that we say such things as "The boat was capsized by a large wave" and "The cat knocked the vase off the shelf." He does, however, make a number of remarks which we can compare with cases in which we speak of causal necessities and physical impossibilities.

In the *Investigations* he issues the following advice: "One cannot guess how a word functions. One has to *look at* its use and learn from that. But the difficulty is to remove the prejudice which stands in the way of doing this" (PI, §340). Our question is: Did Wittgenstein *look* at what we say or did he allow empiricist prejudices to stand in the way? More particularly, did he continue to think, as he had in the *Tractatus*, that "just as the only necessity that exists is *logical* necessity, so too the only impossibility that exists is *logical* impossibility" (TLP, 6.375)?

There are various cases to consider here, and we may begin by considering Wittgenstein's treatment of cases in which we say that something *cannot* happen or *cannot* be done. In The Blue Book, commenting on the fact that we say, "An iron nail can't scratch glass," he declares:

We could write this in the form "experience teaches that an iron nail *doesn't* scratch glass," thus doing away with the "can't" (BB, p. 49).

This shows us Wittgenstein's attitude toward our ordinary use of the word "can't." Instead of being instructed by what we say, he explains it away, declaring that we don't mean what we appear to mean.[9] Why? Because what we are saying in this case cannot be reconciled with his ontology: if we reside in an acausal world of 'sensible qualities,' we cannot rightly speak of something being *physically impossible*, for in such a world anything can happen at any moment, e.g., on the very next try we may find that an iron nail scratches glass or find that a blazing fire does not ignite paper.

Wittgenstein treats similar cases in more or less the same way: he either dismisses – or simply ignores – our talk about physical impossibilities and necessities. The best illustrations of this are found in his remarks about machines and what we say about them, in his so-called 'machine-as-symbol' argument. To understand this argument, we must bear several things in mind. First, Wittgenstein directs this argument at anyone who might think that human beings have certain intellectual *capacities* and that they do so by virtue of having in them a *mechanism*, the brain, which determines, for example, how they will go on to use a word once they've been taught it.[10] Second, his argument purports to show that, in order to think that humans have such intellectual powers, one must already have a misconception about machines, namely, the misconception that if a machine is in proper working order, its movements are *determined*, in the sense that, once it is set in motion, its parts *must* move, *can only* move, in certain ways (and that one can, by inspecting the machine, foresee, can *know*, how its parts *will* move). Third, this is a misconception, according to Wittgenstein, because the words "must," "can," and "cannot" are used properly only in speaking of *logical* necessities and impossibilities.[11] Fourth, Wittgenstein held this view of these words because his phenomenalistic view of the world obliged him to think that an unheard-of event (a metaphysical nightmare) can occur at any moment and thereby interrupt any regularity that has been observed in past instances, e.g., that the cogwheels of a machine can, unaccountably and unforeseeably, turn to mush or vanish or pass through one another, so that the machine, instead of going according to plan, suddenly runs amuck. Given these four presuppositions, Wittgenstein was bound to think that, in talking about machines, we say some very strange things.

Suppose, for instance, that a screwdriver has fallen into a machine and jammed there. While trying to remove it, someone says, "If we turn this wheel this way, it will come loose." A mechanic, more familiar with the machine, says, "It *can't* turn in that direction; there's a ratchet that prevents it from going backward." Here, in speaking of an actual machine, one might say, "It *can't* turn that way." We might also say in such a case, "It can only turn clockwise." Judging by his treatment of "A nail can't scratch glass," we should expect to find Wittgenstein explaining this away, and this is precisely what he does in the following passage.

If we know the machine, everything else, that is its movements, seem to be already completely determined.
"We talk as though these parts *could* only move in this way, as if they could not do anything else."
How is this – do we forget the possibility of their bending, breaking off, melting, and so on? Yes; in *many* cases we don't think of that at all (RFM, pp. 84–85).

What are these 'possibilities' that we allegedly ignore? Wittgenstein was not thinking that these are well-known possibilities that a mechanic, in a fit of absent-mindedness, might forget. (If his argument depended on his introducing possibilities of *that* sort, one could easily get around his argument by assuming that the mechanism is quite a simple one and that the defects to which it is subject had been carefully checked and eliminated.) He means that in an acausal world there are possibilities that (as he puts it) we don't think of at all – such as the possibility of the ratchet in my example suddenly and unaccountably turning to mush. What, then, is Wittgenstein's conclusion about the fact that we say, for example, "The wheel *can't* turn that way; there's a ratchet preventing it from going backward"? In the passage from which I am quoting he goes on to say:

But we do not say this kind of thing [i.e., we don't say "can't" or "can only"] when we are concerned with predicting the actual behaviour of a machine. Here we do not in general forget the possibility of a distortion of the parts and so on (RFM, p. 85).

He goes on in this passage to say that it is only when we are treating the machine as a 'symbol' that we say, "The wheel *can't* turn like that."[12] He is, of course, entirely wrong about this, for we say "can't" in a case such as the one I described, where we are trying to free a screwdriver from the cogs of an *actual* machine. So in the passage last quoted Wittgenstein, in order to cover up the conflict between his metaphysics and what we actually think and say, simply denies that we say what we do say.

Let us turn now to cases in which we say that we *know* what is going to happen. In the following passage Wittgenstein takes notice of such cases:

> In many cases we think of a thing in terms of a mechanism. The point of thinking of it in these terms is that from the way it looks and from certain tests I shall call static (handling, looking, etc.) and which are made before we test the behavior of the mechanism, we draw conclusions as to how it *will* behave. For example, when we have examined a screw and found, say, that its threads are not broken, we say we *know* what it is going to do if certain things are done to it (WL35, p. 82; emphasis added).

Here Wittgenstein acknowledges that we say we *know* what will happen if certain things are done to the machine. (The situation might be as follows. A machine operator, in a careless moment, allows his sleeve to catch in the cogs of his machine, whereupon it jams and stops. Other workers gather about, offering advice. One of them makes several futile attempts at freeing the sleeve, then looks more closely at the gears and says, "Ah, *now* I know what to do. If this gear is turned clockwise, this other one will turn counter-clockwise, and the sleeve will come free.") That we speak of *knowing* such a thing could only have puzzled Wittgenstein, and accordingly the above passage continues as follows:

> Yet it does not *follow* from the way it looks that it *will* behave so-and-so. For we can imagine a fountain pen, for example, which looks like mine and yet will not unscrew. We examine its screw and cap and predict that it will behave in such-and-such a way, but whether it *will* behave in this way is a hypothesis, a conjecture. There is *no* static test, i.e., one to which we submit a mechanism before it is put into use, which will enable us to *know* it is going to work in a certain way. This is always hypothetical. We may be wrong in expecting a certain behavior.
>
> We are accustomed to think of things in terms of a very few definite possibilities. . . .
>
> When we see a diagram of a wheel connected with a piston rod we have one idea of how it will behave. We do not assume that the wheel is made of dough or will suddenly become elliptical. Yet how do we know that these things will not happen? (WL35, pp. 82–83).

So in the first part of this passage he acknowledges that "we say we know what [the machine] is going to do if certain things are done to it." Yet he goes on in the latter part of the passage to insist that there is no way "to *know* it is going to work in a certain way." That is, instead of taking a lesson from what we say, his own prejudices (the four presuppositions of his argument that I listed above) force him to deny that we say what even *he* has acknowledged we do say.

An important feature of the above passage is that Wittgenstein says that "we are accustomed to think of things in terms of a very few definite possibilities," and he goes on to explain that we do not ordinarily consider the possibility that the wheel "will suddenly become elliptical." Here we find him taking for granted the fourth of the presuppositions listed above. He made this more explicit in his 1939 lectures by saying: "You might think the cogs [of the machine] would vanish away, or explode. But you don't" (LFM, p. 195). And in the *Investigations* he writes:

. . . A misleading analogy lies at the root of this idea; the causal nexus seems to be established by a mechanism connecting two parts of the machine. The connexion may be broken if the mechanism is disturbed. (We think only of the disturbances to which a mechanism is *normally* subject, not, say, of cog-wheels suddenly going soft, or passing through one another, and so on) (PI, §613, emphasis added).

Here Wittgenstein makes explicit the distinction on which his argument turns, namely, between "disturbances to which a mechanism is normally subject," such as worn bearings, and those of a very different sort, such as cogwheels "passing through one another." It is by invoking the possibility of the latter 'disturbances' – those we never think of – that he means to prove that we never *know* how a machine will behave.

So we must ask what he means by "cogwheels passing through one another." A philosopher might talk this way if, like Wittgenstein, he were thinking of a cogwheel as a 'bundle of sense-impressions' that are related to one another only by certain regularities in our past experience. Such a philosopher would think that on some future occasion past regularities might cease. Impenetrability is one such regularity: in the past when we have seen certain shapes approach each other, they haven't coalesced, but they might do so in the future. So Wittgenstein says:

. . . suppose I wanted to call this chair Jacob. What did I really give the name to? The shape or the chair? . . . If two chairs that looked absolutely alike moved towards each other, penetrated each other, and then separated again – how could I know, then, which of them was Jacob? The possibility of giving names to things presupposes very complicated experiences. (Impenetrability!) (WVC, p. 51).

What Wittgenstein says here about the two chairs resembles what one might say about a cartoon film involving two chairs (or two cogwheels), where the images on the screen coalesce. Plainly, he was thinking of the chairs as a phenomenalist *would* think of them. And this is how, in the earlier passage, he was thinking of the cogwheels when he says that we normally do not take into consideration the possibility of their 'passing through' one another: he was thinking of them as phenomenal objects.

Because Wittgenstein thought that we reside in a phenomenal, and hence an acausal, world, he was obliged to think that what we say about an actual machine should not be taken at face value, for metaphysical nonsense results when one does take it at face value. Thus, he writes:

When does one have the thought: the possible movements of a machine are already there in it in a mysterious way? Well, when one is doing philosophy.

And what leads us into thinking that? The kind of way in which we talk about machines. We say, for example, that a machine *has* (*possesses*) such-and-such possibilities of movement. . . .

We pay attention to the expressions we use concerning these things [i.e., machines]; we do not understand them, however, but misinterpret them. When we do philosophy we are like savages, primitive people, who hear the expressions of civilized men, put a false interpretation on them, and then draw queer conclusions from it (PI, §194).

It is, however, Wittgenstein who is confused in what he says about machines, for he thinks of them as phenomenal entities. It never occurred to him to consider that, in talking as we do about machines, we are *not* talking about his phenomenal, indeterministic world.

Let us consider, finally, examples in which we say that something must be causing what is happening. Wittgenstein comments:

We are accustomed to think of things in terms of a very few definite possibilities. If two cylinders are such that one is smaller than the other, we say that one will turn inside the other. If it does not, we say something must be stopping it. It might be very puzzling why it does not turn, and we might say that there must be a *cause* for its not turning (WL35, p. 82).

We could suppose that Wittgenstein has in mind here an old-fashioned ice cream freezer, the kind turned with a hand crank. Anyone who has used such freezers will recall that they very often get stuck, that the crank won't turn. And Wittgenstein remarks, quite rightly, "If it does not [turn], we say something must be stopping it."[13] We can anticipate what Wittgenstein says about this by recalling his remark (see above) that anything "can be the case or not the case while everything else remains the same." In conformity with this Wittgenstein was obliged to think that despite the fact that everything else has remained the same as when the crank turned freely, the crank will now not turn at all. Thus, he continues the above-quoted passage by saying:

But what more does this mean than that in some circumstances it will turn and in others not. To say it will turn if nothing is wrong means nothing. Can't I assume that it does not turn [even if nothing is wrong]? We do not have here a case of one thing [i.e., there being a *cause* of its not turning] following logically from another [from the fact that it won't turn]. It is a conjecture [that something is preventing the cylinder from turning] (WL35, pp. 82–83).

In the earlier part of the passage Wittgenstein acknowledges that we say in cases of the sort in question, "Something must be stopping it," but in this latter part of the passage he seems to be saying that this use of "must" is a *mis*use because "Something is stopping it" does not follow logically from "It won't turn." And he adds that, if the cylinder does not turn, it is only a *conjecture* that something is stopping it. Here again we find Wittgenstein presupposing that the world we live in is a phenomenal, and hence an indeterministic, world, so that nothing *need* be stopping it. And although he notices what we say in cases of the sort in question, he dismisses it and thus fails to learn a lesson from it.

In the passages we have considered thus far Wittgenstein meant to be criticizing only philosophers. He took himself to be saying that ordinary people do not talk about machines in the ways he criticizes. But the matter is otherwise when it comes to science, for he thought that scientists make the same mistake as philosophers, i.e., they think that events do not happen causelessly.

The 'Causal Point of View'

We find Wittgenstein's attitude toward science displayed in the following passages:

Lavoisier makes experiments with substances in his laboratory and now he concludes that this and that takes place when there is burning. He does not say that it might happen otherwise another time. He has got hold of a definite world-picture – not of course one that he invented: he learned it as a child (OC, §167).

The insidious thing about the causal point of view is that it leads us to say: "Of course, it had to [*musste*] happen like that." Whereas we ought to think: it could have happened like that and also in many other ways (CV, p. 37).

Wittgenstein claims that Lavoisier has a 'world-picture' inasmuch as he does not say that combustion might occur in a different way on some other occasion. This seems to be what Wittgenstein, in the second passage, calls "the causal point of view," which he declares to be "insidious." What are we to make of this?

There are two points to be borne in mind here, the first of which comes to light when Wittgenstein says:

Physics is not history. It prophesies. If you tried to conceive of physics as a mere report on the facts observed to date, it would be lacking its most essential element, its relation to the future (WVC, p. 101).[14]

He also says that natural laws "refer to the future *ad infinitum*" (WVC, p. 100). Thus we find that when he gives an example of a law of nature, he employs the future tense: "The statement that a mechanism made of iron *will* when tested in a certain way behave so-and-so is a law of nature" (WL35, pp. 83–84, emphasis added). I assume that he here states the "law" without reference to *past* cases merely to simplify the example. For in fact what he actually thinks about laws of nature is (i) that they are what logicians call "universal propositions" (having the form "All A is B" or "If A, then B")[15] and (ii) that the generalization covers future instances as well as past instances of the conjunction. As regards the past instances, Wittgenstein sees no problem: "Whatever may happen in the future, however water may behave in the future, we *know* that up to now it has behaved *thus* in innumerable instances" (OC, §558). His problem about laws of nature concerns the (as yet unobserved) future instances that are 'prophesied' by the generalization that *all* As are Bs. For if the scientist's generalization covers future instances in an *indeterministic* world, how is he to know that his generalization is true?

Wittgenstein's problem, then, with 'the causal point of view' is the following. Because Lavoisier does not content himself with saying that combustion has, in the past, always occurred in such-and-such a way, but instead 'prophesies' about future instances, it looks to Wittgenstein as though what Lavoisier and other scientists say, in formulating laws, flies in the face of the Humean view of the world. It looks to Wittgenstein, in other words, as though scientists are regularly implying that he is mistaken in regarding the world as indeterministic. This is why he declares 'the causal point of view' to be insidious.

How did Wittgenstein propose to deal with this? He explains himself most clearly in his example of the seeds, which he discusses briefly in *Zettel* (§608) but much more fully in a notebook, from which I here quote:

Think of two different kinds of plant, A and B, both of which yield seeds; the seeds of both kinds look exactly the same and even after the most careful investigation we can find no difference between them. But the seeds of an A-plant always produce more A-plants, the seeds of a B-plant, more B-plants. In this situation we can predict what sort of plant will grow out of such a seed only if we know which plant it has come from. Are we to be satisfied with this; or should we say: "There *must* be a difference in the seeds themselves, otherwise they *couldn't* produce different plants; their previous histories on their own *can't* cause their further development unless their histories have left traces in the seeds themselves"?

But now what if we don't discover any difference between the seeds? And the fact is: It wasn't from the peculiarities of either seed that we made the prediction but from its previous history. If I say: the history can't be the cause of the development, then this doesn't mean that I can't predict the development from the previous history, since that's what I do. It means rather that we don't call *that* a 'causal connection,' that this isn't a case of predicting the effect from the cause.

And to protest: "There *must* be a difference in the seeds, even if we don't discover it," doesn't alter the facts, it only shows what a powerful urge we have to see everything in terms of the cause and effect schema [*durch das Ursache und Wirkung Schema*].

When people talk about graphology, physiognomics and such like they constantly say: ". . . clearly character must be expressed in handwriting somehow. . . ." "Must": that means we are going to apply this picture come what may.

(One might even say that philosophy is the grammar of the words "must" and "can," for this is how it shows what is a priori and what a posteriori.) . . .

And now suppose that in the foregoing example someone had at last succeeded in discovering a difference between the seed of an A-plant and the seed of a B-plant: he would no doubt say: "There, you see, it just isn't possible for *one seed* to grow into two different plants." What if I were to retort: "How do you know that the characteristic you have discovered is not completely irrelevant? How do you know *that* has anything to do with which of the two plants grows out of the seed?" (CE, pp. 410–411).

Wittgenstein is not here suggesting that the discovered difference in the seeds may be an inessential difference and that further tests might show this. Rather, he is challenging 'the causal point of view' by saying: Even if you have found *all* the differences there are between the seeds, how do you know that when a cabbage grows from this seed, it does so because of the structure of the seed, i.e., how do you know that the sprouting of the cabbage isn't an uncaused event?

We can get a better understanding of what Wittgenstein is getting at by recalling that Berkeley, in his *Principles*, entertained the question: "Might not vegetables grow, and shoot forth leaves and blossoms, and animals perform all their motions, as well without . . . all that variety of internal parts so elegantly contrived and put together. . . ?" (§60). He answers that "those parts and organs [are] not absolutely necessary to the producing [of] any effect" (§62). Similarly, Wittgenstein says that a plant "might come into being even out of something quite amorphous, as it were causelessly" (Z, §608). And in his 1946–47 lectures he said that we might be unable, even with the use of a microscope, to find any difference between seeds from which lilies grow and those from which roses grow (WL47, p. 90), thus implying that when a lily sprouts from a seed it does so causelessly. His point, then, in the above passage, is that science does not show that it is a mistake to think that an uncaused event occurs when a cabbage sprouts from a seed. Accordingly, he says:

What a curious attitude scientists have: "We still don't know that [e.g., whether the seeds of lilies and roses differ]; but it is knowable and it is only a matter of time before we get to know it!" As if that went without saying (CV, p. 40).

What are we to make of this argument? I suppose we can concede that science does not show – or even try to show – that the world is not indeterministic. But Wittgenstein was surely wrong if he thought that this provides support for his Humean view of the world, for as we saw in the preceding chapter, this view of the world is a complicated piece of metaphysics which results from the (wrong-headed) way in which Berkeley, Hume and Wittgenstein rejected Locke's causal theory of perception.

In a further discussion of the seed example, Wittgenstein makes a rather startling suggestion about 'the causal point of view,' namely, that it might be abandoned altogether:

Imagine we had seeds which came from two plants. We find that the two plants have exactly the same seed. But if it comes from a poppy, the seed produces a poppy again; if it comes from a rose it produces a rose. . . .

There is something like action at a distance here – which shocks people. The idea would revolutionize science. "A seed that has come from a poppy will produce a poppy" – this is all right. But not: "It will produce a poppy *because* it came from a poppy."

Today, in case we actually discovered two seeds which we could not distinguish, we should look frantically for a difference. But in other circumstances we might give this up – give up looking for a difference. This would be a tremendous thing to do – as great as recognizing indeterminacy. We would no longer *look* for the difference, and so we would no longer say there *must* be a difference.... (CE, pp. 433–434).

What is Wittgenstein proposing here – merely that we might close up our laboratories and stop doing science? No, for that would not 'revolutionize science.' He is proposing, rather, that we might abandon 'the causal point of view,' meaning that we might come to embrace the following idea: even if we do find a difference between, for example, a cabbage seed and a carrot seed, this discovery has no bearing on the fact that different plants grow from these seeds.

What Wittgenstein had in mind comes out more clearly in the following passage from his 1932–33 lectures:

If an explosion occurs when a ball is dropped, we say that some phenomenon must have occurred to make the cause proportional to the effect. On hunting for the phenomenon and not finding it, we say that it has merely not yet been found. We believe we are dealing with a natural law *a priori*, whereas we are dealing with a norm of expression that we ourselves have fixed. Whenever we say that something must be the case we have given an indication of a rule for the regulation of our expression....

The statement that there must be a cause shows that we have got a rule of language. Whether all velocities can be accounted for by the assumption of invisible masses is a question of mathematics, or grammar, and is not to be settled by experience.... It is a question of the adopted norm of explanation. In a system of mechanics, for example, there is a system of causes, although there may be no causes in another system. A system could be made up in which we would use the expression "My [emotional] breakdown had no causes." If we weighed a body on a balance and took the different readings several times over, we could either say that there is no such thing as absolutely accurate weighing *or* that each weighing is accurate but that the weight changes in an unaccountable manner. If we say we are not going to account for the changes, then we would have a system in which we would have no causes. We ought not say that there are no causes in nature, but only that [once we have ceased to account for the difference in weight] we have a system in which there are no causes. Determinism and indeterminism are properties of a system which are fixed arbitrarily (WL35, pp. 15–16).

This passage suggests that Wittgenstein had the following idea: science is a language game, one of whose rules is that one may always ask (and seek an answer to), "What causes this?" But since rules are man-made, we can always alter the rules by which we play, and in particular we could drop the rule that permits the question "What causes this?" i.e., we could adopt an 'indeterministic system.'

To understand how Wittgenstein thought of this, it will be useful to consider how he would have answered the following three questions: (i) What would it be like for us to adopt an 'indeterministic system'? (ii) Don't scientists go on, in case after case, asking (and seeking to answer) "What causes this?" because there are causes in nature awaiting discovery? (iii) If we were to abandon 'the causal point of view,' wouldn't we be consigning ourselves to a life of ignorance – to ignorance, for example, of the causes of various diseases? Let us take these questions in order.

(i) Did Wittgenstein think that, if we adopted an 'indeterministic system,' we would stop saying, for example, that a wave capsized the boat, that the cat knocked the vase off the shelf, and so on? No, I think he meant that we would go on saying such things but would not do what scientists do, namely, look for 'hidden causes,' those not apparent to the plain man, to nonscientists. More particularly, he thought that our lives would then resemble those of people who lived many hundreds of years ago, before there existed anything resembling modern science, for he thought that those people regarded many events as occurring causelessly. To understand this, it is useful to consider something Hume said about the peasants of his own time. He said: "The vulgar, who take things according to their first appearance, attribute the uncertainty of events to such an uncertainty in the causes as makes them often fail of their usual influence, tho' they meet with no obstacle nor impediment in their operation." He means that the vulgar often think that something has happened *causelessly*. Hume then goes on to contrast this with the way in which scientists think:

But philosophers [i.e., scientists] observing that almost in every part of nature there is contain'd a vast variety of springs and principles, which are hid, by reason of their minuteness or remoteness, find that 'tis at least possible the contrariety of events may not proceed from any contingency in the cause, but from the secret operation of contrary causes. This possibility is converted into a certainty [for them] by farther observation, when they remark that upon an exact scrutiny, a contrariety of effects always betrays a contrariety of causes, and proceeds from their mutual hindrance and opposition. A peasant can give no better reason for the stopping of any clock or watch than to say, that commonly it does not go right. But an artisan easily perceives, that the same force in the spring or pendulum has always the same influence on the wheels; but fails of its usual effect, perhaps by reason of a grain of dust, which puts a stop to the whole movement. From the observation of several parallel instances, philosophers [i.e., scientists] form a maxim, that the connexion betwixt all causes and effects is equally necessary, and that its seeming uncertainty in some instances proceeds from the secret operation of contrary causes (*Treatise*, I, III, 12).

What Hume refers to here as the scientist's "maxim" is what Wittgenstein called "the causal point of view" or "the cause and effect schema." And the point is that Hume held that it is this that distinguishes scientists from uneducated peasants: the latter believe that many things happen for no reason at all – they 'just happen.'

I suspect that Hume is here distorting the facts, that the peasants of whom he speaks meant only that they hadn't the faintest idea of why this or that has happened. Nevertheless, Wittgenstein seems to have shared Hume's view of this matter, so that in suggesting that we might abandon 'the causal point of view' and adopt an 'indeterministic system,' he meant that we might come to think of things in the way Hume's peasants did.[16]

(ii) Don't scientists go on, in case after case, asking (and seeking to answer) "What causes this?" because there are causes in nature awaiting discovery? To understand Wittgenstein's answer to this question, we must bear in mind that he regarded science as a language game, one rule of which is that one may always ask (and seek to answer) "What causes this?" and, because he regarded this rule as being man-made, he regarded it as being arbitrary, so that we could drop it and adopt an 'indeterministic system.' Because he thought of science in this way, he rejected the idea that we go on searching for, say, the cause(s) of cancer because there are causes in nature awaiting discovery. This is what he is getting at when he says: "We have the idea that language is kept in bounds by reality. . ." (WL32, p. 103), i.e., we have the mistaken idea that scientists inquire after causes because *there are* causes. Speaking against this idea, he says:

> . . . causality is at the bottom of what [physicists] do. It is really a description of the style of their investigation. Causality stands with the physicist for a style of thinking. Compare in religion the postulate of a creator. In a sense it seems to be an explanation, yet in another it does not explain at all. Compare a workman who finishes something off with a spiral. He can do it so that it ends in a knob or tapers off to a point. So with creation. God is one style; the nebula another. A style gives us satisfaction; but one style is not more rational than another. . . .
> . . . The whole chain of our reasoning is not supported any more than the earth is supported; the whole of grammar is not supported in the sense that a sentence is supported [i.e., shown to be true] by reality. You can't in fact call language or grammar unsupported because there is no question of its being supported. But the rules of grammar are not a deduction from the nature of reality (WL32, pp. 103–104).

Wittgenstein is saying that science is an optional language game in the sense that, while scientists search for hidden causes, there is nothing in the nature of the facts that *obliges* anyone to do so, i.e., we can imagine people playing a language game that differs from ours in that they do *not* seek out hidden causes and yet their language game does not, on that account, come in conflict with how things are in the world.[17]

What are we to make of this argument? It is, of course, easy to imagine people – like those who lived two thousand years ago – who knew nothing about science. But it seems absurd to say that they were not missing anything that is there in the world to be discovered. We now know, for example, that scurvy is caused by a dietary deficiency – a deficiency of vitamin C. Because people who lived long ago knew little about dietary requirements, they remained ignorant (until 1753) of the cause of scurvy. How could Wittgenstein, in the argument outlined above, deny this? This brings us to our third question.

(iii) If we abandoned science, wouldn't we be consigning ourselves to a life of ignorance? Wittgenstein's answer to this should now be obvious. He would say that we do *not* today know anything about the *cause* of, for example, scurvy, for there is no such thing to be known.[18] Why would he have given this answer? Because, like Berkeley, he thought that we live in a world of uncaused sensible qualities, so that, as he put it in the *Tractatus*, "all that happens and is the case is accidental" (TLP, 6.41).

At the end of Chapter 8 I said that Wittgenstein dealt with philosophical problems by simply taking it for granted that his empiricist ontology is correct. His treatment of 'the causal point of view' is a case in point. Because it never occurred to him to challenge the Humean view of the world, he thought that if we were to abandon the pursuit of science, we would not thereby fail to notice (genuine) causal connections, because there are no causal connections to be found. But because he did not recognize that he was himself in the grip of a philosophical muddle, he believed that he saw in our scientific pursuits a profound confusion, and this led him to adopt a pessimistic – a Spenglerian – attitude toward mankind.[19]

Notes

1. Wittgenstein's way of stating his point here appears to have been borrowed from Karl Pearson's *The Grammar of Science*, op. cit., esp. pp. 119–121. Pearson says, in part: "Primitive man placed a sun-god behind the sun . . . because he did not see how and why it moved. The physicist now proceeds to describe how the sun moves. . . . The description of that motion is given by Newton's law of gravitation, but the *why* of that motion is just as mysterious to us as the motion of the sun to the barbarian. . . ." In the Preface to the third edition Pearson sums up this point by saying: "Nobody believes now that science *explains* anything. . ." (p. xi). Schopenhauer said much the same thing: "Every explanation in natural science must ultimately end with . . . a *qualitas occulta*, and thus with complete obscurity" (*The World as Will and Idea*, Book I, Sec. 12).
2. Jean Paul Sartre, *Nausea* (New York, 1964), pp. 158–159.
3. It is noteworthy that in his later writings, when illustrating what could actually occur, he gives examples derived, apparently, from something Russell said about dreams. In "The Relation of Sense-Data to Physics" Russell remarks that "it often happens that dream-objects fail to behave in the accustomed manner: heavy objects fly, solid objects melt, babies turn into pigs or undergo even greater changes" (op. cit., p. 177). In the *Investigations* Wittgenstein speaks of the cogwheels of a machine unaccount-

ably "melting" (PI, §193) or "going soft" (PI, §613). And where Russell speaks of dreaming that babies turn into pigs, Wittgenstein proposes that he might see men turn into trees (OC, §513).

4. Jorn Bramann has made the following observation about this passage: "It may not be entirely unimportant that Wittgenstein says in 1.2 'Die Welt zerfällt in Tatsachen.' It is usually translated as 'The world divides into facts.' This translation is correct, but 'zerfällt' is a much more expressive word than 'divides.' It literally means 'falls apart,' or 'disintegrates,' thus connoting an image of the world which stresses the world's lack of cohesion. . . ." (Jorn K. Bramann, Wittgenstein's Tractatus and the Modern Arts (Rochester: Adler, 1985), p. 84).

5. In this connection see the conversation with Wittgenstein reported by Norman Malcolm in Ludwig Wittgenstein: A Memoir, op. cit., p. 88.

6. Wittgenstein says: "Causality rests on an observed uniformity. Now, that doesn't mean that a uniformity we have observed until now will go on forever" (PG, p. 66).

7. An Enquiry Concerning Human Understanding, Sec. VII, Part II.

8. This passage from Philosophical Investigations has a rather long history. It occurs in Philosophical Grammar (§67), which makes its date of composition to be no later than 1933. An earlier version of it is found in Wittgenstein's conversations with Waismann in 1930. That version runs, in part, as follows: "Now, if I am asked, Had you any right to make the boiler 15mm thick? can you sleep soundly? – then I cannot help replying with a counter-question: What does 'right' mean here? If what you mean by it is that we know that an explosion of the boiler is impossible, then I had no such right" (WVC, p. 172).

9. It is noteworthy that fifteen years later, in 1949, he still clung to this Humean view. Commenting on "It isn't possible for pears to grow on an apple tree," he explained away the words "isn't possible" by saying that "this only means that . . . apples grow on apple trees and pears grow on pear trees" (quoted by O. K. Bouwsma in Wittgenstein: Conversations 1949–1951, op. cit., p. 37).

10. It was evidently Wittgenstein's reading Wolfgang Kohler's Gestalt Psychology in 1930 (Chapter 7, note 4, this volume) that led him to cast the problem in these terms. In the chapter entitled "Dynamics as Opposed to Machine Theory," Kohler attributes to introspectionists and behaviorists what he calls "machine theories of life." In discussing what such theories amount to, Kohler talks about machines, saying that "the machines of our factories . . . cause movement" and that "the form and order of this movement are prescribed by the anatomy of the machines" (op. cit., pp. 62–63). To illustrate this, he says: "In a steam engine . . . the piston can move only in one fashion, which is prescribed by the rigid walls of the cylinder" (ibid., p. 64, emphasis added). In such a system, he adds, the structure of the machine excludes "all possibilities except one," for "the motion of [the piston] is prescribed by the walls of a cylinder" (ibid., p. 65). These remarks contain the key words and phrases Wittgenstein is concerned with in his machine-as-symbol argument, namely, "can only," "rigid" and "possibilities." He even uses Kohler's piston example (LFM, p. 195).

11. In conversations he said: "The word 'can' is obviously a grammatical (logical) concept, not a material one" (WVC, p. 67).

12. Treating a machine as a symbol, Wittgenstein explains, means treating it as a diagram of a machine is used in kinematics, where the relationships in question are geometrical, so the question "Can this rod move like this?"

would be a question whether it was, for example, long enough, not whether it was strong enough (see LFM, p. 196).

13. Consider some examples. Suppose that I am not very experienced with these freezers and have little or no idea of what may go wrong with them. In that case, when I find that the crank won't turn, I will perhaps say, "Something is stopping it" or "Something must be jamming the mechanism." Suppose, however, that I have had experience with hand-crank freezers, and each time that I've encountered a problem turning the crank I have found a piece of ice lodged in the gears and that the crank turned freely once the ice was removed. Now when the crank gets stuck again, I will most likely say, "There must be some ice caught in the gears." But if I then fail to find anything caught in the gears, what will I say? I will very likely say, "Well, *something* is stopping it!" and then find a clump of ice jammed between the cylinder walls, which is the most common cause of the problem.

14. Wittgenstein's friend, Frank Ramsey, said something similar: "As opposed to a purely *descriptive* theory of science, mine may be called a *forecasting* theory. To regard a law as a summary of certain facts seems to me inadequate; it is also an attitude of expectation for the future" ["General Propositions and Causality," in F. P. Ramsey, *The Foundations Mathematics* (London: Routledge and Kegan Paul, 1931), p. 255].

15. That he thinks of laws as being what logicians call "universal propositions" comes out when he begins a passages as follows: "Does a proposition such as 'All bodies move . . .' (Law of Inertia) . . ." (LW, I, §9). This gross misconception of science is owing to the empiricists" idea that any 'proposition' must find a niche in the logician's categories.

16. William James, one of Wittgenstein's favorite philosophers, may have influenced his attitude toward science. James writes: "The aspiration to be 'scientific' is such an idol of the tribe to the present generation, is so sucked in with his mother's milk by everyone of us, that we find it hard to conceive of a creature who would not feel [that aspiration], and harder still to treat it freely as the altogether peculiar and one-sided subjective interest which it is. But as a matter of fact, few even of the cultivated members of the race have shared it; it was invented but a generation or two ago. In the middle ages [science] meant only impious magic. . ." [*The Principles of Psychology*, Vol II (Dover, 1950), p. 640, fn.].

17. Commenting on the "arbitrariness of grammar" Wittgenstein says: "The thing that's so difficult to understand can be expressed like this. *As long as* we remain in the province of the true–false games a change in the grammar [e.g., to an indeterministic system] can only lead us from *one* such game to another, and never from something true to something false" (PG, pp. 110–111). See in this connection the first paragraph of Z, §331.

18. Wittgenstein quotes from Ernest Renan's *History of the People of Israel* the following passage: "Birth, sickness, death, madness, catalepsy, sleep, dreams, all made an immense impression [on primitive peoples] and, even nowadays, only a few have the gift of seeing clearly that these phenomena have causes within our constitution." Renan meant that people with a scientific education know what causes the various things he mentions and are, for that reason, no longer wonder-struck by such things. Commenting on this, Wittgenstein remarks acidly: "As though lightning were more commonplace or less astounding today than 2000 years ago. Man has to awaken to wonder – and so perhaps do peoples. Science is a way of sending him to sleep again" (CV, p. 5). He evidently meant that we do *not* know that

the phenomena in question have natural causes – not, of course, because he thought that further research is needed, but because he thought that no amount of research leads to a knowledge of causes.
19. See G. H. von Wright, "Wittgenstein in Relation to His Times," in *Wittgenstein and His Times*, ed. Brian McGuinness (Chicago: University of Chicago Press, 1982), pp. 108–120, esp. p. 113.

13

The Problem of Induction

In his post-*Tractatus* years Wittgenstein represented himself as solving – or dispelling – philosophical problems by paying close attention to the use of those words that lead to philosophical puzzlement. We have seen that very often, at least, he did not do what he claimed to be doing. In this chapter I want to call attention to another instance in which, rather than paying attention to what we actually say, he simply invented something in order to reach conclusions that suited him, namely, his way of dealing with philosophical skepticism regarding 'induction.'

Induction and Skepticism

Induction is itself one of the myths invented by empiricists. There could never be any such thing. A philosopher could think that scientists (and others) employ 'the inductive method' only if he also thinks that nothing *causes* anything (except in Hume's ersatz sense). The idea behind speaking of 'the inductive method' is this: we experiment in order to discover regularities in nature, and the point of seeking out regularities is that we have to deal with the future in various ways. The more instances we have found of a given regularity, the better equipped we are to predict and to act. But what does "better equipped" mean here? Empiricists (Humeans) have differed widely on this matter. Some have said that the more instances we have found of a regularity the more probable it is that the regularity will persist in the future. Wittgenstein, however, rejected this view on the grounds that past experiences of a regularity can never make it at all *likely* that it will continue into the future. His reason for so insisting comes directly from his ontology. For if the world is indeterministic, then anything can happen at any time, regardless of what has happened before. (Compare: if you are tossing a *fair* coin, then it is always a 50–50 chance that it will come up heads, even if it has come up tails on the first n tosses.[1]) This means that he is obliged to think that regardless of the fact that water has *always* become hot when placed in a kettle above a hot flame, it may not do so in the future. That water has always behaved in such-and-such a way is nothing more than a long lucky run. We find Wittgenstein explaining this point in the following passage:

If a man struggles against having his hand put in the fire, you can ask "Why does he struggle against it when he hasn't been burnt yet?." . . .

. . . We could say that he has good reason to kick if his reason is that he has been burnt before. But he still may or may not be burnt this time. There is no justification yet.

If he says he "is likely" to be burnt, this seems to be a new suggestion. The reason why it's likely [he might say] is that he has been burnt a thousand times before. But we can omit the "likely"; for whatever reason he gives, he still may be burnt or not.

Evidence is always in the past. A general proposition is justified by the reasons we can give, not by the results. However far the reasons go, they stop short before the facts. Trains of reasoning go on and then something either happens or does not [i.e., he gets burnt or he doesn't] (WL32, pp. 87–88).

In the *Investigations* Wittgenstein makes this point rather cryptically: "We are misled by this way of putting it: 'This is a good ground, for it makes the occurrence of the event probable' " (PI, §482). In saying that we are *misled* by this, he means: past experience does not make anything *likely* to happen in the future.

Yet we do put the kettle on and wait for it to heat up. And a doctor, having cured scurvy before by prescribing citrus fruit (or vitamin C) in the diet, prescribes it again with each new patient who has scurvy. So Wittgenstein concludes: we *do* go by past experience in such matters *despite* the fact that anything at all could happen on each new occasion. He says:

People have killed animals since the earliest times, used the fur, bones, etc., etc. for various purposes; they have counted definitely on finding similar parts in a similar beast.

They have always learnt from experience; and we can see from their actions that they believe certain things definitely, whether they express this belief or not. By this I naturally do not want to say that men *should* behave like this, but only that they do behave like this (OC, §284).

But what are we to make of the fact that people act in certain ways when they have had certain experiences? One possibility Wittgenstein considers, and rejects, is that people go about their lives believing the so-called "law of induction," i.e., believing that, as regards regularities, the future, even in this indeterministic world, will *in fact* resemble the past. Wittgenstein says several things about this. He says that the 'law of induction' cannot be "grounded" (OC, §499), meaning that it cannot be proved that the future will resemble the past. He adds that "it would also strike me as nonsense to say 'I know the law of induction is true' " (OC, §500).

But he also says this:

The squirrel does not infer by induction [i.e., by employing a general premise about the dependability of the future] that it is going to need stores next winter as well. And no more do we need a law of induction to justify our actions or our predictions (OC, §287).

So Wittgenstein dismisses the suggestion that we count on certain regularities to continue because we believe the "law of induction." And yet he does want to say that in our *actions* we definitely count on certain particular regularities, e.g, that the same animals will have the same parts, etc. But then the squirrel gathers acorns each fall. The squirrel, we say, does this *instinctively*, rather than by reasoning. And Wittgenstein draws a parallel to our own case:

I want to regard man here as an animal; as a primitive being to which one grants instinct but not ratiocination. As a creature in a primitive state. Any logic good enough for a primitive means of communication needs no apology from us. Language did not emerge from some kind of ratiocination (OC, §475).

What does this mean? For surely we do give reasons. A doctor, if he were challenged regarding his prescription of vitamin C for people with scurvy, could cite a great fund of experience with this treatment – experience going back to 1753, when James Lund discovered that scurvy results from this dietary deficiency. Wittgenstein does not, of course, mean to say that we are like the squirrel in never giving such reasons. The comparison he wants to make, rather, is this: that we do give such reasons is a fact about us and a fact of the *same kind* as the fact that squirrels gather acorns in the fall. In what way are these alike? Well, just as the squirrel's nut-gathering is not grounded in reasoning, so our giving reasons of the sort just mentioned is not grounded in some *further* reasoning, i.e., in an appeal to 'the law of induction.' Wittgenstein explains:

What does man think for? What use is it? Why does he *calculate* the thickness of the walls of a boiler and not leave it to chance or whim to decide? After all it is a mere fact of experience that boilers do not explode so often if made according to calculations. But just as having once been burnt he would do anything rather than put his hand into the fire, so he would do anything rather than not calculate for a boiler. Since we are not interested in causes [of human behavior], we might say: human beings do in fact think: this, for instance, is how they proceed when they make a boiler. Now, can't a boiler produced in this way explode? Certainly it can.
   We expect something, and act in accordance with the expectation; must the expectation come true? No. Then why do we act in accordance with the expectation? Because we are impelled to, as we are impelled to get out of the way of a car, to sit down when we are tired, to jump up if we have sat on a thorn (PG, p. 109).

Our language game, says Wittgenstein, is "groundless" (OC, §166).
   It is at this point that we encounter Wittgenstein's reply to the skeptic. He writes:

If it is now asked: But how *can* previous experience be a ground for assuming that such-and-such will occur later on? The answer is: What general concept have we of grounds for this kind of assumption? This sort of statement about the past is simply what we call a ground for assuming that this will happen in the future (PI, §480).

   If anyone said that information about the past could not convince him that something would happen in the future, I should not understand him. One might ask him: What do you expect to be told, then? What sort of information do you call a ground for such a belief? What do you call "conviction"? In what kind of way do you expect to be convinced? If *these* are not grounds, then what are grounds? If you say these are not grounds, then you must surely be able to state what must be the case for us to have the right to say that there are grounds for our assumption (PI, §481).

Wittgenstein makes other remarks of this sort, in which he claims to be appealing to what we commonly say. For example, he writes:

This is how we acquire conviction, this is called "being rightly convinced"? (OC, §294).

   So hasn't one, in this sense, a *proof* of the proposition? But that the same thing has happened again is not a proof of it; though we do say that it gives us a right to assume it (OC, §295).

   This is what we *call* an "empirical foundation" for our assumptions (OC, §296).

This is supposed to discourage the skeptic. Should it? More importantly, is what Wittgenstein says here correct?

   The answer to this last question is plain: there is nothing at all right in what Wittgenstein says here. He claims to be appealing to something we all ordinarily say, but in truth we never say such things. For we never make predictions of the kind Wittgenstein is thinking of, namely, predictions into the supremely chancy future of an indeterministic world. In fact we are not making predictions about the future at all when we say, for example, that scurvy is caused by a dietary deficiency. When researchers make studies of the kind that lead to such a conclusion, they are not looking for correlations in order to claim a 'constant conjunction.' Rather, they are wanting to find out something about the human body – about how it works and what it needs. To conclude from such a study that the human body, to function normally, needs vitamin C is not to say something about what *has* happened and *is going to* happen; rather, it is to say something about the make-up of the human body, which is why the next step in research is to go looking within the human body for the 'mechanisms' involved in a dietary deficiency. While it is true that such researchers may proceed, in the initial stage, by compiling statistics, these are not an end in themselves. The conclusion drawn from them is not stated in the form Wittgenstein would have us believe, namely, in a form containing the future tense. Wittgenstein said that, in framing its 'laws,' science "prophesies" (WVC, p. 101). He said this because he was thinking that a statement like "Scurvy is caused by vitamin C deficiency" is a misleading form of words, that its true logical form would be shown in what logicians call a "general proposition," and that the 'generality' of the proposition covers the future as well as the past. What is true, of course, is that if we know that vitamin C deficiency causes scurvy, we may warn someone by saying, "If you do not get some vitamin C soon, you will come down with scurvy." But this is no reason to think that the future tense is hidden in the 'logical form' of "Scurvy is caused by vitamin C deficiency."

Assessment of Wittgenstein's Treatment of Skepticism

We can now assess Wittgenstein's way of dealing with the problem of induction. As we saw above, he replies to the skeptic: A properly conducted piece of inductive reasoning is what we *call* a justification for making claims (or assumptions) about the future – i.e., for the prophecies implicit in statements such as "Vitamin C deficiency causes scurvy." Should the skeptic accept this reply?

To understand the nature of the problem, we must consider what both Wittgenstein and the skeptic understand by "inductive reasoning." The model for this is an ordinary sampling procedure, the procedure employed, for example, in sampling a batch of milk for its butterfat content. The trouble is that an essential part of any *genuine* sampling procedure is necessarily excluded from what philosophers call "inductive reasoning." For in any genuine sampling procedure it is essential to ensure that the sample that is drawn be a *fair* one. If one is sampling a batch of milk for its butterfat content, one does not simply plunge in a dipper and test the dipperful of milk drawn. If someone did that, we would have no reason to think his 'sample' was representative of the whole batch. The reason, of course, is that milk separates; the cream rises to the top. In order, therefore, to draw a fair sample, one must first stir the milk, and additional stirring is required if the milk is very cold. To be a competent sampler, one must obviously know a good deal about the kind of thing one is sampling. Only a person who is knowledgeable in this way can be counted on to draw samples we can rightly regard as representative of the whole batch. But it is just this that both Wittgenstein and the skeptic think of as being out of the question when it comes to 'induction.' For the whole idea behind speaking of 'induction' here is that the 'batch' one is 'sampling' includes the *future*, i.e., the supremely chancy future of an indeterministic world, a world in which anything at all – including metaphysical nightmares – may happen in the next moment. For both Wittgenstein and the skeptic, then, it is a given in the problem of induction that 'inductive reasoning' *cannot* be based on samples we can rightly regard as *fair* ones. It is just for this reason that the skeptic declares that inductive reasoning is not rational. And surely the skeptic is right! For Wittgenstein and the skeptic are agreed on three points: (i) everything that happens is 'accidental,' (ii) statements such as "Scurvy is caused by a deficiency of vitamin C" make prophecies about future instances, and (iii) our past experience leads us to make such prophecies. Accordingly, the skeptic's view is that a proper analogy for inductive reasoning would be this: I have created a table of random numbers, and now, in going through them, I find a sequence of even numbers, and then, despite knowing that the table is perfectly random, I gamble heavily that the next number will also be an even one *because the previous three were*. This, of course, would be a perfectly crazy thing to do. And yet it is just this *sort* of thing that Wittgenstein is speaking of when he says: Our past experience is "simply what we *call* a good ground for assuming that this will happen [again] in the future" (PI, §480). He says to the skeptic: If you refuse to regard past experience as a ground in a case like this, what sort of ground are you looking for? And Wittgenstein expects the skeptic to be turned around by this. But the skeptic, of course, who shares Wittgenstein's ontology, has a perfectly good reply, namely, that no sampling procedure can rightly be regarded as sound where we have no idea whether the sample drawn is a fair one. This, of course, is a truism, but Wittgenstein flies in the face of it. In short, he concedes everything needed for making an air-tight case for skepticism but then pulls back from the appropriate conclusion.[2]

As I have already pointed out, Wittgenstein's appeal to what we *call* a good ground is an 'appeal' to something we never, in truth, say or think, for we do not call *anything* a good ground for assuming something about the future in an indeterministic world. But inasmuch as both Wittgenstein and the skeptic imagine that we *do* call something a good ground for that, the question *they* should ask is this: Is what we *call* "a good ground" *really* a good ground? And Wittgenstein should answer, as the skeptic does, that it is *not* a good ground. For, as I said above, it is a mere truism that no sampling procedure can rightly be regarded as sound where we have no idea whether the sample drawn is a fair one, and in an indeterministic world, no sample drawn from the past could rightly be regarded as a fair sample of what the future will be like.

Wittgenstein's 'Naturalism'

Having failed to draw the conclusion that his empiricist assumptions require, Wittgenstein goes on to invent a story about 'language-games,' a story that has come to be called Wittgenstein's "naturalism." The story is comprised of two parts, the first of which comes to light in the following passages:

You must bear in mind that the language-game [of induction] is so to say something unpredictable. I mean: it is not based on grounds. It is not reasonable (or unreasonable) (OC, §559).

A *reason* can only be given *within* a language-game. The links of the chain of reasons come to an end, at the boundary of the game (PG, p. 97).

Applying this to the present issue, he says:

Is induction justifiable? . . . The whole chain of our reasoning is not supported any more than the earth is supported; the whole of grammar in not supported in the sense that a sentence is supported by [i.e., shown to be true by] reality. You can't in fact call language or grammar unsupported because there is no question of its being supported (WL32, p. 104).

This is Wittgenstein's final word for the skeptic: language games are neither supported by grounds nor lacking such support, for to give grounds for something is to make a move *within* a language game.

The second part of Wittgenstein's story, and the reason he is often compared with Hume, is that he insists that a language-game is at bottom something animal: it has its origin, not in thought, but in instinct. In OC, §475, quoted above, he says that he wants "to regard man . . . as an animal; as a primitive being to which one grants instinct but not ratiocination."[3] That is, we act instinctively, and our actions, like the squirrel's laying up acorns in the fall, are performed, not with doubt, but with certainty. And as for this certainty, says Wittgenstein, "I want to conceive it as something that lies beyond being justified or unjustified; as it were, as something animal" (OC, §359).[4]

This, as we can now see, is all mere invention.[5] Wittgenstein's 'naturalism' comes, in the first place, from his ontology and, in the second place, from his unwillingness to acknowledge that an acceptance of that ontology is all that is needed for making skepticism irrefutable.[6]

Wittgenstein said to Drury in 1948: "My fundamental ideas came to me very early in life."[7] One of his early ideas, dating from 1912, was that even if matter does not exist, "that doesn't hurt, since physics and astronomy and all the other sciences could still be interpreted so as to be true."[8] In other words, he believed that science is possible even in a world of uncaused sense-data, a world in which a metaphysical nightmare can occur at any moment and defeat our expectations. In this chapter and the previous one we have seen some of the consequences of his sticking to this idea, and in the two chapters that follow we will review the consequences of this idea on his view of philosophical method and his epistemology.

Notes

1. In the *Tractatus* Wittgenstein put this point this by saying: "Two elementary propositions give one another the probability ½." He adds: "In itself, a proposition is neither probable nor improbable. Either an event happens or it does not: there is no middle way" (TLP, 5.152–5.153). In *Philosophical Grammar* Wittgenstein introduces the coin tossing analogy and makes the following point. If someone were to say, "It is *likely* that the sun will rise

tomorrow because it has always done so," he cannot rightly mean that there is a *good chance* – better than a 50–50 chance – that the sun will rise tomorrow, for there is no such probability here (PG, p. 224).

2. Wittgenstein is not, of course, alone in this. Another offender is Strawson, who, although insisting on the rationality of "induction," says: "There is nothing self-contradictory in supposing that all the uniformities in the course of things that we have hitherto observed and come to count on should cease to operate tomorrow. . . ." P. F. Strawson, *Introduction to Logical Theory* (London: Methuen, 1952), p. 260.

3. Hume says that our causal reasoning "is nothing but a wonderful and unintelligible instinct in our souls. . . . This instinct, 'tis true, arises from past observation and experience [of constant conjunctions]; but can anyone give the ultimate reason why past experience and observation produces such an effect, any more than why nature alone should produce it? Nature may certainly produce whatever can arise from habit; nay, habit is nothing but one of the principles of nature, and it derives all its force from that origin" (*Treatise*, I, iii, 16).

4. Although others have regarded Hume as the source of Wittgenstein's comparison of men and animals, the immediate source is almost certainly Russell's *Our Knowledge of the External World*, where Russell writes:

> . . . have we any reason to believe that a particular causal law, such as the law of gravitation, will continue to hold in the future?
>
> Among observed causal laws is this, that observations of uniformities is followed by expectation of their recurrence. A horse who has been driven always along a certain road expects to be driven along that road again; a dog who is always fed at a certain hour expects food at that hour and not at any other. Such expectations, as Hume pointed out, explain only too well the common-sense belief in uniformities of sequence, but they afford absolutely no logical ground for beliefs as to the future. . . . If Hume's account of causation [i.e., that we have no logical ground for beliefs as to the future] is the last word, we have . . . no reason to suppose that the sun will rise tomorrow. . . . (op. cit., pp. 224–225).

Russell adds: "I do not see how such a view could be disproved" (ibid.). What we would need for overcoming this skeptical view, he says, is "an *a priori* logical law" – a law, he explains, which cannot be "proved or disproved by experience" – which would enable us to make inferences about the future. In the *Tractatus* Wittgenstein dismissed this way of avoiding skepticism, saying: "The so-called law of induction cannot possibly be a law of logic, since it is obviously a proposition with sense [i.e., its negation, as Russell admits, is possibly true]. Nor, therefore, can it be an *a priori* law" (TLP, 6.31). And having allowed that skepticism cannot be overcome by means of 'an a priori logical law,' he was content to say that we are like the horse and the dog in Russell's two examples: having had such-and-such experiences, we then act *without* grounds.

5. I have discussed these matters much more fully in "Wittgenstein and Religious Belief," *Philosophy* (October, 1988), pp. 427–452.

6. David Pears, in his defense of Wittgenstein, acknowledges that "Wittgenstein's naturalism leaves many people dissatisfied," and he goes on to speculate that their dissatisfaction springs from the fact that "the habit of theorizing is so deeply rooted in their minds" that they would rather challenge Wittgenstein's naturalism than leave off theorizing (*The False Prison*, op. cit., p. 513). This, as we can now see, is not at all the reason for

dissatisfaction. The trouble with Pears is that he, like Wittgenstein, wants to accept empiricism but avoid the skepticism it entails. It seems never to have occurred to him that empiricism is rotten to the core. On the contrary, he constantly says or implies that the only alternative to empiricism is some sort of rationalism.

7. See Introduction, note 2, this volume.
8. See above, Chapter 1, note 24, this volume.

IV

Logical Possibilities and the Possibility of Knowledge

14

Logical Possibilities and Philosophical Method

In the *Tractatus* Wittgenstein said: "What can be described can also happen" (TLP, 6.362). As we saw in Chapter 12, he intended the phrase "what can be described" to include metaphysical nightmares – bizarre events such as one might find in fairy tales or in the telling of dreams. Did he continue to hold this view? Many passages in his later writings suggest that he never abandoned the view that metaphysical nightmares could actually occur. The following passage from *Zettel* plainly suggests this:

It is easy to imagine and work out in full detail events which, if they actually came about, would throw us out in all our judgements.

If I were sometimes to see quite new surroundings from my window instead of the long familiar ones, if things, humans, and animals were to behave as they never did before, then I should say something like "I have gone mad"; but that would merely be an expression of giving up the attempt to know my way about (Z, §393).

Consider also the following passage from *On Certainty*:

What if something *really unheard-of* happened? – If I, say, saw houses gradually turning into steam without any obvious cause, if the cattle in the fields stood on their heads and laughed and spoke comprehensible words; if trees gradually changed into men and men into trees. Now, was I right when I said before all these things happened "I know that that's a house" etc., or simply "that's a house"? (OC, §513).

Despite such passages, it is a much disputed question whether Wittgenstein continued to think that such metaphysical nightmares – which he also speaks of as "irregularities in natural events" (OC, §619) – could actually happen. Some commentators have said, in effect: "Oh, come now! A man turning into a tree! Only someone out of his senses would think that such a thing could actually occur."[1] What are we to make of this objection?

Wittgenstein's Distinction between Two Ways of Thinking

When Wittgenstein says in the *Tractatus* that what can be described can also happen, this has the same meaning as his remark that "the only impossibility that exists is *logical* impossibility" (TLP, 6.375). He means that nothing whatsoever is *physically* impossible. In Chapter 12 we saw that Wittgenstein continued to hold this view. For one thing, both in The Blue Book and in a conversation in 1949 (see Chapter Twelve, note. 9) he maintained that when "cannot" occurs in a nonlogical context it means "does not," which shows that he was unwilling to accept the idea of *physical* impossibilities. For another thing, his machine-as-symbol argument plainly presupposes the *Tractatus* view of possibilities, for its point is that a machine *could* run amok in ways that a person familiar with the machine would never think of or would regard as impossible, e.g., a cogwheel might unaccountably vanish. The aforementioned objection, then, is surely wrong.

There are other ways to see that that objection is wrong. For example, in a passage written in 1949 Wittgenstein says that "the philosopher's task [is] imagining possibilities" (LW I, §807), having just given the following as an illustration: "Suppose humans became more intelligent the more books they owned – suppose that were a fact, but that it didn't matter at all what the books contained" (LW, I, §806). We would normally dismiss this as being impossible, but Wittgenstein presents it as a real possibility.

Yet there is *something* right about the foregoing objection. For Wittgenstein was not, of course, a man out of his senses. And he himself recognized that the 'possibilities' he spoke of when doing philosophy are not among those he contemplates in his nonphilosophical moments. Recall here his saying that *normally* "we think of things in terms of [only] a few definite possibilities" (WL35, p. 82). He did not think that this holds only for other people. Indeed, he insisted that in the normal course of his activities he, too, did not entertain the possibility of metaphysical nightmares occurring. This is the point of his saying: "If I do a calculation I believe, without doubts, that the figures on the paper aren't switching of their own accord. . ." (OC, §337). He is saying that in his nonphilosophical moments he thinks in terms of only a few possibilities, not in terms of *all* the possibilities there are. He also says: "I can easily imagine someone always doubting before he opened his front door whether an abyss did not yawn behind it, and making sure about it before he went through the door (and he might on some occasion prove to be right) – but that does not make me doubt in the same case" (PI, §84). The "abyss" (*Abgrund*) he is speaking of here is not to be thought of as a ditch made by some road construction crew, but rather as a bottomless pit, an immeasurable void – in short, its occurrence would be a metaphysical nightmare. And Wittgenstein is saying: Even though this doubter might one day prove to be right, *I* do not have this worry when I open my door. As he says in another context: " 'But, if you are *certain*, isn't it that you are shutting your eyes in face of doubt?' They are shut" (PI, p. 224). He means: "I simply *do not* doubt, i.e., this is a fact about me." As regards the abyss, Wittgenstein means that it simply does not occur to him to worry about an abyss yawning beyond his door – even though he knows that an abyss *could* be there. He is making the same point when he writes: "Why do I not satisfy myself that I have two feet when I want to get up from a chair? There is no why. I simply don't. This is how I act" (OC, §148). He means: although my feet *could* vanish (causelessly) while I'm writing at my desk, I normally never look to see whether they *have* vanished.

This is what Wittgenstein says he is like in his nonphilosophical moments. It echoes what Hume said about this, namely, that nature has determined him to live and act like other people, even though he can find no reason to exclude the possibility of a change in the course of nature.

In his remarks about the human nervous system we again find Wittgenstein invoking this distinction between his normal and his philosophical mode of thinking. When he is doing philosophy he is prepared to say: It is possible that if my friends' heads were opened, their heads would be found to be empty or full of sawdust. For example, he says that when doing philosophy he finds useful "the thought that I don't know at all whether the humans I am acquainted with actually have a nervous system" (RPP, I, §1063). He also says that "it is imaginable that my skull should turn out empty when it was operated on" (OC, §4). Elaborating on this idea, he writes: "Why should not the initial and terminal states of a system be connected by a natural law, which does not cover the intermediary state? (Only don't think of *agency*)" (RPP, I, §909). Here he means to be suggesting that it is perfectly *possible* for someone to behave like a normal human being even if he has no brain. He says of the contrary view: "The prejudice in favour of psycho-physical parallelism is also a fruit of the primitive conception of grammar" (RPP, I, §906). What Wittgenstein is maintaining here (see Chapter 17, this volume) is the traditional phenomenalist view of dispositions (or capacities), namely, that dispositions require no physical basis. But he does not want to think of this as setting him apart from other people – from people who never think philosophically. And so he says:

I, L. W., believe, am sure, that my friend hasn't sawdust in his body or in his head, even though I have no direct evidence of my senses to the contrary. I am sure, by reason of what has been said to me, of what I have read, and of my experience. To have doubts about it would seem to me madness – of course, this is also in agreement with other people; but *I* agree with them (OC, §281).

The fact that Wittgenstein italicizes "I" twice in this passage shows that he means to be telling us something about *himself*. Consistently with this he could have added: If another person were to doubt that my friends have brains, he might prove to be *right*, but *I* do not have this doubt.

Many people reading Wittgenstein's later writings overlook the fact that he, like Hume, makes this distinction between what he thinks *qua* philosopher and what he thinks as he goes about the business of living, and this oversight has led them into serious misunderstandings. For having noticed what Wittgenstein says about his normal (nonphilosophical) mode of thinking, they conclude that he would, *qua* philosopher, think it impossible for a metaphysical nightmare actually to occur. But this is plainly a mistaken reading of Wittgenstein. He did not think that as a philosopher he was a captive of our 'normal' way of thinking. On the contrary, he says: "The philosopher is not a citizen of any community of ideas [*Denkgemeinde*]. That is what makes him into a philosopher" (Z, §455). Similarly, he says: "If we look at things from an ethnological point of view, does that mean we are saying that philosophy is ethnology? No, it only means that we are taking up a position right outside so as to be able to see things *more objectively*" (CV, p. 37). So he plainly thought that, *qua* philosopher, he could stand outside our 'normal' way of thinking and thereby see things more objectively, i.e., realize things we normally fail to realize. And one of the things he thought he could see from the outside is that "we are accustomed to think of things in terms of a very few definite possibilities," i.e., that we do not, in our practical affairs, take account of such a possibility as that an abyss yawns just beyond our door or that our feet have vanished.

A Difference between Philosophy and Science

To understand how he could think and reason in this way, we need to notice first of all Wittgenstein's view of the difference between science and philosophy. In his conversations with Waismann he said:

> Physics wants to determine regularities; it does not set its sights on what is possible.
>   For this reason physics does not yield a description of the structure of phenomenological states of affairs. In phenomenology it is always a matter of possibility, i.e., of sense, not of truth and falsity. Physics picks out certain points of the continuum, as it were, and uses them for a law-conforming series. It does not care about the rest [of the possibilities] (WVC, p. 63).[2]

What are these 'possibilities' that science allegedly ignores and philosophy (phenomenology) needs to consider? Plainly, Wittgenstein is here thinking of such things as he himself mentions in a passage quoted above: trees turning into men and men into trees, etc., i.e., things which scientifically literate people would say couldn't happen. But Wittgenstein, as we saw in Chapter 12, never abandoned the *Tractatus* view that nothing is physically impossible: "An iron nail can't scratch glass" just means it *doesn't* happen, not that it *couldn't* (BB, p. 49). And so we find him saying:

> Not only does epistemology pay no attention to the truth or falsity of genuine propositions, it's even a philosophical method of focusing on those propositions

whose content seems to us as physically impossible as can be imagined (e.g. that someone has an ache in someone else's tooth). In this way, epistemology highlights the fact that its domain includes everything that can possibly be thought (PR, p. 90).

Wittgenstein makes a similar point about philosophy when he writes: "We feel as if we had to *penetrate* phenomena: our investigation, however, is directed not towards phenomena, but, as one might say, towards the 'possibilities' of phenomena. We remind ourselves, that is to say, of the *kind of statement* that we make about phenomena" (PI, §90). He also says: "One might also give the name 'philosophy' to what is possible *before* all new discoveries and inventions" (PI, §126). In speaking of 'discoveries and inventions,' Wittgenstein was no doubt thinking of science (see WL32, p. 42), so that what he says here comes to this: In philosophy we are to allow as possible even what science might lead us to think is *not* possible.[3]

Here is one example. Naive and gullible people occasionally return from a trip to India with stories of having seen a man levitate or climb up an unsupported rope (the famous Indian rope trick). What do we say in such cases? A physicist, of course, would say that such things are impossible. "Believe me," he might say to his gullible cousin, "it just can't be done!" So people say they have seen things happen which a physicist says *cannot* happen. Wittgenstein's view is that although such things *do not* happen, they *could* happen. And philosophy, says Wittgenstein, is concerned with these very possibilities that science writes off.

We will understand this better if we consider the following passage from Wittgenstein's lecture on ethics:

... we all know what in ordinary life would be called a miracle. It obviously is simply an event the like of which we have never yet seen. Now suppose such an event happened. Take the case that one of you suddenly grew a lion's head and began to roar. Certainly that would be as extraordinary a thing as I can imagine. Now whenever we should have recovered from our surprise, what I would suggest would be to fetch a doctor and have the case scientifically investigated and if it were not for hurting him I would have him vivisected. And where would the miracle have got to? For it is clear that when we look at it in this way everything miraculous has disappeared; unless what we mean by this term is merely that a fact has not yet been explained by science which again means that we have hitherto failed to group this fact with others in a scientific system. This shows that it is absurd to say "Science has proved that there are no miracles." The truth is that the scientific way of looking at a fact is not the way to look at it as a miracle (EL, pp. 10–11).

For present purposes, the interesting feature of this passage is Wittgenstein's view of science in relation to 'miracles,' i.e., metaphysical nightmares. He says that science cannot rule out the occurrence of such events. And the reason he gives is that science, when it explains something, merely *groups* events of one sort with events of another sort. By this he means that science does no more that discover *correlations*. We would ordinarily think that when biologists uncovered the mechanisms of reproduction and variation, they had proof that, say, a pumpkin seed could not grow into a pine tree. And if a biologist were asked by an inquiring child whether a boy could suddenly grow a lion's head, he would say that this could not happen because a human being does not have the genetic material needed for growing a lion's head. But Wittgenstein is rejecting this. He does so, of course, because (i) he thought that we live in a world of (uncaused) sense-data, so that anything could happen at any moment, and (ii) he crafted his account of science to accommodate his indeterministic ontology, thereby arriving at the view that science merely *correlates* facts of one kind with facts of another and so cannot show anything to be impossible.

It should not surprise us that Wittgenstein allowed that metaphysical nightmares could actually occur. After all, an empiricist, given his ontology, can only think of two ways of avoiding this view: (i) finding a noncircular proof – and that means an *a priori* proof – that the future will resemble the past, and (ii) invoking probability theory to prove that if a regularity in nature has a great longevity (and no known exceptions) we can be sure that it will continue indefinitely. Wittgenstein rejected (i), saying: "It would ... strike me as nonsense to say 'I know the law of induction is true'" (OC, §500). What about (ii)? As I remarked in the preceding chapter, this view has been held by some empiricists. Karl Pearson is a case in point. He writes:

Our discussions of the probability basis for routine in the sequences of perceptions ... may perhaps suffice to indicate that the odds in favor of that routine being preserved in the immediate future ... are overwhelming. We may be absolutely unable to demonstrate any inherent necessity for the routine from our perceptions themselves, but our complete ignorance of such necessity, combined with our past experience, enables us by aid of the theory of probability to gauge roughly how unlikely it is that the possibility of knowledge ... will be destroyed in our generation by those breaches of routine which, in popular language, we term miracles.[4]

Wittgenstein discussed in many places Pearson's notion of probability and flatly dismissed it (e.g., WVC, pp. 98–99; PR, pp. 289–297; PG, p. 224ff., and PI, §§482 and 484). His view of the matter is that, contrary to Pearson, it is not *in the least* unlikely that a 'miracle' will occur, i.e., that an observed regularity will cease to hold. "Causality," he said, "depends on an observed uniformity. This does not mean that a uniformity so far observed will always continue ..." (PG, p. 227). This comes to: past experience of uniformities, however extensive, provides no assurance that we won't see such a thing as men turning into trees. So given his ontology and his rejection of both (i) and (ii), Wittgenstein had no way to rule out metaphysical nightmares.

Wittgenstein's Indifference to What We Actually Say

Wittgenstein's refusal to rule out metaphysical nightmares was, of course, in no way original. He was merely agreeing with Hume, who says in the *Treatise* that "it is an established maxim in metaphysics that *whatever the mind clearly conceives includes the idea of possible existence* or, in other words, that *nothing we imagine is absolutely impossible*" (I, II, 2). Some philosophers, having recognized that Wittgenstein thought it possible for a man to turn into a tree or for a boy suddenly to grow a lion's head, have maintained that Wittgenstein is *right* to adopt this Humean view.[5] As we saw in Chapter 12, however, Wittgenstein is *not* right about this; the only reason he thinks that such things *could* happen – that there are no physical impossibilities – is that his ontology dictates this way of thinking. I want now to make this point in an additional way.

Wittgenstein imagines that his philosophical view of this matter does not conflict with the fact that we say that such-and-such *could not* happen. To accommodate our saying such things, he declares that what we *mean* when we say that something could not happen is merely that it never does happen (his iron nail example). There are, however, examples of another sort that he should have, but did not, consider – examples that plainly conflict with his idea that whatever can be described can also happen. If he were *right* about this, and if our ordinary way of thinking could be *reconciled* with this idea, then we should expect to find the following: whenever someone insists that he has witnessed some very bizarre event, we always remain entirely open minded about it, i.e., we say something like, "Well, that *could* happen, but I would have to see it with my own eyes." This is what a Wittgensteinian view would lead us to expect. But the fact is that we often do not receive in this way reports of bizarre events. I have already mentioned the case of someone returning from India claiming to have seen a man climb an unsupported rope: we would say, "That couldn't happen. The man must have been an illusionist."

Consider also the following example. For many years people have reported seeing UFOs, and many have thought that the objects sighted are some sort of manned space ships. And yet it is also often reported that these same UFOs are seen to maneuver in extraordinary ways: not only is their rate of acceleration and deceleration astonishingly great, but they also make right-angle turns at enormous speeds. How would an empiricist, like Wittgenstein, want us to receive such reports? With an open mind! Wittgenstein would not have expected us to say something like, "Whatever it was that you saw, it *cannot* have been a solid spacecraft if it behaved like *that!*" And yet this is just what *is* said. Consider, for instance, the following passage from a book by Philip

Klass, who maintains that many of the UFOs sighted are in fact only an unusual electrical phenomenon known as "plasmas." He writes:

Every automobile driver knows that he cannot possibly bring a car moving at 60 mph to an instant halt, no matter how hard he presses on the brakes. Every pilot knows that it is impossible to execute a sharp right-angle turn. This merely demonstrates one of Newton's laws. . . . The sole exception seems to be the UFO, if it is a solid spacecraft.

If, however, UFOs are really plasmas, it would be quite easy for them to "stop on a dime," reverse direction and make right-angle turns. Despite the illusion of large size, *the total mass of material in the plasma is almost infinitesimal.* In a television set the beam of very-low-mass electrons which creates the picture is caused to sweep across the screen more than 15,000 times every second. This requires the electron beam to halt its sweep at the right-hand edge, stop and reverse its direction more than 30,000 times every second. Such movements would be completely impossible for a solid object with the same general dimensions.[6]

Wittgenstein's view of nature and science in no way prepares us to find a scientist reasoning in this way – saying that it would be "completely impossible" for a manned space ship to maneuver as reported. If we were to follow Wittgenstein, we would have to think: since laws of nature are only statements about regularities, one should consider *two* possibilities here: (i) that in the case of these UFOs a regularity has failed, i.e., they *are* solid objects but behave like no solid object we have ever observed; and (ii) that these UFOs are plasmas rather than solid spacecraft. But we do not always keep an 'open mind' in this Wittgensteinian sense. We often say, "That *couldn't* happen!" The U.S. Patent Office does not keep an open mind about patent applications for machines that are alleged to put out more energy than goes into them (perpetual motion machines). As Milton Rothman points out, "the Patent Office . . . lays down the rule: Perpetual motion is impossible, so we will waste no time looking at any applications on the subject."[7]

What, then, should be our attitude if we are meant to regard Wittgenstein's nightmarish examples as events in the physical world? If we are asked to suppose, for instance, that a boy grows a lion's head, we will surely have to decline, saying something like, "I can't suppose such a thing, for I wouldn't know *what* I was supposing if I 'supposed' it." Or we might say, "I can't suppose that, for I don't know what you are talking about. How *could* a boy grow a lion's head?" But this would be only the beginning of a proper reply. An adequate reply would have to include the full discussion in Chapters 11 and 12.

This point will become clearer if we consider Norman Malcolm's attempt to show that Wittgenstein's nightmarish examples could be events in the physical world. In support of this view, Malcolm asks us to suppose that one night after G. E. Moore had gone to bed, a member of his family looks in on him and finds him missing. Hours of searching fail to locate Moore, but later he is found to be back in his bed. As a result, says Malcolm, his family is "convinced that Moore had disappeared for two hours."[8] Malcolm's aim here is to persuade us by this account that an unheard-of event involving, not a phenomenal man, but a flesh-and-blood human being could actually occur. But what has Malcolm described? He does not mean that Moore disappeared in the sense that a fugitive from justice is said to have disappeared, for a few lines later he explains that Moore's family thought that his "body must have ceased to exist." But what does this mean? In what ways can a human body "cease to exist"? Was Malcolm thinking that this would be like a soap bubble's bursting, in which case the material of Moore's body would be scattered far and wide? If so, Moore would be dead and far beyond help from heroic measures of resuscitation, and of course his family would not find him back in his bed. Or was Malcolm thinking that the matter comprising Moore's body is not scattered about but "ceases to exist"? What could that mean? If it means anything at all, it must mean that the atoms comprising his body are transformed into energy. But were *that* to happen, the energy released would exceed that released by an atomic bomb. Not only would Moore be annihilated but his family would too. It is not at all clear, then, what, if anything, Malcolm means by "disappear" or "cease to exist." Perhaps he was thinking of Moore's 'disappearance' much as a phenomenalist would, namely, as a purely 'phenomenal' event, so that we needn't think about the *matter* that comprises Moore's body. But if so, Malcolm hasn't given us what he promised to: a *physical* event that would be like Wittgenstein's unheard-of events. In any case, we can see here why, if we are invited to suppose that a metaphysical nightmare has occurred in the physical world, we must reply by saying, "I don't understand what I'm meant to suppose."

Logical Possibilities and Phenomenalism

It is noteworthy that Wittgenstein, in giving examples of 'unheard-of' events, did not feel obliged to construct the examples in such way that we can follow them as we follow episodes in an ordinary narrative, where sufficient detail is given to enable us to understand what is being described. For example, he tells us that he might sometimes see from his window quite new surroundings instead of the long familiar ones (Z, §393). Similarly, he thought he could present a situation by saying that when he goes to fetch a chair from across the room, it suddenly vanishes, then reappears, then vanishes again (PI, §80). And he thought he could pose (and expect us to understand) the question: "What would I say if I saw cows talking or saw men changing into trees or trees into men?" (OC, §513). But what are we to think has happened in these situations? Wittgenstein does not tell us. Nor did he think that he was obliged to explain how such things could occur.

To understand his attitude toward these examples, we must bear in mind that Wittgenstein thought he inhabited a phenomenal, and hence an indeterministic, world – a world in which whatever happens 'just happens.' In the *Tractatus* Wittgenstein makes this clear when he says: "The world disintegrates [*zerfällt*] into facts" (TLP, 1.2), meaning that no fact has any connection with any other fact. He adds: "Each item can be the case or not the case while everything else remains the same" (1.21). He is saying here that in order for a state of affairs to come into being, no *other* state of affairs is required, i.e., states of affairs come into being *ex nihilo*. This comes to the same as Hume's claim that we can "conceive any object to be non-existent this moment and existent the next, without conjoining to it the distinct idea of a cause or productive principle" (*Treatise*, I, III, iii). This, then, is the formula for the way in which Wittgenstein constructs his examples of metaphysical nightmares. So if we ask why he regarded these 'examples' as presenting 'logical possibilities,' the explanation must be that he meant to be describing events in the fractured world of Hume's phenomenalism and therefore thought he could present 'examples' without providing the details we need for understanding *what* it is that is supposed to have happened.

We might compare Wittgenstein's 'examples' to certain comically bizarre episodes we see in cartoon films, as when one character paints an open door on a wall, hoping to foil his adversary, but the latter then runs through the painted doorway as though there were no wall. This analogy, or something like it, is needed for understanding why Wittgenstein thought he could pose the question: "What kind of reason have I to assume that my finger will feel a resistance when it touches the table?" (PI, §478), and also why he assumed he would be understood when he said: "Take the case that one of you suddenly grew a lion's head and began to roar." It was because he thought of his metaphysical nightmares as occurring in a phenomenal world that he could say in regard to them: "It is easy to imagine and work out in full detail events which, if they actually came about, would throw us out in all our judgments" (Z, §393). Certainly it would not be easy to describe and work out in full detail a situation in which a boy grows a lion's head or my hand meets with no resistance when I try to grasp the table next to me. But Wittgenstein was not thinking of boys and tables as we normally do; he meant to be speaking of phenomenal boys and tables. That is why he thought there is nothing more to tell about how these nightmarish events come to pass, i.e., why he thought it is "easy" to describe them. This is also why he thought he could present examples of events which, if they were actually to occur, would "throw us out in all our judgments" and lead us to say, "I have gone mad" (Z, §393). So if we eschew Wittgenstein's ontology, we will also eschew his night-marish examples – along with Hume's examples of 'changes in the course nature.'

Why is it that Wittgenstein's use of nightmarish examples does not immediately suggest that he meant to be speaking of a phenomenal world? A part of the answer, surely, is that in presenting his examples he allows himself to use words such a "table," and "tree," and "lion's head." (You can't tell a phenomenalist by his nouns.) Another part of the answer may lie in a similarity with fairy tales. We have all been entertained by such tales, and surely it would be perverse to say that we cannot follow them, can make no sense of them. In fairy tales, of course, frogs turn into princes, straw is spun into gold, and so on. Moreover, such passages in fairy tales are not the occasion for wondering how such things could come about – how, for example, the atomic structure of straw could be so altered as to yield gold and how this could be accom-plished on a spinning wheel. We would not be entering into the spirit of a fairy tale were we to go back over it in that way with the thought: Let me see if I understand exactly what happened here. That we follow a fairy tale from beginning to end does not mean that we can supply details that render it consistent with what we already know. Nor does it mean that we simply let certain matters pass provisionally, thinking that an explanation could be given on demand. In that respect there is a resemblance between fairy tales and Wittgenstein's presentation of his nightmarish examples, and this may make his examples seem accept-able.

There are, however, important differences between the two cases. For one thing, if a child who is being told a fairy tale should ask, "Could that really happen? Could straw be spun into gold?" we would answer, "No, that couldn't happen." Wittgenstein, by contrast, expected us to allow that metaphysical nightmares could actually occur: we are to imagine *ourselves* seeing a man change into a tree, etc. and are to ask what *we* would say in that situation. He is not asking: What would this character in a fairy tale say if such-and-such happened to her? (In a fairy tale, of course, the characters say whatever furthers the author's plot develop-ment, which is why they do not say what Wittgenstein imagines *he* would say were he to encounter an 'irregularity in natural events,' namely, "I have gone mad.") So, on the one hand, Wittgenstein presents meta-physical nightmares as things that could happen, but, on the other hand, he did not want us to cast about for a fuller account of the supposed happening, e.g., for a biological explanation of how a boy could grow a lion's head. And it is this combination that brings our understanding to a halt. For when we are asked to suppose that some bizarre event has actually occurred, we are entitled to be told how such a thing *could* occur, for otherwise we will dismiss it out-of-hand, as we dismiss eye-witness reports of a man climbing an unsupported rope. So when presented with Wittgenstein's nightmarish 'examples,' we can protest: "I don't see how I can suppose that, for I wouldn't know what I was supposing."

Wittgenstein, as we have seen, understands his nightmarish examples to be illustrations of what could happen in a phenomenal world. A teller of fairy tales, of course, is not asking us to think of such a world, and in that respect Wittgenstein's examples bear no resemblance to fairy tales. That we read and are entertained by such tales, then, provides no grounds for thinking that we shouldn't balk at Wittgenstein's examples. When he says, "Suppose that I were to see men changing into trees," he is not speaking of men and trees. He is supposing that he sees 'phenomenal men' changing into 'phenomenal trees' – rather as one might see a transformation in a cartoon film. Plainly, then, one cannot agree to make Wittgenstein's 'supposition' unless one is prepared to think of men and trees as he does. Accordingly, the appropriate comment to be made about Wittgenstein's 'irregularities in natural events' is that we cannot make sense of, cannot explain to ourselves, the notion of "phenomenal men and trees" and so cannot make sense, either, of irregularities in a 'phenomenal world.'[9]

Philosophical Method

In 1948 Wittgenstein wrote: "What is important about depicting anomalies precisely? If you cannot do it, that shows you do not know your way around the concepts" (CV, p. 72). It was his view, in other words, that to get a proper understanding of a concept, one must consider whether and how it would be used if one were to encounter a metaphysical nightmare.[10] In Chapter 7 we considered an instance of Wittgenstein's employing this 'method': his example of the chair (or seeming chair) that disappears and reappears (PI, §80). He proposed this 'example' in order to raise the question: "Have you rules ready for such cases – rules saying whether one may use the word 'chair' to include this kind of thing?" That is, his 'example' was intended to teach the philosophical lesson that the use of a word is not everywhere bounded by rules. What are we to think of this?

The place to begin is with Wittgenstein's own question. He asks whether we have rules ready for *such cases*. But what sort of case has he presented us with? In PI §80 he tells us only that what he at first takes to be a chair disappears and then reappears. Is this the whole story, or is Wittgenstein holding something back, namely, that a magician is trying out on a friend a new illusion he has devised by the use of mirrors? We can easily eliminate this latter alternative. For suppose that Wittgenstein had had in mind a case in which a magician is using concealed mirrors which reflect an image of a concealed chair. (The trick is carried out by his swiftly draping one of the mirrors with black velvet.) There would then be two sorts of questions to consider: (i) Given the aforementioned details, what did the magician's friend actually see, a chair or a mirror image of a chair? and (ii) What would his friend say if he didn't know *what* he had just seen? The answer to (i) is obvious: he saw a mirror image of a chair. The answer to (ii) would depend on what the protagonist suspected or guessed or knew. If he knows he is witnessing a magician's illusion but does not know how the illusion has been created, he might say, "How did you *do* that?" or "What a *great* illusion!" If, on the other hand, he knows he is witnessing a magician's illusion and can detect an ill-concealed mirror, he might say to his friend, "I could tell that I was looking into a mirror." Suppose, however, that he does not know about the magician: in that case he is likely to say, "What's going on here?!"[11] But when he walks over and catches sight of the magician's mirror, he will know that he had seen a mirror image of a chair. My point is that in none of these cases does Wittgenstein's question arise, i.e., the question: Do you have rules saying whether one may use the word "chair" to include this kind of thing? So we can exclude the possibility that in PI §80 Wittgenstein held back the fact that a magician was using mirrors.

Wittgenstein, then, meant to be telling *the whole story* when he said that what he at first takes to be a chair begins disappearing and reappearing, i.e., there is nothing more to know or find out about how this comes about, for it does so *ex nihilo*. But that means that he was thinking of his story as a story about what might happen in a phenomenal world, where nothing happens *because of* anything else. And that being the case, it is easy to see why Wittgenstein was disposed to ask: May we use the word "chair" to include this kind of thing? For his view is that *ordinarily* what he calls "a chair" is a certain sort of *experience*, and now, in the anomalous case, his experience is chair-like for a moment and then, unaccountably, becomes quite unchair-like. And it is for this reason that he thought that 'anomalies' were methodologically important, i.e., that they can teach us certain lessons about our concepts.

My question was whether Wittgenstein was right to claim that philosophical lessons can be learned by contemplating metaphysical nightmares. The answer is now obvious: to employ this method, one must first agree with Wittgenstein that "the world we live in is the world of sense-data," for in order to think that one could describe a metaphysical nightmare, one would have to think of it as a phenomenal event, so that one could describe it in the way one describes comically bizarre events in cartoon films. In the next chapter we will find that in *On Certainty* Wittgenstein tied himself in knots when he tried to employ this method in epistemology.

Notes

1. This view was expressed to me by John Hunter, author of several books on Wittgenstein. See also Richard Scheer, "What If Something Really Unheard-of Happened?" *Philosophical Investigations* (April, 1990), pp. 154–164.
2. This, it should be noted, is contrary to what physicists themselves say. For instance, the physicist Milton Rothman writes: ". . . physics is the science of deciding what is possible and what is not possible. . . . [T]he laws of physics are quite precise in telling us what kind of things *cannot* happen. Therefore I am on perfectly safe ground when I predict that none of my readers is suddenly going to levitate to the ceiling – no matter what kind of cult he or she may belong to" ("Myths About Science and Belief in the Paranormal" in *The Skeptical Inquirer*, Vol. 14, No. 1, p. 30). Rothman discusses this point in much greater detail in his book *A Physicist's Guide to Skepticism* (Prometheus Books, 1988).
3. One does not, of course, need a scientific education to know that all sorts of things are impossible. A child knows how far he can throw a baseball, how high he can jump, how fast he can run (e.g., that he can't run as fast as his brother). He may also know that his dog cannot outrun a horse (or an automobile), that a fish cannot live out of water, and that a bird with a clipped wing cannot fly. And most people know, without the benefit of science, that a man cannot live without air or survive a fall to the pavement from atop a tall building. Why did Wittgenstein fail to take account of such examples? The answer, surely, is that he persisted in his view that "the word 'can' is obviously a grammatical (logical) concept, not a material one" (WVC, p. 67) and so was prepared to explain away the foregoing examples, as he does with "A nail can't scratch glass." This led him to think that a philosopher must not count as *knowledge* the sort of thing illustrated by the foregoing examples.
4. *The Grammar of Science*, op. cit., p. 149.
5. See, for example, Norman Malcolm, "Reply to Scheer," *Philosophical Investigations* (April, 1990), pp. 165–168 and also Malcolm's *Nothing is Hidden*, op. cit., Chapter 11.
6. Philip J. Klass, *UFOs – Identified* (New York, 1968), pp. 127–128.
7. *A Physicist's Guide to Skepticism*, op. cit., p. 22. See also p. 141.
8. *Nothing is Hidden*, op. cit., pp. 224–225
9. David Pears, commenting on Wittgenstein's attitude toward "logical possibilities," says that the point of his nightmarish examples "was . . . to show that there is no *intellectual* obstacle in their way" (*The False Prison*, op. cit., p. 514). Pears is plainly in agreement with this, evidently because he shares Wittgenstein's Humean metaphysics.
10. In 1947 he said that in philosophy "you have to think of situations you wouldn't normally think of and remember what you would and would not say in them" (WL47, p. 301).
11. The exclamations of the unsuspecting victims of the television program "Candid Camera" were never such as to warrant the idea that they thought they had just witnessed an uncaused event. They invariably inferred that some sort of prank had been played on them.

15

The Search for a Phenomenalist's Theory of Knowledge

In *On Certainty* Wittgenstein was concerned, as he said, with how to show that "we *know* truths, not only about sense-data, but also about things" (OC, §426). Why did he think there was a difficulty about this? Since he was not a dualist, he was not faced with Moore's problem about how one could know what there is beyond one's sense-data. In Chapter 7, where I traced the history of Wittgenstein's epistemological concerns, we saw that his problem was one that is peculiar to phenomenalists.

Generating Wittgenstein's Problem

I will identify his problem by describing an example in which the verb "to know" plays a role and by then introducing, in several stages, considerations of the sort that generate Wittgenstein's problem. The example is as follows. One foggy morning a friend and I are strolling along a country road. A dark shape looms in the fog ahead, and my companion says, "It must be a large tree." I say, "No, it's a house. Don't you see the lines of the roof?" He demurs, and I say to him, "I know that's a house; I've walked along this road before." When we draw closer, I retract this, saying, "You were right; it *is* a tree. It certainly *looked* like a house. I guess we're not where I thought we were." Here is a case in which a knowledge claim gets retracted because of what is found on closer inspection. Had I held my tongue until we had drawn closer, I would have had nothing to retract. So in cases of this sort we sometimes say, "I spoke too soon." I will refer to this as our Primary Example.

The phenomenalist's problem can now be stated in part as follows: Is it not inevitable that we speak 'too soon' *whenever* we make knowledge claims about such things as houses, tables, and chairs, so that we really ought never to make such claims? To understand this question as a phenomenalist does, a further step is needed. In our Primary Example, if I walk up to what I at first took to be a house shrouded in fog and find it to be a tree, there would seem to be no way of raising a skeptical problem about my *now* exclaiming, "You were right; it *is* a tree!" or my calling out to my companion somewhere in the fog, "Oh, now I know what it is; it's Mr. Johnson's chestnut tree." And yet for the phenomenalist it is just here, where we have, so to speak, the best 'evidence of the senses,' that the problem begins. For on the phenomenalist's view the *course* of one's sense-data is not determined by anything. So although *until now* one's sense-data may have taken a manageable course, one that has contained no shocking surprises, there is no guarantee that it will continue in this way. On the contrary, it is possible that the course of one's sense-data will suddenly (and unaccountably) take uncanny twists and turns of the sort one finds in dreams. Wittgenstein calls such uncanny twists and turns "unheard-of" events (OC, §513). So the problem Wittgenstein sees himself faced with is this: Suppose that I make no hasty judgment but, instead, wait until I've drawn very near the fog-shrouded object and then say, "Oh, it's a tree" or "Oh, now I know what it is; it's Mr. Johnson's chestnut tree." Would I still have to retract this if there *then* occurred an unheard-of event, such as finding that when I go to tap the tree with my walking stick it meets with no resistance and passes right through the tree (or 'tree')? Wittgenstein poses this question as follows:

What if something *really unheard-of* happened? If I, say, saw houses gradually turning into steam without any obvious cause, if the cattle in the fields stood on their heads and laughed and spoke comprehensible words; if trees gradually changed into men and men into trees. Now, was I right when I said before all these things happened "I know that that's a house" etc. or simply "that's a house" etc.? (OC, §513).

Here, then, is Wittgenstein's problem: Is the occurrence of an unheard-of event – a metaphysical nightmare – a reason to retract a prior knowledge claim about a tree or a house? And if so, doesn't that mean that, since such an event could occur *at any moment*, we are *never* entitled to make such knowledge claims? Are we not, that is, obliged to be skeptics about the existence of such things as trees and houses? Hence Wittgenstein's question about how it can be shown that "we *know* truths, not only about sense-data, but also about things" (OC, §426).

We could formulate the problem in another way. As Wittgenstein sees the matter, there seem to be two ways in which future experience can pose a problem for the assertion "It's a house" or "I know that's a house": one of these is the familiar way in which, having drawn closer and looked more carefully, we realize that we spoke too soon, for it wasn't a house but a tree that we saw through the fog; the other is the possibility that, even after we have drawn closer and had a good look and said, "You see, I was right; it *is* a house," something unheard of then occurs, such as the 'house' floating away or suddenly vanishing. Wittgenstein is alluding to this difference when he writes: "There is a difference between a mistake for which, as it were, a place is prepared in the game, and a complete irregularity that happens as an exception" (OC, §647). In cases of the first sort, which we are all familiar with, we often say in regard to our too-hasty judgment, "I was mistaken," meaning that we didn't take sufficient pains, that if we had waited to get a better look, etc., we would have found that it wasn't what we took it to be. But in cases of the other sort it would be wrong to say we were mistaken, for these are stipulated to be cases in which we have gotten as good a look as one could hope to get. This poses a dilemma for Wittgenstein which can be set out as a choice between what I shall call Alternatives I and II. Alternative I says: Since we cannot, where we've gotten the best look possible, be said to be *mistaken*, it would seem that we shouldn't have to retract a prior knowledge claim when the 'house' (or the 'tree' or whatever) floats away or vanishes or offers no resistance when we go to touch it. Alternative II says: It would seem that I can't be said to have *known* that it was a house if in fact it was about to float away or vanish, for it can't have been a *house* if it does *that*. (This is what Mill meant in saying, somewhat misleadingly, that a material object is a permanent possibility of sensations. This is not to say that a tree won't be destroyed by fire or cut up for lumber, but rather that we wouldn't say that there is a *tree* in the front yard if we found that our hand passes right through it so that we have no tactile sensations when we go to feel its bark. This is also what Wittgenstein had in mind when he said in PI, §80 that if something we had taken to be a chair were suddenly to disappear, we would say, "So it wasn't a chair, but some kind of illusion.") The choice between these alternatives constitutes Wittgenstein's dilemma. For Alternative I argues that there is good reason for saying that, prior to the unheard-of event, I was right to say I knew it was a house, while Alternative II argues that I was wrong to say I knew this.

We can better appreciate the problem if we consider what Wittgenstein must have taken to be implied by Alternative II, which says that an unheard-of event can always defeat one's claim to know that this a tree or a house. It implies the view Wittgenstein himself had adopted in the 1930s, namely, that "This is a house" or any similar proposition is a hypothesis and therefore can never be completely verified.[1] But, given Wittgenstein's belief that unheard-of events could actually occur, this is tantamount to embracing skepticism. So if Wittgenstein is to avoid skepticism, he must embrace Alternative I and allow that the occurrence of an unheard-of event is *not* a reason for retracting a prior knowledge claim (that it was a house or whatever). But in order to adopt this alternative he would either have to abandon his earlier analysis of propositions about houses and the like as being *hypotheses* (about future sense-data) or find some other way out of the difficulty.

On Certainty is the record of Wittgenstein's struggle with these alternatives, and we find him taking now one stance and now another, never feeling sure he has found the right one. The trouble is, however, that the question he was putting to himself is a bogus one, for it presupposes that unheard-of events *could* actually occur. As we have seen in previous chapters, Wittgenstein's unheard-of events could never occur. So there was no chance of his finding the *right* answer to his question; there is no correct account to be given of what we would (or should) say if a metaphysical nightmare occurred. Not realizing this, Wittgenstein tormented himself through the final two years of his life in pursuit of a chimerical goal.[2]

Let us consider now Wittgenstein's various solutions – there are four in all – to the dilemma I have described and its attendant problem about the analysis of "This is a tree," "That's a house," etc. I have quoted *On Certainty* §513 in which he mentions several unheard-of events and then asks: Now, was I right when I said before all these things happened "I know that that's a house" etc. or simply "that's a house" etc.? Here is his problem plainly stated, and we will see that he sometimes adopts the first alternative (I was *right* when I said "I know . . .") and sometimes the second (I must retract "I know . . ." and say "I *thought* I knew . . .").

Wittgenstein's First Solution

The first of Wittgenstein's proposed solutions is one in which he adopts the first of these alternatives:

May not the thing that I recognize with complete certainty as the tree that I have seen here my whole life long – may this not evolve into [*entpuppen*] something different? May it not confound me?

And nevertheless it was right, in the circumstances that give this sentence meaning, to say "I know (I do not merely surmise) that that's a tree." To say that in strict truth I only believe it would be wrong (OC, §425).

The wording of this passage is somewhat vague, but I think we can make out the following points. First, he is plainly thinking of his example as being like our Primary Example once I have drawn close to the fog-shrouded object for a good look: he was making no *mistake*. Second, we are to think of what happens to the tree in this case as like what happens to the trees in §513, where Wittgenstein says the trees "change into" men.[3] Third, so Wittgenstein regards this as a case in which, after the unheard-of event, he would say "It *was* a tree, but now it has evolved into something different." (In OC, §503 Wittgenstein suggests that one alternative would be to say: "It *was* a tree but now it isn't any longer.") Fourth, because he is prepared to say, in retrospect, that it *was* a tree, he also allows that it was "right" for him to say, prior to the unheard-of event, "I know that's a tree." In other words, as his verb "*entpuppen*" suggests, Wittgenstein was thinking of the situation as being like this: one's saying, "That's a caterpillar," isn't something we retract when the caterpillar turns into a butterfly – since it *was* a caterpillar *then*. Fifth, as regards the analysis of "That's a tree" Wittgenstein is here adopting the following view: when he said it was a tree, he didn't mean to be forecasting that it would *remain* a tree (any more than when we say "Here's a caterpillar" we mean that it will *remain* a caterpillar). So we can take Wittgenstein to be abandoning his earlier view that "That's a tree" is a hypothesis. As we will presently see, there are many passages in *On Certainty* in which Wittgenstein insists that there are in our language propositions which, although having the "form of empirical propositions," are not *hypotheses*. Just what this alternative analysis comes to is not spelled out in the passage we are considering, but at least he is saying that a tree is *not*, contrary to Mill, a permanent possibility of arboreal sensations, for even if it changes into a man, it was right to say, "I know what it is; it's a tree."

Wittgenstein's Second Solution

The second of Wittgenstein's proposed solutions is one in which he embraces Alternative II, which says that an unheard-of event would defeat a prior knowledge claim. (The knowledge claim would be defeated because it involved a hypothesis about future experience, which turns out to be false.) In the following passage Wittgenstein is confronting his dilemma:

"Do I know or do I only believe . . . ?" might also be expressed like this: What if it *seemed* to turn out that what until now has seemed immune to doubt [e.g., that that's a tree] was a false assumption? Would I react as I do when a belief has proved to be false? . . .
Would I simply say "I should never have thought it!" – or would I (have to) refuse to revise my judgment. . . ? (OC, §492)

A few passages later he takes this up again:

I look at an object and say "There is a tree," or "I know that that's a tree." Now if I go nearer and it appears to be something different [*es stellt sich anders heraus*],[4] I may say "It wasn't a tree after all" [and thereby retract my prior claim] or alternatively I say "It *was* a tree but now it isn't any longer" [and thereby stick to my prior claim]. But if all the others contradicted me, and said it never had been a tree, and if all the other evidences spoke against me – what *good* would it do me to stick to my "I know"? (OC, §503).
Whether I *know* something depends on whether the evidence backs me up or contradicts me (OC, §504).
It is always by favor of nature that one knows something (OC, §505).

Here Wittgenstein is addressing the question posed in the first of the above passages (§492), namely, whether one can be said to have known it was a tree if later events take a nightmarish turn, i.e., if one is *not* 'favored by nature.' And his answer in these passages is that a nightmarish experience (things behaving in an unheard-of way) would oblige one to retract the prior knowledge claim.

When he wrote these passages, he must have been thinking that we would continue to regard something as having been a *tree* only so long as there remained a 'permanent possibility' of arboreal sensations, i.e., that "It's a tree" is a hypothesis to the effect that arboreal sensations will be available here in the future. What would make this view attractive to Wittgenstein? He does not say much about this, but I think we can see its attraction by considering its alternative, for a phenomenalist who holds that "It's a tree" or "It's a house" is *not* a hypothesis will have to swallow a nasty consequence. To declare that "It's a house" is not a hypothesis amounts to abandoning Mill's suggestion about this matter, namely, that such a thing as a house is "a permanent possibility of sensations." As I remarked above, Mill's formulation is somewhat misleading, for we all know that a house can burn to the ground or be destroyed by a wrecking crew or simply rot away. And an ice cube can melt, a pencil mark be erased, a piece of cake be eaten, etc., etc. So what Mill must have meant is this: although such a thing as a house or an ice cube may meet its end in one these *familiar* ways, we won't persist in saying that it was a *house* if it suddenly vanishes or floats a way. (If it meets its end in some unheard-of way, then it wasn't a house after all, but some sort of extraordinary illusion.) We can now see the nasty consequence a phenomenalist would be faced with were he to abandon Mill's position. When a realtor has sold me a house and then, as I am about to move in, I see it float away or simply vanish, I can't complain that it wasn't a *house* that he sold me and refuse to pay off the thirty-year mortgage. On this view, where it is allowed that a house may meet its end not just by fire or demolition but also by unheard-of events, the realtor could rightly insist that he did indeed sell me a house, that its floating away (or vanishing) proves nothing to the contrary.

We could easily think of similar inducements for a phenomenalist to adopt Mill's analysis, i.e., to hold that in speaking of trees, automobiles, etc., we imply various things about the future. And yet, this analysis creates an obvious difficulty for Wittgenstein, who had set out to show that "we know truths, not only about sense-data, but also about things." For if, in the cases in question, "It's a tree" is a hypothesis, then (given Wittgenstein's phenomenalism) when we say "I know it's a tree," we are claiming to know something one could not *possibly* know, namely, that no unheard-of event will seem to count against our knowledge claim. So this analysis of "It's a tree," makes it seem perfectly absurd that we should say, "I *know* it's a tree," even in those cases in which we have the very best 'evidence of the sense.' Accordingly, this analysis leads one straight into skepticism.

We can see Wittgenstein wrestling with this difficulty in various ways in the following passages:

Even a proposition like this one, that I am now living in England, has these two sides: it is not a *mistake* – but on the other hand, what do I know of England? Can't my judgment go all to pieces? (OC, §420).
I am in England. Everything around me tells me so; wherever and however

I let my thoughts turn, they confirm this for me at once. But might I not be shaken if things such as I don't dream of at present were to happen? (OC, §421).[5]

What is odd is that in such a case I always feel like saying (although it is wrong): "I know that – so far as one can know such a thing." That is incorrect, but something right is hidden behind it (OC, §623).

One might also put this question: "If you know that that is your foot, do you also know, or do you only believe, that no future experience will seem to contradict that knowledge?" (That is, that nothing will seem to *you yourself* to do so.) (OC, §364).

Here we can see Wittgenstein worrying about whether the words "I know" can be followed by a proposition that is properly to be analyzed as a hypothesis about future experience and hence is falsifiable by a future unheard-of event.

Wittgenstein's Third Solution

This brings us to the third of Wittgenstein's proposed solutions. There are many passages in *On Certainty* in which he explicitly dismisses his earlier view that *all* propositions about physical objects are hypotheses. This is what he is getting at when he says, "Our 'empirical propositions' do not form a homogeneous mass" (OC, §213) and "I am inclined to believe that not everything that has the form of an empirical proposition *is* one" (OC, §308). What he means by such remarks is that not all of our empirical propositions are *hypotheses*. This becomes apparent when he says that "it is wrong to say that the 'hypothesis' that this is a bit of paper would be confirmed or disconfirmed by later experience" (OC, §60). Similarly, with reference to Moore's example, "Here is a hand" (where the hand is his own), he says that it "can't be called a hypothesis" and contrasts it in this respect with a proposition about a planet (OC, §52). He is making the same point when he remarks that Moore could be interpreted as saying quite *rightly* that "a proposition saying that here is a physical object may have the same logical status as one saying that here is a red patch" (OC, §53). Wittgenstein's most explicit remarks along these lines are the following:

If I say "Of course I know that that's a towel!" I am making an utterance [*Äusserung*]. I have no thought of a verification. For me it is an immediate utterance.

I don't think of past or future. (And of course it's the same for Moore, too.)

It is just like directly taking hold of something, as I take hold of my towel without having any doubts (OC, §510).

Here, then, is Wittgenstein's third proposed solution: he retracts his earlier analysis of such propositions as "That's a towel" or "It's a house" as being hypotheses about future experience, and in this way seeks to avoid the skepticism inherent in his second solution.

What we need to consider here is how this third solution differs from the first one, which *also* rejects Wittgenstein's earlier view that "It's a towel" is a hypothesis. The peculiarity of that first solution is that it (by way of the phrase "evolve into something different") compares "It's a tree [or towel]" with "It's a caterpillar" in that, just as we wouldn't say "That can't have been a caterpillar" when it evolves into a butterfly, so we won't say "That can't have been a towel" if it suddenly and unaccountably dissolves or vanishes. But this comparison fails, in an important way, to address the problem that confronts Wittgenstein. For a caterpillar's evolving into a butterfly is not an unaccountable and unheard-of event. On the contrary, its evolving into a butterfly is just what we *expect* of a caterpillar. What Wittgenstein should have asked himself is this: If I've said "It's a caterpillar," what would I say if, in the next moment, it turned into a tree or a man? My point is that Wittgenstein's first solution fails to address his real problem, which is: What are we to say when we encounter an *unheard-of* event? This becomes obvious if the unheard-of event is that what one has taken for a caterpillar (or a towel) simply *vanishes*. In such a case one couldn't think that what's happened is similar to a caterpillar developing into a butterfly.

The difficulties I have just pointed out regarding Wittgenstein's first solution do not beset his third, which says that "That's a towel" is an *Äusserung*. For while this denies that the proposition is a hypothesis, it does not attempt to justify this by introducing the idea that things sometimes "evolve" into others. Rather, what Wittgenstein is doing here is calling upon a distinction he had made in the early 1930s, namely, between sense-datum propositions and hypotheses. The difference, he said, is this: "A hypothesis goes beyond immediate [i.e., present] experience. A [sense-datum] proposition does not" (WL32, p. 110). So in the passage we are considering (OC, §510), he means to say that "That's a towel" is like "Here is a red patch" in that it does not go beyond present experience. This is why Wittgenstein also says in this passage that, in saying "That's a towel," he does not "think of past or future" and has "no thought of a verification." This, then, is what he meant when he suggested that "a proposition saying that here is a physical object may have the same logical status as one saying that here is a red patch" (OC, §53). Wittgenstein's third solution, then, resembles the first by denying that "That's a towel [or house, etc.]" is a hypothesis, but differs from the first solution by justifying this analysis by comparison with "Here is a red patch."

As I remarked in discussing Wittgenstein's second solution, a phenomenalist will be faced with a nasty consequence if he abandons the analysis of "Here's my house" as a hypothesis, for if we buy a house, for example, we expect to be able to move in and live there. Or, as Mill would put it, we expect it to be a permanent possibility of sensations.

(That, so to speak, is what we're *paying* for.) Wittgenstein's third solution ignores this and thereby suggests that he would have to allow that what he had been sold was indeed a *house* (or a towel) even if it unaccountably dissolves or vanishes.

Wittgenstein's Fourth Solution

Wittgenstein proposed a fourth solution: one that resembles the second by retaining the view that "That's a house" is a hypothesis but seeks to avoid the skepticism inherent in the second solution by protecting "I know it's a house" against being falsified by an unheard-of event. His solution here is to say that if one were later to have seemingly conflicting experiences, one could treat *them* as illusory (OC, §361). He adds: "But doesn't it come out here that knowledge is related to a decision?" (OC, §362). At one point he writes:

I can't be making a mistake [i.e., I'm not being careless in my observations]; but if after all something should appear to speak against my proposition I shall stick to it, despite this appearance (OC, §636).

It is plain that Wittgenstein is here thinking that his "proposition" implies something about the future, for otherwise he could not think that some future experience might "appear to speak against" it. So in this fourth proposed solution Wittgenstein reverts to his earlier analysis of "It's a house" and proposes that a *decision* can protect it from being falsified by an unheard-of event. In his conversations with Malcolm in 1949 Wittgenstein formulated this solution as follows: "I might refuse to regard anything as *evidence* that there isn't a tree [over there]. If I were to walk over to it and feel nothing at all, I might say that I was *then* deluded, not that I was previously mistaken in thinking it a tree. If I say that I would not *call* anything 'evidence' against that's being a tree, then I am not making a psychological prediction – but a *logical* statement."[6]

In order to assess this fourth solution, we have to be clear about the following point. Wittgenstein can't have intended this solution as being relevant to an ordinary case of illusion. Surely, he did not mean to say: If I were crossing the desert and, because of a mirage, thought I saw a grove of palm trees in the distance, and if, as I drew closer, the 'trees' faded away and disappeared, I would say: "There *were* trees here. I *know* there were." What, then, was he thinking of? He was thinking of his situation as being one in which he has gotten as good a look at something as one could ever care to get. So what is his fourth solution intended to solve? Like his first three, it is intended to answer the question: In situations in which we can't be making a mistake, what should we say if there suddenly occurred an unaccountable, completely unheard-of event? And his fourth solution is this: In such a situation I would stick to saying that I'd seen a house (or tree or whatever). But let us ask: How does one determine that this is the *right* answer, the *correct* solution to his problem? I have no idea, for his problem is predicated on a philosophical misunderstanding, and for that reason it has no *correct* solution. In any case, Wittgenstein himself does not offer anything to show that this *is* the correct solution. He does, it is true, try to make it plausible by saying that when he encounters the unheard-of event he could treat *that* "as illusory" (OC, §361). But what is the word "illusory" doing here? It is surely not our ordinary word, for what we normally speak of as illusions are things we can explain, as in the case of a mirage in the desert, for example. But Wittgenstein had in mind an event that *cannot* be explained. Moreover, we discount our illusions (by saying, for example, "It only looked like there were trees on the horizon") *because* we can explain (or hope to explain) them, whereas Wittgenstein can have no such reason for discounting a metaphysical nightmare. (After all, if he thought he could *explain* the experience in question, he wouldn't have to *decide* what to say.) So I think we must in the end say that this fourth solution is in no way preferable to the first three.

As I said, the question he was putting to himself is a bogus one, for it presupposes that 'unheard-of events' *could* actually occur. So there is no chance of his finding the *right* answer. There is no correct account of what we would do or say if, in real life, we were confronted by a metaphysical nightmare. It is hardly to be wondered at, then, that Wittgenstein kept on proposing solutions which sound utterly contrived and left him dissatisfied. Nor should we be surprised at the expressions of despair (§400 and §532) that we find toward the end of *On Certainty*, as when he asks himself: "Is my understanding only blindness to my own lack of understanding? It often seems so to me" (OC, §418).

Wittgenstein's Theory of Hinge Propositions

I have not as yet mentioned a related view of propositions that Wittgenstein develops mainly in the middle part of *On Certainty*. I refer to his idea that our language is a system or structure at the bottom of which are certain *propositions* that are excluded from doubt (or that no reasonable man would doubt). At one point he explains this by saying that "about certain empirical propositions no doubt can exist if making judgments is to be possible at all" (OC, §308). He also says:

When Moore says he *knows* such and such, he is really enumerating a lot of empirical propositions which we affirm without special testing; propositions, that is, which have a peculiar logical role in the system of our empirical propositions (OC, §136).

This "peculiar logical role" Wittgenstein describes as follows: ". . . the *questions* that we raise and our *doubts* depend on the fact that some propositions are exempt from doubt, as it were like hinges on which those turn" (OC, §341). As an illustration of this he says:

If I make an experiment I do not doubt the existence of the apparatus before my eyes. I have plenty of doubts, but not *that*. If I do a calculation I believe, without any doubts, that the figures on the paper aren't switching of their own accord (OC, §337).

We can see here that Wittgenstein is thinking that someone, perhaps someone who is not entirely sane, *could* doubt these propositions but that reasonable men do not. He is here harking back to something he had written years earlier in the *Investigations*:

I can easily imagine someone always doubting before he opens his front door whether an abyss [i.e. a bottomless pit] did not yawn behind it, and making sure about it before he went through the door (and he might on some occasion prove to be right) – but that does not make me doubt in the same case (PI, §84).

Wittgenstein is here suggesting that someone (albeit, not a *reasonable* person) could, even though he is not philosophizing, conceive of, and fear that he is about to encounter, an unheard-of event: a bottomless pit beyond his front door. The relevance of this is that Wittgenstein thinks that one could give a great many additional examples of metaphysical nightmares that *someone* might fear but that reasonable men never entertain as real possibilities. And in every such case, he thinks, the correct philosophical account to give is this: A reasonable man is never beset by doubts about p, where "p" contains a description of some metaphysical nightmare. We can illustrate this by means of his own example. Wittgenstein is saying: The reasonable man is not beset by doubts about there being *terra firma* (rather than a bottomless pit) beyond his door, i.e., he does not doubt the proposition "There is *terra firma* (rather than a bottomless pit) beyond my door." It is, then, propositions of *this* sort which have, according to Wittgenstein, "a peculiar logical role in the system of our empirical propositions." It is these propositions that are "as it were, like hinges" on which everything else in our lives and our language turns. I will speak of these henceforth as Wittgenstein's "hinge propositions."

In what way, according to Wittgenstein, does our system of language "contain" these hinge propositions? It is not that we ever *say* these things, for hinge propositions, says Wittgenstein, have been "removed from the traffic ... shunted onto an unused siding" (OC, §210), by which he means that they are "never called in question, perhaps not even ever formulated" (OC, §87). They are, he also says, thoughts that are "never thought" (OC, §159). (No one ever says or thinks: "Beyond my door lies *terra firma*, rather than an abyss.") How, then, can they belong to our language? Wittgenstein's way of thinking of this comes out in his remarks about what he calls our "conviction that the earth

exists" (OC, §210). What conviction is he speaking of here? To understand this, we must bear in mind that hinge propositions, when properly
spelled out, contain the description of some metaphysical nightmare
(e.g., "Beyond my door there is *terra firma*, rather than an abyss").
Presumably, then, Wittgenstein meant something like the following: We
go about our daily rounds without seeing much more than streets and
buildings (including the interiors of rooms) and the moon and stars
above, so the huge globe we call the earth could have ceased to exist
(metaphysical nightmare) without our knowing it. And yet we send
letters off to distant cities, make phone calls to distant lands, and go on
telling children, "The earth is round." In doing and saying such things,
Wittgenstein thinks, we show that we are of the conviction that the earth
exists, i.e., if I say to a child, "The earth is round," I thereby imply the
proposition "The earth exists (and has not vanished)."

It is this that Wittgenstein is getting at when he says: "The existence
of the earth is . . . part of the whole *picture* which forms the starting point
of belief for me" (OC, §209). Hinge propositions, then, are such that "we
don't . . . arrive at any of them as a result of investigation" (OC, §138).
"I do not explicitly learn the propositions that stand fast for me" (OC,
§152), says Wittgenstein, adding by way of illustration: "No one ever
taught me that my hands don't vanish [*vershwinden*] when I am not
paying attention to them" (OC, §153). So in the matter of the proposition "The earth exists," a child "swallows this consequence down, so to
speak, together with *what* it learns" (OC, §143), i.e., when it learns that
the earth is round and that China is on the other side of the earth.

Plainly, Wittgenstein is thinking here that when we teach our children that the earth is round and that it is larger than the moon, we
thereby implicitly "affirm . . . propositions . . . which have a peculiar
logical role in the system of our empirical propositions (OC, §136). And
the children also "affirm" these hinge propositions when they write in
a school examination, "The earth is larger than the moon."

Given the foregoing explanation, it is understandable that Wittgenstein also says that one could not doubt a hinge proposition without
thereby "toppling all other judgments with it" (OC, §419), for he thinks
that the possibility of the truth or the falsehood of the various things we
do say depends (logically) on hinge propositions being (accepted as)
true. (For example, it couldn't be true that the earth is larger than the
moon if the proposition "The earth has vanished" is true.) This is why
Wittgenstein speaks of such propositions as being the *foundations* of our
language: "I want to say: propositions of the form of empirical propositions, and not only propositions of logic, form the foundation of all
operating with thoughts (with language)" (OC, §401). Accordingly, he
says that it is fundamental to "any understanding of logic" to "realize
that complete absence of doubt at some point, even where we would say

that 'legitimate' doubt can exist, need not falsify a language-game" (OC, §375). He also puts this by saying that "a doubt is not necessary even when it is possible [as it is possible, for example, that a man should doubt whether there isn't an abyss just beyond his door] . . . . [T]he possibility of the language-game doesn't depend upon everything being doubted that can be doubted" (OC, §393).

Many of Wittgenstein's followers have taken the account I have just sketched (the theory of hinge propositions) to be Wittgenstein's final view of language and his final answer to skepticism. They have also tried to defend this theory as one we all ought to accept. I will comment on both of these ideas.

First of all, it is important to be clear that Wittgenstein's theory of hinge propositions is not a proposed solution, as were the four we considered above, to the problem with which we began. That problem was stated in terms of our Primary Example, in which, having drawn near enough to the fog-shrouded object to get a good look at it, one says, "You were *right*! It's a tree" or "Now I know what it is. It's Johnson's chestnut tree." The original problem, then, concerned things of the sort we *do* say and so had nothing to do with hinge propositions. The problem Wittgenstein was addressing in the four solutions discussed earlier is whether we have a right to say what we do say in such cases or whether, instead, the prospect of unheard-of events undermines our right to say such things. By contrast, when Wittgenstein introduces his theory of hinge propositions, it does not have even the appearance of pertaining to examples like our Primary Example.[7] Rather, Wittgenstein had noticed a second kind of problem that is posed for him by his assumption that unheard-of events could actually occur and by his acceptance, further, of the idea that *someone*, albeit not a reasonable man, could live in fear that he will be victimized by one of these nightmarish events. This problem, as Wittgenstein saw it, is this: Given that many of the things we say, such as "The earth is larger than the moon," imply hinge propositions, such as "The earth exists, i.e., has not vanished," and given that these (unspoken) hinge propositions are such that (i) their truth is presupposed by the things we *do* say and yet (ii) we can't be said to *know* that hinge propositions are true, how can we go on saying the things we do say? His answer, as we saw above, is that it is fundamental to "any understanding of logic" to "realize that complete absence of doubt at some point, even where we would say that 'legitimate' doubt can exist, need not falsify a language-game" (OC, §375). This is also where he introduces the idea of "the groundless of our believing" (OC, §166), saying, for example: "At the foundation of well-founded belief lies belief that is not founded" (OC, §253).

As I remarked above, Wittgenstein's followers have maintained that his theory of hinge propositions is correct and should be accepted by all of us. But who needs such a theory? Surely, only phenomenalists. Philosophers who reject the idea that Wittgenstein's unheard-of events could actually occur have no reason to agree that many of the things we say imply hinge propositions, i.e., propositions which could be falsified by the occurrence of metaphysical nightmares. For that reason we are in no need of the whole apparatus of his theory, including what he says about "the groundlessness of our believing."

Notes

1. As we saw in Chapter 7, Wittgenstein explained the term "hypothesis" as follows: "What is essential to an hypothesis [such as 'That's a tree'] is . . . that it arouses an expectation by admitting of future confirmation. That is, it is of the essence of an hypothesis that its confirmation is never complete" (PR, p. 285). He also said: "If I were to describe the grammar of an hypothesis, I would say that it follows from no single [sense-datum] proposition and from no set of single propositions" (WVC, p. 211). Accordingly, hypotheses "refer to the future *ad infinitum*. They never count as proved; we always reserve the right to drop or alter them" (WVC, p. 100). Wittgenstein also states this view by saying that a tree or a man cannot be the content of experience, i.e., one cannot just look at something and *see* that it is a tree or a man (since it could in the next moment vanish). This is the way Wittgenstein put this matter in his 1946–1947 lectures (WL47, pp. 61–62 and 187), which shows that at this late date he still held that "This is a tree" is a hypothesis. This is the view he began wrestling with a year later in *On Certainty*.
2. Another phenomenalist, A. J. Ayer, had been worrying these same questions for some years before Wittgenstein wrote *On Certainty*. See Ayer's *The Foundations of Empirical Knowledge* (London: Macmillan, 1940), esp., pp. 239–243, and his essay "Phenomenalism," *Proceedings of the Aristotelean Society*, XLVII (1946–1947), esp. pp. 171–172. The relevant passages are quoted in my essay "The Metaphysics of Wittgenstein's *On Certainty*," op. cit., pp. 103–105; they are very much worth reading as a background for understanding Wittgenstein's cryptic remarks.
3. The German verb *"entpuppen,"* which I have translated as "evolve into," suggests that Wittgenstein was thinking of the change of the tree into "something different" as being like the metamorphosis of a caterpillar into a butterfly. The prefix *"ent-"* indicates establishment of a new state or abandonment of an old one, and the root comes from the noun *"Puppe,"* meaning "chrysalis" or "pupa."
4. I have altered the translation of this clause because the given translation ("it turns out that it isn't") makes nonsense of the passage. The German verb *"herausstellen"* can mean either "prove to be" or "appear to be." The context clearly demands the latter translation.
5. What sort of thing did Wittgenstein think would leave him shaken? In *Zettel* he gives this example: "If I were to see quite new surroundings from my window instead of the long familiar ones, . . . then I should say something like 'I have gone mad'. . ." (Z, §393). Presumably he was thinking that he might return from a walk where all the surroundings were familiar, then enter his rooms, step to the window and see the Hong Kong waterfront spread out before him.

6. Norman Malcolm, *Ludwig Wittgenstein: A Memoir*, op. cit., p. 88.
7. The reason for this is that Wittgenstein's theory of hinge propositions grew out of his reflecting on G. E. Moore's attempt to answer philosophical skeptics by saying, for example, that he knows he has two hands and that he knows he is dressed and not naked. The relation of Moore and Wittgenstein on this topic is extremely complex, and, as I have discussed it in detail elsewhere, I will say nothing about it here. (See my "Moore and Skepticism," op. cit., "Notes on Wittgenstein's *On Certainty*," op. cit., "Malcolm's Misunderstandings," op. cit., and "The Metaphysics of Wittgenstein's *On Certainty*," op. cit.) What is important to recognize is that, although his *soi-dissant* followers strongly endorse Wittgenstein's theory of hinge propositions, he himself, on the last day of his conscious life, began to see where this theory goes wrong. See OC, §§655–659, written on April 26, 1951. What he began to recognize is that he had been right, much earlier in *On Certainty*, when he had said: "In certain circumstances a man cannot be making a mistake" (OC, §155), and also: "One may be wrong even about 'there being a hand here.' Only in particular circumstances is it impossible" (OC, §25). This is very different from saying, as his theory of hinge propositions requires, that there are in our language certain *propositions* that are immune from doubt or that no reasonable person would doubt.

V

The Past, Memory, and the Private Language Argument

16

Memory, Tenses, and the Past

In this chapter and those that follow we will be concerned with Wittgenstein's argument against the possibility of a private language. Among Wittgenstein scholars there is no topic more hotly debated than the nature – and validity – of this argument, and many versions of it have been offered by both his detractors and his disciples. No one, however, has recognized that his argument depends on the following aspects of Wittgenstein's philosophy: (i) his reductionist accounts of memory and the past; (ii) his attack on intellectual capacities, such as the capacity to learn and retain what one has learned; and (iii) his conclusion from (i) and (ii) that in order to hold that the use of a word such as "red" or "pain" is rule-governed, it is necessary to accept a reductionist account of "same color" (or "same sensation"). The first of these aspects will be elucidated in the present chapter. The remaining two aspects will be dealt with, respectively, in Chapters 17 and 18. In Chapter 19 these will be shown to be the basis of Wittgenstein's private language argument.

Solipsism of the Present Moment

Philosophers have had difficulty understanding Wittgenstein's private language argument because his views about time and memory have gone largely unnoticed or been misunderstood. To understand these views, we must begin by seeing what prompted them. As with so many of his other views, it was a form of skepticism that led him to embrace a peculiar view of time and memory. More particularly, in order to avoid skepticism with regard to the past, he opted for reductionist accounts of memory and the past.

To understand why Wittgenstein adopted these reductionist accounts, it will be useful to consult Russell's 1914 essay, "On the Nature of Acquaintance," where the problem that troubled Wittgenstein is stated as follows:

How do we come to know that the group of things now experienced is not all-embracing? . . .

. . . At first sight, it might seem as though the experience of each moment must be a prison for the knowledge of that moment, and as though its boundaries must be the boundaries of our present world. Every word that we now understand must have a meaning which falls within our present experience; we

can never point to an object and say: '*This* lies outside my present experience.'
We cannot know any particular thing unless it is part of present experience. . . .
On this ground, we may be urged to a modest agnosticism with regard to
everything that lies outside our momentary consciousness. . . . [T]he principles
of solipsism and of the older empirical philosophy would seem, if rigorously
applied, to reduce the knowledge of each moment within the narrow area of
that moment's experience.[1]

Rather than embracing the 'agnosticism,' i.e., the *skepticism*, Russell
speaks of here, Wittgenstein was drawn, if only briefly, to what he later
called "solipsism of the present moment" (WL35, p. 25), which comes to:
"Nothing exists but the present experience." This metaphysical statement, however, is formulated in the material mode, and for that reason
Wittgenstein could not have remained satisfied with it. He was, nevertheless, sympathetic with what one would *mean* were one to say this.
Moore, reporting on Wittgenstein's lectures of the early 1930s, writes:
". . . he said that he himself had been often tempted to say 'All that is real
is the experience of the present moment' . . . and that anyone who is at
all tempted to hold Idealism or Solipsism knows the temptation to say
'The only reality is the present moment' or 'The only reality is *my*
present experience'."[2] In this chapter we will see how Wittgenstein dealt
with this temptation.

One can identify – in a rough way, at least – three phases in his
treatment of solipsism of the present moment. By this I do not mean
that his fundamental view of time and memory changed but only that
he used three different methods of presenting his view. The first of
these is found in the *Tractatus*. The second is found in his conversations,
lectures and writings from the period 1929 to approximately 1934,
wherein he undertook to explain and defend his reductionist view of
time and memory. The third phase, which overlaps with the second, is
developed in his later writings and lectures, wherein he invokes the
verificationist theory of meaning and, somewhat later, his technical
notion of *criteria*. During all three phases, as we will see, Wittgenstein's
aim was to show that the realist view of the past, to which Russell
subscribed, involves a mistaken conception of both time and memory.

Phase One – the *Tractatus*

The skeptical view sketched by Russell is that "the boundaries" of the
world are the boundaries set by language and do not extend beyond the
present. Russell's formulation was later echoed in the *Tractatus*:

. . . what the solipsist *means* is quite correct; only it cannot be *said* [in the material
mode], but makes itself manifest.

That the world is *my* world is manifest in this: that the limits of *language* (of
that language which alone I understand) signify the limits of *my* world (TLP,
5.62).

These remarks about solipsism apply also to solipsism of the present moment: what it *means* is quite correct; only it cannot be expressed in the material mode but must show itself in the features of language.

What feature, then, of the logically perspicuous language envisioned in the *Tractatus* signifies the limits – the *temporal* limits – of the world? A striking feature of the Tractarian ideal language is that it contains no verbs and hence no tensed verbs. (Elementary propositions are said to be configurations of names.) If we tried to *say* what is shown by this feature of language, we might try to say something like this: In the world *as it is* (as opposed to our conceptual world) there is no past or future – there is only the experience of the present moment. Or, putting the matter in the formal mode, one might say: A language by means of which the world can be described nonmisleadingly must be a language whose sentences are atemporal. This is how Wittgenstein thought of the (tenseless) elementary propositions of the *Tractatus* and of the facts that comprise the world.

Why did he adopt such a view? An alternative had been proposed by Russell in the essay quoted from above, namely, that by means of definite descriptions one can refer to things one is not presently experiencing. As we have seen, however, Wittgenstein dismissed Russell's claim to be able in this way to 'transcend immediate experience' (Chapter 1, note 35, this volume). Accordingly, he thought that a philosopher who holds a realist view of the past must succumb to the 'agnosticism' Russell describes and ought to conclude that (as Wittgenstein put it in 1949) the *only* language possible would be to gape and exclaim, "This!"[3] – i.e., one could not say anything using the past tense. His view, then, was that in order to accommodate the things we commonly say by using the past tense, one must reject the realist view of the past. This is why in the *Tractatus* the specifications for a logically perspicuous language allow no verbs and hence no tenses.

This was not, however, a way of declaring that we cannot say all the things we commonly do say using the past tense. On the contrary, Wittgenstein held that the propositions of everyday language, although misleading in form, are "in perfect logical order" (TLP, 5.5563). This point had to hold also, of course, for our past-tense statements, such as, "I was given a pony when I was a child." In saying such a thing, one *seems*, at least, to be stating a fact which is not a fact of *present* experience. Yet the Tractarian position was that our past-tense statements can be analyzed into propositions containing no past-tense verbs.

To understand the nature of the problem Wittgenstein meant to solve in this way, it is useful to review a point about empiricism. Empiricists hold a peculiar view of 'facts,' which is dictated by Hume's account of causation. Hume's account leads to the idea that whatever happens is unrelated to what went before – or, in other words, that whatever happens comes into being *ex nihilo*. In the *Tractatus* Wittgenstein stated this view as follows: "The world disintegrates [*zerfällt*] into facts. Each item can be the case or not the case while everything else remains the same" (TLP, 1.2–1.21). Wittgenstein is saying here that in order for a state of affairs to come into being, no *other* state of affairs is required, i.e., states of affairs come into being *ex nihilo*, not *because* something else has occurred. Now, it is easy to see that this Humean view of the world leads straight to skepticism if it is combined with a realist view of the past. For our memories – say, of childhood – are among the events that (on this view) come into being *ex nihilo*, so that although I recall – or seem to recall – many events from my childhood, no such events *need* have occurred in order for me to have these 'memories.' Indeed, I *need* not have had any childhood at all – or even any *past* at all. And the same goes for photographs, diaries, and birth records: that these things exist *now* is no reason for thinking that other events occurred in the past – if, that is, the events they purport to record are events whose very nature requires that they be described (now) in the past tense.

How was Wittgenstein to avoid this plunge into skepticism? Inasmuch as he shared Hume's view of the world, his only alternative was to reject the realist's view of the past and to adopt in its place the view that past-tense statements are misleading forms of words and so will not retain this form in a proper analysis. This, then, is the solution Wittgenstein adopted in the *Tractatus*. He held that propositions apparently about (irreducibly) past events turn out, when stripped of their misleading phraseology, to be propositions whose hidden logical form allows them to be translated into tenseless propositions. Accordingly, he could hold that skepticism about the past can seem plausible only so long as one makes the realist's mistake of thinking that the grammatical form of our past-tense statements is also their *logical* form.

Phase Two – Explaining Reductionism

After returning to philosophy in 1929 Wittgenstein devoted considerable time to explaining the *Tractatus* view. Because he soon abandoned the idea that an *explicitly* phenomenalistic language could be constructed, he could no longer explain himself by saying, simply, that an ideal language would be a tenseless language. He needed, therefore, to explain himself by elaborating his view of tenses and by saying what he found to be wrong with a realist interpretation of past-tense propositions.[4]

A useful place to begin a survey of this second phase is with the following passage from *Philosophical Remarks*:

What belongs to the essence of the world cannot be expressed by language [i.e., in the material mode]. . . .

We are tempted to say: only the experience of the present moment has reality. And then the first reply must be: As opposed to what?

Does it imply I didn't get up this morning? (For if so, it would be something one could doubt.) But that is not what we mean [when we make the *a priori* claim]. Does it mean that an event that I'm not remembering at this instant didn't occur? Not that either.

The proposition that only the present experience has reality appears to contain the last consequence of solipsism. And in a sense that is so; only what it is able to say [in the material mode] amounts to just as little as can be said by solipsism. For what belongs to the essence of the world simply *cannot* be said. And philosophy, if it were to say anything, would have to describe the essence of the world.

But the essence of language is a picture of the essence of the world; and philosophy as custodian of grammar can in fact grasp the essence of the world, only not in the propositions of language. . . .

If someone says, only the *present experience* has reality, then the word 'present' must be redundant here, as the word "I" is in other contexts. For it cannot mean *present* as opposed to past and future. Something else must be meant by the word, something that isn't *in* a space, but is itself a space. That is to say, not something bordering on something else [namely, 'the past'] (from which it could therefore be limited off). And so, something language cannot legitimately set in relief (PR, pp. 84–85).

Plainly, Wittgenstein held that the word "present" is being misused by philosophers who say: "Only the present is real." He was not, however, dismissing solipsism of the present moment. Rather, his point here is that it is a mistake to say that there are only *present* facts, for in an important sense there can be no *present* facts, either. (Compare: in the ideal language of the *Tractatus* there are no *present*-tense verbs.) Commenting on what might seem to be a paradigm of a present fact, he said: "It appears to me that the present, as it occurs in the proposition 'the sky is blue' . . . is not a form of time, so that the present in *this* sense is atemporal" (PG, p. 217).

Because he held that it is a mistake to use the word "present" to express solipsism of the present moment, Wittgenstein required some other way of doing so, some other terminology. Thus, in some places we find him using the phrase "immediate experience" in place of "present experience." Because this phrase could be misunderstood, I shall, instead, expound his views by availing myself of a specialized use of the word "present," flagging it with an asterisk. This use of the word is to be understood in the light of Wittgenstein's remark, quoted above, that if we say that only the present is real, we cannot "mean present as opposed to past and future. Something else must be meant by the word, something that isn't *in* a space, but is itself a space." Or as he puts it in his remark about "The sky is blue": "the present in *this* sense is atemporal."

To see the point of this convention, it is useful to notice how flagging the word "present" with an asterisk saves Wittgenstein's position, as just

stated, from being utterly paradoxical. For it certainly would be paradoxical to say that if I now remember some event from my childhood I
am remembering a present event. If we mean to be using "present" in
its ordinary sense, where it is used in contrast to "past" and "future,"
then necessarily the events of my childhood are past, not present. Wittgenstein, anticipating an objection of the sort Moore was prone to make,
makes the same point about the ordinary use of the word "present":

Anyone wishing to contest the proposition that only the present experience is
real . . . will perhaps ask whether then a proposition like 'Julius Caesar crossed
the Alps' merely describes my present mental state which is occupied with the
matter. And of course the answer is: no, it describes an event which we believe
happened ca. 2,000 years ago. That is, if the word "describes" is construed in
the same way as in the sentence "The proposition 'I am writing' *describes* what
I am at present doing" (PR, pp. 86–87).

Wittgenstein is not here rejecting a reductionist account of the past. He
is simply making the point that "present" and "past" are ordinary words
and that in their ordinary use "present" goes with our present tense and
"past" with our past tense. He might have made his meaning clearer
had he said that our ordinary word "present" is so used that if I am
asked, "What is he doing at present?" I answer in the present tense (e.g.,
"He is writing") and that our ordinary word "past" is so used that if I am
asked, "Has he done this in the past?" I answer in the past tense (e.g.,
"He did so yesterday"), and therefore it makes no sense to use our word
"present" to say that a *past*-tense statement is about one's *present* experience. And yet, using our asterisk convention, we can say that Wittgenstein's view is that when one says one remembers something from
childhood, one's statement, *despite* the past tense, is about the present*,
i.e., the past tense is a misleading form of words.

The Analysis of Tensed Verbs

Here we may ask: How could Wittgenstein have thought that a language without past-tense verbs can capture what we mean when we say,
for example, "I had a pony when I was ten"? He cannot have thought
that our tenses correspond to *nothing* in the world, for he would not
have wanted to deny that we speak of *something* real when we speak of
a sound's growing louder, and we do so by using tenses: "It *was* very soft,
but now it's quite loud." So he must have thought that there is some sort
of ordering of states of affairs that corresponds to our tenses but that this
ordering is not of the sort that our tenses suggest to philosophers who
fail to distrust this feature of our grammar.

The *Tractatus* provides no hint of the way in which Wittgenstein
thought that the tensed verbs of ordinary language could be translated
into a tenseless language. He does say: "Space, time, and colour (being

coloured) are forms of objects" (TLP, 2.0251), but the inclusion of time in this list merely acknowledges that it must be possible *somehow* to accommodate what we commonly say by the use of tenses. He was presumably thinking that in carrying out a proper reduction of propositions with tensed verbs, they would pass through a stage in which such verbs would be replaced by terms such as "now" and "earlier" and "later" (or "before" and "after"). Thus, in his conversations with Waismann in 1929 he illustrated a point about "temporal specifications" (WVC, p. 53) by giving as an example "Caesar before Augustus" (WVC, p. 55). Presumably he did not regard this sentence, which contains no verb, as being an incomplete sentence but regarded it as showing something about the logical form of time as it occurs in the past-tense sentence "Caesar *was born* before Augustus."[5]

We needn't speculate how Wittgenstein might have thought that replacing tenses with the terms "earlier" and "later" brought him a step closer to atemporal propositions.[6] But we do need to bear in mind that he regarded tensed verbs and the words "past" and "present" as being *misleading* forms of words and as being, therefore, unsuitable for use in philosophy.

Criticizing Russell's Realist View of the Past

An important part of the second phase of Wittgenstein's development was his criticism of Russell's realist view of the past and of the corresponding view of memory. Understanding this requires some background, which can best be provided by considering Russell's famous argument to the effect that, for all we know, the world might have sprung into existence five minutes ago complete with our 'memories' of childhood, etc. Russell states the argument as follows:

It is not logically necessary to the existence of a memory-belief that the event remembered should have occurred, or even that the past should have existed at all. There is no logical impossibility in the hypothesis that the world sprang into being five minutes ago, exactly as it was then, with a population that "remembered" a wholly unreal past. There is no logically necessary connection between events at different times; therefore nothing that is happening now . . . can disprove the hypothesis that the world began five minutes ago. Hence the occurrences which are *called* knowledge of the past are logically independent of the past; they are wholly analysable into present contents, which might, theoretically, be just what they are even if no past had existed.

I am not suggesting that the non-existence of the past should be entertained as a serious hypothesis. Like all sceptical hypotheses, it is logically tenable, but uninteresting. All that I am doing is to use its logical tenability as a help in the analysis of what occurs when we remember.[7]

An essential step in this argument is the statement: "There is no logically necessary connection between events at different times," where the events he is speaking of are, e.g., (a) one's remembering something from childhood and (b) the events (if there be any) of one's childhood. In saying that there is no logically necessary connection between such events, Russell was assuming that there could be nothing philosophically objectionable in his speaking of these as being "events at different times." And yet this realist view of time is precisely what Wittgenstein found unacceptable.

Wittgenstein made plain his opposition to Russell's argument when he wrote: "Does it now make sense to say I could have been deceived by a demon and what I took for a description wasn't one at all, but a memory delusion? No, that can have no sense. A delusion that, *ex hypothesi, cannot* be unmasked isn't a delusion" (PR, p. 104). In his writings, lectures and recorded conversations one can find a rather complicated response to Russell's argument.

To understand his criticisms of Russell, we must put into the record Russell's views about time and memory. One can discern two stages in Russell's thinking about these matters. In 1912, in *The Problems of Philosophy*, he gave the following account:

Sense-data . . . are among the things with which we have acquaintance. . . . But if they were the sole example, we should only know what is now present to our senses: we could not know anything about the past – not even that there was a past. . . . We have therefore to consider acquaintance with other things besides sense-data if we are to obtain any tolerably adequate analysis of our knowledge.

The first extension beyond sense-data to be considered is acquaintance by *memory*. It is obvious that we often remember what we have seen or heard or had otherwise present to our senses, and that in such cases we are still immediately aware of what we remember, in spite of the fact that it appears as past and not as present. This immediate knowledge by memory is the source of all our knowledge concerning the past: without it, there could be no knowledge of the past by inference [as when we infer from footprints on a beach that someone *was* here], since we should never know that there was anything past to be inferred.[8]

Two aspects of this passage bear notice. First of all, it is plain that Russell takes it for granted that a sense-datum he sees now is necessarily in the present and that what he remembers – in remembering, say, some event in his childhood – is necessarily something in the past. Second, Russell is also saying that in remembering something we have seen or heard we are "immediately aware of what we remember," so that we can no more be in error about it than we can be in error about a sense-datum of which we are immediately aware. This second feature is introduced by Russell in order to explain how we can have *knowledge* of the past.

The skeptical argument regarding the past which Russell set out in *The Analysis of Mind* shows that at some time between 1912 and 1921 his views underwent a change, for that argument is plainly inconsistent with his early view that in memory we are "immediately aware" of the past and thereby *know* that this or that happened. By 1921, then, he had dropped this view of memory. And yet in another respect Russell's views had not changed, for he continued to think that *what* one remembers, in remembering some event in one's childhood, is something in the past. (In *The Analysis of Mind* he makes this explicit when he says that "my memory is true (or false) in virtue of a past event. . . ."[9]) This is the realist view of the past, and it is, in part, because he retained this feature of his early view that he could formulate his skeptical argument. Russell's analysis of the situation is as follows:

> Remembering has to be a present occurrence [which is] in some way . . . related to what is remembered. And it is difficult to find any ground . . . for supposing that memory is not sheer delusion, if, as seems to be the case, there is not, apart from memory, any way of ascertaining that there really was a past occurrence having the required relation to our present remembering. . . . [T]he past event which we are said to be remembering is unpleasantly remote from . . . the present mental occurrence in remembering. There is an awkward gulf between the two, which raises difficulties for the theory of knowledge.[10]

The difficulty Russell is thinking of here is this: if (i) remembering and *what* we claim to remember are events at different times and (ii) there is no logically necessary connection between events at different times, then it is logically possible that nothing we *think* we remember ever occurred, so that memory is "sheer delusion."

One way Wittgenstein deals with this is to provide a diagnosis of how a philosopher comes to accept (i), i.e., a realist view of the past. His diagnosis is formulated in terms of an analogy Russell had introduced for giving an analysis of time. In his 1915 essay "The Ultimate Constituents of Matter" Russell said that "the immediate data of sense are . . . in a state of perpetual flux" and then proceeded to explain this as follows:

> My meaning . . . may perhaps be made clearer by the use of Bergson's favorite illustration of the cinematograph. . . . When, in a picture palace, we see a man rolling down hill, or running away from the police . . . we know that there is not really only one man moving, but a succession of films [i.e., *frames*], each with a different momentary man. The illusion of persistence arises only through the approach to continuity in the series of momentary men. . . . The real man too, I believe, however the police may swear to his identity, is really a series of momentary men, each different one from the other. . . . And what applies to men applies equally to tables and chairs, the sun, moon and stars. Each of these is to be regarded, not as one single persistent entity, but as a series of entities succeeding each other in time, each lasting for a very brief period, though probably not for a mere mathematical instant. In saying this I am only urging the same kind of division in time as we are accustomed to acknowledge in the case of space. . . . [A] thing which persists for an hour is to be regarded as composed of many things of less duration.[11]

Russell is saying: the flux of experience is like the succession of the frames of the film strip passing before the lens of the projector. It is in terms of this analogy that Wittgenstein formulates his diagnosis of the mistake made by philosophers who embrace a realist view of the past.

Stated in its most general form, his diagnosis of Russell's mistake is as follows:

> The worst philosophical errors always arise when we try to apply our ordinary – physical – language in the area of the immediately given. . . .
> All our forms of speech are taken from ordinary, physical language and cannot be used in epistemology or phenomenology without casting a distorting light on their objects (PR, p. 88).

To understand this, one must be aware that several pages earlier (PR, p. 80) Wittgenstein has spoken of the world of data as being *timeless*. So in the passage just quoted he meant to say that if a philosopher uses ordinary forms of speech when trying to say something, not about our conceptual world, but about the world of *data*, this will result in philosophical errors. He then goes on to say that one error that arises in this way "stems from taking the time concept from time in physics [i.e., in speaking of men and tables] and applying it to the course of immediate experience. It's a confusion of the time of the film strip with the time of the picture it projects" (PR, p. 81). This is plainly a reference to Russell's analogy, and in explanation of this Wittgenstein says:

> We can speak of present, past and future events in the physical world [i.e., in speaking of our conceptual world, where our forms of expression are not to be taken at face value], but not of present, past and future sense impressions. . . .
> Thus [philosophers] cannot use the concept of time, i.e., the syntactical rules that hold for the names of physical objects, in [speaking of] the world of sense impressions – not, that is, where we adopt a radically different way of speaking [i.e., where our propositions must be tenseless] (PR, p. 82).[12]

Russell introduced his film-strip analogy to explain his remark that "the immediate data of sense are . . . in a state of perpetual flux," and what this suggests is that each present datum quickly passes and becomes a *past* event. But this is a misuse of the analogy, according to Wittgenstein:

> If I compare the facts of immediate experience with the pictures on the screen and the facts of physics with pictures in the film strip, on the film strip there is a present picture and past and future pictures [i.e., the frame being projected and those on either side of it]. But on the screen, there is only the present [or: present*] (PR, p. 83).

Wittgenstein is objecting to Russell's use of his analogy to explain what he meant in saying that "the immediate data of sense are . . . in a state of perpetual flux." Russell's way of picturing the flux of experience is bound to lead one into skepticism regarding the past, Wittgenstein thought, because it suggests that in speaking of one's childhood, one is speaking of events that were *once* on the screen but have *now* receded beyond the reach of experience. This is the point he is making when he says:

> It is noteworthy that in ordinary life we are not troubled by the feeling that the phenomenon is slipping away from us, [by] the constant flux of appearance, but only when we philosophize. This indicates that what is in question here is an idea suggested by a misapplication of our language [i.e., by using "past" when speaking of experience].
>
> The feeling we have is that the present disappears into the past without our being able to prevent it. And here we are obviously using the picture of a film strip remorselessly moving past us, that we are unable to stop. But it is of course just as clear that the picture is misapplied: that we cannot say 'Time flows' if by time we mean the possibility of change. What we are looking at here is really the possibility of motion: and so the logical form of motion [rather than time].[13]
>
> In this connection it appears to us as if memory were a somewhat secondary sort of experience, when compared with experience of the present. We say 'We can *only* remember that.' As though in a primary sense memory were a somewhat faint and uncertain picture of what we originally had before us in full clarity (PR, pp. 83–84).

Wittgenstein is saying: Russell leaves himself open to skepticism regarding the past because he mistakenly thinks that there is a temporal parade of events passing us by just as a parade of horses can pass one by, with the difference being that one can chase after the horses for a second look at them but cannot chase after parading events (cannot return to the past) to verify one's memories of them. It is this comparison, according to Wittgenstein, that led Russell to think of memory as no better than an "uncertain picture of what we originally had before us."

Initially, Russell had held a different view. He had said, in 1912, that we can have *knowledge* of the past because, in remembering something, we are "immediately aware of what we remember." Accordingly, we can expect to find Wittgenstein, in his determination to avoid skepticism, trying to devise a position similar to that of the early Russell. What we need to understand, then, is how Wittgenstein could embrace Russell's early view and think of memory as something other than an *uncertain* picture of what we originally had before us. For this purpose Wittgenstein needed to separate memory from Russell's realist view of the past, i.e., the view that there is a temporal "gulf" separating a childhood event and our memory of it. How did he go about this?

Separating Memory from the Realist View of the Past

In *Philosophical Remarks* Wittgenstein stated his views about memory as follows:

> . . . 'time' has one meaning when we regard memory as the source of time, and another when we regard it as a picture preserved from a past event.

. . . . [In the latter case] I compare [my memory] with other evidence of what happened [such as a photograph]. In this case, memory is not the source of time [i.e., not our *grounds* for a past-tense statement] but a more or less reliable custodian of what "actually" happened; and this is something we can know about in other ways, [because it is] a physical event. It's quite different if we now [as regards *non*physical events] take memory to be the source of time [i.e., as our reason – our *criterion* – for using the past tense].[14] Here it [i.e., memory] isn't a picture, and it cannot fade either – not in the sense in which a picture fades, becoming an ever less faithful representation of its object [i.e., where memory is our *sole* criterion, it cannot be regarded as possibly faulty]. Both ways of talking are in order, and are equally legitimate, but cannot be mixed together. It's clear of course that speaking of memory as a picture [preserved from the past] is only a metaphor; just as the way of speaking of images as 'pictures of objects in our minds' . . . is a metaphor. We know what a picture is, but images are surely no kind of picture at all. For, in the first case I can see the picture and the object of which it is a picture. But in the other, things are obviously quite different. We have just used a metaphor and now the metaphor tyrannizes us [i.e., leads us to say we have *only* a picture of the past] (PR, pp. 81–82).[15]

Russell's mistake, he is saying, is that of thinking that when we rely solely on memory in making a past-tense statement, our memory could be faulty – as a photograph could be faulty because it has faded. In *Philosophical Grammar* he makes a similar point about recognizing:

It is easy to have a false concept of the process called "recognizing"; as if recognizing always consisted in comparing two impressions with one another [e.g., one's present sense impression of a person and a mental picture of him preserved from the past]. It is [we think] as if I carried a picture of an object with me and used it to perform an identification of an object as the one represented by the picture. Our memory seems to us to be the agent of such a comparison, by preserving a picture of what has been seen before, or by allowing us to look into the past (as if down a spy-glass). . . .

Perhaps someone will say: if I hadn't kept his image in my memory, I couldn't have recognized him. But here he is either using a metaphor, or expressing a hypothesis (PG, pp. 167–168).

In support of his claim that one's memory of, say, a person's face is unlike having a photograph of him, Wittgenstein says:

'I can *merely* remember.' As if there were some other way and memory not the *only* source from which we draw.

Memories have been called pictures. A picture can be compared with its original, but a memory cannot. Experiences of the past are after all not like objects in the next room; although I do not see them [there] now, I can go there. But can I go into the past? (WVC, p. 48).

Wittgenstein is saying here that someone who says he can "merely remember," i.e., that he can't verify his memory, has made the mistake of thinking that memory images are like photographs in being representative of something, which, in the case of memory, one cannot get back to. In rejecting this, Wittgenstein meant to imply that in those cases in which we rely solely on memory in making a past-tense statement, it makes no sense to suggest – as Russell's skeptical argument does – that one may be mistaken. This, then, is one element in his criticism of the idea that (as he put it in a passage quoted above) memory is "a somewhat secondary sort of experience, when compared with experience of the present." To complete this criticism, we must turn to another aspect of Wittgenstein's argument.

It will be recalled that in the passage in which Russell formulates his skeptical argument he says that his purpose is to show that the occurrences we call "remembering" are "wholly analysable into present contents." But in speaking here of "present contents," he meant to be using "present" as a term which contrasts with "past," and Wittgenstein held this to be a mistake. Wittgenstein's own view could be stated as follows, using the asterisk convention introduced earlier: "The occurrences called 'remembering' (and 'recognizing') are wholly analyzable into something present*." The difference between this formulation and Russell's is that Russell, because he meant to use "present" in contrast to "past," thought he had discovered an "awkward gulf" between one's remembering, which is in the present, and *what* one remembers, which is in the past. Wittgenstein, because he regarded it as illegitimate to use "present" and "past" (as he puts it) "in the area of the immediately given" ("our forms of speech are taken from ordinary . . . language and cannot be used in epistemology") could maintain that there can *be* no such gulf. Which is to say that, on his view, it is not merely the remembering that is present*, but also *what* one remembers – and this *despite* the fact that we use the past-tense in saying *what* we remember.[16]

To understand how Wittgenstein could take such a position, one needs to understand his view about meaning and verification, namely, that how one verifies a proposition determines its meaning. His position regarding the issue at hand is that when a proposition – even a past-tense proposition – is verified, it is verified by present* experience, and therefore it is *about* the present*. He writes:

If the world of data is timeless, how can we speak of it at all?
The stream of life, or the stream of the world, flows on and our propositions are so to speak verified only at instants.[17]
Our propositions are only verified by the present [i.e., by the present*].
So they must be so constructed that they can be verified by it. And so in some way they must be commensurable with the present [i.e., with the present*]. . . . (PR, p. 80–81).

This is put forth as an entirely general claim and so is meant to hold not only for our ordinary *present*-tense statements but also for those of our ordinary *past*-tense statements that can be verified. (The exception would be past-tense propositions of the sort he calls "hypotheses," which, as we saw in Chapter 7, he did not regard as being (completely) verifiable because they imply various things about *future* experience.) What Wittgenstein is saying, then, is that past-tense statements which can be verified must be so constructed that they can be verified by the present*.

In saying that propositions must be *so constructed* that they can be verified by the present*, he means that their *logical form* must be such that they can be so verified. And this, in turn, means that the logical form of our ordinary past-tense statements must be such that they are really about something present*. To understand how he explains this, we must take account of the fact that Wittgenstein believed that past-tense propositions come in several logically different varieties, which he distinguished as follows: some past-tense propositions, he said, "I can verify . . . only by means of memory" and others, namely, those regarding *physical* events, "I can verify . . . by other means, e.g., by reading a document, or by asking someone, and so forth" (WVC, p. 53).[18] (This is a *logical* differentiation, he explains, because "where there are different verifications there are also different meanings" (ibid.).[19]) Cases of the latter sort – those in which one can verify the proposition by consulting a document or other people – are those in which he regards the past-tense proposition as a 'hypothesis,' and I will present his account of these cases first.

As we saw in Chapter 7, Wittgenstein regarded the statements we make about such things as trees and houses and chairs as being 'hypotheses,' meaning that such a statement "goes beyond immediate [i.e., present*] experience" (WL32, p. 110), so that "its confirmation is never complete" (PR, p. 285). In saying this he was thinking that if I say, "There's a chair," I imply that if I reach for it, my hand *will* meet with resistance. Similarly, if a museum curator, relying on documentary evidence, says, "This chair was made for Abraham Lincoln," additional evidence may be found which *will* support or undermine his claim. Accordingly, Wittgenstein says of such cases: "The verification of a proposition about the past is a set of propositions involving present *and future* tenses" (WL35, p. 28, emphasis added). And he makes a point of saying that for this reason it would be a mistake to maintain that such propositions are really about one's *present** experience (PR, pp. 86–87). [To illustrate the point, he says (PR, p. 87) that the *sense* of the proposition "Julius Caesar crossed the Alps" includes such *future* possibilities as our finding his corpse or, conversely, finding a manuscript which convinces us that no such person ever existed.] So in regard to past-tense propositions of *this* sort Wittgenstein's position is that they are not threatened by Russell's skeptical hypothesis regarding the past because their subject matter is the present* and the future.

What about past-tense propositions of the other sort – those which (as he says) I can verify only by means of memory (or, alternatively, where memory is our only criterion)? As I have already suggested, Wittgenstein held that these escape the clutches of skepticism because they are solely about the present*. He is making this point in the following passage:

> How do I know that the colour of this paper, which I call 'white,' is the same as the one I saw here yesterday? By recognizing it again; and recognizing it again is my only source of knowledge here. In that case, 'That is the same' *means* that I recognize it again.
>
> Then of course you also cannot ask whether it really is the same [as the color seen yesterday] and whether I might not perhaps be mistaken; (whether it *is* the same or doesn't just *seem* to be.) (PR, p. 60).

Wittgenstein is making two claims here, the first of which is that the *past*-tense statement "It was this color yesterday" means the same as the *present*-tense statement "I recognize it as the same color." His second claim is that "I recognize it" is not to be understood as though it could be true or false, i.e., one is not to think that in saying "I recognize it" he is alluding to something at another time about which he might be right or wrong. What we find in this passage, then, is that Wittgenstein is giving a reductionist account of a past-tense statement and in that way aims to protect it from Russell's skepticism.

As we will see in Chapter 19, his analysis of such cases forms the basis of his 'private language argument.' The relevant points emerge in notes he made in the late 1940s, where he deals with an example by giving a similarly reductionist account of the past-tense:

> But isn't there such a thing as a kind of private ostensive definition for feelings of movement and the like? E.g. I crook a finger and note the sensation. Now someone says to me: "I am going to produce certain sensations in your finger in such and such a way, without its moving; you tell me when it is *that* one that you have now in crooking your finger." Mightn't I now, for my own private use, call this sensation "S," use my memory as criterion of identity and then say "Yes, that's S again" etc.? (RPP, I, §393).
>
> I can certainly, e.g., raise my knee several times in succession and say I have had the same sensation each time. . . .
>
> Being the same here of course means the same thing as seeming the same (RPP, I, §395).

His point here is that, because there is no way to test one's recollection of what the sensation was like the first several times, if one says, speaking from memory alone, "It was the same each time," this cannot mean what it appears to mean, for although it appears to support the realist view that it is a statement about what was felt on *successive* occasions, it is really a statement about one's present* state.

In the *Investigations* Wittgenstein discusses another case of the sort that concerns us here. He writes:

> Let us assume there was a man who always guessed right what I was saying to

myself in my thoughts. (It does not matter how he manages it.) But what is the criterion for his guessing *right*? Well, I am a truthful person and I confess that he has guessed right. But might I not be mistaken, can my memory not deceive me? And might it not always do so when – without lying – I express what I have thought within myself? But now it does appear that 'what went on within me' is not the point at all. (Here I am drawing a construction-line.)

The criteria for the truth of the *confession* that I thought such-and-such are not the criteria for a true *description* of a process. And the importance of the true confession does not reside in its being a correct and certain report of a process. It resides rather in the special consequences which can be drawn from a confession whose truth is guaranteed by the special criteria of *truthfulness*.

(Assuming that dreams can yield important information about the dreamer, what yielded the information would be truthful accounts of dreams. The question whether the dreamer's memory deceives him when he reports the dream after waking cannot arise, unless indeed we introduce a completely new criterion for the report's 'agreeing' with the dream, a criterion which gives us a concept of 'truth' as distinct from 'truthfulness' here.) (PI, pp. 222–223).

What Wittgenstein means to say here, regarding the thought-guessing example, is this: Whereas some philosophers may conceive of the past (and the past tense) in such a way as to produce the idea that in such a case my memory could be deceiving me (although nothing whatsoever could prove whether it was or wasn't), the truth is that this realist conception of the past is mistaken because, although I say, "You're right; that's what I thought," which seems (because of the tense) to be about something that is *not* now present*, what I am actually *saying* is something about my present* recollection, and since I cannot be in error about *that*, there is no room here for skepticism about my memory. We will consider this example in greater detail later in the chapter.

What about cases in which we decide that our memory is faulty? Wittgenstein sketches such a case as follows:

Imagine that you were supposed to paint a particular colour "C," which was the colour that appeared when the chemical substances X and Y combined. Suppose that the colour [that appeared when X and Y combine] struck you as brighter on one day than on another; would you not sometimes say: "I must be wrong, the colour is certainly the same as yesterday"? This shews that we do not always resort to what memory tells us as the verdict of the highest court of appeal (PI, §56).

Wittgenstein does not work out the details of his example, and it is not clear that he could do so consistently with his view that we inhabit an indeterministic world. (Why, on Wittgenstein's view, should someone think that a chemical mixture will *always* produce the same color?) But leaving that matter aside, I take it that Wittgenstein's point in this passage is that one will think his memory is faulty only in case he has some *other* criterion, and in his example the criterion is the present* fact that he is seeing a mixture of the chemical substances X and Y (not X and Z, for example). Presumably, however, Wittgenstein did not think that this could be the end of the matter, for we still have to deal with the statement that this man has run the same test each day, i.e., that he has combined the same chemicals today as yesterday (and in the same proportion, etc.). And if we say that each time he conducts the test, he does so on the basis of what he *remembers* being told of the procedure (which chemicals, what proportion, etc.), then we are once more back to a case in which everything depends on memory and in which references to the past reduce to present* 'memories.' On the other hand, if we say that he performs the test each day by consulting a manual which describes the procedure, then (so Wittgenstein would say) he trusts his memory that the printed instructions have not unaccountably altered, so that again we are back to a case in which everything depends on taking one's memory as the final court of appeal. That this is how Wittgenstein thought of such cases can be seen from the following passage:

> Of course, it would also be possible to say that the colour is the same [not on the basis of memory but] because chemical investigations do not disclose any change. So that if it doesn't look the same to me then I am mistaken. But even then there *must* still be [i.e., it is *logically* necessary that there be] something that is *immediately recognized* [namely, that the chemical tests produced the same results] (PR, p. 60, emphasis added).

Wittgenstein's point in the final sentence of this passage (where the phrase "immediately recognized" harkens back to Russell's early view of memory, in which he said that we are "immediately aware of what we remember") is that even in cases like this, in which memories are checked against physical evidence, memory must *in the end* play a role as the final criterion.[20] So cases of this sort turn out to be, in Wittgenstein's view, not essentially different from his thought-guessing example. In cases of both sorts we depend, in the final analysis, on memory, and about this we cannot, in such cases, be in error.

His view, then, was that there are two basic types of past-tense propositions: those in which the past-tense is misleading because they are, in the last analysis, about one's present* 'memory,' and those in which the past-tense is misleading because the propositions are 'hypotheses' and so are about future as well as present* experiences.[21] What Wittgenstein is maintaining, then, is that there is *no* case about which Russell is right to say that "my memory is true (or false) in virtue of [an irreducibly] past event," and therefore Russell's skeptical argument rests on a misconception.

Phase Three – Verification and Meaning

We can now turn to the third phase in Wittgenstein's attempt to deal with skepticism regarding the past. As I said at the beginning of the chapter, this phase overlaps somewhat with the second phase. Moreover, it differs from the first two phases, *not* because Wittgenstein came to accept a realist view of the past, but because he became dissatisfied with a methodological feature of the second phase. In a passage quoted above from *Philosophical Remarks*, Wittgenstein says that our propositions (including past-tense ones) must be *so constructed* that they can be verified in instants. The phrase "so constructed" suggests that he was, at this point, still thinking along the lines of the *Tractatus*, i.e., still thinking that it is the construction, i.e., the *hidden logical form*, of a proposition that determines its meaning. This view, as we saw in Chapter 7, was abandoned by Wittgenstein in the early 1930s. In its place he began talking about the *use* of language and about how *part* of the use is the way in which we verify propositions. Accordingly, he began saying the following sort of thing:

The question, "What is its verification?", is a good translation of "How can one know it?" Some people say that the question, "How can one know such a thing?" is irrelevant to the question, "What is the meaning?" But an answer gives the meaning by showing the relation of the proposition to other propositions. . . . It gives the grammar of the proposition, which is what the question, "What would it be like for it to be true?" asks for (WL35, pp. 19–20).

This passage, from a lecture in 1932, is very similar to what Wittgenstein says in the *Investigations*: "Asking whether and how a proposition can be verified is only a particular form of the question 'How d'you mean?' The answer is a contribution to the grammar of the proposition" (PI, §353). There are three points that need to be made about the view expressed in these passage as it relates to memory and the past-tense.

First, Wittgenstein thought that the points he had made in what I have called "Phase Two" could be made by talking about the verification of (or criteria for) such propositions instead of talking about their *construction*. Thus, his discussion of the thought-guessing example (PI, pp. 222–223), which is meant to attack the realist view of time and memory, turns on his claim: "The criteria for the truth of the *confession* that I thought such-and-such are not the criteria for a true description of a process. And the importance of the true confession [in which the past tense is used] does not reside in its being a correct and certain report of a process."

Second, he also thought that by talking about the verification of propositions (or the criteria for their truth) he could make it plain that he had not abandoned his rejection of Russell's realist view of the past. Many philosophers, including those close to Wittgenstein, have thought that he eventually abandoned his early views and that when he says that there are criteria for this or for that he is not advancing a reductionist account.[22] In Chapter Nine we saw that this is not the case in his treatment of 'other minds.' On the contrary, in that instance his saying that we have *criteria* for the thoughts and feelings of other people is part of his reductionist campaign, i.e., his behaviorism. We will find that the same is true in his treatment of the past. To see that this is so, it is necessary to understand why in the passages quoted above Wittgenstein connects verification with "meaning" and "grammar." What do these words mean in this context?

This brings us to my third point. When Wittgenstein talks about "meaning" in this context, he is not using that word in any familiar way. Nor is he using "grammar" and "grammatical" in a familiar way. Rather, he is using the word "grammar" in his technical sense, where it depends on his view that ordinary language contains misleading forms of words, i.e., grammatical forms that lead philosophers (i.e., realists) to misinterpret the meaning of things we say in everyday life (see WL35, p. 31). In other words, his insistence that there is an essential connection between verification (or criteria) and *meaning* or *grammar* is his way of deciding questions about the *philosophical interpretation* of certain disputed forms of words, such as past-tense verbs. "When we do philosophy," he says, "we are like savages, primitive people, who hear the expressions of civilized men, put a false interpretation on them, and then draw the queerest conclusions from it" (PI, §194). This is why he also speaks of criteria as grounds "which are grammatically related to the proposition and tell us what proposition it is" (Z, §437). Why do we need something to tell us *what proposition it is*? Because, he thought, their grammatical form is misleading. The relevance of this to the case at hand is that Wittgenstein poses the question: "How could the *meaning* of a sentence about the past be given by a sentence about the present?" and answers that how a proposition is verified "determines the *meaning*, i.e., determines its use, or *grammar*" (WL35, pp. 28–29, emphasis added). His point, as we saw earlier, is that Russell's realist *interpretation* of past-tense propositions is mistaken because it fails to connect the *meaning* of such propositions with something that is present*, which is to say that Russell's mistake is to think that what makes a past-tense proposition true is something that is not present*.

We are now in a position to consider Wittgenstein's most direct comment on Russell's skeptical argument. In lectures he said of this argument:

By examining Russell's hypothesis that the world was created five minutes ago I shall try to explain what I mean in saying that it is meaningless. Russell's hypothesis was so arranged that nothing could bear it out or refute it. Whatever our experience might be, it would be in agreement with it. The point of saying that something has happened derives from there being a criterion for its truth. To lay down the evidence [that is to serve as a criterion] for what happened five minutes ago is like laying down rules for making measurements. The question as to what evidence there can be is a grammatical one. It concerns the sorts of actions and propositions which would verify the statement. It is a simple matter to make up a statement which will agree with experience because it is such that no proposition can refute it, e.g., "There is a white rabbit between two chairs whenever no observations or verifications are being carried out." Some people would say that this statement says more than "There is no white rabbit between the chairs," just as some would say it means something to say the world was created five minutes ago. When such statements are made they are somehow connected with a picture, say, a picture of creation. Hence it is that such sentences seem to mean something. But they are otiose, like wheels in a watch which have no function although they do not look to be useless (WL35, pp. 25–26).

Wittgenstein says here: "The point of saying that something has happened derives from there being a criterion for its truth." What he means by the term "criterion" is such that there can *be* a criterion for something only if the criterion does not transcend one's immediate experience. Indeed, this is the whole *point* of introducing the term "criterion." Put differently, Wittgenstein's reason for introducing this term was to provide him with a way of making the same point that he also makes when he says: "It is only apparently possible 'to transcend any possible experience'; even these words only seem to make sense, because they are arranged on the analogy of significant expressions" (Z, §260). That his notion of criteria is connected in this way with 'immediate' (i.e., present*) 'experience' can be seen from the following considerations. Russell was proceeding on two assumptions: (i) if he did have a childhood, then the events of his childhood now transcend his immediate experience; and (ii) there is no logically necessary connection between events at different times. Wittgenstein is saying in regard to (i): this realist interpretation of having had a childhood is nonsense, for the very *meaning* of the statements one makes about the events of one's childhood is determined by the *criteria* for the truth of those statements, and these criteria, which are not themselves something doubtful but rather are given in immediate (present*) experience, show us what those propositions about one's childhood *are*.

So what, on Wittgenstein's view, *is* the meaning, i.e., the proper philosophical *interpretation*, of statements an adult makes about his or her childhood? Or, put differently, how would Russell's view of the meaning of such statements have had to change in order for him to accept Wittgenstein's claim that there are *criteria* for the truth of such statements?

To answer this question, we may note that Russell himself held a misconception about this. Commenting on Wittgenstein's view, he wrote:

There is a theory that the meaning of a proposition consists in its method of verification. It follows (a) that what cannot be verified or falsified is meaningless, (b) that two propositions verified by the same occurrences have the same meaning.
    I reject both, and I do not think that those who advocate them have fully realized their implications.
    . . . Other people's observations [i.e., their sense-data] are not data for me.

The hypothesis that nothing exists except what I perceive and remember is for me identical, in all its *verifiable* consequences, with the hypothesis that there are other people who also perceive and remember. If we are to believe in the existence of these other people . . . we must reject the identification of meaning with verification.

. . . The hypothesis that there are other people, having thoughts and feelings more or less like my own, does not have the same significance as the [solipsistic] hypothesis that other people are only parts of my dreams, and yet the verifiable consequences of the two hypotheses are identical.[23]

Russell says here that Wittgenstein and others have not realized the "implications" of holding that a proposition's meaning is determined by the way it is verified. And one of those implications, says Russell, is that one cannot believe in the existence of other people. This is implied, he says, by the following: the two propositions "Nothing exists except what I perceive and remember" and "There are other people who also perceive and remember" are identical in all their verifiable consequences. But Russell, in saying this, is assuming a further premise, namely, that *if* there are other people, they are not given in immediate experience. He is, in other words, assuming a *realist* interpretation of 'other people.' Had he realized that Wittgenstein had put forth a doubly reductionist account of "other people," so that other people *are* given in immediate experience, Russell would not have thought that Wittgenstein's view of meaning and verifiability has the implication that one cannot believe that 'other people' exist. Put differently, Wittgenstein, had he been confronted with Russell's argument, would have said that the very fact that one *can* verify statements about other people's thoughts and feelings, etc. shows that such statements do not have the meaning Russell thinks they have, i.e., shows that such statements must be interpreted behavioristically (in the sense explained in Chapter 9, this volume).

This provides the answer to the question posed above about the way in which Russell's 'interpretation' of past-tense statements would have had to change in order for him to accept Wittgenstein's claim that there are criteria for the truth of such statements. Russell would have had to accept the following Wittgensteinian theses: (a) past-tense statements do not mean what they appear to mean, for in saying, "I remember having thought him a fool," I appear to be speaking of an event that now transcends present* experience, so that what I say appears to be unverifiable; but (b) the criterion for the truth of such a past-tense statements is something present*; and (c) criteria determine the *meaning* of past-tense statements, so that they do *not* refer to events that aren't present*.

To understand these theses, we must begin from a rather obvious point regarding Wittgenstein's term "criterion," namely, that if one wanted to say what the criterion is for a past-tense statement, one could not formulate the criterion in the past tense. For example, Wittgenstein would not allow that when I now say, "I had a pet when I was a child," my criterion for this is that my father gave me a dog when I was ten years old. The reason for this becomes obvious as soon as one takes account of the role Wittgenstein's term "criterion" was meant to play in replying to philosophical skepticism. What the skeptic says, in effect, is that a certain class of propositions – which I will call "the disputed class" – can never be known to be true. Obviously, therefore, if "p" and "q" were *both* propositions of a disputed class, it would be pointless to reply to the skeptic by saying: "You say that we cannot know that p, but you are wrong, for there is a *criterion* for the truth of 'p,' namely, the fact that q." This would be pointless because it would allow the skeptic to reply quite simply that one cannot know that q because "q" *also* belongs to the disputed class. So if one is going to reply to the skeptic by invoking criteria, then *what* one invokes as a criterion must be something the skeptic allows we *can* know, for otherwise the appeal to criteria would be question begging and hence pointless. To know what may count as a criterion, then, one must consult the skeptic's argument regarding the case in question. Thus, as regards the problem of other minds, if one wants (as Wittgenstein did) to invoke criteria in order to defeat skepticism, one is obliged to consult the skeptic's argument to determine what may count as criteria here, and what one finds in doing so, of course, is that the skeptic says: Even if other people exist, all one can *know* of them is what one could know of beings who *have* no thoughts or feelings, namely, their bodily movements, including the sounds they make. Accordingly, Wittgenstein is obliged to hold that we have *behavioristic* criteria for another person's being worried or in pain, etc. But this, in turn, means that it lies in the very notion of what a criterion is that it can only be described in philosophical (e.g., behavioristic) terms, and that makes a criterion altogether different from anything that we ordinarily say in support of our knowledge claims about other people's thoughts, emotions, pains and so on, i.e., very different from our saying, "I know his back is still hurting because he winces whenever he stoops over." (Wincing, as I pointed out in Chapter 9, is not 'behavior' in the relevant sense.) But if, as Wittgenstein would have it, criteria give the *meaning* of what we say in the sense of determining *the philosophical interpretation* of what we say, it follows that he would have us interpret "His back is still hurting" behavioristically (in the sense explained in Chapter 9). And this, as we have seen, is precisely what he does.

Similarly, a philosopher who would invoke criteria as an answer to skepticism regarding the past must, to avoid begging the question, consult the skeptic's argument to discover what he may relevantly take as criteria. And in this case what we find is that the only thing the skeptic allows to be beyond doubt is his immediate (i.e., present*) experience.[24] So as regards the meaning of past-tense statements, Wittgenstein would have said that there is an alternative Russell has failed to consider, namely, that (a) past-tense statements do not mean what they appear to mean, for (b) the criterion for the truth of a past-tense statement is something present*, and (c) these criteria determine the *meaning* of past-tense statements.[25] But (to conclude the parallel) if, as Wittgenstein would have it, criteria determine the *meaning* of what we say in the sense of determining *the philosophical interpretation* of what we say, it follows that what we say in the past tense is about the present* (except in the case of 'hypotheses'). In short, Wittgenstein continued to think that he had got things mostly right in the *Tractatus* when he envisioned a language without tenses.[26]

Criteria and Meaning

Let us now consider what to think about all of this and in particular what Wittgenstein says about criteria (or verification) and meaning. If there is any reason to agree with what he says about this, there ought to be something to which he can call our attention which would show that he is right. Yet in none of the passages I have quoted above does Wittgenstein provide any reason for thinking that there *are* meaning-determining criteria. Let us, therefore, undertake an investigation of our own, using as our guinea pig what Wittgenstein's says about his thought-guessing example (PI, pp. 222–223), which was quoted earlier. The relevant features of his example are (a) that it deals with (as Wittgenstein puts it) what someone says to himself in his thoughts and (b) that when he later says what he had thought, he does so on the basis of memory alone, i.e., there is nothing else in present experience to take as a criterion for what he had thought. Wittgenstein's conclusion is that in this case there can be no distinction between truth and truthfulness. As a way of testing this, let us duplicate features (a) and (b) in a somewhat more realistic example.

Suppose, then, that while giving a speech I think to myself that the audience does not seem interested in what I have to say. Later, recalling the episode, I tell a friend that this thought occurred to me during my speech. I do so to reassure him, for he is distraught about the reception of a speech which he has just given. I say to him, "We sometimes misjudge an audience. I recall giving a speech to a group of lawyers and thinking: I'm boring them to *death*! But I learned afterward that they were enthralled." In saying this, I am going only on my memory of having had that thought; there is nothing else that Wittgenstein would regard as a criterion for my having had it. What would he have said of such a case?

He would have said that the meaning of my past-tense statement, "I thought to myself: I'm boring them to *death*!" is such that there can be no distinction here between truth and truthfulness. The "importance" of what I say to my friend, accordingly to Wittgenstein (see above), "does not reside in its being a correct . . . report."

To see whether this is plausible, let us ask: Would my friend be reassured about the success of his own speech if he merely took me to be *truthful* (i.e., sincere) in what I say? Surely, not! It is not my truthfulness that would reassure him but only the conviction that what I relate to him did actually happen, that I did misjudge my audience while I was speaking. If he were to take reassurance from what I tell him and wanted to explain to his wife the grounds for his new-found confidence, what would he tell her? He would say: "Cook once misjudged the effect of a speech he was giving, so perhaps I've misjudged the effect of mine as well." To see that this is very different from his merely taking me to be truthful (sincere), consider a case in which he does regard what I say as being (merely) sincere. If he thought I was terribly befuddled, he might say to his wife: "Cook tried to reassure me about my speech by telling me how he once misjudged an audience. He was terribly *sincere*, dear man, but you know how dotty he's become. So I wasn't reassured in the least." Plainly, there is an important difference between truth and sincerity as regards past-tense statements. And therefore Wittgenstein's account, which assimilates truth to (mere) sincerity will not do.

Why did Wittgenstein embrace such a wrong-headed view? He did so because he thought that if he were to adopt a Russellian view of past-tense statements, he would be opening the door to skepticism, for then, he thought, it could be said that possibly our memory always deceives us. But why does the specter of skepticism arise here?

The Source of Skepticism Regarding the Past

The answer lies in the way Russell frames the issue. As I remarked earlier, Russell's position consists of two parts. He held both that (i) if he did have a childhood, then the events of his childhood now transcend his present* experience, and (ii) *given* the truth of (i), there is no *logically* necessary connection between what happened in his childhood and any present* (or future) events, including his recollecting his childhood doings. Wittgenstein had no quarrel with (ii), for it is a dogma of empiricism that there can be no *necessary* connection between two different facts. So, to avoid Russell's skepticism, he declared in regard to (i): this realist interpretation of having had a childhood is nonsense. To understand why, in regard to (i), he resorted to reductionist measures, it is essential to recognize why, as regards (ii), he was in agreement with Russell. He thought that skepticism would be unavoidable *if*, as Russell held, the past tense is *not* a misleading form of words, i.e., if past-tense statements were *irreducibly* about the past. He was obliged to agree with Russell to this extent simply because he, like Russell, accepted a Humean view of the world, a view in which every fact (or event) is independent of every other one. In such a world the fact that one now recollects such-and-such is an event which could occur regardless of what else has occurred, for in such a world whatever occurs comes into being *ex nihilo*.[27] Or to put the matter more exactly, had Wittgenstein agreed with Russell that past-tense propositions are *irreducibly* about past events, he would have had to allow that the fact that one now recollects that p (where "p" is in the past-tense) is logically compatible with "p" being false in every such case. On a Humean view, then, it is conceivable (if the past tense is irreducible) that I *seem* to remember having had a pony when I was a child *regardless* of what sort of life I have had – and even if I had no childhood at all. So the specter of skepticism rears its head for Russell and Wittgenstein just because they accepted a Humean view of the world, which, in turn, engenders their notion of 'logical possibility' and the idea that we speak in propositions.[28] And it was to forestall skepticism in a *Humean* world that Wittgenstein invoked meaning-determining criteria.

We can now see how to avoid both Russell's concession to skepticism and Wittgenstein's reductionist alternative, namely, by dismissing their Humean assumptions. What this amounts to in the present case is the following. Instead of thinking of a person as a being whose life (including one's remembering and forgetting things) is made up of wholly *unrelated* events, we must allow that one's remembering and forgetting and recognizing and believing, etc., etc. belong essentially to a complex personal *history*. What this means is that if, in our philosophizing, we want to present a case in which someone seems to remember an event from his childhood although no such event actually occurred, we must be prepared to construct the example with details of a sort which will make this understandable. And, to broaden the point, if we conduct our philosophizing, not in terms of Humean assumptions (i.e., past-tense *propositions*) but in terms of detailed stories that have an internal coherence, we will find that, while the details of *some* examples (stories) allow us to depict the person's recollection as faulty on certain matters, the details of other examples – other stories – preclude this. In other words, we must supply such details as whether the person is senile and perhaps, in recollecting, confuses one person with another, whether he has a good memory for the sort of thing he says he remembers, whether something has happened that has led him to confuse one event with another (or one date with another), whether at the time of the alleged event he or she was old enough to have understood what was happening, and so on. The point here is that if we make it our policy[29] to include such details in our examples and make them internally *coherent*, we cannot get so far as supposing that our recollections may invariably be wrong. In short, we cannot get so far as entertaining Russell's 'hypothesis' about the world being five minutes old as a 'logical possibility.' And that being so, we will not find it necessary, in order to avoid skepticism, to resort to the reductionist alternative that Wittgenstein sets forth in terms of meaning-determining criteria.

Some Consequences of Wittgenstein's Reductionism

In what I have just said I have taken it for granted that we may credit human beings with having, in varying degrees, a (genuine) capacity for remembering various things, i.e., that we needn't adopt a reductionist analysis of remembering. Wittgenstein, however, would not have conceded this point, for like Hume he found that his ontology precludes there being powers or capacities of any sort.

We have already seen how he deals with remembering a past thought: he offers a reductionist account. And as we will see in the next chapter, he also gives reductionist accounts of what it is to have memorized a poem, to have learned how to play chess, and in general what it is to have learned or mastered a skill or acquired an ability. The mistake we are prone to make in such cases, he says, is that ". . . we can hardly help conceiving of memory as a kind of storehouse. Note also how sure people are that to the ability to add or to multiply or to say a poem by heart, etc., there *must* correspond a peculiar state of the person's brain. . . . We regard these phenomena as manifestations of this mechanism. . . ." (BB, p. 118). He adds: "There is a kind of disease of thinking which always looks for (and finds) what would be called a mental state from which all our acts [e.g., reciting a poem] spring as from a reservoir" (BB, p. 143). His criticism of this idea plays a crucial role in his discussions of what is involved in learning a new word or acquiring a language. When we think about having learned a new word, says Wittgenstein, "we tend to think of the mind as a sort of receptacle in which things are stored" (WL35, p. 77).

That he should regard this as a mistake was inevitable, given his reductionist view of the past. Because he has, as it were, collapsed the past into the present* and the future, he cannot think of people as possessing skills or certain other abilities or capacities, such as knowing how to play chess. Put differently, when he comes to analyze those words by which we speak of such an ability as being able to recite from memory Wordsworth's "Tintern Abbey," he cannot allow that we are speaking of something a person has *learned* and *retained*, for were he to do so, he would have to think of the past in a nonreductionist way, and *that*, he thought, would invite skepticism in regard to the past. Accordingly, as we will see in the next chapter, he offers a reductionist account of such matters, so that he would say, for example, that when I remark that my daughter can speak French, although the *form of words* I use ("can speak French") suggests that she has something stored up in her (something she has learned and retained), I mean only that she *does* (on occasion) speak French and *would* respond in French if she *were* asked a question in French.

Notes

1. Op. cit., pp. 133–134.
2. G. E. Moore, "Wittgenstein's Lectures in 1930–33," reprinted in *Philosophical Papers*, op. cit., p. 311.
3. Quoted from a conversation with Wittgenstein by O. K. Bouwsma in *Wittgenstein: Conversations 1949–1951*, op. cit., p. 13. It is not easy to see that Wittgenstein meant to be alluding to a consequence of the realists' view of the past unless one recognizes that he was alluding to Russell's view when he said to Bouwsma: "The present is the picture which is before the light [of the film projector], but the future is still on the roll to pass, and the past is on that roll. It's gone through already" (ibid.). See below for the explanation of this analogy.
4. In the passage which I have called his "Methodological Reassessment," he declares that ordinary language is itself a phenomenological language.
5. In *Our Knowledge of the External World* Russell says: "Immediate experience provides us with two time-relations among events: they may be simultaneous, or one may be earlier and the other later. These two are both part of the crude data. . . . The time-order, within certain limits, is as much given as the events. . ." (op. cit., pp. 121–126). Wittgenstein seems to have accepted this part of Russell's view, although he had objections (see WVC, pp. 214–215) to other things Russell said about time.
6. His conversations with Waismann contain a hint of what he may have had in mind, for he said: "My memories are ordered. *Time is the way memories are ordered.* Time is, as it were, the form in which I have memories" (WVC, p. 98). He goes on to say that where no one's memory is involved "an ordering can also be achieved in a different way" and gives as two of his examples "historical statements or the time of geology," adding: "Here the sense of a temporal specification depends entirely on what is admitted as a verification." [In an earlier conversation he had said that a historical statement could be verified by "reading a document" (WVC, p. 53).] Perhaps the relevance of these remarks is that Wittgenstein was thinking: It is a bed rock fact about us – one that can't be explained – that we often *say* "I remember p" where "p" is in the past-tense and also that, upon reading a document, we make past-tense statements, so that the 'ordering' of memories and historical events is to be regarded as a product of our *saying* things in the past tense. See PI, §§654–656 and Z, §667.
7. *The Analysis of Mind*, op. cit., pp. 159–160.
8. Op. cit., pp. 48–49
9. Op. cit., p. 165.
10. Ibid., pp. 163–164.
11. Reprinted in *Mysticism and Logic*, op. cit., pp. 128–129.
12. In the English edition of *Philosophical Remarks* the Schopenhauerian term "*Vorstellung*" has been translated as "idea," but as this could be misleading, I have chosen to translate it as "sense impression."
13. In lectures he explained this remark as follows: "The puzzles about time are due to the analogy between time and motion. There is an analogy, but we press it too far; we are tempted by it to talk nonsense. We say time 'flows', and then ask where to and where from, and so on" (WL32, pp. 60–61). In a later lecture he said:

Why does one feel tempted to say "The only reality is the present"? . . . The person who says only the present is real because past and future are not here has before his mind the image of something moving [past him].

past   present   future

←————————————————

This image is misleading. . . . That the statement "Only the present experience is real" seems to mean something is due to familiar images we associate with it, images of things passing us in space (WL35, p. 25).

In addition to Russell, Wittgenstein may have had in mind (see BB, pp. 107–108) Augustine's use of spatial idioms in Book XI of the *Confessions*, where he makes the following comparison of God's timelessness with our perceived world: "Thy years do not come and go; while these years of ours do come and go. . . . All thy years stand together, for they stand still, nor are those going away cut off by those coming, for they do not pass away, but these years of ours shall all be [i.e., be present for God] when [for us] they are no more." Having said that our years "come and go," rather than stand still, Augustine goes on to ask: ". . . when the present comes out of the future, does it proceed from something secret, and, when the past comes about from the present, does it recede into something hidden? If future and past things exist, I would like to know where they are." Finding this question hopeless, Augustine comes around to a view that anticipates Wittgenstein's (see note 21 below).

14. This distinction between remembering a physical event, which could be photographed or witnessed by others, and a *non*physical event, such as a thought that crossed my mind, is critical for understanding Wittgenstein's private language argument, as we will see later.

15. Augustine employs this metaphor in saying that "when past things are recounted as true, they are brought forth from memory, not as the actual things which went on in the past, but as words formed from images of these things; and these things have left their traces, as it were, in the mind while passing through sense perception. . . . [W]hen I recall and tell about [my boyhood], I see its image in present time, for it is still in my memory" (op. cit.).

16. Moore, in his report of Wittgenstein's lectures, writes: ". . . he made a distinction . . . between what he called 'memory-time and what he called 'information-time,' saying that in the former there is only earlier and later, not past and future" ("Wittgenstein's Lectures in 1930–33," op. cit., p. 319). See also PR, p. 104. This means that if I now recall that in childhood I had a secret fantasy about being Superman, what I recall cannot rightly be said to be *past*, for there is no past in 'memory-time.'

17. A comment on the standard translation, which I have quoted here, is in order. Wittgenstein's qualifying phrase "as it were" is not a qualification of the English word "instants." The German word which has been translated as "instants" is "*Augenblicken*," which would in most contexts be translated as "instants." But it can also be translated as "glimpses," so that the line could be translated as: ". . . our propositions are so to speak verified only in glimpses." As thus translated, the qualifier "so to speak" would have its point because it is not only *visual* sense-data (glimpses), but also tactile and other sense-data that are relevant here.

18. In later years, when he had begun speaking more often of criteria than

verification, he spoke of the first of these cases as those in which we take memory as our criterion, e.g., RPP, I, §393.

19. In lectures he explained this as follows: ". . . a statement gets its sense from its verification. . . . To find out with what meaning a word is used, make *several* investigations. For example, the words 'before' and 'after' mean something different according as one depends on memory or on documents to establish the time of an event" (WL35, p. 17).

20. That Wittgenstein regarded remembering as being fundamental in this way comes out in notes that he made in 1949, in which he said in an entirely general way that remembering "is really the *criterion* for the past" (LW, I, §837).

21. Wittgenstein's view is remarkably similar to that of Augustine, who writes (*Confessions*, Book XI): "What is now plain is that neither future nor past things are in existence, and that it is not correct to say there are three periods of time: past, present, and future. Perhaps it would be proper to say there are three periods of time: the present of things past, the present of things present, the present of things future. For, these three are in the soul and I do not see them elsewhere: the present of things past is memory; the present of things present is immediate vision; the present of things future is expectation." Augustine goes on to explain that, in saying that neither future nor past things are in existence, he is not criticizing what we commonly say, for "there are few things which we express properly; more frequent are those that we express improperly, though making our intentions understood." In Wittgensteinian terms, what Augustine is saying here is that although we misleadingly speak of remembering past wars or past worries, we are speaking only of present* recollections.

22. Among the philosophers who have failed to understand this point is G. E. M. Anscombe. In "The Reality of the Past" [in *Philosophical Analysis*, ed. Max Black (Ithaca: Cornell University Press, 1950), pp. 38–59] she maintains that because Wittgenstein no longer held the analytic version of reductionism he had espoused in the *Tractatus*, his insistence that there are *present* criteria for past-tense statements does not commit him to the view that such statements aren't about the past. And of course she is right in the sense that Wittgenstein insists that "Caesar crossed the Alps" describes (as he puts it) "an event which we believe happened about ca. 2000 years ago." But he is here making a point only about the 'surface grammar' of ordinary language. As regards the 'depth grammar' of past-tense propositions his point is that we must not take their surface grammar as our guide to their depth grammar because the subject matter of propositions about Caesar is present* and future experience. Anscombe's misunderstanding of Wittgenstein, it would seem, is due to her failure (see Chapter 1) to recognize his life-long obsession with skepticism. Her colleague at Oxford, A. J. Ayer, whose interpretation of Wittgenstein [see his *The Problems of Knowledge* (Penguin, 1956), pp. 154ff.] Anscombe is evidently replying to, was better attuned to Wittgenstein's empiricist views, and I believe that he states Wittgenstein's views correctly.

23. "Logical Positivism" in *Logic and Language*, op. cit., p. 375–376, emphasis added. To make his disagreement with Wittgenstein as clear as possible, Russell added: "The hypothesis that the starry heavens exist at all times, and the hypothesis that they only exist when I see them, are exactly identical in all those of their consequences that I can test. It is especially in such cases that meaning is identified [by the positivists] with verification, and that, therefore, the two hypotheses are said to have the same significance. And it is this that I am specially concerned to deny" (p. 376).

24. Reporting Wittgenstein's discussion of Russell's skeptical argument, Moore writes: "Now Wittgenstein pointed out, quite justly, that . . . Russell's view requires that it is equally true that [the world] might have 'sprung into being' two minutes ago or one minute ago, or, says Wittgenstein, that it might have begun to exist *now*: he actually said that Russell *ought* to have said 'The world might have been created *now*' " ("Wittgenstein's Lectures in 1930–33," op. cit., p. 320). It is worth noting here that Wittgenstein himself was a connoisseur of skeptical arguments. In a 1912 letter Russell said of Wittgenstein: "He is the only man I have ever met with a real bias for philosophical scepticism; he is glad when it is *proved* that something can't be known" (quoted by Brian McGuinness in *Wittgenstein: A Life*, op. cit., p. 106).

25. There is a question to be raised here which I have systematically evaded in this chapter: What *is* the present* (or immediate) experience Wittgenstein would regard as the criterion for (the truth of) past-tense statements. It is an important – and revealing – fact that he remained quite vague about this.

26. Anscombe reports that "Wittgenstein used to say that the *Tractatus* was not *all* wrong." *An Introduction to Wittgenstein's Tractatus*, op. cit., p. 78.

27. It was because Wittgenstein held such a view of the world that he could say that we might see trees "change into men" (OC, §513). He wasn't thinking of a biological process like that in which a tadpole *develops* into a frog. He was thinking that where there is *now* a tree a man might suddenly spring into being *ex nihilo*. And my point is that he also thought of 'mental' events – such as its suddenly occurring to me that I left my keys in the car – in this way, as occurrences in Hume's fractured world.

28. The philosophical conception of propositions is that they are the counterparts of Humean facts, which is why Wittgenstein, in the *Tractatus*, held that they are 'independent' of one another (see Chapter 3, this volume). Later he allowed that there are exceptions in the case of, e.g., "This man is 3m tall" and "This man more than 2m tall," and also in the case of "This is red" and "This is green" (WVC, p. 64; PR, §§76–86; and RLF, pp. 36–37). But he seems never to have got rid *completely* of the idea that there are propositions in the sense of there being *units of meaning* which we can contemplate, when doing philosophy, by thinking about single sentences. Here the idea is that there is something about *language* – its rules or whatnot – that determines *what* we are saying or believing when we say or believe that *p*. (See, for example, my discussion of Wittgenstein's 'hinge propositions' in Chapter 15.) As Ebersole has been endlessly at pains to demonstrate, this conception of language only generates confusion. It prevents us from conducting our philosophizing in terms of detailed examples of people talking (or writing), and it is just such examples that can free us from our difficulties. Ebersole's most explicit comments on the idea of propositions are found in his *Language and Perception*, op. cit., Chapters 6 and 7. Here and elsewhere the moral of his story is that to escape one's philosophical confusions one must develop a good ear for dialogue and pay attention to the background against which any bit of dialogue takes place (who is speaking to whom and to what purpose; what do they know (of eachother or of what they are speaking of), and so on). One might summarize Ebersole's point by saying that there is no such thing as what philosophers call "ordinary language."

29. I have discussed this policy in "Malcolm's Misunderstandings," *Philosophical Investigations*, Vol. 4, No. 2 (Spring, 1981), esp. pp. 82–88.

17

Wittgenstein's Analysis of
Mental States and Powers

In this chapter we will be concerned with Wittgenstein's account of what were once called "the intellectual powers of man." This phrase is now archaic but there is none better for designating the topic that needs discussion here. It refers to certain human abilities, capacities, and 'know how.' The reason for concerning ourselves with this is that Wittgenstein's philosophy of mind consists largely of denying that people have intellectual powers. (In this he is not singling out human beings for special treatment, for, like Hume, he denies powers to anything whatsoever.) The larger relevance of his denial of intellectual powers, as we will see in the next two chapters, is that it forced him to adopt a peculiar view of our linguistic capacities, a view that lies at the heart of his private language argument.

Historical Background

As we saw at the end of the preceding chapter, Wittgenstein was intent on dismissing the following idea: if one knows how to play chess or is able to recite a poem from memory, one is in a particular state (perhaps it is a state of one's brain), and when one plays a game of chess or recites a poem, this is a manifestation of that state. Because Wittgenstein's view of intellectual powers may seem wildly implausible to a modern reader, it is important to understand the historical context in which his view developed. Wittgenstein, as we have seen, held Berkeley in high esteem, and in *The Principles of Human Knowledge* Berkeley formulates very clearly an important feature of Wittgenstein's own position. He begins by entertaining the following objection:

... it will be demanded [of me to explain in conformity with my principles] to what purpose serves that curious organization of plants, and the animal mechanism in the parts of animals. Might not vegetables grow, and shoot forth leaves and blossoms, and animals perform all their motions, as well without, as with, all that variety of internal parts so elegantly contrived and put together; – which, being ideas, have nothing powerful or operative in them, nor have any *necessary* connexion with the effects ascribed to them? If it be a Spirit that immediately produces every effect by a *fiat*, or act of his will, we must think [that] all that is fine and artificial in the works, whether of man or nature, to be made in vain. By this doctrine, though an artist hath made the spring and wheels, and every movement of a watch, and adjusted them in such a manner as he knew would produce the motions [of the hands] he designed; yet he must think all this done to no purpose, and that it is an Intelligence which directs the index, and points to the hour of the day. If so, why may not the Intelligence do it, without *his* being at the pains of making the movements and putting them together? Why does not an empty [watch] case serve as well as another? And how comes it to pass, that whenever there is any fault in the going of a watch, there is some corresponding disorder to be found in the movements, which being mended by a skilful hand all is right again? The like may be said of the Clockwork of Nature, great part whereof is so wonderfully fine and subtle as scarce to be discerned by the best microscope. In short, it will be asked, how, upon our Principles, any tolerable account can be given, or any final cause assigned of an innumerable multitude of bodies and machines, framed with the most exquisite art, which in the common philosophy . . . serve to explain abundance of phenomena? (§60).

Berkeley, in reply to this objection, concedes that "the fabrication of all those parts and organs be not absolutely necessary to the producing [of] any effect" (ibid., §62), i.e., he concedes that we might operate on someone's pet dog and find that it is hollow or filled with sawdust. He adds:". . . it cannot be denied that God . . . might, if He were minded to produce a miracle, cause all the motions on the dial-plate of a watch, though nobody had ever made the movements and put them in it" (ibid.).[1] Berkeley is saying: if we see that the hands of a watch are moving, we cannot know until we have opened it whether there is a mechanism inside the case.[2] Similarly, we cannot know whether the person whose lecture we are listening to has a brain inside his skull, for it *could* turn out that, when operated upon, he is found to have no brain.

That Berkeley should take such a view is not surprising since he holds that, in the case of such things as clockworks and brains, their very *existence* consists in their *being perceived*. Since we cannot perceive the works of a watch that is closed, it follows that its works *do not exist while the watch is closed*. Berkeley – and Wittgenstein – would object here that *of course* the works may exist while the watch is closed, for all that can be *meant* here by "exist" is this: "if at any time while the watch was closed we *had* opened it, we *would* have seen the works." But this counterfactual analysis does not make the clockworks available to do any work while the watch is closed. So on Berkeley's view, even if a watchmaker installs a mechanism inside a watch case, it is perfectly irrelevant to the functioning of the watch. This holds also for a person's brain: his having (or not having) a brain is irrelevant to such things as, say, his reading aloud from a text or doing calculations on a blackboard. This is a view Wittgenstein often reiterated.

The Role of Wittgenstein's Ontology

We have already seen one manifestation of Wittgenstein's view in his discussion of seeds, which we considered in Chapter 12. He insists that two seeds which are alike in every way could grow into plants of different kinds – one into a pine tree and the other into a cabbage. Even if all the seeds that grow into cabbages have a unique structure, it is a mistake, says Wittgenstein, to think that the seeds grow into cabbages *because of* their structure. He thinks this, of course, because he regards their growing into cabbages as something that happens in an 'indeterministic' world. A seed's DNA structure is irrelevant, then, to the way it will develop when planted and nourished. This also means that nothing is *needed* in a seed in order for it to grow into a plant of a particular kind, for it could grow into a cabbage regardless of its structure and even if it is wholly amorphous. And what holds for seeds holds for other things as well:

So an organism might come into being even out of something quite amorphous, as it were causelessly; and there is no reason why this should not really hold for our thoughts, and hence for our talking and writing (Z, §608).

There is no physical complexity we *need* in order to think or converse about politics or to write books about philosophy.

But do we not need a brain? Wittgenstein thought that brains are as superfluous as the inner structure of a seed. In *On Certainty* he says that "it is imaginable that my skull should turn out empty when it was operated on" (OC, §4). Elsewhere he says that when trying to think about psychological concepts he finds it helpful to reflect that "I don't know at all whether the humans I am acquainted with actually have a nervous system" (RPP, I, §1063). Elaborating this idea, he writes:

Why should not the initial and terminal states of a system be connected by a natural law, which does not cover the intermediary state? (Only don't think of *agency*!) (RPP, I, §909).

If the initial state is that I read the instructions on a vending machine and the terminal state is that I follow the instructions, Wittgenstein's idea is that this could occur regardless of the state of my brain – and even if I had no brain. He is suggesting that it would be perfectly *possible* for someone to behave like a normal human being even if he had sawdust in his head – just as a seed may grow into a cabbage whatever its internal structure may be and even if it is quite amorphous. The idea that a brain of some complexity is essential for thinking, writing, calculating, understanding a poem, and so on, Wittgenstein treats as a confusion: "The prejudice in favour of psycho-physical parallelism is also a fruit of the primitive conception of grammar" (RPP, I, §906).

It is not difficult to understand how Wittgenstein could think this way. For as we saw in Chapter 8 he held that propositions about unperceived objects are equivalent to what I there called "bastard" counterfactual conditionals. This means that a person's having a brain is not a matter of what is currently inside his or her skull but only a matter of what experiences a doctor would have *if* he opened the skull.[3] So Wittgenstein's view, like Berkeley's, is that even if one has a brain, it isn't available, so to speak, to perform any functions as one goes about one's normal activities with one's skull unopened. But if brains are *that* sort of thing, who needs them?! Why should it matter whether, when a mathematician's skull is opened, it is found to be empty? For during all those years that he was devising proofs and writing books his skull was closed and no brain was functioning. On this view, then, having a brain is entirely inessential for the possession of intellectual powers.

There is another reason Wittgenstein was obliged to adopt a reductionist view of powers and capacities. As we saw in Chapter Ten, Wittgenstein, like Kohler, thought that the people we credit with having various powers and capacities are what Kohler calls "perceptual bodies." They are not truly flesh-and-blood beings but only bundles of sensible qualities. This poses no problem, says Kohler, for understanding how we can say, for example, that someone is happy or has a happy disposition, for we are only speaking of what we can perceive of the perceptual body – a smile, a brisk gait, a hearty laugh. But other cases, he hints, are not so easily accounted for:

The present account needs amplification at one point. When saying that common social understanding refers to certain perceptual events, we seemed forced to assume that such events occur only on the surface of another person's body. And yet, as a matter of phenomenological description, this would not always be entirely true; for the events in question sometimes seem to emerge from the interior of the body. Does this observation contradict our analysis? The answer follows from another question. What is "the interior" from which those events seem to issue? Obviously, it is the interior of the body as a perceptual entity. Now, if events emerge from a volume which is surrounded by a certain surface, the volume and the surface clearly belong to the same world – which, in the present case, is the world of perceptual facts. Thus it is still the body as a percept, from the interior of which such events emerge.[4]

Kohler does not provide examples of what he is speaking of here, but presumably he was thinking of such things as the following: a woman unleashes at her husband the pent up fury that has been building through years of abuse; a man lets flow tears of grief held back since the death of his son; someone pours out his heart to the woman he has loved for years from afar; a child recites a poem she has memorized; a student demonstrates his ability to do mental arithmetic by correctly solving several multiplication problems without using pencil and paper.

It is not clear how Kohler hoped to accommodate examples such as these, but it is clear enough what his problem is. For how could one think of a 'perceptual body' as having memorized a poem or as having pent up emotions? A perceptual body, after all, is of the same class of things as, for example, an afterimage. It is supposed to differ in complexity, of course, in that it is comprised of other sensible qualities as well as color and shape. But this wouldn't seem to make it a better candidate than an afterimage for having anything memorized or pent up.[5]

This is also Wittgenstein's problem, for he too thought of people as 'perceptual bodies.' Let us consider, then, how he deals with this problem.

Wittgenstein's Master Premise

I will begin by making explicit the structure of his argument as it applies to both physical and intellectual states and powers. His basic premise comes to light in the following passage:

The word "can" in a great number of cases is used to refer to a *state*. Suppose we had a glass box [i.e., a box of *transparent* glass] with a ball in it, and that instead of saying "The ball is in the box" we said "The ball can be taken out of the box." This alludes to an activity without saying it is performed. Compare the ball in the box [which we can see] with a chemical which when heated gives off drops. When the chemical stops giving off drops we say that there are more drops to come and that these can be drawn from it. This [use of "can"] differs from the case of the ball in the glass box where we had something we could call a state but which we could see. In the case of the chemical there is not a state which we can see when the chemical is not giving off drops. We thus have here a use of the word "can" in two different ways to describe a state, in the one case [i.e., the visible ball] being more obviously a state than in the other.

To take another and somewhat different case, suppose a doctor on examining my muscles and finding them red says they are in perfect health. He expresses this by saying they can contract [i.e., he uses the form of words "can contract"]. In this instance one might say he is describing a state, but one that is hypothetical [i.e., my muscles *will* contract when . . .]. It is not one that can be seen, as can the color of my muscles or the ball in the glass box. To say that the ability to contract is a state, only it cannot be seen, misuses language (WL35, p. 95).

Here Wittgenstein's phenomenalism is clearly in evidence, for he is saying that only sensible qualities are real, that nothing may count as a (true) state unless it can be described in terms of sensible qualities, e.g., the ball that is visible in the glass box, the redness of muscles. And he is saying that where we employ phraseology which suggests that we are speaking of a state, but one that cannot be described in terms of sensible qualities, we are not speaking of a (true) state but only using a misleading form of words.[6] I will refer to this henceforth as Wittgenstein's "Master Premise."

Armed with this premise, he can then argue that many things that are treated grammatically as states are not really states, for they do not fulfill the condition of being perceivable (or, in the case of mental states, 'introspectable'). This comes out clearly in his treatment of mental states, as when he says: "The view I wish to argue against in this context is that understanding is a *state* inside me, like, for instance, toothache" (WVC, p. 167). Placing this stricture on what is to count as "a state inside me" is a critical move in his argument, and he reiterates it with regularity, as when he explains what he regards as mental states by saying: "Depression, excitement, pain, are called mental states" (PI, p. 59), where by "depression" and "excitement" he evidently means "*feelings* of depression and excitement." By taking such cases as his paradigm, he can then proceed to argue that if we find that knowing the ABC, knowing how to play chess, being able to solve quadratic equations, and so on are *not* introspectable states, we must conclude that they are not states at all and that humans *have* no intellectual powers. This is how he proceeds to show that understanding, for instance, is not a state:

> When we try to get clear about understanding ... , we ask ourselves what happens when we understand. But we are dissatisfied with descriptions of what happens. Everything we bring up, such as images, seems irrelevant. ... Images are not part of understanding, but symptoms of understanding. ... It is because of the form of words, 'I understand this' ... that we suppose the grammar of these words is that of describing a state, whereas it is not (WL35, p. 92).

Wittgenstein's argument is this: understanding is not an introspectable state, so (given his Master Premise) it is not a state at all.

Wittgenstein intends, of course, that we should reach the same conclusion about all manner of other things. He wants us to agree, for example, that the fragility of a glass vase is not a state of the glass (i.e., something that would change only if something about the glass changed), that a storage battery's being fully charged is not a (true) state of the battery, and that ether does not have the power to anesthetize. The reason for this, of course, is that Wittgenstein imagines himself to be living in Sense-Data Land, where there is nothing real but sensible qualities. In Wittgenstein's world, then, there can be no powers or capacities or dispositions, except in some ersatz sense in which these are not (occurrent) states of things.[7]

Human Beings

Let us turn now to Wittgenstein's way of thinking about human beings. The problem here is that mentioned by Kohler in the passage quoted above: it may seem as though a phenomenalistic analysis could not account for the way in which we normally understand human beings because in some cases the behavior seems (as Kohler puts it) "to emerge from the interior of the body." That is, it sometimes seems to us that a person acts as he does because of some 'interior' state he is in. As Wittgenstein puts it:

> ... we want to say that being able to recite a poem is a state of our memory. Memory is a characteristic picture for the word "can." And when we are able

immediately to continue a series, say 2, 4, 6, 8, without even seeing the formula, we also want to say that there must be something and it must be a state of the brain (WL35, p. 95).

What a phenomenalist must show, then, is that there are no such "interior" states, and this is what Wittgenstein undertakes to show.

We can most easily see how he goes about this by considering first what he said in lectures (WL35, pp. 90–92) about love. He undertakes to show that, contrary to what we may think, when we say that we love another person we do not mean that we are in a state from which certain of our conduct flows, i.e., we cannot rightly *explain* our conduct by saying, "I put up with her bouts of depression because I loved her." If we think otherwise, says Wittgenstein, we have fallen into confusion:

A disposition is thought of as something always there from which behavior follows. It is analogous to the structure of a machine and its behavior. There are three different statements which seem to give the meaning of "*A* loves *B*": (1) a non-dispositional statement about a conscious state, i.e., feelings, (2) a statement that under certain conditions *A* will behave in such-and-such a way, (3) a dispositional statement that if some process is going on in his mind it will have the consequence that he behaves in such-and-such a way. . . . We seem to have distinguished here three meanings for "*A* loves *B*", but this is not the case. (1), to the effect that *A* loves *B* when he has certain feelings, and (2), that he loves him when he behaves in such-and-such a way, both give meanings of the word "love." But the dispositional statement (3), referring to a mechanism, is not genuine. It gives no new meaning. Dispositional statements are always at bottom statements about a mechanism, and have the grammar of statements about a mechanism. Language uses the analogy of a machine, which constantly misleads us. In an enormous number of cases our words have the form of dispositional statements referring to a mechanism whether there is a mechanism or not. In the example about love, nobody has the slightest idea what sort of mechanism is being referred to. The dispositional statement does not tell us anything about the nature of love; it is only a [misleading] way we describe it. Of the three meanings the dispositional one is the only one that is not genuine. It is actually a statement about the [misleading] grammar of the word "love" [when we say we did such and such *because* we loved him] (WL35, pp. 91–92).

Here we see Wittgenstein's formula for solving the problem Kohler posed about human beings. He maintains that if we imagine that certain behavior has its source in an 'inner' state, we have fallen into confusion about the meaning of some word, such as "love."

What are we to make of this? We see here once again Wittgenstein's ontology at work. Because he has the idea that the world disintegrates into phenomenal states which are (necessarily) independent of each other, he can find no place in the world for true dispositions, since a disposition (e.g., a happy disposition or being in love) is a state which, given the right circumstances, leads to something further, such as a lover making sacrifices for his beloved. And of course Wittgenstein does not think that even a machine, such as a clock with its spring wound, is in such a state. He would think it a mistake to regard the tension of the wound-up spring as exerting a force that makes the hands go round. As he thinks of it, a wound-up piece of spring steel is a state which we can survey by looking into the back of the clock, but he regards it as a mistake to imagine that in seeing the spring tightly wound we thereby see what, under usual conditions, is bound to happen to the hands of the clock. Seeing a present state, he might have said, cannot give us any insight into the future.

Intellectual Powers

Let us turn now to Wittgenstein's treatment of intellectual powers. As a preliminary to this it is necessary to observe that he addresses himself to this topic for two reasons. At times he is interested in the general problem posed by Kohler, i.e., the problem of how to give a phenomenalistic account of such things as having memorized a poem, knowing how to play chess, and so on. At other times, and perhaps most often, he is interested in a more specific question, which might be put as follows: In giving an account of what is required for speaking a language, is it necessary to allow that speaking a language involves various mental powers?

Wittgenstein is answering this last question when he writes: "In our study of symbolism [i.e., language] there is no foreground and background; it isn't a matter of a tangible sign with an accompanying intangible power or understanding" (PG, p. 87). In the present chapter we will consider Wittgenstein's treatment of the general problem about intellectual powers and will turn to his treatment of the more specific question about language in the chapter that follows.[8]

The best general account that he gives of his position is the following:

There are . . . various reasons which incline us to look at the fact of something being possible, someone being able to do something, etc., as the fact that he or it is in a particular state. Roughly speaking, this comes to saying that "A is in the state of being able to do something" is the form of representation we are most strongly tempted to adopt; or, as one could also put it, we are strongly inclined to use the metaphor of something being in a particular state for saying that something can behave in a particular way. And this way of representation, or this metaphor, is embodied in the expressions "He is capable of . . .", "He is able to multiply large numbers in his head", "He can play chess": in these sentences the verb is used in the *present tense*, suggesting that the phrases are descriptions of states which exist at the moment when we speak [as when we say of a sleeping man that he can (or knows how to) play chess].[9]

The same tendency [to use a misleading form of words] shows itself in our calling the ability to solve a mathematical problem, the ability to enjoy a piece of music, etc., certain states of mind; we don't mean by this expression 'conscious mental phenomena.' Rather, a state of mind in this sense is the state of a hypothetical mechanism, a mind model meant to explain the conscious mental phenomena. (Such things as unconscious or subconscious mental states are features of the mind *model*.) In this way also we can hardly help conceiving of memory as a kind of storehouse. Note also how sure people are that to the ability to add or to multiply or to say a poem by heart, etc., there *must* correspond a peculiar state of the person's brain, although on the other hand they know next to nothing about such psycho-physical correspondences. We regard these phenomena as manifestations of this mechanism, and their possibility is the particular construction of the mechanism itself (BB, pp. 117–118).

He goes on to say: "There is a kind of general disease of thinking which always looks for (and finds) what would be called a mental state from which all our acts spring as from a reservoir" (BB, p. 143).

How does Wittgenstein go about showing that this way of thinking *is* diseased? He goes about this by two steps. The first step is that in which he eliminates the brain as the seat of the mental state, and he does this, as we have already seen (pp. 271–272), by maintaining that one could memorize poems and calculate and write books even if one had no brain at all. Then, with the brain eliminated as a contender (and for Wittgenstein it was never a *serious* contender), he turns his attention to the question whether knowing how to play chess, having memorized a poem, knowing the ABCs, and so on are *psychological* states. In this second step he invokes what I have called his "Master Premise," namely, that if intellectual powers are genuine states of a person, there is only *one* way for them to be so: they must be phenomenal ('introspectable') states, like being in pain. Then, having taken such states as his paradigm, he proceeds to argue that understanding, knowing how to play chess, and so on are *not* 'introspectable' states and therefore are not states at all. Thus, in the *Investigations* he argues as follows:

How should we counter someone who told us that with *him* understanding was an inner process? How should we counter him if he said that with him knowing how to play chess was an inner process? We should say that when we want to know if he can play chess we aren't interested in anything that goes on inside him. And if he replies that this is in fact just what we are interested in, that is, we are interested in whether he can play chess – then we shall have to draw his attention to the criteria which would demonstrate his capacity, and on the other hand to the criteria for the 'inner states.'

Even if someone had a particular capacity only when, and only as long as, he had a particular feeling, the feeling would not be the capacity (PI, p. 181).

Wittgenstein is, of course, right that in such cases we are interested in what someone can actually do. But he is wrong in thinking that if the capacities he mentions are (truly) states, then they must be 'introspectable' states. There is no good reason to think that if we grant that knowing how to play chess is not a matter of silently rehearsing the rules of chess, we thereby concede that knowing how to play chess isn't a state. And we can readily grant that one's knowing the ABC is not a matter of silently rehearsing the alphabet (or having an image of it) without thereby conceding that this is not a state. After all, in order to take a view different from Wittgenstein's, we need only reject his Master Premise, i.e., his idea that the only things that are real (the only things we can properly, unmisleadingly, speak of in the present indicative tense) are such things as sensible qualities and toothaches. Who but a phenomenalist ever thought *that*?

Wittgenstein's Additional Arguments

In order to be sure that his position depends entirely on his Master Premise, let us consider the other arguments he advances.

At one point Wittgenstein puts the matter as follows: "The general differentiation of all states of consciousness from dispositions seems to me to be that one cannot ascertain by spot-check whether they [i.e., dispositions] are still going on" (RPP, II, §57).[10] This is the criterion he would have us apply to determine whether knowing the ABC, knowing how to play chess, and so on are states.[11] But here he is once more invoking his Master Premise, for by "spot-check" he has in mind *perceiving* the state itself (e.g., a sensation), so that putting someone (or something) to a test is not to count as a spot-check. By this I mean the following. To determine whether a storage battery is holding a charge, one cannot simply *look* at a battery; one must employ a battery tester or connect the battery to a light, and so on. Any time you want to know whether the battery has held its charge, you can check it in this way, but Wittgenstein would not allow that this is a spot-check, for by "spot-check" he means perceiving the state itself. He would say, then, that a battery's being fully charged is not a (true) state but only a state in a grammatical sense (see PI, §572), since its being fully charged is not something we can directly perceive. Similarly, he insists that knowing how to play chess is not a state, for one cannot directly perceive this state in oneself.

When Wittgenstein says that a state is the sort of thing that is subject to spot-checks, he is both right and wrong. He is right that states are subject to spot-checks, but he is wrong in thinking that spot-checks must be like noticing that one's back still aches. One can reject his phenomenalist view of spot-checks, i.e., reject his Master Premise, and take the proper view that spot-checks include tests of the sort I have just mentioned, such as employing a battery tester. Wittgenstein's ontology would not permit him to regard such tests as revealing a power or capacity, because in his indeterministic world the fact that an instrument's needle jumps up is a fact that is independent of anything else, i.e., it comes into being *ex nihilo* and is not the consequence of a preexisting state of, e.g., a battery.

Another of Wittgenstein's arguments calls attention to the following difference between pains and knowing how to play chess: we say, "He has been in continuous pain since yesterday," but we do not say, "He knew how to play chess throughout the entire game" (PI, p. 59). This observation might be relevantly addressed to a philosopher who thinks of intellectual powers as being introspectable states, i.e., who accepts Wittgenstein's Master Premise, but it goes no distance toward showing what Wittgenstein wants it to show, namely, that there are no intellectual powers. We don't speak of powers and capacities as we do of pains, for pains may come and go in a short span of time, whereas knowing how to play chess, like knowing how to ride a bicycle, is something that, once acquired, is pretty much a lifetime affair. We needn't be puzzled about this if we refuse to accept Wittgenstein's Master Premise. For, in order to allow that knowing how to play chess is pretty much a lifetime affair, we needn't think that we go through life – or a chess game – constantly rehearsing the rules of chess.

His final argument consists of his pointing out that one can be mistaken in thinking that one knows how to do something or in thinking that one knows the meaning of a word (PI, p. 53, below the line). We are supposed to think: Since I can be mistaken about such things, knowing how to do something and knowing the meaning of a word cannot be mental states, for a mental state is something given in experience, like a toothache, and it makes no sense to think one is mistaken about such things. Here again Wittgenstein's Master Premise plays the pivotal role, for in order to escape the clutches of this argument we need only refuse to agree that nothing can be a (true) state, i.e., be spoken of nonmisleadingly in the present indicative, unless it is something like a toothache. *Of course* a person can think he still knows how to solve quadratic equations and discover, on trying, that he has forgotten too much. But trying to solve a quadratic equation is a perfectly good 'spot-check' for a genuine state.

Let us now try to understand why arguments based on Wittgenstein's Master Premise should have been found so persuasive – not only by himself but by others as well. The reason is that Wittgenstein was writing in an era in which dualism was still a commonly held view. It was a tenet of dualism that intellectual powers are powers of the mind. One reason for this was that dualists were generally persuaded that a person can survive death, and this was taken to mean that when his body, including his brain, is buried and decays, his mental powers will live on: he will remember his life (in particular, his sins) and will still be able to think and reason. It was therefore necessary for the dualist to hold that intellectual powers are not dependent on the brain, that the locus of such powers is in the mind. But what is *in* the mind, it seems, should also be *present* to the mind, available to "the inner sense." So if knowing how to play chess were a power of the mind, then it would seem that this could be so only if one could 'look within' and thereby discern one's ability to play chess. This, it seems to me, is why Wittgenstein's Master Premise – or arguments based on it – came to seem so plausible to philosophers wanting to reject dualism. For what is a dualist to reply once he has acknowledged the obvious fact that a person who is sleeping or who is occupied with matters other than chess can be said to know how to play chess? At such times the rules of chess are certainly not before his mind; he is not rehearsing them to himself. Similarly, a person who can rightly be said to have memorized a poem or a piece of music may be asleep or be occupied with other matters and not thinking of the poem or the piece of music at all. In what sense, then, can these powers be 'in the mind'? Must the dualist not agree that when the chess player is asleep (or is otherwise occupied) there is *in his mind* nothing of chess at all? But if so, what can it mean to say that he *at that time* knows how to play chess? How could it mean anything other than that *if* he were awake and sitting at a chess board he *would* make appropriate moves. But if *that* is what it *means* to say that someone knows how to play chess, then the whole notion of intellectual powers must evaporate. For what this talk of mental powers comes down to, then, is simply that someone who *can* play chess will *do* certain things in certain circumstances. And what remain to be counted as mental states are things of the sort Wittgenstein himself holds up as his paradigm: being in pain, feeling nauseous, feeling depressed, and the like.

Wittgenstein makes this view seem more compelling by suggesting that the only alternative to it is a rather absurd one. Thus, in opposing the idea that knowing the ABC is a state, he depicts his opponent as having to take the view that since knowing the alphabet is obviously not a *conscious* state of mind (one is not always silently rehearsing the alphabet or visualizing it written on a blackboard), it must be an *unconscious* state, i.e., one must have in one's unconscious mind something like a visual image of the written alphabet. [Wittgenstein takes this line in both *Philosophical Grammar* (p. 48) and in *Philosophical Investigations* (§149).] And such an idea has certainly been adopted by some philosophers.[12] What is objectionable (and revealing) is that Wittgenstein considers no *other* alternative to his analysis. As a result he thinks that those who oppose his view can be debunked in the way he (unfairly) debunks psychoanalysts in The Blue Book: "The psychoanalysts . . . were misled by their own way of expression into thinking that they had done more than discover new psychological reactions; that they had, in a sense, discovered conscious thoughts which were unconscious" (BB, p. 57).

An Alternative to Wittgenstein's Account

There is surely an alternative to his own view which Wittgenstein overlooked entirely, for our options are not limited to embracing dualism or phenomenalism. The trouble with Wittgenstein's view is that, being a phenomenalist, he has bargained away people – real flesh and blood people – so that he has no proper place for intellectual powers and is obliged to maintain that ordinary language, where we appear to speak of powers, contains misleading forms of expression.[13] But if we allow that when we attribute intellectual powers we are attributing them, not to a Cartesian mind or to 'a perceptual body,' but to a flesh and blood human being (and if we reject the phenomenalistic analysis of what it is to have a brain), there is no general problem about how intellectual powers *can* be attributed to ourselves and others. The point that needs to be made here is the same as needs making in the case of physical powers and capacities: if we dismiss the phenomenalistic account of material objects, no reason remains for being puzzled about our saying that a battery is fully charged or about our telling a child, whose toy we have just wound up, "It's ready to go," i.e., there is no reason to think that we are here employing misleading forms of words. After all, if the wind-up toy takes off across the floor when the child releases the brake, what are we to think? That this is some 'causeless happening'?

It was not by paying attention to language that Wittgenstein decided that knowing how to play chess is not a state. He was forced to this conclusion by embracing a Humean view of the world. For Wittgenstein, as for Hume, human life is a matter of discrete, momentary, phenomenal states, each independent of what went before. Hume put this by saying that a person is "a bundle or collection of different perceptions, which succeed each other with an inconceivable rapidity, and are in a perpetual flux . . ." (*Treatise*, I, IV, 6). Wittgenstein, even as late as 1949, spoke similarly of life as "the flux of life" ("*Fluss des Lebens*") (LW, I, §913).[14] In such a 'life' there can *of course* be no intellectual powers, for there is nothing enduring to sustain any powers at all. For there to be powers, whether intellectual or otherwise, there must be something that endures through time to acquire and retain those powers. Wittgenstein's metaphysics does not allow for this, and accordingly he had to give a spurious account of 'the grammar' of such phrases as "knows how to play chess," "can speak French," and similar phrases.

A final point needs to be made here regarding the role of the brain. In a passage quoted above, Wittgenstein says: "Note also how sure people are that to the ability to add or to multiply or to say a poem by heart, etc., there *must* correspond a peculiar state of the person's brain, although on the other hand they know next to nothing about such psycho-physical correspondences." It is, of course, true that most people know nothing at all about brain states. But is this a reason for dismissing intellectual powers and capacities, i.e., for saying that *after* memorizing a poem (or learning to speak French) a person may be in the *same state* as beforehand? In the *Investigations* Wittgenstein argues that if a philosopher says that knowing the alphabet is a state, this can be objected to by pointing out that "there ought to be ... a knowledge of the construction of the apparatus, quite apart from what it does" (PI, §149). By parity of reasoning, we ought to say that a battery's being fully charged is not a *state* of the battery since a person may know that a battery is charged without knowing anything about the construction of a storage battery or what changes take place in it when a battery is charged. This, of course, would be an absurd argument. The point is that when we say that someone has memorized a poem or can do mental arithmetic, we are not describing the state of his or her brain, any more than we are describing the chemical state of a battery when we say that it is holding a charge. Nonetheless, even if I knew nothing about the construction of a storage battery or about how the reagents in it are restored when a battery is charged, I could still be sure that *some sort of change* is taking place in the battery when it is being charged and that, whatever its new state may be, it lasts as long as I can power a light bulb with the battery. And in similar fashion, although I know nothing about brain states, I can be sure that *some sort of change* takes place in a person when he or she learns how to play chess or memorizes a poem. To think otherwise, one would have to imagine, as Wittgenstein did, that a person's reciting a poem from memory is an event in an indeterministic world, i.e., that the recitation comes into being *ex nihilo*.

In his 1946–47 lectures Wittgenstein scoffed at the suggestion that there must be some physiological difference between two people if one of them has learned to speak French and the other has not. There need not be any such difference between them, said Wittgenstein, adding that he did not, in saying this, mean to imply that they may differ in some other way, namely, that there may be a difference in their souls (WL47, p. 330). This is reminiscent of what he says about two seeds from which different plants grow, namely, that the seeds may differ in no way at all, which implies that the cabbage that grows from one and the pine tree that grows from the other both come into being *ex nihilo*. I think we may take it, then, that Wittgenstein is implying the same sort of thing about speaking, namely, that the words that form on one's lips come into being *ex nihilo*, so that there is no accounting for the fact that I answer, "Red," rather than "Blue," when I am asked the color of something that I see before me. In the next two chapters we will see that this idea plays the central role in his private language argument.

Notes

1. Berkeley further explains that, although God *could* produce such miracles on a regular basis, that would deprive Him of using miracles to strike awe into men (ibid., §63).

2. Wittgenstein, in his 1934–1935 lectures, appears to have had in mind Berkeley's example of the clock which contains no clockworks:

> When a child is able to use a word we say that he has got hold of an idea, that he *understands* the word. This may be a way of saying that his being able to use the word is a hypothesis, and we then give him tests to find out whether we can rely on his using it aright in the future. The hypothesis that he has the general idea [of a plant] corresponds to the assumption of a hypothetical mechanism which we do not know [of] because it is seen from the outside, like the works of a watch which no one has ever been able to open. The hands are seen to go round and we then make the hypothesis that they do so because there are works inside. And we could make a model of them. We very often think of ideas in this way. An idea [we think] is like a mechanism whose workings we do not know (WL35, p. 80).

3. Moore, in his 1914 essay "The Status of Sense-data," had given this example in characterizing the phenomenalists' view, saying that on their view the proposition that I *now* have in my body blood and nerves and a brain "does *not* assert, in the proper sense of the word 'existence,' the *present* existence of anything whatever . . . , but only makes assertions as to the kind of experiences a doctor *would* have, if he dissected me" (op. cit., pp. 191–192).

4. *Gestalt Psychology*, op. cit., pp. 143–144.

5. Kohler would encounter the same difficulty, of course, with inanimate objects. For him a wind-up toy is also a perceptual object, and so he would no doubt have said that when we release the toy and it begins moving, "the events in question . . . seem to emerge from the interior of the body." But how could a perceptual object be wound up and ready to go? How, indeed, could perceptual objects, whether animate or inanimate, have any powers at all? If we had to think of, say, a storage battery as a perceptual object, how could we think of it as holding an electrical charge? Hume, of course, was also faced with this problem and said that powers of all kinds are metaphysical fancies: "The distinction which we often make betwixt *power* and the *exercise* of it is . . . without foundation" (*Treatise*, I, III, xiv). Wittgenstein, too, dismisses physical powers (e.g., BB, pp. 100–104). See also his way of treating the statement that something has a certain weight (NFL, p. 287, CE, pp. 423–424, and PI, §§182 and 572). In addition, Wittgenstein bargains away the atomic structure of things by treating scientific terms as another misleading forms of words. He holds that when we say (using the present indicative) that water "consists of hydrogen and oxygen," what this means is analyzable into subjunctive propositions about tests we might perform. At one point he imagines his interlocutor asking in astonishment: "You are surely not going to deny that rust and water and sugar have an inner nature!" (RPP, I, §104). This refers back to his remark a few passages earlier: "Think of the sense in which water 'consists' of H and O" (RPP, I, §97). In this connection see PG, p. 223; PI, §422; RPP, II, §643; and CV, p. 71.

6. Compare: "Expectation is, grammatically, a state; like: being of an opinion, hoping for something, knowing something, being able to do something" (PI, §572). He means to say: these are not (true) states; they are only treated by the grammar of our language as if they were states.

7. Wittgenstein is merely taking the view common to phenomenalists. As Elizabeth Prior remarks, "The phenomenalist says that there are disposi-

tions but that they are nothing over and above the holding of certain conditionals," so that phenomenalism is the view that "two items could be alike in *all* their causally relevant properties and one item possess a particular disposition . . . but the other item *not* possess that disposition." *Dispositions* (Aberdeen: Aberdeen University Press, 1985), pp. 29 and 31.

8. Separating these two issues in Wittgenstein's writings is not always easy, for he often lumps them together, treating the latter as a particular case of the former, as in his discussions of whether *understanding* is a state. This comes about because Wittgenstein, in addressing the more specific question about language, commonly boils it down to this: Is one's being able to use such-and-such a word the manifestation of a *state*? And this, in turn, he frequently takes up in the form: What is it to *understand* a word, i.e., is *understanding* a word a *state*? (See WVC, p. 167.) This, of course, is a rather odd question, for we do not commonly speak of understanding a *word*. We speak of understanding (or not understanding) what someone has said (as when someone has spoken very cryptically or has spoken in a foreign language or muttered something), but it is difficult, at best, to think of cases in which we speak of understanding (or not understanding) a word. Wittgenstein seems not to have noticed this, for although he never gives examples in which we actually speak of understanding a word, he often poses the question "How do we actually use the word 'understand'?" and then proceeds to talk in a general way about understanding a word, as if we were supposed to know what he is talking about. It appears that Wittgenstein uncritically copied this misuse of "understand" from Russell's *The Analysis of Mind*, op. cit., esp. pp. 197ff.

9. The emphasis on "present tense" is Wittgenstein's, and this is important. What is at issue is the way (as Wittgenstein would put it) our language uses the present tense in these cases. He would say that what we mean by "He *is* capable of . . ." would be better, less misleadingly, expressed in subjunctives.

10. The reader will have noticed that Wittgenstein was not consistent in his use of the term "disposition." In his remarks (quoted above) about love he so defined "disposition" that, given his ontology, there *could not* be dispositions. Later on, however, he used "disposition" to mean a certain grammatical category, and in this latter use he could say that "This vase is fragile" is a dispositional statement without thereby allowing that fragility is a state of – a liability inherent in – the vase. Given this change of meaning, Wittgenstein could speak of understanding as a *disposition* without allowing it to be a *state*. Indeed, at times he even extended the meaning of "state" along these lines, as when he wrote: "We might speak of 'functional states'. (E.g.: Today I am very irritable. If I am told such-and-such today, I keep on reacting in such-and-such a way. In contrast with this: I have a headache the whole day.)" (RPP, I,§61). One might have thought that the need for such verbal juggling would have suggested to Wittgenstein that he had somewhere gone wrong, but he had no such insight.

11. Wittgenstein makes this clear as follows:

> We are inclined to call understanding a mental state or a state of mind. This characterizes it as a *hypothetical* process, etc., or rather as a process (or state) in the sense of a hypothesis. That is, we banish [relegate?] the word "understanding" to a particular region of grammar.
>
> The grammar of a mental state or process is indeed in many respects similar to that of e.g. a brain-process. The principal difference is perhaps

that in the case of a brain-process a direct check is admitted to be possible; the process in question may perhaps be seen by opening the skull. But there is no room for a similar "immediate perception" in the grammar of mental process. (There is no such move in this game.) (PG, p. 82).

12. A. S. Pringle-Pattison, the editor of an abridged edition of Locke's *Essay*, comments in a footnote: "Psychologists are pretty well agreed that the facts of memory cannot be stated without invoking the hypothesis of subconscious dispositions." John Locke, *An Essay Concerning Human Understanding* (Oxford: Oxford University Press, 1924), pp. 79–80, footnote 1. Pringle-Pattison appears to endorse this view.

13. In lectures he said:

> ... the statement "he understands" is of the dispositional form. Although it does not refer to a mechanism *as it seems to*, what is behind the [misleading] grammar of that statement is the picture of a mechanism set to react in certain ways. ...
>
> It is because of the form of words "I understand," "I have an idea," that we suppose the grammar of these words is that of describing a state, whereas it is not. "I understand" is used quite differently [from words used to ascribe a state] (WL35, p. 92, emphasis added).

14. The German word "*Fluss*" can also be translated "stream" and has been so translated in the passage cited. I have used "flux," thinking that Wittgenstein was echoing Hume or perhaps Russell, who had said that "the immediate data of sense are ... in a state of perpetual flux" (*Mysticism and Logic*, op. cit., p. 128). In 1930 Wittgenstein not only spoke of the "constant flux of appearance" ["*Fluss der Erscheinung*"] (PB, p. 83), but also said: "Der Strom des Lebens, oder der Strom der Welt, fliesst dahin, und unsere Sätze werden, sozusagen, nur in Augenblicken verifiziert" (PB, p. 81). So regardless of the translation, his use of the phrase "*Fluss des Lebens*" in 1949 is a pretty clear indication that his metaphysics remained unchanged at the end of his life. In his pre-*Tractatus* notebooks he had said: "The World and Life are one. ... Life is the world" (NB, p. 77), and he went on to say: "All experience is world" (NB, p. 89). In the *Tractatus* he retained the line "The world and life are one" (TLP, 5.621), adding: "I am my world" (TLP, 5.63). See in this connection NFL, p. 297.

18

Following a Rule

The two preceding chapters have provided the background needed for understanding Wittgenstein's change of mind about a basic tenet of the *Tractatus* theory of language. In his post-*Tractatus* years he came to realize that when the implications of his phenomenalism are carefully thought out, it becomes necessary to abandon what he had said about logically proper names (color words, for instance), namely, that such words are "correlated" with objects (TLP, 2.1514, 2.1515, 5.526) and "represent" them (TLP, 3.221, 4.0312). His abandonment of this view can be discerned in a 1932 conversation with Waismann, in which he said: "In the *Tractatus* logical analysis and ostensive definition were unclear to me. At that time I thought that there was 'a connection between language and reality'" (WVC, pp. 209–210). In this chapter and the next we will see why he came to think that there cannot be such a connection.

To understand Wittgenstein's attack on his earlier view of the connection of names and objects, one must consider how such a connection might be established. Philosophers have often said that once one has correlated, say, a color and its name, one can *continue* using the name to denote that color. The idea is that we have within us an *ability* to continue applying the same name to the same color on successive occasions. One account of this ability is that offered by John Locke, and to understand what Wittgenstein says on this topic, it will be useful to review Locke's account.

Locke's Account

Its starting point is the mind's acquisition of simple ideas. This acquisition, says Locke, involves two steps. First, the 'original' of those ideas must be received from sensation or reflection and attended to. Second, the mind must *retain* the ideas that are impressed upon it. Here he distinguishes two sorts of retention. One he describes as the mind's keeping "the idea ... for some time actually in view, which is called *contemplation*." The other he describes as "the power to revive again in our minds those ideas which, after imprinting, have disappeared, or have been as it were laid aside out of sight. ... This is *memory*, which is, as it were, the storehouse of our ideas" (*An Essay Concerning Human*

Understanding, II, x, 1 and 2). It is this second sort of retention that plays a role in his account of language:

When children have by repeated sensations got ideas fixed in their memories, they begin by degrees to learn the use of signs. And when they have got the skill to apply the organs of speech to the framing of articulate sounds, they begin to make use of words to signify their ideas to others (II, xi, 8).

Conveying one's ideas to other people, Locke thinks, is "the chief end of language":

Men learn names, and use them in talk with others, only that they may be understood: which is then only done when by use or consent the sound I make by the organs of speech excites in another man's mind who hears it, the idea I apply it to in mine when I speak it (III, iii, 3).

How am I to know that what another person calls "yellow" or "pain" is the *same* idea that *I* call by those names? Locke answers that "this could never be known, because one man's mind could not pass into another man's body, to perceive [the other's sensations]" (II, xxxii, 15). Even so, men

suppose their words to be marks of the ideas in the minds also of other men, with whom they communicate; for else they should talk in vain, and could not be understood, if the sounds [the speaker] applied to one idea were . . . by the hearer . . . applied to another, which is to speak two languages (III, ii, 4).

What is implied here is that, for all we can know, each of us may be speaking a *different* language. And in any case each of us is speaking a *private* language, since the meanings of one's words can be known only to oneself. Locke imagines that such a private use of words is possible because he thinks that the meanings of words are the ideas stored up in our memories.

How does Locke think of ideas being stored there? He explains:

. . . this laying up of our ideas in the repository of the memory, signifies no more but this, that the mind has the power, in many cases, to revive perceptions which it has once had, with this additional perception annexed to them – that it has had them before. And in this sense it is that our ideas are said to be in our memories, when indeed they are actually nowhere, but only there is an ability in the mind, when it will, to revive them again (II, x, 2).

Locke acknowledges that an idea whose object we have experienced only once or which we have taken little notice of may be quickly forgotten (II, x, 4). He also acknowledges that we may find that "a disease quite strip[s] the mind of all its ideas" (II, x, 5). But such cases aside, says Locke, where there is constant repetition, as with heat and cold, our ideas "are seldom quite lost" (II, x, 6). This is not to say that the ideas of heat and cold and red are constantly before one's mind, in the way that a severe toothache may hold one's attention for a considerable time, but that the mind's power to revive these ideas remains throughout one's life.

Let us consider why it is that Locke introduces ideas into his account of language. There are perhaps several reasons for this, but for our purposes the important reason is that Locke supposed that if what I am doing *now* is something I do from memory, such as singing a song without following a printed score, then I must have in my mind a 'pattern' that I am going by, i.e., a 'pattern' preserved from the past. In other words, he thought that singing a song I have memorized and singing a song by following a printed score must be alike in the following respect: in both cases I follow a score, although in one case it is a *printed* score and in the other an *internal* score.[1] And what holds for singing a song holds also for using a word: when I now use a word I learned in childhood, I must have in my mind an exemplar of what I was taught to call by that name. On Locke's view, then, the role of ideas in accounting for our linguistic capacities was something like this: when I hear someone speaking my native tongue, I hear sounds that trigger my memory in reviving the ideas I once associated with those sounds and which serve as exemplars of what the word stands for, and it is the revival of these ideas in my mind that enables me to act on the request "Fetch a red flower" or "Bring me some blue thread," whereas if I have no idea of green, I cannot act on the request to bring green thread.

It is useful to observe that Locke's account of language contains two elements: (i) his insistence that in order to acquire language one must have the power of retention – what we might also call "the capacity to learn" and (ii) his account of this capacity in terms of 'ideas.' We will presently consider whether we could we accept (i) while rejecting (ii).

Names and Rules

When Wittgenstein, in the *Tractatus*, said that names are "correlated" with objects, he may have been assuming a Lockean view. And he seems still to have held this view in 1930, for in lectures that year he said: "If I use a symbol I must be committing myself. . . . If I say this is green, I must say that other green things are green too. I am committed to a future usage" (WL32, p. 37), and he went on to say: "We need in addition to the word 'green' something else. . . . [T]he word, the noise, 'green' alone won't help you to find a pot of green paint. The word 'green' . . . must be connected by an explanation to a symbol in another language, e.g., the totally different language of memory-images" (ibid., p. 38).

In saying here that, to be using a *symbol*, one must be committed to a future usage, Wittgenstein meant that this is what distinguishes using a word from making a meaningless sound or mark. On the *Tractatus* view of names, this difference would seem to be that a name is correlated with a *particular* object and that each time that name is used it is used to denote the *same* object, so that, in giving a name to something, one commits oneself to using it *consistently* thereafter and that is how words differ from random noises. The importance he attached to consistency is why Wittgenstein spoke of ostensive definitions as *rules* and said that in using a word one is *following* a rule.[2] He also used the word "rule" in another context, saying for example that "+1" (where this is given to generate a number series) is a rule (RFM, p. 319). Wittgenstein spoke of both sorts of things as "rules" because he thought of them as telling us that we are to do something consistently and because we are corrected if we do otherwise. Thus, when a student is told to write down the number series "n, n+1, . . . ," he is to do the *same* thing at each step, and if he fails to do what's expected of him, he is corrected. Similarly, defining a word, says Wittgenstein, "is something which shows us how to use a word at some other time as well" (LSD, p. 39). "If I have once grasped a rule I am bound in what I do further" (RFM, p. 328). Also, ". . . giving a name should show the way I am going to use it [in the future]" (LSD, p. 109).[3]

It is here that Wittgenstein began to see that some of his other views – those reviewed in the two preceding chapters – make it difficult to understand *how* there could be a difference between saying something and merely making random noises. At one point he formulates his problem as follows:

But it is remarkable that I don't lose the meaning of the rule as I [apply] it. For how do I hold it fast?
But – how do I know that I do hold it fast, that I do not lose it?! It makes no sense at all to say I have held it fast unless there is such a thing as an outward mark [a *criterion*] of this (RFM, p. 351).

Locke would have seen no difficulty here, for he was prepared to say that our memory is a capacity for reviving a past exemplar and that, unless some disease has robbed us of this capacity, it stays with us always. Wittgenstein, as we saw in Chapter 17, dismissed the very idea of intellectual capacities and powers, and therefore this Lockean explanation was unavailable to him. His genuine perplexity about this matter is revealed in a remark written in the early 1940s: " 'How can one follow a rule?' That is what I should like to ask" (RFM, p. 341). As we will see, Wittgenstein solved this problem, in part, by taking the view that if "following a rule" means using, say, "green" always as the name of the *same* color, then a reductionist account must be given of "same color."[4]

To understand Wittgenstein's remarks about using a word according to a rule, it is useful to divide the problem into two aspects. In one aspect, using a word is considered *retrospectively*, and Wittgenstein's problem, which is generated by his view of memory (see Chapter 16), is this: If using a word correctly means using it consistently, how, if at all, could one know that one *has* used a word correctly or know that one's present use is consistent with one's *past* use? In its other aspect, using a word is considered *prospectively*, and Wittgenstein's problem, which is generated by his rejection of powers (see Chapter 17), is this: How, if at all, can one undertake to use a word (or teach a child to use a word) correctly *in the future*, if using it correctly means using it consistently? I will begin by presenting the retrospective aspect of his problem.

The Retrospective Aspect of Wittgenstein's Problem

To understand Wittgenstein's problem, it is important to know that the passage, quoted in Chapter 16, in which Russell posed the problem about the reality of the past is immediately preceded by the following:

Why do we believe that images [or Lockean ideas] are, sometimes or always, approximately or exactly, copies of [our earlier] sensations? What sort of evidence is there? And what sort of evidence is logically possible? The difficulty of this question arises through the fact that the [earlier] sensation which an image is supposed to copy is [already] in the past when the image exists, and can therefore be known only by means of memory, while, on the other hand, memory of past sensations seems only possible by means of present images. How, then, are we to find any way of comparing the present image and the past sensation? The problem is just as acute if we say that images *differ* from their prototypes as if we say that they *resemble* them; it is the very possibility of comparison that is hard to understand. We think we can know that they are alike or different, but we cannot bring them together in one experience and compare them. . . . In this way the whole status of images as "copies" is bound up with the analysis of memory.[5]

Russell, as I said above, goes on immediately to propose, as a 'logical possibility,' that the universe may, for all we know, have come into being five minutes ago. (Wittgenstein was later to comment that Russell *should* have said that the universe may have come into being *now*.) The passage quoted above, if applied to Locke's account of using words, suggests as a 'logical possibility' that if I now say, "This is green," and later say, "Here is some green thread," the color I call "green" may, for all I can know, be different each time, for the image I *take* to be an exemplar may not be the same on both occasions.

We know how Wittgenstein dealt with Russell's 'hypothesis' of a five-minute-old world: he rejected Russell's realist view of the past, i.e., the view which says that if a past-tense statement is true, what makes it true is something that is (irreducibly) in the past. He maintained that if a past-tense statement can be known to be true, what makes it true is something that is now present*. But having given this reductionist account of the past, how was Wittgenstein going to provide for any regularity in the use of a word? Plainly, he could not hope to show that his present use of "red" conforms to his *past* use of it (if "past" is taken in the realist's sense), for given his Humean view of the self (and hence of memory), if past events are, as Russell thought, irreducibly past, they are unknowable. His alternative was to hold that a past-tense statement *can* be known to be true but only because one takes one's present* 'memory' of the event as a *criterion* for its truth, in which case the past-tense statement is really about one's present* recollection. But this latter alternative, he came to realize, provided him with no way of showing that his present* use of "red" conforms to a rule.

The first step in this realization came in 1931, when he wrote:

> If we can talk of using a sign twice with the same meaning, this meaning must be laid down somehow. The problem is that of recognition (Frege). But here recognition must be autonomous, which in the ordinary sense it is not, as ordinarily we acknowledge other criteria – as, e.g. if I recognize Mr. Smith. But if I say "This is brown" my recognition is the only criterion, not one of several. Compare Russell on memory (WL32, p. 61).

What did Wittgenstein mean in saying here that recognition must be *autonomous*? He meant that there is nothing against which to test one' 'recognition' for accuracy, so that there can be no distinction between actually recognizing that this is the color one has previously called 'red' and merely thinking that one recognizes it. But in that case, there would be no difference between using a word repeatedly according to a rule and merely thinking one does so. He drew out the import of this as follows:

> Perhaps someone will say: if I hadn't kept his image in my memory, I couldn't have recognized him. But here [with the phrase "kept . . . in my memory"] he is either using a metaphor, or expressing a hypothesis.
> We say "we couldn't use words at all, if we didn't recognize them and the objects they denote." If (because of a faulty memory) we didn't recognize the color green for what it is, then we couldn't use the word "green." But have we any sort of check on this recognition, so that we know that it is really a recognition? If we speak of recognition, we mean that we recognize something as what, in accordance with other criteria, it is. "To recognize" means "to recognize what it *is*" [not what it *seems* to us to be] (PG, p. 168).

This passage contain three related points. (i) In the first paragraph Wittgenstein rejects the Lockean view that memory is a "storehouse" from which memory images arise. (ii) Because of this, he is led, in the second paragraph, to pose the skeptical problem raised by Russell: Is our 'recognition' of a color really a recognition? (iii) He concludes the passage by implying that since there is no check on whether we have correctly recognized a color, we cannot speak of *recognizing* colors.

This led Wittgenstein eventually to declare that memory (or recognition) plays no role in the use of such words as "red," "sweet," and "pain." He made this point in various ways, one of which was to declare that one cannot place implicit trust in memory images:

If the use of the word "red" depends on the picture that my memory auto-matically reproduces at the sound of this word, then I am as much at the mercy of this reproduction as if I had decided to settle the meaning by looking up a chart in such a way that I would surrender unconditionally to *whatever* I found there (PG, p. 95).

He is saying: identifying colors by means of 'memory' images would not ensure that we use "red" and "green" consistently, for there is no guarantee that our memory will serve up images of the *right* color each time. In the *Investigations* he repeats this point:

How is he to know what color he is to pick out when he hears "red"? Quite simple: he is to take the colour whose image occurs to him when he hears the word. But how is he to know which colour it is "whose image occurs to him"? Is a further criterion needed for that? . . . .
" 'Red' means the colour [*whatever* it may be] that occurs to me when I hear the word 'red' " would be a *definition*. Not an explanation of *what it is* to use a word as a [rule-governed] name (PI, §239).

Wittgenstein is saying here that since there is no guarantee that images of the *same* color will occur to one each time one hears the word "red," one cannot explain what it is to use "red" *consistently* by saying that it means the color whose image occurs to one upon hearing the word.

Wittgenstein was also denying that memory or recognition plays a role in the use of color words when he wrote:

Searching with a sample which one places beside objects to test whether the colours match is one game; acting in accordance with the words of a word-language without a sample is another. Think of reading aloud from a written text (or writing to dictation). We might of course imagine a kind of table that might guide us in this; but in fact there isn't one, there's no act of memory, or anything else, which acts as an intermediary between the written sign and the sound.
Suppose I am now asked "why do you choose *this* colour when given this order; how do you justify the choice?" In the one case I can answer "because *this* colour is opposite the word 'red' in my chart." In the other case [where I use no chart] there is no answer to the question and the question makes no sense [i.e., I have no reason or justification for choosing the color I do]. But in the first game there is no sense in *this* question: "why [when reading aloud] do you [audibly] call 'red' the colour in the chart opposite the [written] word 'red'?" A *reason* can only be given *within* a game (PG, pp. 96–97).

Here Wittgenstein is saying: just as memory plays no role when we pronounce the words we read aloud from a text, so memory plays no role in our use of color words in giving descriptions. He later made the same point about tastes: ". . . when I say 'It tastes exactly like sugar,' in an important sense no remembering takes place. So I do *not have grounds for* my judgment or my exclamation" ['Sugar!'] (RPP, II, §353).

Plainly, if Wittgenstein is going to say that memory or recognition plays no role in the use of color words, he is also going to say that Russell's skeptical problem cannot arise, that the question cannot arise whether (as he puts it) our recognition "is really a recognition."[6] But this solved, at most, only half the problem, for Wittgenstein still needed to give an account of what it is to use a word, as opposed to mouthing noises, i.e., what it is to use color words *according to a rule*.

One might think that another option was available to him: he could reject the idea that we *recognize* colors when we speak their names and yet hold that being *taught* the name of a color establishes a permanent connection between the name and the color, so that henceforth we invariably use the name correctly. This brings us to the other aspect of his problem.

The Prospective Aspect of Wittgenstein's Problem

For a brief period in 1930 Wittgenstein believed that the problem of following a rule could be solved in the way just mentioned. In lectures he said that the way we actually learn a word's meaning is not essential to "our future understanding" of it. Rather, he said, "what is essential . . . to the understanding of a symbol [is what] sticks to it." And what is that? When we are taught a word, he explained, "what remains [with us] is our *understanding*" (WL32, p. 23, emphasis added). He also said that explanations of words "give us something which completes the symbol . . . , and this stays with us" (ibid., p. 27). Within a few months, however, Wittgenstein came to see that such an account was precluded by certain of his other views. As we saw in the preceding chapter, his Humean ontology forced him to conclude that we have no intellectual powers, that although we *talk* as though we had such powers, we are only using misleading forms of words. Philosophers, he concluded, are led by these forms of words to the erroneous idea that "the understanding itself is a state which is the *source* of the correct use" (PI, §146). Accordingly, he declared that "in our study of symbolism [i.e., language] there is no foreground and background; it isn't a matter of a tangible sign with an accompanying intangible power or understanding [which guides our use of a word]" (PG, p. 87). He means that in our use of words there is only the 'foreground,' i.e., we speak or write words, but there is nothing at all 'behind' our doing so.

So Wittgenstein came to reject the idea that when a child is taught his colors, a permanent connection is established between colors and color words. But this left him with a major problem, for if no such connection is established, how can I count on anyone, including myself, to call the same color by its name on future occasions? In the *Investigations* he explains his problem as follows:

"I don't see anything violet here, but I can shew it you if you give me a paint box." How can one *know* that one can shew it if . . . , in other words, that one can recognize it if one sees it? . . .

How do I know that I shall be able to do something? that is, that the state I am now in is that of being able to do that thing? (PI, §388).

Because Locke did not hold a Humean view of the world he was not, as we have seen, troubled by this problem. It will be recalled that Locke acknowledged that the mechanism (memory) which serves up the idea of red or sweet on appropriate occasions is subject to failure. He explicitly allowed that an illness may affect the mechanism in such a way as to rob a person of his or her command of language. He did not, then, hold that once a child has learned his colors, his future use of color words is absolutely guaranteed. What Locke did take for granted, however, is that a child will retain his learning unless some kind of brain damage occurs. [Locke says: "He that knows once that whiteness is the name of that colour he has observed in snow or milk, will not be apt to misapply that word, as long as he retains that idea" (III, iv, 15).] This is what Wittgenstein came to find unacceptable.

To understand why Wittgenstein found this unacceptable, it is useful to consult the *Tractatus*, the relevant passages of which are the following:

5.135 There is no possible way of making an inference from the existence of one situation to the existence of another, entirely different situation.

5.136 There is no causal nexus to justify such an inference.

5.1361 We *cannot* infer the events of the future [including a person's future behavior] from those of the present. . . .

5.1362 . . . future actions cannot be known now.[7] We could know them only if causality were an *inner* necessity like that of logical inference.

6.362 What can be described can also happen [even in the case of human behavior]. . . .

6.3631 It is clear that there are no grounds for believing that the simplest eventuality will in fact be realized.

6.37 There is no compulsion making one thing happen because another has happened. The only necessity that exists is *logical* necessity.

An important part of Wittgenstein's problem about following a rule can be generated by applying this Humean view to the case in which we teach a child a new word and he then uses that word in the future. For the remarks I have just quoted imply that, contrary to Locke, a child who is taught the word "red" as others are taught it may yet go on to use that word in some wildly deviant way. Thus, we find Wittgenstein saying:

The correct use of the word "red" is thought of as a consequence of its meaning, which is given in one act, all at once [when the word is taught]. . . . *However,* note that the [subsequent] use of the word is not actually fixed by giving someone, by ostensive definition, what is supposedly the meaning. For he may now use "red" when he sees a square (WL35, p. 87).

Or, says Wittgenstein, he might use "red" as the name of the complementary color (LFM, p. 193). The same problem arises for Wittgenstein if I invent a word by deciding to call a muddy shade of brown "blah": my so deciding in no way guarantees what color I will call "blah" on future occasions, for according to Wittgenstein, there is nothing to *compel* my future actions. How, then, can I *ensure* that I will use "blah" in a *consistent* way in the future or ensure that a child will use color words with consistency from one occasion to the next? His answer is that *nothing* can ensure this.

Wittgenstein's clearest exposition of this aspect of his problem was given in a lecture, where he introduced the topic as follows:

> One of the chief difficulties we have with the notion of a general idea [e.g., of a plant] or with understanding a word is that we want it to be something present at some definite time, say when the word is understood, and the idea we have is supposed to have consequences and to act *as time goes on*. For example, the idea of a plant is supposed to enable me to identify something as a plant, bring a plant when ordered to, . . . etc. (WL35, pp. 84–85, emphasis added).

He then went on to say:

> We have been puzzled by the notion that when we understand a word the idea we have makes us use the word in a particular way. It is as if the idea contains the use, which is then spread out in time. I tried to trace this [faulty] notion to that of a mechanism. Now what a mechanism *does* does not follow from what it is in any important sense. What it *will* do can only be conjectured [i.e., cannot be known] from what it is. . . . Before we realize that we can only *hypothetically* infer [i.e., cannot know] what a mechanism does from what it is, we tend to compare an idea with a mechanism. This notion must be discarded (WL35, p. 87).[8]

It must it be discarded, he means, because nothing *makes* us use a word in a particular way, i.e., "there is no compulsion making one thing happen because another [the ostensive definition] has happened."

Wittgenstein registers his opposition to the Lockean view in several ways. He does so at one point by asking: "How does an ostensive definition work? Is it put to work again [anew?] every time the word is used, or is it like a vaccination which changes us once and for all?" He answers that it is *not* like a vaccination: "A definition as a part of the calculus cannot act at a [temporal] distance" (PG, pp. 80–81). He is saying: An ostensive definition cannot have effects into the future. He is making the same point when he says: "Teaching as the hypothetical history of our subsequent actions . . . drops out of our considerations. . . . A rule [e.g., an ostensive definition] . . . does not act at a distance" (BB, p. 14). The teaching drops out, he is saying, because it does not guarantee a consistent use of the word over a stretch of time. In a related context Wittgenstein remarks that, when we give someone a rule, "there is no such thing here as, so to say, a wheel that he is to catch hold of, the right machine which . . . will carry him on automatically" (RPP, II, §407).

Wittgenstein's point is this: Even if, like Locke, we suppose there to be a mental mechanism involved in learning a word, that does not explain how we could use a word *consistently*, because, in an indeterministic world, any mechanism is subject to unaccountable deviations from what it was designed to do, so that regardless of how a child is taught the word "red," and regardless of the fact that he later suffers no brain damage, his subsequent use of it is in no way assured, i.e., there is no guarantee that he will use the word consistently thereafter.

One must be careful in thinking about this matter. One might think that, once a child has been taught the word "red," there are three possible scenarios: (i) the child goes on to use "red" as everyone else does; (ii) he uses "red" with the correct grammar and uses it perfectly consistently but in an idiosyncratic way, i.e., whenever he is told, "Fetch a red flower," he brings a blue one; and (iii) he puts "red" together with other words in a grammatical fashion, but when he points to things and says, "This is a red flower," etc., the things he points to are of *various* colors. And one might think that we could readily tell whether the child was doing (i), (ii), or (iii). But Wittgenstein cannot allow this. For how are we to tell the difference between (ii) and (iii)? Wittgenstein's problem here is that if it seemed to us that the child brings flowers of various colors when he is told, "Fetch a red flower," how are we to decide whether it is the *child's* use of "red" or *our own* that is inconsistent? Can we say: "*We* at least have a Lockean capacity which ensures that we are using color words consistently, so if the child is out of step with us, he is *not* being consistent"? Of course not, for in Wittgenstein's view it is not merely the child, but everyone, who has no Lockean capacity guaranteeing a consistent use of color words.[9]

But now what about (i), i.e., the senario in which the child uses "red" just as the rest of us do? Let us ask: Are all of us using the word consistently on successive occasions, i.e., always as the name of the *same* color? Since Wittgenstein holds that we do not have a Lockean capacity which ensures that we use color words consistently, is he not obliged to say that it is *equally possible* that (iv) we all use the word as the name of the same color on successive occasions and (v) we use the word in *agreement* with one another but there is no *consistency* in our use of the word on successive occasions? If, of course, he *is* obliged to say that (iv) and (v) are equally possible, he will then have to abandon the idea that we use words according to a rule.

Following a Rule – Part One

In a passage quoted above, Wittgenstein asks himself: "How do I know that I do hold [the meaning of the rule] fast, that I do not lose it?" We can now understand why this was a problem for him: he was hemmed in from both the retrospective and the prospective sides of the problem.

He could say neither that we *recognize* a color as the one that has always been called "red" *in the past* nor that being taught "red" established in us a capacity to call red things "red" *in the future*. What account could he possibly give, then, of using a word according to a rule?

Before turning to the solution he finally adopted, we can profit from considering one he eventually abandoned. It seems that in an early attempt to solve his problem, Wittgenstein considered the idea that one could employ a color chart – a chart in which names of colors are written opposite samples of the colors named (see PG, pp. 85–86). His idea was that this would eliminate both aspects of his problem. It eliminates the prospective aspect because the color chart could serve in place of a mental mechanism which empowers one to use color words correctly in the future. It also gets around Russell's problem about memory images. For if the criterion for using "green" *correctly* is that the color sample opposite the word "green" on the chart matches the color of the thing I *now* describe as "green," their matching is something I can take in (to use Wittgenstein's phrase) in the blink of an eye (*Augenblick*). There is no room for a possibly fallible memory to create a problem here.[10] So saying, "His hat is *green*," would seem to be as secure against Russell's skeptical doubt as would saying, "This is the same color as that," where I can see this and that simultaneously. Wittgenstein eventually discarded this solution for two reasons, the first of which he states as follows: "When we work with a sample [in a color chart] instead of our memory there are circumstances in which we say that the sample has changed colour and we judge of this by memory" (PI, §56), so the color-chart solution is really no help (see PG, p. 95). His second reason for dismissing this proposed solution is stated in The Blue Book: we simply do not use color charts this way. Instead, when told to fetch a red flower, we "look about us, walk up to a flower and pick it, without comparing it to anything" (BB, p. 3). He makes the same point in the *Investigations*: "We do not usually carry out the order 'Bring me a red flower' by looking up the colour red in a table of colours . . ." (§53). So Wittgenstein was obliged to find another way to explain what it is to use a color word correctly.

Following a Rule – Part Two

His alternative solution resembles the color-chart solution in that it, too, aims to finesse Russell's skeptical problem by making something in present experience the criterion for whether one is using a word correctly, i.e., according to a rule. This solution is to declare that one is using a color word (not merely making a noise) if one uses it in *agreement* with other people. By "agreement" he means, for example, that if one is told, "Bring a red flower," the flower one brings is accepted, not rejected, and if one tells another, "Press the red button," he does what is wanted of him.

We can see Wittgenstein formulating this view – for the first time, I believe – in his 1936 lectures. He introduces the problem of what it *means* to say that on several occasions someone has called the *same* color "green" (LSD, p. 113), and then characterizes the problem in a way that suggests he was thinking of his reductionist account of the past:

> It is all bound up with the notion of *'recurring'* and the word "the same"; with the words "already" and "again" [in "same colour again"].
>
> What do we *define* as being a recurrence [of, for example, a colour]? How do we *use* the word "recur"?
>
> Suppose Adam when he was naming the animals said "This is the lion again" – is this a definition of "lion", or of "again"? (LSD, p. 114).

He then declares that, if there is to be language, there must be agreement among two or more speakers:

> Suppose someone just learns by heart the names of colours, without using a colour chart – "impressing them on his memory." If you say he *learns* this, then you distinguish between a correct and a wrong remembering; if not, there is no learning. He has colours in a row and says "blue, green, yellow, . . ." etc. Perhaps he asks himself, "Do I *know* it now?." If he can know it, it must be possible for him to be wrong.
>
> After a bit he says "Now I know it. Therefore what I call blue is now blue. There is no further criterion for checking up." Then he is not using any language at all. He simply goes about and makes noises.
>
> If he and I played the game *together*, then it would become a language, for then I could say, "No, you were wrong [this time]." Otherwise [i.e., where he is left to his own devices] we can't say "he calls blue what *is* blue." He just makes a noise which he has made three times before. The point of repeating it is to "get it right" – otherwise it has no point: he [simply] said the word three times and later said it again.
>
> You might object, "He said the word and it was the same." But what is 'being the same' here [where he does not play a game with anyone]?
>
> He would be using a language just as much and just as little as if he were to go about and say "Hello" to various objects. But it would not be a case of using the word "blue" correctly, as we may do in our language [where we use it with other people] (LSD, pp. 114–115).

Wittgenstein is saying that if we *try* to tell a story in which color words are learned and used, but make it a story in which the words are used in accordance only with one man's 'memory' of colors, this attempted story fails to become a story about someone learning and using color words, whereas if we make it a story about *two* people and allow them to give each other orders, such as "Fetch a red flower," and if they generally regard what the other does as complying with the orders, then the story succeeds as one in which color words are learned and used, for now there is something to regard as their using these words *correctly*, namely, their agreement. He means: given that they agree, skepticism cannot arise here.

In the *Investigations* Wittgenstein arrives at this position over a span of passages. In §199 he says that two conditions must be met in order for there to be language: "Is what we call 'obeying a rule' something that it would be possible for only *one* man to do, and to do only *once* in his life? This is of course a note on the grammar of the expression 'to obey a rule'." Wittgenstein's use of italics here shows that he is saying: in order for there to be language, at least *two* people must be involved and also they must use words on *several* occasions. In §202 he repeats these two points, saying both that obeying a rule is a "practice" and that "it is not possible to obey a rule 'privately'," i.e., all by oneself. In §§240–242 it finally comes out that the requirement that there be several people involved in speaking a language is the requirement that there be *agreement* amongst them (see also §§224–225). Elsewhere Wittgenstein says: "If there did not exist an agreement in what we call 'red', etc. etc., language would stop" (RFM, p. 196). He means: if agreement ceased, but we went about 'saying' "It's red," "This is blue," etc., we would not be *talking*, would not be *saying* anything.

In declaring that there must be agreement if there are to be color words, Wittgenstein is not, of course, saying something like: Two heads are better than one when it comes to remembering which color is called "green." After all, Russell's skeptical problem regarding memory would arise for two people no less than for one. Rather, Wittgenstein is finessing Russell's skeptical problem by declaring that the agreement among speakers is sufficient to overcome the problem about whether they always call the *same* color "green." But what does this mean? Is Wittgenstein equating "The chameleon is still green" with "We (now) *say*, 'It's still green'"? Before addressing this question, let us consider the implications of the foregoing.

To understand what Wittgenstein is saying about the role of agreement in our use of words, it is essential to realize that he regarded this agreement as being inexplicable. Thus, he speaks of "spontaneous agreement" (RPP, II, §699) and says that we should not look for an explanation but should look upon what happens as a "proto-phenomenon" (PI, §654; see also *Zettel*, §§310–315.) Norman Malcolm, in expounding Wittgenstein's view, puts this point by saying that normally, in the application of color words, "we *agree*! Nothing could be more astonishing!"[11]

To understand Wittgenstein's thinking on this point, one must bear in mind that he thought of the world as being indeterministic. That our agreement in the use of words should be inexplicable did not strike him as highly peculiar for the reason that in an indeterministic world *every*-

thing that happens is inexplicable. It would be just as inexplicable if we did *not* agree. Consider, for instance, the following case. To illustrate one sort of linguistic impairment that can result from brain dysfunction, the neurologist Oliver Sachs reports the following episode. Having examined a patient who suffered impairment of the right brain hemisphere, he asked the man to put on his shoe, which Sachs had removed to test his reflexes. Noticing that the man made no move to put his shoe on, Sachs offered to help. Their ensuing conversation Sachs reports as follows:

> 'Help what? Help whom?'
> 'Help you put on your shoe.'
> 'Ach,' he said, 'I had forgotten the shoe,' adding *sotto voce*, 'The shoe? The shoe?' He seemed baffled.
> 'Your shoe,' I repeated. 'Perhaps you'd put it on.'
> He continued to look downwards, though not at the shoe, with an intense but misplaced concentration. Finally his gaze settled on his foot: 'That is my shoe, yes?'
> 'No, it is not. That is your foot. *There* is your shoe.'
> 'Ah! I thought that was my foot.'[12]

This incident was typical of the man's linguistic impairment – an impairment caused by a dysfunction of the right hemisphere of his brain. Wittgenstein, of course, would not accept this explanation (or would not regard this as an *explanation*), because in an indeterministic world nothing *can* explain anything else. And for the same reason he would have scorned anyone who said: That we agree in our use of color words is not, as you think, unaccountable, for we all learn our colors in the same way and have suffered no impairment of brain function. Wittgenstein would have rejected this by saying that it presupposes 'the causal point of view.' It involves the mistake, he would have said, of thinking that there is within us a mechanism which enables us to use and understand words.[13] It is for this reason that he held that our agreement in the use of words is inexplicable.

This is the point I was making at the end of the preceding chapter when I said that we could expect to find Wittgenstein saying that the words that form on one's lips come into being *ex nihilo*, so that there is no accounting for the fact that I answer, "Red," rather than "Green" or "Blue," when I am asked the color of something I see before me. Thus, we find Wittgenstein saying:

> When someone asks me "What colour is the book over there?" and I say "Red," and then he asks "What made you call this colour 'red'?" I shall in most cases have to say: "Nothing *makes* me call it red; that is, *no reason*. I just looked at it and said 'It's red' " (BB, p. 148).

Or, as Wittgenstein also puts it, "I obey the rule *blindly*" (PI, §219). What goes for one person, of course, goes for all: nothing *makes* anyone say "Red" when asked the color of something; we all just say it – blindly.

Following a Rule – Part Three

At this point a Lockean might complain that Wittgenstein's emphasis on people agreeing in their use of color words fails to achieve its aim, for if this agreement is inexplicable, it in no way guarantees that people use color words *consistently* over a stretch of time. This is the problem we raised earlier by means of the question: Was Wittgenstein not obliged to say that we are unable to tell whether (iv) we all use "red" consistently, i.e., as the name of the *same* color, day after day, or (v) although we use the word in *agreement* with one another, we do so inconsistently: what we all call "red" one day we all call "blue" the next? To see how Wittgenstein dealt with this difficulty, it is useful to recall his view about meaning and verification. He says: "According to my principle two suppositions must have the same sense if every *possible* experience that confirms the one also confirms the other, if, that is, no decision between the two is conceivable on the basis of experience" (PG, pp. 219–220). Accordingly, he would have said that (iv) and (v) have the same sense. But what, then, *is* that sense? Did he mean to suggest that talk of consistency and inconsistency must drop out of (iv) and (v), leaving only the common (and verifiable) element: we agree in our use of the word "red"?

Wittgenstein was answering this question when he wrote in 1947:

When [a child] first learns the names of colours – what is taught him? Well, he learns e.g. to call out "red" on seeing something red. But is that the right description; or ought it to have gone: "He learns to call 'red' *whatever we too* call 'red' "? Both descriptions are right.[14]

... But what then is something red? "Well *that* (pointing)." Or should he have said, "*That*, because most of us call it 'red' "? Or simply "*That* is what most of us call 'red' "?

This information doesn't help us at all. The difficulty we sense here with respect to "red" reappears for "same" (RPP, II, §312).

To understand what Wittgenstein is getting at in these three paragraphs, it is useful to know that in the next paragraph he placed within parentheses the word "Relativity." He was thinking of Einstein's relativity theory, and he meant to suggest that what he says about the need for agreement if a color word is to be used always as the name of the 'same color' is importantly similar to Einstein's theory, which requires that statements about spatial and temporal magnitudes have a *meaning* only when referred to a particular observer. Elsewhere he says: "This is the similarity of my treatment [of following a rule] with relativity-theory, that it is so to speak a consideration about the clocks with which we compare events" (RFM, p. 330). Wittgenstein, we might say, is rejecting the 'absolute' identity of sensations on successive occasions and proposing a 'relativized' account.

How does this 'relativized' account come to light in the three paragraphs of §312? The problem posed in the first paragraph is this: if one is to say that the child who is taught "red" proceeds thereafter to follow a rule, i.e., proceeds to call the *same* color "red," it would seem that we must use the *first* description to say what he learns, i.e., must say that the child thereafter calls *red* things "red." And yet Wittgenstein's own view seems to require that we use, instead, the *second* description, i.e., that we say that the child subsequently calls "red" whatever (i.e., *whichever color*) we (at any moment) call "red," i.e., that he is in *agreement* with us. But if we give this second description, do we not imply that the child may *not* thereafter always call the *same* color "red" and thereby imply that he does *not* follow a rule? This is Wittgenstein's problem. He solves it by saying: "*Both* descriptions are right." But how can that be? It seems clear that Wittgenstein meant to say that the first description has *the same meaning as*, i.e., is reducible to, the second description. *That* is how both can be right. This, then, is Wittgenstein's "relativity theory" and his way of salvaging the notion of following a rule: he equates "He learns to call red things 'red' " with "He learns to call 'red' *whatever we too* call 'red'," thereby eliminating any suggestion of consistency of reference (over a span of time) in the use of "red."[15]

To understand Wittgenstein's thinking here, consider an objection that might be put to him. It might have been said to him: "Your account of using color words correctly, Wittgenstein, would seem to allow that, even if we are in agreement in our use of color words, it *could* still be that on successive days we (unwittingly) alternate between calling first one color and then another color 'red.' And the result is that if on Monday I place an order for flowers, saying, 'A dozen red roses, please, and I'd like them delivered tomorrow,' and if on Tuesday a delivery of flowers arrives and I say, 'Ah, red roses – just what I ordered,' and if all my friends admire them, saying, 'What beautiful red roses,' then although we all *agree* that the roses are red, we may be *wrong*, for the flowers may *not* be the color I ordered but some *other* color (say, yellow), which on Tuesday we happen to *call* 'red.' This, of course, is absurd, but your account of using color words seems to *imply* this absurdity. Or, to put the matter another way, your account seems to allow that I may, unwittingly, be equivocating on the word 'red' if I reason as follows: 'I ordered red roses yesterday, and today the florist delivered red roses, so he delivered what I ordered'."[16]

It is not difficult to figure out how Wittgenstein would have responded to this. He would have said: "I agree that your scenario is an absurdity, but the reason it *is* an absurdity is that you have provided no criterion for determining whether the flowers delivered on Tuesday are or are not the right color, i.e., no criterion that is different from and independent of what we *say* about a thing's color. But in trying to saddle me with this absurdity, you overlook the fact that I am dismissing the idea that the following are two separate questions: (a) 'Given that *red* roses were ordered on Monday, were roses of the *right* color delivered on Tuesday?' and (b) 'Given that red roses were ordered on Monday, do those who speak of the flowers on Tuesday use the word 'red' to describe them or do they, instead, say, 'These roses are *yellow*'?' Indeed, my whole *point* is that nonsense results from trying to make the meaning of (a) independent of (b). Had you understood this, you would also not have thought that I must allow that unwitting equivocations may occur when people reason using color words."

Why do we feel that this reply to the above objection fails to address the troublesome feature of Wittgenstein's account? We want to say that if someone were to ask whether the florist delivered roses of the right color, i.e., the color I ordered, this would be a question about the roses, one to be settled by looking at the roses (and, if need be, at a copy of my order) and so has nothing to do with several people *saying* the roses are red.

Wittgenstein was not insensitive to this objection, and in the *Investigations* he addressed it as follows:

"So you are saying that human agreement decides what is true and what is false?" It is what human beings *say* that is true and false. That is not agreement in opinions but in form of life (PI, §241).

Wittgenstein does not here disown what appears to be the implication of his view, namely, that if the roses are red it is because people *say* they are. Instead, he merely says: if people speak of the roses as being red, they are not of the (possibly false) *opinion* that "red" is the right word to use; rather, they all (unaccountably) *react* to the roses with the word "red." This does not, of course, answer the objection I have posed, but given his Humean metaphysics, Wittgenstein could make no other reply.

Wittgenstein says: "If there did not exist an agreement in what we call 'red,' etc. etc., language would stop" (RFM, p. 196). By considering two implications of this statement, we can bring into sharper focus Wittgenstein's view of the necessity of agreement in the use of words. One implication is that I would no longer be using color words if I and those with whom I converse ceased to agree in our color judgments. A second implication would seem to be that I could not go on keeping a diary or keeping a record of the weather if I were the sole survivor of a worldwide plague. What does Wittgenstein say about these two matters?

What Would Happen If Agreement Ceased?

He was addressing the first of these matters in his 1936 lectures when he said:

It seems as though, however the outward circumstances change, once the word is fastened to a particular personal experience it now retains its meaning; and that therefore I can now use it with sense whatever may happen. . . .

It seems [that], whatever the circumstances, I always know whether to apply the word or not. It seems, at first it was a move in a special game [in which we agreed in our use of the word] but then it becomes independent of this game. . . .

But can't the old game lose its point when the circumstances change, so that the expression ceases to have a meaning, although of course I can still pronounce it. . . .

We learn the word 'red' under particular circumstances. Certain objects are usually red, and keep their colors; most people agree with us in our color judgments. Suppose all this changes: I see blood, unaccountably sometimes one sometimes another color, and the people around me make different statements. But couldn't I in all this chaos retain my meaning of 'red,' 'blue,' etc., although I couldn't now make myself understood to anyone? Samples, e.g., would all constantly change their color – 'or does it only seem so to me?' "Now am I mad or did I really call this 'red' yesterday?" (NFL, p. 305–306).[17]

The aim of this passage is to show that it is a *mistake* to think that if agreement were to cease we could "retain the meaning of" color words.[18] In the *Investigations* Wittgenstein is addressing this issue when he says:

Does it make sense to say that people generally agree in their judgments of colour? What would it be like for them not to? One man would say a flower was red which another called blue, and so on. But what right should we have to call these people's words "red" and "blue" *our* colour-words? (PI, p. 226).

His point is that if we say that people generally agree in their judgments of color, we must not think that we are stating a matter of fact, so that their *not* doing so could be described by saying: "People might regularly *disagree* in their color judgments," as if they could still be using color words despite the lack of agreement. What are we to make of this?

In the first of the above passages Wittgenstein speaks of the 'chaos' he describes as coming about *unaccountably*. This confirms a point I made earlier in connection with the example from Oliver Sachs, namely, that Wittgenstein was obliged to say that whether or *not* we agree in the use of color words, there is no accounting for what we do. This is essential to his claim that we would no longer be using color words if our agreement were to cease. To see that this is so, let us set aside his Humean view of the world and represent the 'chaos' he describes as having an identifiable cause. Suppose, then, that an explosion occurs at a chemical plant, and a variety of caustic and toxic chemicals are released into the air, some of which affect the colors of things, while others have an effect on people's vision, sense of smell, and so on. Not all the employees are affected by the same chemicals, and so some people exhibit one sort of symptom and some other sorts. For example, when asked to sniff vinegar, some say it smells smoky, others say it smells like violets, while others say it smells like vinegar. Similarly, when shown a sheet of fresh typing paper, some say it's yellow, others say it's grey, and still others say it's white. Now it so happens that at the time of the explosion Harvey was wearing protective gear and so was not affected by any of the chemicals. In that case, of course, nothing has happened to Harvey to make him think that he can no longer determine whether something has changed color or only looks different to him now. If he encounters people who say that the sky is greenish, he can assure them that they're wrong, that their vision has been affected. ("The sky is as blue as ever," he assures them.) It might even be that everyone Harvey encounters thinks the sky is some color other than blue, so that there is no longer any agreement between him and the others. But that would not be a reason for Harvey to think that he had lost the ability to use color words. Nor would it be a reason for the others to think that they had lost that ability. In fact, if Harvey were a doctor attending these victims, he might make a quick assessment of each patient by asking him or her to tell him the color of the walls of his office. From his experience with cases of this sort he might know that those who say the walls are yellow have been affected by such-and-such a gas and require such-and-such an antidote, while those who say the walls are gray require a different antidote. In short, he would rely in this way on their color judgments.[19]

How, then, does Wittgenstein's story differ from mine in such as way as to warrant his thinking that the people in his story must think they have lost command of their color vocabulary? The difference lies in the way he thinks of the people in the story: because he has dismissed the idea that, in learning our colors, we have the capacity to *retain* what we've learned, he thinks of the people in his story as having a color vocabulary *only* insofar as they use color words *in agreement* with others. So when their agreement ceases, they must, he thinks, cease to have any command of color words.

To better understand Wittgenstein's thinking, let us consider how he would have regarded my account of the chemical plant explosion. I can imagine him protesting as follows:

If we could accept the Lockean view that memory is a mechanism that invariably provides us with the right word whenever we see a certain color, then your story might be unproblematic, i.e., there would be no problem about whether a person uses color words consistently over a stretch of time. But such a view of memory is untenable because it imbues mechanisms with causal necessity (see PI, §§191–197), and once we have dismissed the notion that there is in us a mechanism that *guarantees* our continued correct use of a word, we are confronted with the following puzzle: What is the difference between a person's using "blue" in a consistent way and his only *thinking* that he so uses it? In your story you provide no criterion by which to distinguish these. Perhaps you thought you had provided such a criterion by offering a causal explanation of why people began seeing different colors and smelling different smells and by then saying that Harvey, because he wore protective clothing, was unaffected by the chemicals. But here you are the unwitting captive of the causal point of view, and if you will put that aside, you will see why your story is flawed. For how is it to be decided that Harvey's color vision remained unchanged? It is no use your saying that the 'protective clothing' he wore had been tested and could be relied on to protect his vision, for all regularities are subject to breakdown, i.e., his color vision could have changed *unaccountably*. So your causal account doesn't solve the problem. But if you say that the proof of Harvey's unchanged color vision lies in the fact that, following the explosion, the walls of his office do not appear to him to have changed color, you must still address the challenge: What would show that his memory is not deceiving him? If you answer by saying that his office was not in the vicinity of the explosion, you are again assuming the causal point of view, i.e., assuming that things couldn't change color *causelessly*. So, you see, you have nowhere provided a criterion for distinguishing between Harvey's using "blue" in a consistent way and his only thinking he so uses it. And therefore you cannot tell a story like the one you tried to tell, i.e., a story about a man who goes on using color words over a stretch of time although he does not agree with others in his color judgments. By making it a story in which there is no agreement in the use of color words, you have left us with a story in which Harvey is no longer *saying* anything when he utters "blue," "red," etc.

We can see Wittgenstein making this kind of point in the following passage:

But what if the lack of agreement was not the exception but the rule? How should we think of that?
   Well, a rule [such as the ostensive definition of a color word] can lead me to an action only in the same sense as can any direction in words, for example, an order. And if people did not agree in their actions according to rules, and could not come to terms with one another [about, for example, the colors of things], that would be as if they could not come together about the sense of orders or descriptions [e.g., orders for meals in restaurants]. It would be a 'confusion of tongues,' and one could say that although all of them accompanied their actions with the uttering of sounds, nevertheless there was no language.[20]

Wittgenstein is here implying that, in my story, Harvey was not *saying* anything when he said to his co-workers, "The sky is as blue as ever."

We can now see why Wittgenstein insisted that if there is to be language there must be agreement in judgments. He thought of those who speak a language as having no capacity to learn and to *retain* what they have learned. Consequently, he thought that we are exercising no capacities when we speak or write. Accordingly, to escape Russell's skeptical problem, he was obliged to think that, if there is to be language, there must be several people who, not only make sounds or marks, but also agree in their reactions to one another, for in that case a reductionist account, in terms of agreement, can be given of their using words *correctly*. But, as we can now see, the 'agreement' he speaks of is an 'agreement' amongst a very strange cast of characters: they are beings who must be thought of very differently from the way we think of Harvey and of ourselves.[21]

The Impossibility of a Solitary Speaker

Let us turn now to the question whether one could continue keeping a diary if one were the last person on earth. Various passages quoted above, in which Wittgenstein says that there can be rules or language only where several people agree in their judgments, seem to imply that there *could* not be a solitary individual – e.g., the last person alive – who keeps a diary of some sort. Wittgenstein addressed this point as follows:

Could a solitary person calculate? Could a solitary person follow a rule?
Are these question perhaps like this one: 'Can a solitary person carry on a trade?' (RFM, §349).

In the *Investigations* (§§199 and 202) Wittgenstein makes his answer plain: in order for there to be rules that are followed, there must be more than one person involved. Wittgenstein did not, of course, mean that a person would give up reading and writing for his own pleasure if there were no longer anyone with whom to converse. He meant unless *several* people are involved language is *logically* impossible – as would be carrying on a trade. So there *could* not be a person who, once all other humans had died, went on keeping a diary or keeping records of the weather, etc.

This implication of Wittgenstein's view is highly counterintuitive. After all, here I am alone in my study writing: if everyone else suddenly perished, why should it be that, at that very moment, what I'm doing ceases to be *writing*? We have seen why Wittgenstein was committed to this strange conclusion. Locke thought of people as learning to speak a language and as *retaining* what they had learned, so that, as I sit here alone in my study, I am (provided I don't suffer a massive stroke) *able* to read and write. On Locke's view this is a genuine capacity and not something I would lose because everyone else perished.[22] Because Wittgenstein's metaphysics forced him to reject the Lockean view, he was obliged to invent his own account of what it is to use words correctly, and the account he settled on included the necessity of using words in agreement with others.

As I said above, this conclusion is counterintuitive. It conflicts with the way we all think of people and their linguistic capacities. For this reason *soi-disant* Wittgensteinians have tried to save him from this conclusion in two ways. Some have claimed that Wittgenstein's only point about agreement is this: a person who is *now* alone in the world could keep a diary, etc., but only if, in the *past*, he was part of a community in which there was agreement in the use of words. Others have gone further and insisted that Wittgenstein simply did *not* hold the view that agreement with other speakers is a necessary condition for using words correctly, for his *only* requirement is that a person use words in a *regular* way, and therefore he would have allowed that a person could follow a rule even if he had *never* been in communication with others. Let us consider these defenses of Wittgenstein in order.

The first of these is typified by Norman Malcolm, who says that Wittgenstein saw no problem about a solitary speaker (or writer), provided this person is like Defoe's Robinson Crusoe, who grew up and acquired his native tongue in a community of other speakers. Why is there no problem? Because, says Malcolm:

> Most of us follow rules when we are alone. I calculate my income tax alone. I write letters, read, think, when I am alone. I was brought up in the English language and carry it with me wherever I go. If I were shipwrecked, like Robinson Crusoe, on an uninhabited island, I would retain (for a time at least) my knowledge of English and of counting and arithmetic.[23]

Malcolm thinks that with such an explanation he can render Wittgenstein's position plausible, and yet he is here obviously resorting to *just* the sort of explanation Wittgenstein meant to reject. In saying that he carries his language with him wherever he goes and that even on an uninhabited island he "would retain" his knowledge of English, Malcolm talks as though he had a (genuine) power of retention. But anyone who thinks of the matter in this way is fundamentally at odds with Wittgenstein and cannot see what led to all of his wrestling with the problem of following a rule.

The second of the aforementioned defenses of Wittgenstein is presented by G. P. Baker and P. M. S. Hacker. They insist that Wittgenstein found nothing amiss in the idea that an individual could follow a rule *entirely* by himself, provided that, over a period of time, he engages in a 'regular practice.'[24] Their misunderstanding arises from two sources. Like Malcolm, they fail to see that Wittgenstein *rejects* the Lockean view that a speaker can *retain* what he learned as a child or the meanings of words he has invented for himself. In addition, they fail to realize that, for Wittgenstein, there is a problem about the *regularity* of a practice, a problem he thought could be solved only by (a) requiring that several people use words in agreement when they *speak to one another* and (b) giving a reductionist (or 'relativistic') account of "using 'red' in the *same* way on successive occasions." As a result of this dual misunderstanding they undertake to expound Wittgenstein's view by saying that if we were to observe a man who has never had contact with others, *we* might find that he is following a rule, e.g., always uses a sign in the *same* way. But here they are assuming something Wittgenstein would not allow, namely, that *we* have a capacity for recognizing that someone always calls the *same* color "red." Like Malcolm, these authors have failed to understand Wittgenstein's problem.[25]

How the *Investigations* Differs from the *Tractatus*

We can now see how Wittgenstein's later view differed from the Tractarian view that each color word is *correlated* with a particular color. In 1930, before Wittgenstein had abandoned his earlier view, he said: "If I use a symbol I must be committing myself. . . . If I say this is green, I must say that *other green things* are green too. I am committed to a future usage" (WL32, p. 37, emphasis added). Within a few months Wittgenstein had come to think that this made no sense. The difference between his early and later views can be brought out by imagining an advocate of the Tractarian view to protest as follows: "In Wittgenstein's later view, the words 'red' and 'blue' are not really names of *colors*, for in fact they are nothing more than sounds which (a) are used with a certain grammar (e.g., we say, 'I *see* that it's red,' but not 'I *smell* that it's red,' and say, 'It's *red* all over,' but not, 'It's *triangular* all over'); and (b) are used in agreement with others. But these words are not really *connected* to anything in the world, whereas to be names of colors such words would have to be connected to *colors* and each name connected to a *particular* color." How might the later Wittgenstein have responded to this?

He would have been quite ready to agree with part of this, namely, that on his view color words are *not* connected with 'the world.' As I remarked at the beginning of the chapter, this is a point that he made as early as 1932 when, in his conversations with Waismann, he said that when he wrote the *Tractatus* he had mistakenly "thought that there was 'a connection between language and reality'" (WVC, pp. 209–210).[26] In *Philosophical Grammar* Wittgenstein remarks:

One is inclined to make a distinction between rules of grammar that set up 'a connection between language and reality' and those that do not. A rule of the first kind is 'this colour is called "red"' ' – a rule of the second kind is '~~p = p' (PG, p. 89).

Commenting on this supposed distinction, he says: "The connection between 'language and reality' is made by definitions of words, and these belong to grammar, so that language remains self-contained and autonomous" (PG, p. 97). So Wittgenstein would have responded to the objection formulated above by acknowledging that on his later view a word such as "red" is not 'connected to the world' by ostension (or by anything else). Here, then, we find him most explicitly repudiating the *Tractatus* view that color words are 'correlated' with objects and 'represent' them. On his new view of the matter, the correct use of "red" (and also the correct use of the phrase "remained the same color") is governed only by the agreement in our color judgments, not by systematic correlation with features of the world. But he would have insisted that this does not disqualify "red," "blue," etc. from being color words, since words having the *grammar* that these words have are, after all, what we *call* "names of colors." As he puts it: "To call a thing a colour is to say it obeys certain grammatical rules" (WL32, p. 47). He might have responded to the foregoing objection by saying: If you think there is some *other* way a word could be used, one in which it would be correlated with something in experience, then you owe us an account of how that is possible, but don't think that you can do so by invoking the Lockean account of language, for I have blocked that route.

Exemplars and Rules

A final point must be made here. Locke says: "He that knows once that whiteness is the name of that colour he has observed in snow or milk, will not be apt to misapply that word, as long as he retains that idea" (III, iv, 15). He would no doubt have given a similar account of other color words – saying, perhaps, that he that once knows that "black" is the name of the color he has observed in a lump of coal will not be apt to misapply the word. But thinking of color words in this way ignores the great variety of the things we say. Locke makes his account seem plausible because he speaks of colors as being *simple* ideas, which suggests that he was thinking that we learn color words by associating them with the colors found in a child's paint box, and when we are told to paint a red flower or a red ball, we do so by painting with the paint labeled "red." But the actual use of color words is not like this. For if we are told to paint a girl with red hair or a blushing boy with a red face, we would not be doing as we were told if we painted the hair or the blushing face by simply applying the red paint. Similarly, if a police report describes a suspect as a white male, it is not being said that the man was the color of fresh snow. And if I tell someone that I was struck by a door and have a black eye, I am not saying that my eye is the color of coal. Locke's account does not hint at, nor does it seem able to accommodate, the complexity in the use of color words. How could an exemplar of black help me with the use of "black" in these phrases: "two black cats," "a tall black man," and "a black eye"?

But this is only the beginning of the problem. For suppose I am driving and my passenger says to me, "Follow that red car." On a Lockean view, will I know what to do? If, as he has it, I learned the word "red" by associating it with an exemplar of red, that exemplar would have a certain hue, intensity, and saturation. Must I then obey my passenger's instructions by looking for a car whose color has precisely that hue, intensity, and saturation? If so, I would probably search in vain for a car of the right color, even if the car ahead of me was dark red. But this is not, of course, what I would actually do. I would follow the dark red car.[27]

It is not only Locke's account that runs afoul of these difficulties, for the idea that in learning a color word we learn a *rule* seems to run afoul of them also. Wittgenstein said: "If I have once grasped a rule I am bound in what I do further" (RFM, p. 328). If that were true, how would we have come to speak of someone as drinking red wine or having red hair or a black eye? Here one might think that at least this much is true: if I've been shown a color and told that it's called "green," then whenever I want to describe something of *that* color, I will do so by using "green." But this ignores the variety of contexts in which we use color words, for, as I point out at the beginning of this chapter (note 3), if my wife were wearing a green dress, I might, if she were standing with others wearing dresses of various shades of green, point her out to someone by saying, "She's the one wearing the emerald dress." The idea that there are rules of language that dictate what we are to say seems as far off the mark as the idea that we are guided by exemplars. If this does damage to the philosophical notion of semantics, then so much the worse for semantics.

Notes

1. This view of what memory involves comes out nicely in what Locke says about birds mimicking tunes they have heard played on a pipe. That they endeavor in several attempts "to hit the notes right," says Locke, "put it past doubt with me, that they . . . retain ideas in their memory, and use them for patterns." For it cannot be reasonably supposed, he says, that birds could "approach their notes nearer and nearer to a tune played yesterday" unless there is, as they *now* sing, "a pattern for them to imitate" (II, x, 10).

2. Thus, he says: "I can produce a certain patch and say 'this is red.' This is a rule of grammar" (LSD, p. 25) and ". . . when we learn the meaning of a word, we are often given *only* the single rule, the ostensive definition" (PG, p. 61).

3. It should be noted that both Locke and Wittgenstein present a highly artificial picture of our use of words, including color words. They neglect the fact that our choice of a color word depends on a great many contextual factors. For example, whether I point out my wife across the room by saying, "She's the woman over there wearing the green dress," or say, instead, "She's the woman over there wearing the aquamarine dress," will depend on such things as whether I am speaking to a dress designer or a small child, whether in the direction in which I point there are two women, one wearing an aquamarine and the other a jade or emerald dress, and so on. Yet both Locke and Wittgenstein talk as though, in this situation, the word "green" would spring automatically to my lips.

4. Wittgenstein, in his discussions of "following a rule," concentrated on color words for the following reason. His idea in the *Tractatus* had been that the common nouns of our language (e.g., "chair") are reducible, via a chain of

definitions, to words that cannot be further defined and that this reducibility eliminates (as he later put it) "any vagueness in logic" (PI, §101). Colors words are among those supposed to be at the bedrock of language. (Wittgenstein speaks of them as "the signs one wants to call 'primary' " (PG, p. 90). Compare PI, §258, where he says of the name of a sensation, "I will remark first of all that a definition of the sign cannot be formulated.") In his post-*Tractatus* years he came to think that his earlier ideal was misguided, and accordingly we find him saying: "Nor would these questions [about what you mean by words such as "Moses" and "Egypt"] come to an end when we got down to words like 'red', 'dark', 'sweet' " (PI, §87). His discussion of color words, then, was meant to expose the error in the *Tractatus* view. Later, he introduced a subsidiary problem about other words, such as "cube" (see PI, §§74 and 139). This version of the problem, which is that discussed by Saul Kripke in *Wittgenstein on Rules and Private Language* (Cambridge: Harvard University Press, 1982), is predicated on the idea that any rule can always be interpreted in various ways. I have omitted discussion of this version of the problem for the following reason. If one asks what is supposed to be meant by "A rule *can* always be interpreted in various ways," it won't do to say that a *philosopher can always invent* various interpretations, for the problem is meant to hold for anyone who is taught a word. What must be meant, then, is that the plain man (or child) *can*, without philosophical design, always interpret a rule in various ways (or at least in some nonstandard way). But how is it to be shown that this is *true*? Surely this cannot be shown by a philosopher merely *saying* of an imaginary child: "We can *imagine* that he, instead of doing so-and-so, does such-and-such." And yet this is just how Wittgenstein himself proceeds (see PI, §§143–144). The same is true of Kripke. Neither of them, that is, makes any attempt to work out *in detail* what it would be like for someone with a certain kind of history to interpret a rule (or explanation) in a nonstandard way. And if one does try to work this out in detail, the idea becomes implausible. There is, however, a reason why Wittgenstein approached the matter as he did: his Humean metaphysics allowed him to think that humans, no less than inanimate objects, could *unaccountably* behave in unheard-of ways, and this allowed him to think that a case of such behavior can be described without supplying details that make a coherent story. And Kripke, it seems to me, shares this view. (See notes 8 and 20, below, for comments related to this point.) I will, however, say this much for Kripke: he understands Wittgenstein's problem better than those (e.g. Malcolm, Dilman, and Mounce) who have complained of his failure to appreciate the relevance of Wittgenstein's saying in PI, §201 that "there is a way of grasping a rule which is *not* an *interpretation*." What Kripke's critics have failed to see is that when *this* version of his problem is dispatched, Wittgenstein is still faced with the version of it that I discuss in this chapter. In consequence, they fail to see what Kripke (ibid., pp. 66–67) sees very clearly, namely, that Wittgenstein is offering a "sceptical solution" to the problem when he insists that language requires that there be several people who agree in their use of words. (See my discussion, below, of Malcolm's view.)

5. *The Analysis of Mind*, op. cit., pp. 158–159.

6. In the notes he made for his 1936 lectures Wittgenstein posed the skeptical problem as follows: "What if someone asked: 'How do I know that what I call seeing red isn't an *entirely* different experience every time? and that I am deluded into thinking that it is the same or nearly the same?' " (NFL, p. 279). Commenting on this, he wrote: "Is it ever true that when I call a

colour 'red' I make use of memory??" (Unfortunately, this is one of the remarks Rush Rhees omitted when he edited the notes for publication.) I take it that Wittgenstein is suggesting that (a) it is a mistake to think that memory is involved in the use of color words and (b) it is this mistaken idea that would lead one to pose the skeptical problem.

7. I have adopted a version of the Ogden translation of this sentence.

8. Why does Wittgenstein make the odd remark that "what a mechanism does does not *follow* from what it is"? The answer lies in his view that the only necessity is *logical* necessity. This led him to think that a philosopher who, like Locke, invokes a mechanism to account for our using a word consistently must think of this mechanism in an odd way: it must provide (what is plainly impossible) a *logical* guarantee that the word will be used always in the same way. This is why, in explaining the notion of a mental mechanism, he says: "Our notion of it is of a mechanism from the existence of which it *follows* [i.e., follows *logically*] that we will use a general word in this way or that way" (WL35, p. 83). In the *Investigations* (§193), he turned this into the idea of "the machine as symbol." The irony is that, in debunking this idea, what he is debunking is nothing that a Lockean is committed to but is rather the Lockean account *as it looked to Wittgenstein* when he viewed it through his Humean presuppositions. (Recall his remark, quoted above from the *Tractatus*, that a person's future actions could be known now "only if causality were an *inner* necessity like that of logical inference.") In PI, §§139–237 Wittgenstein sets up as the target of his criticism the idea of (what he calls) "logical compulsion" (PI, §140) or of being "logically determined" (PI, §220), but in doing so, he was conjuring up a red herring, for the Lockean view requires no such idea.

9. This has been frequently overlooked in discussions of Wittgenstein, especially (see below) by Norman Malcolm, G. P. Baker, and P. M. S. Hacker.

10. In the *Investigations* Wittgenstein remarks: "This table [with color words written opposite samples] might be said to take over the role of memory and association in other cases" (§53).

11. "Wittgenstein on Language and Rules," *Philosophy*, 64, 1989, p. 14. Elsewhere, in speaking of "the human agreement that is so fundamental for the concept of a rule," Malcolm writes: "Can it be explained? Is there something, even more basic, that could be appealed to as an explanation? I should say, no.... This human agreement... is a particularly apt illustration of Wittgenstein's remark: 'What has to be accepted, the given, is – one could say – *forms of life*.' (PI, p. 226)" (*Nothing is Hidden*, op. cit., p. 159).

12. *The Man Who Mistook His Wife for a Hat* (New York: Summit Books, 1985), p. 9.

13. In his 1947 lectures Wittgenstein said that it would be a mistake to think that if one man has learned French and another has not, there must be some difference between their brains (WL47, p. 330).

14. I have slightly altered the translation of the italicized phrase. The German reads "*was auch wir*." Although "*was*" can be translated as either "what" or "whatever," the latter is required in this case to capture Wittgenstein's meaning. For he clearly did *not* intend that we should take the sentence in question to mean "He learns to call 'red' that color which we too (always) call 'red'."

15. That this *is* Wittgenstein's solution becomes evident in PI, §270, where he says: "And what is our reason for calling 'S' the name of ... a 'particular sensation,' that is, the same one every time? Well, aren't we supposing that we write 'S' every time?" He is saying that the phrase "a particular sensa-

tion" is to be explained, not in terms of correctly *identifying* a sensation, but merely in terms of one's repeatedly *using the same sign,* "S." This will be discussed in the next chapter.

16. Because his relativized account will seem *from a Lockean perspective* to tolerate such unwitting equivocations, Wittgenstein says that his account "seems to abolish logic" (PI, §242). He immediately adds: "but does not do so," thus dismissing the Lockean perspective.

17. Elsewhere Wittgenstein makes the same point about such words as "sweet" and "sour":

> If people were (suddenly) to stop agreeing with each other in their judgments about tastes – would I still say: At any rate, each one knows what taste he's having? Wouldn't it then become clear that this is nonsense? (RPP, II, §347).

18. Wittgenstein's point is *not,* of course, that one has the power of retention if and only if others agree with one's color judgments – as if one could be stripped of a genuine capacity by a change in one's "outward circumstances." Rather, he means: because there *cannot be* such a thing as the power of retention, the agreement of our color judgments is the *only* thing that distinguishes our using color words from our merely making noises.

19. A similar point could be made about the account Oliver Sachs gives of the patient who, because of brain dysfunction, mistook his foot for his shoe: there was no reason for Sachs to think that *he* was losing his grip on the words "shoe" and "foot." Nor would the case be different if a plague had wiped out the earth's human population, except for Oliver Sachs and three of his patients, all of whom had suffered brain damage of the same sort as the patient Sachs described in the passage quoted above.

20. Quoted and translated by Norman Malcolm in "Wittgenstein on Language and Rules," op. cit., p. 8. Malcolm is quoting from Wittgenstein's MS 165, pp. 93–94.

21. The same must be said of the 'pupils' in Wittgenstein's arithmetic examples (PI, §§143–145 and 185) who exhibit what he calls an "abnormal reaction" to the teaching they receive. Wittgenstein intends that we should regard these 'reactions' as inexplicable (see PI, §144). They are, in short, what I have called "metaphysical nightmares." Plainly, he is invoking the notion of 'logical possibilities.' So these examples are pieces of pure metaphysics and do not deserve serious consideration.

22. To take such a view, one need not embrace a full-blown Lockean account of language, including his story about ideas as exemplars. What is needed is only that we not think of the world as indeterministic and allow that human beings have the capacity to learn. In order to allow that we have such a capacity, we must also, as we saw in the preceding chapter, set aside the Humean—Wittgensteinian idea that a person is a bundle or collection of impressions in perpetual flux.

23. "Wittgenstein on Language and Rules," op. cit., p. 17.

24. *Scepticism, Rules and Language,* (Oxford: Blackwell), 1985, esp. pp. 10–27. One result of this misinterpretation is that they fail to see (pp. 21 and 25) that in PI, §202 the word "privately" means "all by oneself."

25. Kripke, in *Wittgenstein on Rules and Private Language* (op. cit.), offers the following odd interpretation of Wittgenstein's position. The isolated Crusoe can (by us) *be said* to follow rules (p. 110), but whether he *does* follow rules is a matter Wittgenstein does not address because "Wittgenstein has no theory of truth conditions" (p. 111). I can find no warrant for such an

interpretation. In any case, Kripke seems not to recognize that this problem about Crusoe arises for Wittgenstein because of his Humean metaphysics and that the problem simply does not exist for those who eschew this feature of Wittgenstein's philosophy.

26. The editor of these notes, Brian McGuinness, appends a footnote to this passage in which he says that there is reason to believe that this topic came up in the conversation because of Rudolf Carnap's article "Die Physikalische Sprache als Universalsprache der Wissenschaft," published in 1931, in which Carnap maintained that "ostensive definition remains within language."

27. For a much more adequate treatment of these matters, see Frank Ebersole, "Seeing Red in Red Things" in *Things We Know*, op. cit., pp. 3–17.

19

The Private Language Argument

In *Philosophical Investigations* Wittgenstein poses the question whether there could be a language which is private in the sense that "the individual words of this language . . . refer to what can only be known to the person speaking; to his immediate private sensations," so that "another person cannot understand the language" (PI, §243). He goes on to argue that there cannot be any such use of words. What Wittgenstein means to criticize here is an idea that is at home in a dualistic view of the world, namely, that whenever I speak of the contents of my mind, I alone can know what I am speaking of. Wolfgang Kohler, himself a dualist, stated the idea as follows:

What is our evidence for assuming that under given conditions the ultimate data of experience are the same for several persons? Unfortunately, we shall never know whether or not this is the case. . . . We have no proof of agreement even in cases in which all imaginable tests give identical results such as precisely the same verbal reports. One person may always report "red" where another person also says "red." Still we know only that the first person has throughout a constant quality wherever and whenever the second person talks about red. We do not know that the first person has the same quality as is called red by the second person. Nor does it help us that what one person calls red seems to have the same exciting character as another person finds in what he calls red. For they may not use the term "exciting" with the same meaning, and actually have different experiences while their expressions are the same.[1]

Kohler takes it to be unproblematic that whenever a person uses "red" to describe what he sees, there is "throughout a constant quality" which he calls "red." He would no doubt have said that once a person has associated the word "red" with a color, he can go on using it always as the name of the *same* color. And if asked how one could do this, he would perhaps have said that one's memory retains the meaning of the words one uses. This would be in agreement with Locke, who, as noted in the preceding chapter, held that each of us is speaking a private language, since the meanings of one's words can be known only to oneself. This is the idea Wittgenstein meant to criticize.

The Relevance of the Argument

Before considering his argument, it will be useful to review an important point. Wittgenstein, by embracing pure realism, came to reject the idea that colors are private (see PI, §§273–277). He held that we can see that we are in agreement with another person in his use of "red" by seeing what he points to when he says, for example, "I would like a dozen of these red roses." And children are taught color words by being shown samples (PG, p. 83). "Red," says Wittgenstein, "can be pointed to. 'Red' is taught by public pointing – to a common object" (WL47, p. 269). Accordingly, Wittgenstein would have dismissed what Kohler says about "red." But what about such words as "tickle" and "itch" and "pain"? These words are not taught by public pointing. So it might seem that if "pain" were substituted for "red" in Kohler's account, Wittgenstein would have to accept the conclusion that no one knows what another calls "pain." As Wittgenstein himself says,

When I have a sample of red, then if you ask me "Well, what *does* 'red' mean?", I can answer "It means *this*." In the case of toothache, the temptation is to say "Well, I know, although I can't express it." There is a suggestion that [unlike the case of red] you have a private ostensive definition [of toothache] (LSD, p. 36).[2]

Were such a view to prevail, it would have grave consequences for Wittgenstein's entire philosophy. For if bodily sensations are private, then other people cannot be merely 'perceptual bodies.' In addition to their bodies, and the behavior of their bodies, they may have private episodes of pain and itching and dizziness and also private thoughts and emotions. But if that is conceivable, then the skepticism Wittgenstein had battled since the days of his pre-*Tractatus* notebooks would have got its foot in the door, for it would mean that we can understand hypotheses which would be unverifiable, such as the hypothesis that what you call "pain" is what I call "tickling." Furthermore, if Wittgenstein had to allow that a dualistic ontology is logically possible, he could no longer remain secure in his defense of pure realism, including his version of behaviorism.

It was therefore imperative that Wittgenstein mount a direct attack on the idea that pains and tickles are private objects. How did he go about this?

He did so in several ways, some which we have considered in earlier chapters. (i) He maintained that sensations have no owners, i.e., that such phrases as "*my* headache" and "*your* headache" are misleading forms of words. So we cannot, he reasoned, hold that pains are private, if this is to be explained by saying, "I can't feel your headache, and you can't feel mine" (PI, §§246–253; see also PG, p. 129). (ii) His second way of dismissing the idea of private objects was to offer a behavioristic account of such third-person statements as "She's dizzy" and "He's in great pain": we have behavioral criteria for another person's being dizzy or in pain. So it is a muddle to say that pains are private if this is to be explained by saying, "I can know that I'm in pain, but I can't know whether you are" (PI, §246). (iii) As we saw in the previous chapter, Wittgenstein maintained (PI, §§138–242) that even in the case of color words it is essential that there be a community of people who agree in their color judgments, for it is only such agreement that distinguishes the *words* "red" and "green" from mere noises. It follows that one cannot rightly think, as dualists do, both that bodily sensations are private and that one can give them names, for giving names to *private* objects would require the impossible, namely, using these names even if there is *not* agreement in the judgments in which these names occur. And from this it follows, in turn, that if it is allowed that "pain" is a *word* (not a piece of gibberish), it cannot be the name of something private (or inner).

One might think that Wittgenstein, having made these three points, would have felt that he had adequately defended neutral monism as a bulwark against skepticism. Yet he saw that he could not rest content here, for he could imagine someone wanting to defend the idea that sensations are private by saying: Since there are no *public samples* of pain or tickling, each of us knows only from his own case what he calls "pain" or "tickling," i.e., one can, as it were, look into oneself and see what these words stand for (see PI, §§293 and 295). This, then, is the crux of the matter. If this counterargument were left unanswered, dualists might think that major parts of Wittgenstein's philosophy could be called into question. Accordingly, he undertook to show that this counterargument is indefensible.

Wittgenstein went about this in three steps, two of which we will consider in this chapter, leaving the third step to the chapter which follows. The first step is essentially a repetition of the argument he had given against the idea that one could undertake to use color words privately, i.e., all by oneself. The second part of his argument is designed to show that in speaking of pains and tickles we are not speaking of private objects. The third part of his argument offers an alternative account of the 'grammar' of sensation words.

The Private Language Argument

As remarked above, Kohler takes it to be unproblematic that although none of us knows what another calls "red," we do know that for each of us there is "throughout a constant quality" whenever one describes something as being red. Presumably, he would have said the same of "pain" and "tickle." He would have said that although what he calls "pain" may differ from what others call "pain," there can be no doubt about whether what he calls "pain" on various occasions is always the same thing. And had he been asked to explain why there can be no doubt about this, it is likely that he, like Locke, would have alluded to the capacity of human beings to *retain* what they have learned. In the preceding chapter we saw Wittgenstein attacking this idea as regards the word "red." Because he rejected the very idea of intellectual powers, he was obliged to abandon the Tractarian idea that color words are "correlated" with colors. The first part of his private language argument is aimed at philosophers who, like Locke, hold that a word such as "pain" is correlated with a certain sensation. He states this part of his argument as follows:

> Let us imagine the following case. I want to keep a diary about the recurrence of a certain sensation. To this end I associate it with the sign "S" and write this sign in a calendar for every day on which I have the sensation. I will remark first of all that a definition of the sign cannot be formulated. But still I can give myself a kind of ostensive definition. How? Can I point to the sensation? Not in the ordinary sense [where I point to a 'public' object]. But I speak, or write the sign down, and at the same time I concentrate my attention on the sensation – and so, as it were, point to it inwardly. But what is this ceremony for? for that is all it seems to be! A definition surely serves to establish the meaning of a sign. Well, that is done precisely by the concentrating of my attention; for in this way I impress on myself the connexion between the sign and the sensation. But "I impress it on myself" can only mean: this process brings it about that I remember the connexion *right* in the future. But in the present case I have no criterion of correctness. One would like to say: whatever is going to seem right to me is right. And that only means that here we can't talk about 'right' (PI, §258).

The argument here is the following. To think that one could undertake to use the name of a 'private object' with regularity, i.e., always as the name of the *same* thing, one would have to think that one could remember the sensation, just as, for example, in naming the puppies in a large litter, one has to remember which dog goes with which name. In the case of the puppies, one could forget and the next time call Rover "Biff" and Biff "Rover." This might come to light by other people reminding me of the puppies' names or by my noticing the description of the pups that I had written, when I named them, on their AKC registration forms. But if one thinks sensations are private, how is one to explain the difference between remembering the sensation right the next time and not doing so? Other people could not correct me, for they could not know which sensation I had given the name to, and there is nothing I could write down that would serve later to show which sensation I had given the name to. That being so, the very idea of *correctly* remembering the sensation on subsequent occasions is a muddle. But in that case there would be no difference between using the name correctly on successive occasions and using it in a merely random fashion. And that means that it could not really be a name at all.[3]

Later in the *Investigations* Wittgenstein says: "Always get rid of the idea of the private object in this way: suppose that it constantly changes, but that you do not notice the change because your memory constantly deceives you" (PI, p. 207). Plainly, Wittgenstein is not proposing here something he takes to be a real possibility (see PI, §271). Rather, he is proposing a conundrum for the dualist: if you think you can again and again *recognize* a private object, how do you distinguish between (a) its constantly changing while you think it's the same and (b) correctly recognizing it? He means to imply that since one cannot distinguish these, it makes no sense to speak of correctly recognizing it.[4]

To understand what Wittgenstein saw in this argument, it will be useful to consider how the passage quoted above from PI §258 might have struck Locke. We needn't introduce here his notion that memory requires 'ideas' (exemplars). But bearing in mind that he thought of memory as a capacity, we can imagine him replying that the capacity to remember things is not so selective that it is reasonable to suggest that, although one has a good memory for most things, one may have a bad memory just for sensations. In short, Locke would have been utterly perplexed by Wittgenstein's argument.

What I mean to bring out by means of this observation is that Wittgenstein did not intend that §258 should be regarded as standing by itself as a cogent argument. On the contrary, in advancing this argument, he was plainly assuming that in PI §§138–242 he had successfully shown that (contrary to Locke) there *are* no intellectual powers, including the power of retention (the capacity to learn). So as an answer to the question whether there can be a private language, §258 is the culmination of an argument that begins with §138. And Wittgenstein's answer is that there cannot be a private language because a language user cannot rightly be credited with a capacity of retention which would enable him to refer to the same sensation (Kohler's 'constant quality') on successive occasions.

Wittgenstein's 'Relativism'

The passage quoted above from PI §258 begins with Wittgenstein saying: "Let us imagine the following case. I want to keep a diary about the recurrence of a certain sensation." Now let us ask: Did he intend, in the remainder of the passage, to argue that one *cannot* keep a diary about the recurrence of a certain sensation? It might seem so. After all, if his argument depends on his having dismissed the very idea of retention, it might seem that he has no way of making sense of the phrase "recurrence of a certain sensation." This was not, however, the way Wittgenstein saw the matter. In PI §§270–271 he presents his alternative. §270 begins as follows:

Let us now imagine a use for the entry of the sign "S" in my diary. I discover that whenever I have a particular sensation a manometer shews that my blood-pressure rises. So I shall be able to say that my blood-pressure is rising without using any apparatus. This is a useful result. And now it seems quite indifferent whether I have recognized the sensation *right* or not. Let us suppose I regularly identify it wrong, it does not matter in the least. And that alone shews that the hypothesis that I make a mistake is mere show.

At first sight this passage seems to contain an inconsistency. For it begins with Wittgenstein supposing that he discovers that whenever he has "a *particular* sensation" his blood pressure rises, but he then goes on to say that it does not matter in the least whether he correctly identifies the sensation. But how could he have discovered that a rise in his blood pressure is correlated with a *particular* sensation if, as he says, he "regularly identifies it wrong"? His point is this: each time he writes "S" in his diary his blood pressure is found (by use of the manometer) to have risen. So what gets *correlated* with the manometer reading is his *writing "S" in his diary* and *not* with something that "S" stands for. He makes his meaning explicit when he continues the passage as follows:

And what is our reason for calling "S" the name of a sensation here? Perhaps the kind of way this sign is employed in this language-game. – And why a "particular sensation," that is, the same one every time? Well, aren't we supposing that we write "S" every time?

So Wittgenstein seeks to remove the apparent inconsistency by saying that the phrase "whenever I have a particular sensation" is to be explained, not in terms of correctly *identifying* a sensation, but rather in terms of one's repeatedly *using the same sign*, "S." Thus, Wittgenstein says: "I do not, of course, identify my sensation by criteria; rather, I use the same expression [*iche gebrauche den gleichen Ausdruck*]" (PI, §290).[5] Here we find Wittgenstein invoking the 'relativism' which, in Chapter 18, we found him invoking in his remarks about using "red" according to a rule: he gets around the problem of memory skepticism by abandoning the Tractarian view that a name is "correlated" with an object.

The wording of the next passage, PI §271, is instructive in this regard. Wittgenstein writes:

"Imagine a person whose memory could not retain *what* the word 'pain' meant – so that he constantly called different things by that name – but nevertheless used the word in a way fitting in with the usual symptoms and presuppositions of pain" – in short he uses it as we all do. Here I should like to say: a wheel that can be turned though nothing else moves with it, is not part of the mechanism.

The first part of this passage, placed within quotation marks, presents the memory skepticism to which, as Wittgenstein sees it, a dualist must succumb. Wittgenstein's own view, by contrast, is that remembering, whether correctly or incorrectly, *does not come in at all*. It is the role dualists, such as Locke, assign to memory that is (given the force of Russell's skeptical argument regarding the past) "a wheel that can be turned though nothing else moves with it" and is therefore "not part of the mechanism," i.e., plays no role in the use of "pain." And when this idle wheel is eliminated, what remains in the use of the word "pain" is only that we use it, as he says, "in a way fitting in with the usual symptoms and presuppositions of pain." This means that when we tell someone we are in pain and are asked, "Where do you hurt?" we will point to some part of our body, that we tell people we have a headache to get them to bring us an aspirin or stop playing the piano so loudly, that when someone asks about our groaning we say, "My head hurts," not "My head itches," and so on.

Assessing Wittgenstein's Argument

Let us now consider whether Wittgenstein's argument in §258 is one that merits acceptance. As I pointed out above, Wittgenstein, in advancing this argument, was assuming that in PI §§138–242 he had successfully shown that there are no intellectual powers, including the power of retention (the capacity to learn). Yet, as we saw in Chapters 16 and 17, his argument to this effect depends in an essential way on his empiricist view of what a person is, namely, a procession of unrelated phenomenal states, so that there is nothing to *retain* any lesson from the past. Accordingly, his argument in PI §258 will carry no weight with philosophers who do not share his empiricist view of what a person is and, hence, his view of intellectual powers. It might seem, moreover, that one could refute Wittgenstein's position by means of a fairly ordinary example. Consider the following.

When I was a child, I was regularly taken to a dentist whose office was on the tenth floor of a tall building. The building had an elevator, and I hated descending in it because its rapid descent brought on an unpleasant sensation that welled up from my abdomen. It was unlike anything I had ever felt. I did not cry out, and, as my parents were of a stoic cast of mind, I made no complaint. Moreover, since none of the other passengers in the elevator complained, I thought I might be alone in suffering this peculiar distress. But even now – many years later – I can still remember that sensation, and it would be implausible to think that if I were now to descend in an elevator, I could be mistaken about the sensation if I said to myself, "Oh, how I dreaded this sensation when I was a child!"

In the *Investigations*, §258 is preceded by a passage in which Wittgenstein entertains the suggestion that a child who showed no "outward signs" of a sensation might "invent a name for it" (PI, §257). And he goes on to suggest that this is a hopelessly muddled idea. Yet there seems to be no difficulty in thinking that, as a child, I might have given a name to the sensation I experienced in the elevator – perhaps, "zing." One day, while waiting for the elevator, I might have said to myself, "Oh, I'm going to have zing again." And following the next visit to the dentist, I might have said to myself as the elevator began to fall, "Here comes zing again!" Also, if I had been taken to a carnival where I saw people riding a roller coaster, I might have said to myself, "I'm not going to ride on that. It would be zingier than the elevator." And years later, when descending in an elevator, I might say to myself, "Elevators *still* give me a zing!"

The fact that we can construct an example such as this would seem sufficient to show that there is something fundamentally wrong with Wittgenstein's argument.[6] But what might Wittgenstein have said had he been presented with such an example? Two things seem quite clear. First, he could not accept the example as I have presented it, for in doing so he would be admitting that his argument in PI §258 – and, indeed, his entire attack on intellectual powers – is fatally flawed. Second, to rescue his argument from this apparent counterexample, he would very likely have insisted that my example contains misleading forms of words, which need to be interpreted in a way consistent with his argument, i.e., in such a way that we are not led to think that the word "zing" and its cognates are used to refer to (in Kohler's phrase) a 'constant quality.'

Given that Wittgenstein would, very likely, have reacted in this way to my example, it is evident that it would not be sound philosophical procedure to hold up this example – and others like it – as a refutation of his argument. Instead, one must try, as I have in the preceding chapters, to trace Wittgenstein's thinking on this matter back to its source in empiricism. Even so, the very fact that it is possible to present in plausible fashion an example such as mine goes to show why dualists have reacted with disbelief when confronted with Wittgenstein's private language argument. Let us review the dualist's position.

A dualist, because he separates minds from bodies and holds that even bodily sensations are properly affairs of the mind, is obliged to think that we cannot know whether there is any similarity between what different people feel when they descend in an elevator or sit on a tack.[7] The dualist, then, will recognize that he is the target of Wittgenstein's argument, but he may think, as Locke would have, that Wittgenstein's view of memory is utterly implausible. So he might protest that his own view does not leave him open to the memory skepticism with which Wittgenstein tries (in PI §§258 and 271) to saddle him. (He might allow that, if, having named the pups in a large litter, one later forgot which pups one had named "Rover" and "Biff," so that one then called Biff "Rover" and Rover "Biff," this would be understandable just because *many* pups were being named at one time. But he might then point out that calling an odd sensation "zing" would not present a similar problem.) And if he were asked what his *criterion* is for remembering a sensation right, he might dismiss the question. He might reply: If I suffered a stroke, *that* might leave me uncomprehending when a doctor asks whether I'm having pain again today, but it's not plausible to think that I might mistake itching for pain, so that I think my pain has returned when in fact I'm only itching.[8] A Lockean, of course, could reply in these ways because he does not share Wittgenstein's notion that the world consists of nothing more than the succession of uncaused phenomenal events and that our language must somehow have a use in such a fractured world.

Regarding Wittgenstein's private language argument, then, two assessments are possible. A Lockean dualist will recognize that the argument is directed at him, but he will find the argument unsound because it presupposes a view of memory which he does not share and because Wittgenstein's criticism of his view is misguided (see note 8 in Chapter 18). A philosopher with no theory to defend will find no merit in the argument for two reasons: first, because it attacks dualism in the wrong place (Wittgenstein opts for behaviorism instead of seeing what is amiss in the Cartesian notion of bodies), and second, because it presupposes a thoroughly implausible view of memory (see the discussion of his thought-guessing example in Chapter 16), i.e., a view of memory that impugns my story about inventing "zing." Moreover, both parties will think that Wittgenstein's 'relativistic' way of getting around memory skepticism (in the manometer passage) is quite unnecessary, and they will think so for much the same reason: neither is obliged to explain how it is possible to give a name to something in a world comprised of unrelated phenomenal states.

The Beetle-in-the-Box Analogy

At this point we may turn to the second step in Wittgenstein's argument, which is designed to show that when we use such words as "pain" and "tickle" we are not speaking of private objects. Here we encounter his beetle-in-the-box argument, in which Wittgenstein is plainly addressing the dualist.

Now someone tells me that *he* knows what pain is only from his own case! Suppose everyone had a box with something in it: we call it [whatever it may be] a "beetle." No one can look into anyone else's box, and everyone says he knows what a beetle is only by looking at *his* beetle. Here it would be quite possible for everyone to have something different in his box. One might even imagine such a thing constantly changing. But suppose the word "beetle" had nevertheless a use in these people's language? If so it would not be used as the name of a thing. The thing in the box has no place in the language-game at all; not even as a *something*: for the box might even be empty. No, one can 'divide through' by the thing in the box; it cancels out, whatever it is.

That is to say: if we construe the grammar of the expression of sensation on the model of 'object and designation' the object drops out of consideration as irrelevant (PI, §293).

This argument is addressed to a dualist, such as Locke, who allows that people do use words such as "pain" and "tickle" in speaking to one another. The first part of the passage, the part about everyone having something in his box, is intended as an analogue for the dualist's way of thinking of pain, tickling, and so on. And Wittgenstein's point is this: inasmuch as dualists allow that "pain" has a use in our language, they cannot *also* maintain that it stands for a 'private object,' for if, in the analogy, the word "beetle" had a use in speaking with other people, then it would *not* stand for what people have in their boxes, since they may have very different things in their boxes or nothing at all. His point here is that in this imaginary language-game the phrase "have a beetle in my box" would be a *misleading* form of words, for although it looks like "have a penny in my pocket," a person may say, in this language, "I have a beetle in my box," regardless of what, if anything, there is in his box. In this respect "beetle" would not be at all the sort of word that "penny" is. This is why, in the middle of the passage, Wittgenstein says: "But suppose the word 'beetle' had nevertheless a use in these people's language? If so it would not be used as the name of a thing."

This passage has led commentators to raise the question whether Wittgenstein held that, in our actual use of "pain" and "itch," the sensations "drop out as irrelevant," i.e., whether he thought that we are not really talking *about* our sensations. And because they have wanted to find merit in Wittgenstein's argument, many commentators have insisted that this is *not* his view, that his meaning, rather, is this: it is only because of the dualist's misconception about *how* a connection is established between a name and a (private) sensation, namely, by private ostensive definition, that sensations seem to "drop out."[9] This interpretation of the passage is surely mistaken. Wittgenstein did not, as these commentators suppose, think that there was some *other* way to set up a connection between a particular sensation and a name. His point, rather, is this: if you allow, as dualists do, that "pain" is a word we use in speaking to one another, then if you think that pain is a *private object*, you can only conclude, *not* that the word "pain" is the name of something private, but that this (supposed) private object drops out as irrelevant to what people are saying to one another.

Wittgenstein anticipated an objection to what he says in the beetle-in-the-box passage, an objection that he formulates and responds to as follows:

". . . you again and again reach the conclusion that the sensation itself is a *nothing*." Not at all. It is not a *something*, but not a *nothing* either! The conclusion was only that a nothing [i.e., an *empty* box, in his 'beetle' analogy] would serve just as well as a something [i.e., the dualist's 'private objects'] about which nothing could be said. We have only rejected the grammar which tries to force itself on us here.

The paradox [i.e., the impression that Wittgenstein is saying that the sensation itself is a nothing] disappears only if we make a radical break with the idea that language always functions in one way, always serves the same purpose: to convey thoughts – which may be about houses, pains, good and evil, or anything you please (PI, §304).[10]

To understand how this passage is meant to answer the objection to which it is addressed, we need answers to two questions. First, what is "the grammar which tries to force itself on us here"? Second, having rejected this grammar, what did Wittgenstein regard as being the actual grammar of a word such as "pain," i.e., what is the 'radical break' we must make?

As regards the first question, Wittgenstein identifies the 'grammar' in question when he says that philosophers construe "the grammar of the expression of sensation on the model of 'object and designation' " (PI, §293). But what does he mean by that? He is here alluding to the dualist's idea that, having once named a sensation, one can later *recognize* it and call it by the same name, and Wittgenstein is saying that the dualist is here thinking of sensations as though they were like puppies, which we *can* on later occasions recognize and call by the right name. He writes:

Suppose someone says: "The sensation passes, and then later on you recognize it again." I would say no. . . . You can't talk of *recognizing* it, because you have no criterion of recognizing correctly or incorrectly.

. . . Suppose there were a way of tracing the sensation's movements: you can see it move about away from him, move around, and then it comes back and you say "Ah yes, he has it again." Here [because you have kept track of it] you can say "He recognizes it." But clearly this is a wrong picture [for sensations]. And it makes plain that there is in our case [i.e., in the case of sensations, where there is no such thing as keeping track of an object] no such thing as *recognizing* it, since there is no criterion for recognizing it wrongly or rightly (LSD, pp. 110–111).

Here we see the meaning of Wittgenstein's remark about construing "the grammar of the expression of sensation on the model of 'object and designation' ": he is alluding to the 'grammar' of a puppy's name, for example. It is this, he means, that we must reject if we are to understand the use of sensation words.

So Wittgenstein is saying in PI §304 that (i) we will think that he is denying the existence of *sensations* only if we assume that the word "sensation" is the sort of word dualists take it to be and (ii) once we see that "sensation" and "pain" and "tickle" are *not* used like that, we will realize that he is not denying the existence of anything but is only maintaining that these words are not names of 'private objects.' "We can," he says, "give a name to a pain – but we can only do this where the pain is not private – where the word is to be used by all of us" (LSD, p. 33), where we all know its meaning. How, then, *is* it used in speaking with others?

This is the second of the questions posed above: If we are to reject the idea that we use such words as "pain" and "headache" to refer to what we feel, what did Wittgenstein intend that we should recognize as the actual 'grammar' of such words, i.e., what is the 'radical break' we must make? We will take up this question more fully in the next chapter, but recalling Wittgenstein's remarks about language being an instrument (PI, §569), we can here anticipate that he will talk about what we *do* with a word such as "headache."

Wittgenstein's Answers to Objections

Wittgenstein was aware that at this point someone might want to make the same objection we considered in the preceding chapter regarding the word "red," i.e., might want to protest that Wittgenstein's account of a word such as "pain" leaves out what is important, the pain itself, for all that he allows is that the word has a certain grammar and that we use it purposefully in speaking to one another, so that he fails to allow that the word is *connected* to anything. Wittgenstein, in the notes he made for his 1936 lectures, explicitly entertains this objection. Having dismissed the idea that one could set up a connection between "toothache" and a 'private object' by means of an ostensive definition, he imagines someone reproaching him as follows: "But aren't you neglecting something – the experience or whatever you might call it? Almost *the world* behind the mere words?" (NFL, p. 296). He responds as follows:

It seems that I neglect life. But not life physiologically understood but life as consciousness. And consciousness not physiologically understood, or understood from the outside, but consciousness as the very essence of experience, the appearance of the world, the world. . . .[11]

Isn't what you reproach me of as though you said: "In your language you're only *speaking*!" (NFL, p. 297).

By this rejoinder Wittgenstein means to say that his not *connecting* "pain" *to something* is not a legitimate ground for complaint. Or, as he put it in 1947: "The *employment* of a word is not: to *designate* something" (RPP, I, §614).

At several places in his notes Wittgenstein returns to this objection (see also PI, §§290–300). At one point he writes:

"But these 'expressions' can't be mere words, noises, which you make; they get their importance only from what's *behind* them (the state you're in when you use them)!" But how can this state give importance to noises which I produce? . . . .

. . . It is very queer that *all* the importance of our expressions seems to come from that X, Y, Z, the private experiences, which forever remain in the *background* and can't be drawn into the foreground. . . .

We labor under the queer temptation to describe our language and its use, introducing into our descriptions an element [the private experience] of which we ourselves say [as in the beetle-in-the-box passage] that it is not part of the language. . . .

"But can't you imagine people behaving just as we do, showing pain, etc., etc., and then if you imagine that *they don't feel pain* all their behavior is, as it were, dead. You can imagine all this behavior *with* or *without* pain."

The pain seems to be the atmosphere in which the expression ["I have toothache"] exists. (The pain seems to be a *circumstance* [of my saying this].) . . .

The 'private experience' is a degenerate construction of our language. . . . And this grammatical monster now fools us; when we wish to do away with it, it seems as though we denied the existence of an experience, say, toothache (NFL, pp. 312–314).

His answer to the reproach, then, is related to something we noticed in the preceding chapter, namely, his saying that "language remains self-contained and autonomous" (PG, p. 97).

This, of course, is a rejection of what Wittgenstein had maintained in the *Tractatus*, where he said that language is pinned to the world by means of simple names. This is what he was alluding to in his conversations with Waismann when he said that he had, at the time of the *Tractatus*, mistakenly thought that there is 'a connexion between language and reality.' It would, I think, be fair to say that *one* aim of the private language argument is to show that there is no such connection. This will be more obvious if we consider the background of the private language argument.

Schlick's Early Version of the Private Language Argument

An early version of the argument, in highly abbreviated form, is found in Wittgenstein's 1931 lectures (WL32, p. 61). The following year Moritz Schlick – probably after discussing the matter with Wittgenstein – set out the argument more fully in his lectures entitled "Form and Content," delivered at the University of London.[12] The theme of Schlick's lectures was that language is not pinned to reality in the way one might think, a theme he stated by saying that propositions express and communicate only form (or structure), not the *content* of experience. According to Schlick, the great mistake of metaphysicians, e.g., dualists, has been to think that propositions express content, that the proposition "I am in pain" refers to something in me, to a 'content' the nature of which I alone can know, and also that the proposition "This is green" refers to a 'content' the nature of which is unknown to persons blind from birth. But this is wrong, says Schlick, for such propositions express only a form: "wherever words like 'colour,' 'sound,' 'feeling' etc. occur in our sentences they can never stand for Content. They have meaning only in so far as they stand for certain structures."[13] It is therefore a mistake, he says, to think that "two data in different minds must either be alike or not alike, and that the question concerning their sameness has a definite meaning, although, unfortunately, it cannot be answered with absolute certainty."[14] This is a mistake because "statements about the Sameness or Diversity of Qualities must by no means be interpreted as dealing with Content."[15] In fact, he says, "it would be best not to use the word 'content' at all," for the word is here used only to explain a certain metaphysical muddle.[16]

Having set forth his arguments for this position, Schlick entertains the following question:

How about the comparison of qualities perceived by one and the same person? ... If I declare that the leaf I see today has the same colour as one I saw yesterday, or perhaps even the same colour as one lying next to it at this moment: am I then not dealing with quality in a deeper, more intimate sense than that of "mere" structure?[17]

Schlick deals with this question by considering the case in which, as he puts it, I "express facts to myself and communicate with myself" by keeping a diary. The question then is whether words such as "green" and "pain," when one writes them in one's diary, stand for 'content.' Schlick answers that "there can be no mention of content" in the diary and that this can be demonstrated by considering how we "ascertain whether a proposition which has thus been transmitted from an earlier to a later self is true or false."[18] His demonstration involves two stages, the first of which runs as follows:

When I keep in mind the colour of a green object, and tomorrow I am shown another object and am asked whether it has the "same" colour as the first one, my memory will give a more or less definite answer to the question. The question has a good meaning, of course, but can it be said to refer to "sameness of content"? Most certainly not. This follows from the way in which the answer given by memory is tested. For in a certain sense we must admit that our memory may "deceive" us. When do we say that it has done so? If there are methods of testing its judgment, and if all these methods fail to verify it. Such methods are: 1) looking again at the object in question and taking into account, on empirical grounds, the probability of its colour having changed in the meantime; 2) comparing my present judgment with a description I wrote down during the first observation; 3) comparing it with the descriptions given by other people.

The criterion of the truth of the judgment [that it is the same colour as the one seen yesterday] is the agreement of all these different propositions; and if we say that the colour is truly the same, that my memory has not deceived me, we mean nothing but that there is this formal agreement between descriptions based on memory and on observation. This is entirely a matter of structures; we cannot speak of a repetition or comparison of "content."[19]

Stated more explicitly, Schlick's point here is this: if he were to write in his diary, "Today I found a leaf of the same color as the one I found yesterday," this would be equivalent in meaning to certain other propositions. And these propositions, he says, are of the following sort: (i) "When I now look at yesterday's leaf, I would say (as I said yesterday) 'It is green,' and there are no empirical grounds for thinking it has changed color"; (ii) "I find in my diary that I described yesterday's leaf in the same way (namely, 'It is green') that I describe today's leaf"; and (iii) "Mary agrees that today's leaf is the same color as yesterday's." What Schlick is saying, then, is, first, that *these* propositions, since they are only about words, do not have even the appearance of referring to 'content,' and, second, that in saying "Today's leaf is the same color as yesterday's" one is saying only that these propositions, which do not mention content, would be found to be true. This, he says, shows that even when we communicate with *ourselves* about qualities we are not communicating 'content,' i.e., shows that "green" is not connected to a 'content.'

Schlick formulates the second stage of his argument, somewhat obscurely, as follows:

> If we knew of a case in which [unlike the preceding case] there were nothing else with which the judgment of our memory could be compared, we should, in this case, have to declare it impossible to distinguish between a trustworthy and a deceptive memory; we therefore could not even raise the question whether it was deceptive or not: there would be no sense in speaking of an "error" of our memory. It follows that a philosopher would be uttering a meaningless question if he were to ask: "Is it not possible that the colour I am seeing now seems to me to be green, while actually it is red?" The sentence "I am seeing green" means nothing but "there is a colour which I remember has always been called green." This recollection, this datum of my memory, is the one and only criterion of the truth of my statement. I recall it so, and that's final; in our supposed case I cannot go on asking: do I remember correctly? for I could not possibly explain what I meant by such a question.
>
> Thus we see that the question "is the green I see today the same colour as the green I saw yesterday?" refers only to the structure of our expressions and not to some content "green" which is supposed to be beyond. Sameness, equality cannot be predicated of content any more than anything else can be predicated of it; and the case of "two data of consciousness in the same mind at different times" forms no exception.[20]

Here we have, in embryo, Wittgenstein's private language argument, but in stating it as he does, Schlick seems to be assuming that when one says, "I'm in pain," one selects the word "pain" because one's memory is telling one: What you've got is called "pain." And it is only at this point that, in Schlick's version of it, the private language argument takes hold. In the early 1930s Wittgenstein stated the argument (PR, pp. 60–62) just as Schlick does. By 1936 he had dropped the idea that one's memory calls up the word "pain,"[21] so that in the version of the argument found in the *Investigations* the idea that memory (or recognition) plays a role when we say "I'm in pain" is attributed only to those philosophers against whom the argument is directed.

My point in calling attention to this background to the private language argument is this: as understood by Wittgenstein as well as by Schlick, the argument is designed to show that when we complain of pains or itching or dizziness we are not speaking of 'content.'

In notes that he wrote in the late 1940s Wittgenstein himself put the matter in these terms:

This is likely to be the point at which it is said that only form, not content, can be communicated to *others*. So one talks to oneself [i.e., *privately*] *about the content*. And what does that mean? (How do my words 'relate' to the [supposed] content I know? And to what purpose?) (RPP, II, §46).

What Wittgenstein meant to suggest here is this: in *neither* case do my words 'relate' to a 'content,' i.e., neither when I am speaking to others nor when I write in my diary, "Today I am still suffering much pain."[22]

We could state Wittgenstein's view in the following way. If on a Monday I write in my diary, "I am in great pain today," and then on Tuesday write, "I am still in much pain today," the correct philosophical view to take is that these are misleading forms of words because they make us think that on both occasions I (*in addition* to using the same word, "pain") am speaking of the *same thing*, i.e., a 'content of experience' called "pain."

Wittgenstein had two aims in dismissing the idea that one speaks of 'content,' the most obvious of which was to undermine dualism and the skeptical question whether two people are speaking of the *same* content. But also, as I pointed out in the preceding chapter, he saw that his Humean ontology required that, if he was to deal with Russell's skeptical argument regarding memory, he had to find an alternative to the Tractarian view that language is pinned to the world by means of names.[23] His alternative, like Schlick's, was to deny that one ever speaks of 'content,' which enabled him to dismiss as absurd the idea that, on successive occasions, one speaks of the *same* content.

It is important to realize that Wittgenstein did not arrive at this view in some wholly idiosyncratic way. Rather, he saw, as did Locke, that dualism cannot avoid the idea that when one complains to a friend or spouse or doctor by saying, for example, "I'm still having a great deal of pain," the other person cannot know *what* we are talking about. This struck Wittgenstein as absurd. But because he remained an empiricist, he could think of no way to avoid this absurdity other than by declaring that when we complain to others of our aches and pains, our nausea or dizziness, we are not talking *about* anything. What, then, was his alternative account? In the next chapter we will see what alternative he proposed.

Notes

1. *Gestalt Psychology*, op. cit., pp. 12–13.
2. In his 1946–47 lectures Wittgenstein made the same point, saying that in the case of colors we point to *public* things and give ostensive definitions, adding: "Contrast in a preliminary way, 'thinking' – do you point to think-

ing? Do you give an ostensive definition, as you do of red?" (WL47, pp. 261–262).

3. Elsewhere Wittgenstein repeats this argument in a slightly different form. He asks:

> Mightn't I now, for my own private use, call this sensation "S," use my memory as criterion of identity and then say "Yes, that's S again" etc? (RPP, I, §393).

He answers that "being the same here of course means the same thing as seeming the same" (RPP, I, §395), giving as his reason that if one thinks "S" means *this* sensation, one must ask: "But which is this [i.e., is it the one I named 'S']? For I pointed to my sensation a minute ago, and how can I now point to *it* again?" (RPP, I, §398).

4. As noted in the preceding chapter, Wittgenstein rejected the idea that memory (or recognition) plays a role in the use of such words as "red," "sweet," and "pain."

5. Wittgenstein adds: "But this is not the *end* of the language-game; it is the beginning." He apparently means: I do not stop here but go on to use the word *in speaking with other people*. We will take this up in the next chapter.

6. Incidentally, I do not intend that my example should present an instance of a 'private' use of words in Wittgenstein's sense, i.e., in the sense that I could not explain to others what I mean by "zing." I am prepared to allow that my parents would have known what I was talking about had I said to them, "I don't like going down in the elevator. It gives me a funny feeling." And I know, too, that had I invented the name "zing," I could have explained it to a schoolmate by telling him that what I call "zing" is that nasty feeling one gets in rapidly descending elevators. (One should recall here how common it is for us to explain what we feel (or have suffered) by referring to a cause, i.e., instead of saying "It tickled" or "It was painful," we commonly say such things as "It felt like there was a great weight on my chest" or "It felt like there was a tight band around my head.") Wittgenstein, by contrast, could not, because of his Humean view of causation, regard such explanations as conveying anything to another person, and for that reason he could only take the view that with my example I have undertaken to show that a word can be given a private meaning, one whose meaning I alone can know.

7. Dualists, if we can judge by what Locke says, appear to hold that although we can know in such instances that people's (Cartesian) bodies will be similarly affected, we have no reason to believe that the 'uniformity of nature' extends to their (Cartesian) minds.

8. Locke, in a passage quoted in the preceding chapter, allows that brain damage can affect one's power of retention. But he would not have allowed that a man who has no ideas in his mind randomly *calls* things by first one name and then another – as though the man were *saying* something but getting it wrong. On the contrary, Locke says that the man who had no ideas would not be speaking at all. So he would have found most peculiar the suggestion that one's memory might 'deceive' one in the way Wittgenstein speaks of in the two passages quoted above. But then Locke was no Humean.

9. This interpretation is found, for example, in Merrill B. and Jaakko Hintikka, *Investigating Wittgenstein*, op. cit., where the authors say:

> On our view, far from trying to get rid of vertical links between language

and reality, the later Wittgenstein emphasized them. On our interpretation, the first and foremost function of Wittgenstein's language-games is to serve as such links.

Thus there really are private experiences, and there really are expressions naming them and referring to them (p. 247).

They go on to say that "Wittgenstein does not deny the reality of sensations or their role in the semantics of our talk about sensations. . . . The beetle in the box does not disappear, except when we try to speak of it independently of a public framework" (p. 249). They conclude that "in the famous 'private language argument' . . . Wittgenstein was thus not essentially modifying the Cartesian account of our inner life. . . . He was . . . criticizing Cartesian semantics, not Cartesian metaphysics" (p. 250).

10. In saying that a sensation is "not a *something*," Wittgenstein is alluding to an earlier passage (§261) in which he anticipates someone saying: when the person keeping a private diary writes 'S,' he "has *something* – and that is all that can be said," i.e., it cannot be named. This is what Wittgenstein is rejecting when he says that a sensation is "not a something." He made this point more clearly in his 1936 lectures when he said:

> If you imagine that [in teaching a child a word] pinching him is an indirect way of calling his attention to something else, A, and that this recurs and he recognizes it [when he says "I have A"], then I say this is wrong. For (in what you are imagining) there can't be a case in which it recurs and he didn't recognize it; and if it didn't recur and he thought he recognized it, it would do just as well. You are talking of a "something." . . .
>
> If by "pain" we mean something *private*, then we ought not to say it means a certain *feeling*, for "feeling" is not a private word – it refers to a certain grammar in our language. We should have to say that by "pain" we mean, not the pinching, but "a certain something." Then it becomes absurd (LSD, p. 112).

11. The wording of these passages – "life" and "the world" – is plainly an allusion to the *Tractatus*, where Wittgenstein had said such things as "The world and life are one" (5.621) and "I am my world" (5.63).

12. These lectures are reprinted in Schlick's *Gesammelte Aufsätze* (Vienna: Gerold), pp. 151–250.

13. Ibid., p. 167.

14. Ibid., p. 175.

15. Ibid., p. 176.

16. Ibid.

17. Ibid., p. 177.

18. Ibid., p. 178.

19. Ibid., pp. 178–179.

20. Ibid., p. 179.

21. See the passage (quoted above) from NFL, pp. 110–111, where he says: "You can't talk of *recognizing* [the sensation], because you have no criterion of recognizing correctly or incorrectly." Recall here that in the discussion of the retrospective aspect of Wittgenstein problem about following a rule (Chapter 18) we found him insisting that memory plays no role in our use of color words.

22. See also RPP, I, §§91 and 109. In his 1947 lectures Wittgenstein said: "Consider now the *content of consciousness*. Some psychological verbs seem

to give it, e.g. 'I've got a pain' and 'I am feeling ill.' ..." (WL47, p. 323). I take it that the word "seem" is important here, i.e., that Wittgenstein did not think that we actually do (ever) speak of 'content.' He also said in these lectures: "I want now to give a reason ... for trying to avoid the idea that our utterance is a description of our experiences. For what follows this idea [i.e., what it suggests] is that there is a private picture, which is close to me and which I can describe (therefore, one in me). The idea of introspection hangs together with the belief that our utterances are descriptions of the content of experience" (WL47, p. 186; cf. pp. 61 and 317).

23. The *Tractatus* view is captured in Waismann's "Theses" as follows: "Elementary propositions describe the *content* of our experience" (WVC, p. 254, emphasis added). The English edition, unfortunately, contains either a mistranslation or a transcription error, as the next sentence reveals.

20

Names of Sensations and the Use Theory of Meaning

In the preceding chapter I left unanswered the following question: If we are to reject the idea that words such as "pain" and "itch" are used to refer to what we feel, what did Wittgenstein regard as being the actual 'grammar' of these words, i.e., what is the "radical break" (PI, §304) Wittgenstein says we must make? The answer to this question lies in his adoption of Berkeley's 'use' theory of meaning.

Berkeley's Use Theory of Meaning

As we saw in Chapter Eight, Berkeley says that, contrary to what is commonly supposed, it is not the chief and only end of language to convey ideas – mental pictures – to the mind of another. Very often, he says, the purpose of saying something to another is, instead, to stir him to (or deter him from) some action, and for this purpose it is frequently unnecessary to convey a mental picture. He declares that if we pay attention to what actually happens, we will find that when we hear or read something said to us, our actions occur immediately "upon the perception of certain words, without any ideas coming between."[1] His point may be illustrated as follows. As I prepare to leave the house, someone may caution, "It's raining," and I then take an umbrella without forming a mental picture of falling rain. Or as I am about to test the electric burner on my stove, another person exclaims, "It's hot!" and I instantly pull back my hand without forming an image of heat. The important point here, I suppose, is that when we review such examples we recognize them as plain cases of being warned or cautioned and of responding appropriately to the warning or caution without having to *picture* anything to ourselves. These are not, then, like the case in which a loud noise startles me and I jump or cringe. The difference is that the speaker could later say, for example, "I *told* him it was raining." So what these examples show is that forming or conveying pictures is not essential to being *told* something. When someone cautions me by saying, "It's raining," I *may* form a picture of falling rain, but it was not his purpose to get me to do so. This is Berkeley's point, and he no doubt intended this as a criticism of Locke, who had maintained that "the chief end of language" is that "men learn names, and use them in talk with others, only that they may be understood: which is then only done when by use or consent the sound I make by the organs of speech excites in another man's mind who hears it, the idea I apply it to in mine when I speak it."[2]

Locke's telepathic view of language, as we might call it, comes easily to most of us when we philosophize about words. Russell, for example, says something very similar: "Speech is a means of producing in our hearers the images which are in us."[3] Berkeley's rejection of this view is, very likely, one reason Wittgenstein held him in high esteem, for one of the first things Wittgenstein does in the *Investigations* is to drive home Berkeley's point.

That was one of his aims when he invented the language game in PI §2. The only words of this language game are "block," "pillar," "slab," and "beam," and when the builder calls out one of them, his assistant brings a stone of the sort he has learned to bring at that call. Wittgenstein comments:

An important part of the training will consist in the teacher's pointing to the objects, directing the child's attention to them, and at the same time uttering a word: for instance, the word "slab" as he points to that shape.... This ostensive teaching of words can be said to establish an association between the word and the thing. But what does this mean? Well, it can mean various things; but one very likely thinks first of all that a picture of the object comes before the child's mind when it hears the word. But now, if this does happen – is it the purpose of the word? Yes, it *can* be the purpose. I can imagine such a use of words (of series of sounds). (Uttering a word [in this atypical case] is like striking a note on the keyboard of the imagination.) But in the language of §2 it is *not* the purpose of the words to evoke images. (It may, of course, be discovered that that helps to attain the actual purpose.)
But if the ostensive teaching has this effect, am I to say that it effects an understanding of the word? Don't you understand the call "Slab!" if you act upon it in such-and-such a way? (PI, §6).

Wittgenstein's point here is that we judge a child to have learned the words he's being taught by seeing how he *acts*. We don't bother ourselves about what imagery, if any, he may have. Wittgenstein is also making Berkeley's point that very often the purpose of words is to stir someone to (or deter him from) some action: when the builder calls out "slab," his assistant brings him a slab.

Wittgenstein is reiterating Berkeley's point about language when he writes:

"We name things and then we can talk about them: can refer to them in talk." As if what we did next were given in the mere act of naming. As if there were only one thing called "talking about a thing." Whereas in fact we do the most various things with our sentences. Think of exclamations alone, with their completely different functions.

> Water!"
> Away!"
> Ow!"
> Help!"
> Fine!"
> No!"

Are you inclined still to call these words "names of objects"? (PI, §27).

This passage is meant not only to show that in speaking we are not always using *names* of things but also to make us see Berkeley's point, namely, that, as Wittgenstein puts it, "we *do* the most various things with our sentences." To drive home the idea that words have *functions*, Wittgenstein makes the following comparison: "Think of the tools in a tool-box: there is a hammer, pliers, a saw, a screw-driver, a rule, a glue-pot, glue, nails and screws. The functions of words are as diverse as the functions of these objects" (PI, §11). As an alternative to Locke's telepathic view of language, Wittgenstein offers a different account. "Language," he says, "is an instrument. Its concepts are instruments" (PI, §569). Accordingly, Wittgenstein issues the following advice in regard to philosophers: "Look at the sentence as an instrument, and at its sense as its employment" (PI, §421).

This advice he now brings to bear on the problem regarding such words as "pain" and "tickle." In opposition to the telepathic view he says: ". . . communication by language is not a process by which I use a drug to produce in others the same pains as I have myself" (PG, p. 107).[4] In place of the telepathic view he recommends another: "You must think about the purpose of words. What does language have to do with pain?" (RPP, II, §655). "The concept of pain," he says "is characterized by its particular function in our life" (Z, 532). He hints at this function by saying:

"I have pain" is syntactically like "I have a match box" or "The chair has a hole." This is a description of something. And "I have pain" sounds like a description of something. When I say it is [instead] like a moan, I want to say the words are used in an utterly different way. In one form it replaces a moan (LSD, pp. 44–45).

If a cry is not a description, then neither is the verbal expression that replaces it (RPP, II, §728).

In these passages Wittgenstein is opposing the idea that the word "pain" functions as the name of an object. What, then, did he think its function is?

Wittgenstein suggests that "I'm in pain" might replace a moan, perhaps thinking of a case in which I simply blurt out, "Oh, I'm in pain." Elsewhere Wittgenstein says that "the words 'I am in pain' may be a cry of complaint, and may be something else" (PI, p. 189). Here we may recall his saying: "we do the most various things with our sentences." So what do I do with the sentence "I have a headache"? I take it that Wittgenstein had in mind such things as the following. If I call out to my wife, "I have a headache," I may be requesting an aspirin or asking her to play the piano more softly. If I say this to a doctor, it may be a way of getting him to examine me for some medical problem. In these ways my words stir someone to (or deter her from) some action. I take Wittgenstein's point, then, to be that by reminding ourselves of such cases we come to see the way (or ways) in which "I have a headache" is an instrument and that our purpose is *not* to convey the 'content' of our experience. This is his 'radical break.'

Wittgenstein's Replies to Objections

Anyone wedded to the telepathic view of language is likely to find the foregoing account bizarre. They will want to protest that in speaking to others of headaches, heartburn, nausea, dizziness and the like we *must* intend to convey a mental image of something. If I explain to a doctor that my wife went to bed because she had a *headache*, doesn't my explanation make sense to the doctor only because I convey *why* she went to bed, i.e., not because she felt nauseous but because she had a headache? And how can I convey that without conveying an image (or idea) of headache?

Before considering Wittgenstein's response to this, we will do well to notice something Kohler says in this regard. In the course of expounding his version of behaviorism, he writes: ". . . I can of course try and deliberately evoke pictures of the way in which Mr. X and Mrs. Y probably have felt on this or that occasion. . . . But during the effort I soon realize that this is an entirely unfamiliar procedure; plainly, I seldom do anything of the kind in normal social life. . . ."[5] This comes at least very close to Wittgenstein's own view, but he evidently found something of interest in Kohler's use here of the word "picture." He writes:

> It is – we should like to say – not merely the picture of the behaviour that plays a part in the language-game with the words "he is in pain", but also the picture of the pain. Or, not merely the paradigm of the behaviour, but also that of pain. It is a misunderstanding to say "The picture of pain enters into the language-game with the word 'pain'." The image of pain is not a picture and *this* image is not replaceable in the language-game by anything that we should call a picture. The image of pain certainly enters into the language-game in a sense; only not as a picture (PI, §300).

Wittgenstein seems to be making several points here, one of which is that (as he puts it) the image of pain is not a picture. It is important to note that he says this in regard to the third-person sentence "He is in pain." This suggests that he meant to be making the same point that he made in regard to Russell's view of memory images,[6] which he criticized as follows: "We know what a picture is, but images are surely no kind of picture at all. For, in the first case I can see the picture and the object of which it is a picture. But in the [case of images], things are obviously quite different. We have just used a metaphor and now the metaphor tyrannizes us" (PR, pp. 81–82). In the case of memory the metaphor (images as pictures) tyrannizes us by leading us to think we have *only* a picture of the past, a picture we cannot compare with the original. In opposition to this he says that "images are no kind of picture at all," meaning that unlike, say, the sketch I make of a building, a memory image does not *represent* something else. This is his point, also, in saying that "the image of pain is not a picture." He means that it would be a mistake to think that if we do have an image when we speak of another's pain, this image *represents* something the other person *has*, something private, which we cannot compare with the image.

The final sentence of §300 reads: "The image of pain certainly enters into the language-game in a sense; only not as a picture." Wittgenstein goes on to say in §301: "An image is not a picture, but a picture can correspond to it." It is not clear to me what his point is here, but he appears to be suggesting that the picture that "corresponds" to an image of pain would be a picture of someone suffering. Perhaps he had in mind something like cartoons drawn of people who have stubbed their toe or have a toothache, where they are shown grimacing and holding their foot or their cheek.[7] His point in all this seems to be that the telepathic view of language goes wrong in suggesting that the use – the *function* – of the word "pain" is to give someone else a pain, the *paradigm* (as he says) of pain.

A second objection one may want to make against Wittgenstein's 'instrument' account of words concerns the way we learn such words as "pain," "tickle," "itch," "sting," and so on. One may want to protest Wittgenstein's behavioristic account of these words by saying: when we are taught these words in childhood, we learn to associate them with particular sensations, and then we can report the occurrence of such sensations by saying, "I have a pain in my knee" or "My foot itches," etc. and can ask others such things as "Does your foot itch, too?" and so on. Wittgenstein responds to this objection in two ways. One of these, as we saw in the preceding chapter, is his argument against the possibility of naming 'private objects,' wherein he attempts to undermine the idea that one associates "pain" with something. His other response is to offer an alternative account of how the word "pain" *is* learned:

How do words *refer* to sensations? There doesn't seem to be any problem here; don't we talk about sensations every day, and give them names? But how is the connexion between the name and the thing named set up? This question is the

same as: how does a human being learn the meaning of the names of sensations? – of the word "pain" for example? Here is one possibility: words are
connected with the primitive, the natural, expressions of the sensation and
used in their place. A child has hurt himself and he cries; and then adults talk
to him and teach him exclamations and, later, sentences. They teach the child
new pain-behavior.

"So you are saying that the word 'pain' really means crying?" On the contrary: the verbal expression of pain replaces crying and does not describe it (PI,
§244).

To understand this passage, it is essential to realize that Wittgenstein is
not here answering, but is in a way rejecting, the question with which he
begins: "How is the connection between the name and the thing named
set up?" He is not saying that "pain" gets connected to something in the
child when it cries and adults then talk to it. On the contrary, he is
saying that what the child learns is a new 'expression of pain.' As he puts
it elsewhere:

Primitive pain-behaviour [in a child] is a sensation-behaviour; it gets replaced
by a linguistic expression. "The word 'pain' is the name of a sensation" is
equivalent to " 'I've got pain' is an expression of sensation" (RPP, I, §313).

His point is that, although it appears that when we say "My foot hurts
terribly" we are talking *about* something (as we do when we say, for
example, "My foot is swollen"), this appearance is due to a grammatical
similarity, for in truth the cases are not analogous: when we use the
word "pain" in such first-person sentences, we are not talking about
something; we are using a *different kind of instrument*, e.g., asking for
medical attention.

A third objection that may occur to one is the following: even if one
were to agree that "I have a headache" is an 'instrument' for getting
others to do something, the same could not be said of *other* uses of
"headache" or "pain," as when one says, for example, "I hope I never
have a headache like *that* again." Wittgenstein responds to this objection
as follows:

"Suppose I have a pain . . ." – that is not an expression of pain and so it is not
a piece of pain-behavior.

The child who learns the word "pain" as a cry, and who then learns to tell of
a past pain – one fine day this child may declare: "If I have a pain, the doctor
comes." Now has the meaning of the word "pain" changed in this process of
learning the word? It has altered its employment; but one must guard carefully
against interpreting this change as a change of object corresponding to the
word (RPP, I, §479).

What Wittgenstein means to oppose here is clear enough: he is opposing the idea that such a remark by the child shows that he has associated
the word "pain" with something – some 'private object' – he occasionally
has. But what is he proposing as an alternative? He is proposing that the
child's words in this case, too, are an 'instrument' of some sort. Perhaps

he was thinking that the child is seeking reassurance, and that its mother might give reassurance by saying: "Yes, when you fell and hurt your head, the doctor came, and he also came when you cut your foot."

Here we may wonder how Wittgenstein deals with the use of a word such as "pain" when we are speaking in the third- rather than the first-person. If "I am in pain" or "I feel dizzy" is an expression of sensation, what about "He is in pain" or "He feels dizzy"? Here Wittgenstein needs a different account, and in Chapter 9 we saw the kind of account he gives: such third-person propositions, he says, are about the other person's behavior (and circumstances). So he is saying that words such as "pain" and "feel" have different meanings in first- and third-person statements. Realizing that this may strike us as peculiar, he comments:

One may have the thought: "How remarkable that the *single* meaning of the word "to feel" (and of other psychological verbs) is compounded of heterogeneous components, the meanings of the *first* and the *third* person."
But what can be more different than the profile and the front view of a face; and yet the concepts of our language are so formed, that the one appears merely as a variation of the other. And of course it is easy to give a ground in facts of nature for this structure of concepts. (Heterogeneous things; arrowhead and arrow-shaft.) (RPP, I, §45).

Wittgenstein does not say which 'facts of nature' would account for our using a single word ("feel" or "pain," etc.) in both the first- and third-person cases, but perhaps he had in mind that we all exhibit the same expressions of sensation: I groan and others groan; I wince and others wince, etc. In any case, this passage makes clear that he did think of "pain," for example, as not being used univocally in the first- and third-person cases.[8]

It is perhaps noteworthy that Wittgenstein makes no attempt at addressing an objection that calls attention to the fact that when we complain to a doctor about, say, abdominal pain, we may be asked: "Can you describe the pain more exactly? Is it sharp or dull? Is it an ache or a burning sensation? Is it steady or does it come and go?" And, of course, we can readily answer such questions. It seems unlikely that even Wittgenstein could persuade himself that the answers "It's an ache" and "It's a burning sensation" correspond to different 'natural expressions of sensation.'

What are we to think of Wittgenstein's behavioristic account of such words as "pain" and "tickle"? He gives such an account for one reason only, namely, because he thinks the only alternatives here are behaviorism and dualism. And wanting to avoid dualism because of the skepticism it entails, he opts for a behavioristic account of a word such as "pain." But if we dismiss, as we should, the premise shared by dualists and behaviorists, i.e., the premise that what we see of another person is a body, then in order to avoid dualism we do not need an account like Wittgenstein's.

Notes

1. Introduction to the *Principles*, Sec. 20.
2. John Locke, *An Essay Concerning Human Understanding*, III, iii, 3.
3. *The Analysis of Mind*, op. cit., p. 206. Wittgenstein alludes to this view of language in PI, §§317 and 363.
4. On an earlier page he had said: "We regard understanding as the essential thing [about language], and the signs as something inessential. But in that case, why have the signs at all? If you think it is only so as to make ourselves understood by others, then you are very likely looking on the signs as a drug which is to produce in other people the same condition as my own" (PG, p. 39). This, obviously, is intended as a caricature of the telepathic view.
5. *Gestalt Psychology*, op. cit., pp. 141–142.
6. Russell says: "How ... are we to find any way of comparing the present image and the past sensation? The problem is just as acute if we say that images *differ* from their prototypes as if we say that they *resemble* them; it is the very possibility of comparison that is hard to understand. We think we can know that they are alike or different, but we cannot bring them together in one experience and compare them" (*The Anaysis of Mind*, op. cit., p. 159).
7. In his 1946–47 lectures he spoke of illustrating the words "man" and "toothache" with pictures and went on to say that "the toothache picture" is a picture of a man "grabbing his cheek" (WL47, p. 60).
8. See G. E. Moore, "Wittgenstein's Lectures in 1930–33," op. cit., p. 253.

Name Index

Subject Index